A Strange World – Autism,
Asperger's Syndrome and PDD-NOS

A Strange World – Autism, Asperger's Syndrome and PDD-NOS

A Guide for Parents, Partners, Professional Carers, and People with ASDs

Martine F. Delfos

Foreword by Tony Attwood

Jessica Kingsley Publishers
London and Philadelphia

The author would like to thank the following publishers and authors for permission to reproduce copyright material: American Psychiatric Association, Blackwell Publishing, Cambridge University Press, *Developmental Medicine and Child Neurology*, Elsevier, The Endocrine Society, R.J. van der Gaag, M. Hadders-Algra, Johns Hopkins Medical Institutions, Johns Hopkins University Press, The McGraw-Hill Companies, K. Momma, The Paedological Institute Amsterdam, T. Peeters, Psychology Press, Random House, Axel Scheffer, Marita Schoonbeek, Simon & Schuster, Inc., Spectrum, Springer, P. Steerneman, Swets and Zeitlinger, Therafin Corporation and P. Vermeulen.

Information about autism (pp. 365–6), Rett's Syndrome (p.371) and disintegrative disorder (p.372) reprinted with permission from the *Diagnostic and Statistical Manual of Mental Disorders, Text Revision*, copyright © American Psychiatric Association 2000.

www.mdelfos.nl

The right of Martine F. Delfos to be identified as author of this work has been asserted by her in accordance with the Copyright, Designs and Patents Act 1988.

First published in 2001 in Dutch by Uitgeveij SWP, Amsterdam, as *Een vreemde wereld: Over autisme, het syndroom van Asperger en PDD-NOS. Voor ouders, partners, hulpverleners en de mensen zelf.*

First published in 2005
by Jessica Kingsley Publishers
116 Pentonville Road
London N1 9JB, UK
and

400 Market Street, Suite 400
Philadelphia, PA 19106, USA

www.jkp.com

Copyright © Martine F. Delfos 2005
Foreword copyright © Tony Attwood 2005

Library of Congress Cataloging in Publication Data

Delfos, Martine F.
   [Vreemde wereld. English]
   A strange world : autism, Asperger's syndrome, and PDD-NOS : a guide for parents, partners, professional careers, and people with ASDs / Martine F. Delfos ; foreword by Tony Attwood.
       p. cm.
   Includes bibliographical references (p.   ) and indexes.
   ISBN-13: 978-1-84310-255-7 (pbk.)
   ISBN-10: 1-84310-255-2 (pbk.)
   1. Autism. I. Title.
   RC553.A88D4513 2005
   616.85'882—dc22

                                                                              2004025826

British Library Cataloguing in Publication Data
A CIP catalogue record for this book is available from the British Library

ISBN-13: 978 1 84310 255 7
ISBN-10: 1 84310 255 2

Printed and Bound in Great Britain by
Athenaeum Press, Gateshead, Tyne and Wear

Contents

Part 2: What can you do about it?

List of figures, tables and boxes

Figures

Tables

Boxes

Foreword

Martine Delfos has written a book for the intelligent reader, explaining the strange world of autism. She reviews each of the theoretical fields of study and then describes our current landscape of knowledge as though from an observation balloon to provide a single explanatory model for autism. The project has been remarkably ambitious but the author has an encyclopaedic knowledge of the academic literature and the various theoretical models, and extensive personal experience as a clinician. The author also has notable respect for those who have autism and Asperger's Syndrome and she is able to challenge and change attitudes as well as increase understanding.

The first part of the book explains the nature of autism from a theoretical perspective while the second part provides a framework for the practical application of our research knowledge. The author also includes quotations and descriptions of individuals with autism that bring life and reality to the text. The summaries at the end of each chapter ensure the reader can quickly access the key points, which will be of considerable value to students studying autism. I suspect that academics will now discuss and test the theoretical model proposed by Martine Delfos, and clinicians will use Part 2 for guidance in the design of remedial programmes. Parents and teachers who want to explore the strange world of autism at a more intellectual level will appreciate the new perspective.

Tony Attwood
Author of Asperger's Syndrome: A Guide for Parents and Professionals

Preface

It is quite a joy that this book has found its way into an English translation. The Dutch edition proved to be very helpful in understanding autism and in helping people with autism and their families; it also proved to be stimulating for research.

The book is intended for parents, partners and professional carers, as well as for people with an autistic spectrum disorder. But the book is also intended for scientific and educational purposes. The choice has been made to make the book as readable as possible for a broad public; therefore references are included. However, for the purpose of deepening insight and scientific purposes, the completely original models (about autism and anxiety) have been elaborated in separate appendices, with the appropriate references. These appendices can be downloaded from the following website: www.jkp.com/catalogue/book.php/isbn/1-84310-255-2.

This book not only examines current theories about autism, it goes a step further. A new model is presented which encompasses all the knowledge that is available into a broad coherent whole. All aspects of autism, from a lack of sense of time or obsessions, to not understanding jokes, are logically brought together here.

Examples from my psychotherapeutic practice are also used in the book. Not only did I include examples from my work with those, often wonderful, people with autism, but also their enriching comments on the way, which I used as examples. I am very grateful to them. I cannot thank them by name, to protect their privacy. But thank you!

My thoughts go especially back to the mother of Joe and her fight to give her child the help he needed. She died before she could enjoy the fruits of her efforts. I carry with me her struggle as a painful but valuable lesson.

I thank all those who helped me during the creation of this book and its translation.

I am convinced that all scientific endeavour flourishes on the work of those who went along the road before. Although this book has been written in the first person, I wish to acknowledge those scientists whose work was the foundation for further scientific insights. I am deeply indebted to Norman Geschwind and Hans Asperger, who inspired me so profoundly. Without their work, it would not have been possible to construct my models and I could not have accomplished this book.

Martine F. Delfos
Utrecht, 2004

People with autism need other people to
slow down

Martine F. Delfos

I am made of so much glass
That every harsh voice
Is a stone and a crack

Gerrit Achterberg

They say that I am rational,
that I should express my feelings,
but they want me to look there where
I'm blind

'Martin'

Part 1
What is it?

1

Introduction

Is my child autistic, does he have a contact disorder or is he mainly struggling with a lack of social skills? Is the child egoistic, does he show signs of a neglected upbringing, or does he have autistic characteristics? There are many labels for the various diagnoses surrounding autism, from autism in a 'pure form' to related disorders such as PDD-NOS. But what is autism and how can I help the child?

These are the questions that form the guidelines for this book. In this book we will talk about the *autistic spectrum*, the group of disorders where the core problem consists of having difficulty with (interpreting) social interaction.

Apart from interpreting social interaction there are many behaviours which can play a part in autistic disorders and none of the theories have, up to now, been able to place all the aspects in one overall explanatory model. This book aims to do just that, so that behaviours such as 'not understanding jokes', the 'need to keep everything as it was', and 'resistance to change' will become clear. The core concept of the model presented in this book is the *socioscheme*. The model is based on differences between men and women and, on a biological level, deals with the influence of testosterone on the development of the foetus in the womb.

The first researchers

The term *autism* emerged for the first time from three different places in the world. The first time was when Dr Chorus (Frye 1968) used it in the annual reports (1937–1938, 1939–1940) of the pedological institute at Nijmegen in The Netherlands. He used the term for children who were excessively withdrawn into themselves.

Independent from this the term was also being used by the two pioneers in the field of autism, the Austrians Leo Kanner (1894–1981) and Hans Asperger (1906–1980), in order to describe children and adults who showed a specific pattern of behaviours. Bleuler (1908) used the term, which means 'withdrawn into oneself', in order to describe schizophrenics being withdrawn into themselves; this is, however, a completely different problem. Kanner and Asperger used this term for a problem that always existed but was never given a name. Autism can be recognized by a fixed pattern of behaviours throughout various countries and various cultures (Frith 1989, 2003).

Figure 1.1 Hans Asperger (Frith 1997a).
Reproduced with permission from Cambridge
University Press.

Figure 1.2 Leo Kanner (Mottar 1954). Reproduced
with permission from Johns Hopkins Medical
Institutions.

It is amazing that both Kanner and Asperger used this term, working in different parts of the world (Leo Kanner emigrated to America at the age of 28) without knowing it. They used the term to describe a specific pattern of behaviours that since that time has been given the name autism. The fact that they both used this term is probably due to the fact that Asperger and Kanner both were originally German speaking and that they had their education in the same time period, when the work of Bleuler was prominent.

Kanner wrote in English, causing his work to be spread internationally much faster. Asperger's article became known about 30 years later thanks to Uta Frith's translation. The similarities between the two articles are striking. The tone, however, is different. Asperger writes in warm and respectful terms about people with an autistic disorder, emphasizing the special aspects more than the deviating ones. This balanced and respectful way of looking at people with an autistic disorder matches very well with the fundamentally humanist scholar that Asperger was. He writes in more general terms than Kanner and his experience is principally based on youngsters (more than 200). In his first article Kanner describes eleven young children (eight boys and three girls) and pays a lot of attention to the parents, of whom he states that the majority come across as 'cold'. It is probably because Kanner dealt a lot with very young children, two and three years old, that he speaks relatively often about feeding problems. In his article, Asperger is a bit more oriented towards understanding what goes on in the children's minds; Kanner, on the other hand, is more oriented towards describing the children's behaviour.

It struck Kanner and Asperger that the children and adults they described were extremely withdrawn into themselves and seemed to live in a different world. They displayed an amazing naïveté and a fundamental lack of knowledge about social interaction and of insight into social behaviour. Kanner (1943) and Asperger (1944) show many similarities in their descriptions, but also differences. The basis is, however, the same: a lack of social intercourse, and a lack of social insight and of social skills. In the course of time it has been discovered that although some characteristics are essential for autism, others occur with some but not all autistic people. In order to do justice to the different forms of autistic behaviour, Lorna Wing (1988) speaks of the *autistic spectrum*, also called the *a-spectrum*, within which there are various *autistic spectrum disorders* (ASDs). In this spectrum the behaviours go from strong to weak in the fields of:

- social interaction

- social communication in verbal and non-verbal behaviour

- imaginary ability

- repetitive characteristics of activities

- language

- response to sensory stimuli

- specific skills (Wing 1997).

Wing, and the researchers around her, found three areas that are characteristic for autism, called the *triad*. These are problems in the fields of *social contact, communication* and *imagination*.

In the course of this book I will describe the various forms and characteristics of autistic disorders. To that end I present a new, overall theoretical framework, in which the common theories have been jointly included and where all the various behaviours of autistic people prove to be pieces of a large puzzle. The core concept is, as I announced, the *socioscheme*. Without having to oppose common theories I will place these in my *metatheory*. With this I hope to show what, for example, a lack of understanding time has to do with badly interpreting social interaction; how anxiety, aggression and depression play a part; how obsessions function and what the role of the eye for detail is.

The structure of the book

The book consists of two parts. In the first part, *What is it?*, I will describe the various autistic disorders, also called *contact disorders*. The emphasis lies on Asperger's syndrome and PDD-NOS. That means people with an autistic disorder who are not intellectually disabled and who have a normal or even above average intelligence (Asperger's syndrome) and those who show only some autistic characteristics (PDD-NOS). The model to be developed applies, however, to autism in general. I decided, for two reasons, to emphasize those autism disorders that are coupled with a normal or above average intelligence. First, a discussion about autism without an intellectual disability explains more clearly what autism is specifically in itself. Second, I wanted to publish a book that could offer help to people with Asperger's syndrome and PDD-NOS, their families and their professional carers. The book is therefore both theoretical and practical. Progress in science is ultimately based on the harmonious relation between theory and practice. To accommodate the scientific practice appendix (IV) is available in electronic form (for access information see p.13).

I will first explain the meaning of *predisposition* and *maturation* in general and to what extent the upbringing plays a part in the child's development (Chapter 2). Subsequently I will look at what is 'normal'. I will do this on the basis of the differences between men and women; because when we talk about making contact, there prove to be many differences between people and certainly between men and women (Chapter 3). Although in Chapters 2 and 3 only indirect references are made to autism, they are of vital importance in order for the reader to place the following chapters in context. It requires some effort from the reader to read a general discussion about the development of and differences between men and women, before we go on to autism. Then I will try to describe the various contact disorders (Chapter 4) and describe the core of the problem (Chapter 5). In this chapter a new model, with the socioscheme as its basic principle, will be presented.

In the second part of this book, *What can you do about it?*, we will discuss how one can deal with the various problems associated with autism and how a child, and his or her parents, can be helped with that. This includes coping better with changes, coping with anxiety and aggression and making friends. With each subject I will work out, as much as possible according to age, what the help could entail. We will focus both on the situation at home and at school. We will not, however, restrict ourselves to children but will also examine the problems of youngsters and adults with an autistic disorder. As autism is a developmental disorder, the chapters of the book follow the process of growing up from the me–other differentiation to friendships and relationships.

We will start with a chapter about the significance of the *diagnosis*, or the lack thereof, for children's growing up (Chapter 6), and continue with the help which is needed.

One of the most important elements of contact problems, and this is characteristic for disorders from the autistic spectrum, is the lack of ability to be able to put yourself into someone else's shoes. This is linked to an inadequate *me–other differentiation*. It is therefore important to stimulate this as much as possible (Chapter 7). The me–other differentiation leads to *social insight* which is necessary to develop *social skills* (Chapter 8). Children with contact problems struggle with poor social skills and it is therefore important to stimulate and develop these skills with them. Being able to put yourself in someone else's shoes and developing social skills are of the utmost importance for striking up *friendships* and forming *loving relationships* (Chapter 9).

A second important aspect with children who have contact problems is often their *resistance to changes*. This aspect in particular is often very aggravating in normal daily life. How do you deal with the child's need to keep everything as it was, his or her resistance to a new pair of pyjamas or a new teacher at school, and also his or her need for *rituals* (Chapter 10)? Contact disorders often go hand in hand with intense *anxiety, obsessions* (Chapter 11) and *aggression* (Chapter 12). In the chapter about anxiety I will present the anxiety scheme (Delfos 2004a) which gives insight into the working of anxiety, aggression and depression with people. In addition I will also discuss the contact problems connected with anxiety and shyness, not to be confused with a lack of interpreting social interaction well, namely *social anxiety*. This problem does not come under the autistic spectrum and is completely different from the contact disorder which forms this book's theme. I will discuss the contact problem of social anxiety in order to explain the difference with the contact problem which plays a part in the autistic disorder. Apart from that, children within the autistic spectrum can suffer a lot of anxiety over social contact due to their inadequate social functioning, and on that basis will develop social anxiety in addition to their autistic disorder (Chapter 13). Finally, in the epilogue (Chapter 14) I will pay attention to the significance of disorders for our society.

Each chapter ends with *focal points*, in which central points are formulated regarding the nature of the problem and the appropriate help. Each chapter has focal points with regard to *attitude*. Before anything else an understanding, respectful attitude is necessary in order to help people with an autistic disorder and their environment. This attitude is partly given, but it can partly be achieved through a better understanding of the problem. One could question if giving help is possible without this attitude. Each chapter, except the introduction and the epilogue, will end with a summary.

Finally, in a number of appendices, we will give a description of the various diagnoses (Appendix I), relevant addresses and websites on the Internet (Appendix II), useful books to read (Appendix III), and, in electronic form, a concise explanation of the socioscheme as explanatory model (Appendix IV) and an extensive version of the anxiety model (Appendix V) (for access information see p.13).

Real-life examples have been included in the book in order to make the subject matter more clear and more expressive. The names of the persons are fictitious. In the examples referring to the same person, I systematically used the same fictitious name, so that an image can be formed of what the problem is like, for example, for 'Alec', 'Martin', or 'Sam'. It also means that I can show some of the development in the process of growing up and ageing and how the various subjects play within one person. At the end of the book an index has been included of the names of the people in these case studies. This way the different aspects of the disorder can be checked per person.

The examples are mainly from the author's therapy practice, which concerns children, youngsters and adults most of whom have Asperger's syndrome or PDD-NOS. Some examples are from the autobiographies of autistic people. Sometimes, in order to clarify things, examples are used of people with *Asperger traits*: that means people with some characteristics of Asperger's syndrome but not the full-blown disorder. The advantage of an example is that it clarifies the subject matter and illustrates it; the disadvantage is that if we recognize a trait in one example we may think that someone with whom we are dealing has the disorder, when this is not the case. Be prepared, therefore: when a child shows the behaviour illustrated in one of the examples, this does not mean that the child has an autistic disorder. We all have traits which to a greater or lesser degree are linked to autism.

This is not a book about how you can 'cure' a contact problem, because that is in principle not possible, but it is about how you can learn to cope with it, how you can give a child, a youngster or an adult the chance of as much happiness as possible and how you can learn from him or her.

Predisposition or upbringing

In recent years more and more scientific research has been carried out in the field of autistic disorders. It has become clear that autism develops from the predisposition of the child or as a result of an illness and is not, as had been thought for a long time before, caused by the child's upbringing (by the mother). Whole generations were brought up with the idea that a dominant or (over-) concerned mother was the cause of autism. A cold, cool, intellectual or over-concerned mother would bring her child up to be someone who had difficulty making contact and lived completely in a world of his or her own. This image was created by Bettelheim (1956, 1967). He did this, however, following the description that Leo Kanner gave of the parents of autistic children. Kanner (1943) had genetic origin in mind and described the parents of autistic children as having autistic traits themselves. He described them as 'cold' and 'cool', not very interested in their children. Kanner was, however, shocked that his work was interpreted as if he was blaming the parents for the autism of their child (Kanner 1969). He therefore exclaimed emotionally in 1969 during a meeting of the American Psychiatric Association: 'Parents, I exonerate you!' He stated that from the beginning he took as his starting point an *organic disorder* and not an *upbringing defect*. He even wrote a book: *In Defense of Mothers: How to Bring up Children in Spite of the More Zealous Psychologists* (Kanner 1958). Given his description of the parents it is, however, not surprising that following his work, behaviour therapists such as Lovaas (1974, 1996) embroidered on the idea of learned behaviour through upbringing. Treatment was developed that was based on the behaviour therapy techniques of *punishment, reinforcement* and *extinction*.

The behaviour of the children concerned has not changed substantially in the course of time, and the characteristics of autistic children have remained, but the causes are being judged completely differently. Predisposition has started to play an increasingly more important part. Asperger (1944) already indicated that autism had to do with a predisposition factor, among other reasons, because the behaviour was very persistent through time. The behaviour of neglected children can sometimes be similar to that of autistic children, but a different approach causes a neglected child to change his or her behaviour rather quickly (Wing 2001). This is not the case with the autistic child. A different approach can lead to different behaviour with an autistic child only with a lot of effort, insight and patience.

Recent research into genes, the bearers of the genetic characteristics that each of us is born with, shows that autism is connected to a deviation of the chromosomes 4, 7, 10, 16, 19, 22 and the X chromosome, where chromosomes 2 and 7 are the most characteristic (Consortium 1998; Barrett *et al.* 1999; Gallagher *et al.* 2003; Gillberg 2000). Gillberg (2000) indicates that it was established that there is a chromosomal deviation with Rett's syndrome. He also indicates that the first man with Rett's syndrome has been diagnosed, where until recently this autistic disorder was only discovered among women. This immediately shows how important predisposition is. It is not the case that these disorders are brought on by the upbringing by the mother: they are already present. Research indicates that there *is* a relationship between the (overly) concerned mother and autism. For a long time this finding was interpreted as being a causal relationship, in the sense that the mother would cause the autism: this proves to be incorrect. In fact the causal relationship is the other way around: it is the child who calls for the (overly) concerned behaviour in his or her mother.

A mother usually senses very well that her child is 'strange', 'odd'. She feels that something is wrong with the child and that is the reason for her concern. She starts to protect the child more than she would another child. You can actually say that a child with autism *makes* a mother concerned, dominant. It is the predisposition that is the foundation, that determines the extent of the space the child has for growth and development. Because predisposition is so important, parents will also recognize characteristics of themselves and of family members in their child. Asperger (1944) indicated that he saw autistic traits in all the parents of autistic children he had been able to meet.

The disposition of the genes proves to be an important factor in autism. The genetic pattern decides upon the way the central nervous system develops and matures. In Chapter 2 we will examine maturing more profoundly.

Autism can also occur in comorbidity with some specific illnesses. The question with this comorbidity is whether the autism is caused by the illness or whether both have been caused by the same factor, indicating a genetic vulnerability. In Chapter 4 we will go into this further.

A different problem is that, previously, disorders were seen as a clearly distinguishable group of characteristics. These disorders that are named after groups of characteristics are called *syndromes*. Nowadays, disorders are regarded differently. Scientists start more and more to take a continuum as a starting point, a gradual scale of characteristics. This means that characteristics and groups of

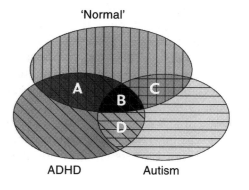

A. Characteristics common to 'normal' and ADHD

B. Characteristics common to 'normal', ADHD and autism

C. Characteristics common to 'normal' and autism

D. Characteristics common to ADHD and autism

Figure 1.3 Disorders as a set of characteristics.

characteristics can occur in a serious and a milder form and that in combination they can form different forms of behaviour patterns, just like a kaleidoscope, where the same pieces of glass can form different figures. In Chapter 4 I explain how disorders and normality relate to each other.

The group of disorders where a number of characteristics of contact disorders occur is, as we saw, called the *autistic spectrum* (Wing 1988). Some characteristics can occur in a mild form without causing serious problems and may even be an advantage, such as a sharp *eye for detail*. Other symptoms, such as a deviant language development, are so important that they immediately constitute an indication of a serious problem. These are symptoms that impede the child's functioning to an important degree. This is definitely true of the way in which the child makes contact with his or her environment, because this is a fundamental issue for all humans.

A clear example of the idea that we are dealing with characteristics which can occur in mild to serious forms, is in a statement by Hans Asperger (1944). He suggested that all men are a little autistic. What he was aiming at was that autistic characteristics are more connected to a male brain structure. This is expressed, for example, in the difference between men and women in the degree that they can put themselves in someone else's position. The male pattern of thinking and feeling occurs in the autistic person in an 'exaggerated' form as it were, according to Asperger. Simon Baron-Cohen (2003) took up this idea and published a book on the extreme male brain. If we say that every man is a little bit autistic we can also find a counterpart 'exaggerated' trait in the female condition and say that all women are a little bit theatrical, without having to diagnose this as a disorder. We will see in Chapter 3 why men are more prone to autistic characteristics and women more prone to theatrical traits.

The idea of a gradual scale of disorders means that it cannot always be clearly established whether someone is suffering from a certain disorder or whether he or she has certain characteristics in a milder form and if we stuck that one 'label' on him or her we would be exaggerating the problem.

Diagnosis or label

To what extent is it useful to make a diagnosis? When does a diagnosis become more than simply putting a label on someone, causing the person more harm than good? A diagnosis is actually only there in order to obtain understanding for certain behaviour, to show others how to deal with it and to mobilize understanding and help. When the diagnosis only serves to put someone in a box and then actually discriminate against him or her, it is counterproductive and harmful. Making a diagnosis can result in all a person's behaviour being placed under one label and for some behaviour being, for example, wrongly blamed on autism. We run the risk of doing someone wrong. We can see this happen when using the term 'autistic' instead of 'autistic person'. In the case of the label 'autistic' the person is subordinate to the diagnosis, and so the risk increases that all of his or her behaviour is being classified under the term 'autism'. It is not surprising, then, that such a term can develop into an abusive word.

Before we make a diagnosis, it is therefore wise to look at what can be gained from it. It seems that during the past few years we have discovered 'the child' and are making more and more diagnoses of disorders (Delfos 2002a). We are consciously choosing whether we want to have children and, if so, how many. This all causes us to be 'on top of our children', and for the first time we really discover what they are like. To our amazement they prove to be much more intelligent than we first thought, but the problem is also that we often expect more from our children. Deviation from the average is maybe judged more harshly than is necessary. Society's development of an increasingly faster living pace, and the emancipation and self-development of men and women which mean that often both parents work, have resulted in busy adults who are often less tolerant and less able to deal well with the deviant and disturbing behaviour of their children. When taking a closer look suddenly it seems that all children are deviant! A correct and balanced diagnosis is therefore even more important.

This book is not meant to further increase the making of diagnoses, to encourage parents or teachers to decide whether a child is suffering from some kind of disorder. When you see disorders being described it seems as though all of a sudden you know very many people who have that disorder, and the same goes with diseases. When a disease comes up in the news it seems that suddenly there are a lot of people with that disease. That is because a layman often has difficulty in seeing exactly how a characteristic works, how strong its presence must be and which other characteristics definitely have to occur or not when making a diagnosis. Reading this book is not supposed to make people suffer from disorders they do not have and make people think that their children have an autistic disorder when they do not! This risk is certainly there because autistic traits are very common, certainly in men. We will easily think that we recognize the traits and think that our nephew, niece or husband is autistic. Labelling someone with a disorder he or she does not have is detrimental and discourages mutual communication.

After this warning I want to say that parents are often experts regarding their children, although their fear and powerlessness sometimes causes them to be unable to reach their expertise. That is where the skill of the professional carer comes in, to expose the wisdom of the parent and to listen well to the child and the parent (Delfos 2000), to subsequently make a correct diagnosis based on that information and to get the right professional help for them. For professional carers this book is intended to give something extra to hold on to, because it puts the various diagnoses and their criteria together and offers handles for professional care.

For parents, it is useful to know what information a researcher needs in order to make a correct diagnosis. To start with, we will deal in Chapter 2 with the conditions when a behavioural problem is more the result of a disorder which is governed mainly by the predisposition or the maturation of the central nervous system (CNS), and when a problem mainly seems to be the result of the environment within which the child is growing up.

The strength and the weakness

Autism is a fascinating subject because basically it is a disorder of true human nature (Happé 1998). It touches humans at their very foundation: social interaction. The term *autism* stems from *autos* and expresses the withdrawal into oneself. Autism is universal and timeless, and can be recognized in a distinct pattern of behaviour in different countries and in different cultures. Social interaction is fundamental to the human being. Wing (1997) indicates that the lack of social skills to any degree can have a large impact on the development of the child as a human being and on his or her chances of being able to function independently later.

Although I am writing about a disorder, I want to make it clear from the beginning that conduct disorders in general, and Asperger's syndrome in particular, do not only contain negative characteristics. They distinguish themselves from an 'average' development, especially as far as having difficulty with social interaction is concerned. At the same time there are particularly valuable characteristics connected to the disorder: the other side of the coin. It would be a shame if we concentrated too much on the problematic characteristics and closed our eyes to the special qualities. The sometimes staggering encyclopaedic knowledge and refined language and manners of people with a disorder from the autistic spectrum, often put people on the wrong track. They expect the same intelligence and skills in the social field and that is where people with Asperger's syndrome have shortcomings. Their intelligence and other strengths make it possible for them to think things out and compensate for their shortcomings. With age social contact will develop if the conditions are favourable, and certainly when help is offered.

An essential, important positive aspect concerns norms and values. People with an autistic disorder, such as Asperger's syndrome, are generally more 'pure' and communicate much more directly, without ulterior motives. It makes them very reliable, a quality which we consider very important in relationships. Birger Sellin (1995), an autistic young man who had not spoken since he was two and who started to communicate using language again with the help of the computer, wrote: 'How often have I wanted to return to the muteness and peace of our valuable, non-deceitful world of autistic people.' Contact with autistic people makes you a better person. The beautiful phrase of Antoine de Saint Exupéry fits very well the connection that can develop between autistic and not autistic people: 'Far from hurting me, you complete me when you differ from me.'

Their pureness also makes autistic people vulnerable. The first three lines of a poem by Dutch poet Gerrit Achterberg (1984) express this vulnerability in autistic people. Their inability to interpret people's behaviour means that they experience everything more purely, without suspicion, and as a consequence they can experience acute injustice.

Without speaking about autism, Achterberg voices the autistic pureness so acutely:

> I am made of so much glass
> That every harsh voice
> Is a stone and a crack

The uncle of Joe, a small boy who we will encounter more often in the course of the book, expressed himself as follows about Joe and his mother: 'They have no filter, they are pure, the world enters them as it is.'

We can try to help people with a contact disorder to use their qualities so that they are less troubled by their problematic characteristics and enjoy their positive characteristics more.

The purpose of the book

The most important purpose of this book is to make autistic disorders in general, and Asperger's syndrome and PDD-NOS in particular, more understandable, by means of theory and examples of the people themselves. I hope that with this book we can create respect and understanding both for people who struggle with such a disorder, and for their environment. I hope that it will stimulate people to let go of their inner statistics of how people should be, and not to approach autistic people armed with those statistics and judge them on those grounds as being strange. The book gives advice and tips on various issues that may occur in daily practice. However, the book is not intended to be an exhaustive book of advice. Each person needs custom-made advice which is attuned to him or her. Something that may work for one parent may be impossible to carry out in a different family. But when the background of the behaviour is understood, people's own creativity can be awakened or they may be enabled to explain to someone else what is going on and ask whether they have an idea of how a certain problem can be dealt with. When parents have problems with a pre-schooler who has not slept through the night since he was born and thereby affects his own and his parents' night's rest, general advice will often be 'let the child cry' while the parents feel that this is not possible. The problem becomes very different when people become aware that the child also misses his (night's) rest and would love to sleep, but has enormous difficulties with learning the sleeping phases of *falling asleep* and *sleeping through*. Advice that is based on linking up to the predisposition, as we will see, is completely different and therefore more effective.

We want to offer a framework which makes people understand why a child becomes angry or cannot orientate him- or herself in time, so that help can be offered which links up to the autistic child him- or herself. For people who struggle with Asperger's syndrome or PDD-NOS it can, I hope, help to show how they are regarded and also how fellow-sufferers have looked for and found solutions.

Focal points

- Autism has always existed and exists in all cultures through all ages.

- Autism goes with a more 'male' brain structure.

- One can also have a few characteristics, 'autistic traits' or 'Asperger traits', without having the disorder as a whole.

- People cannot be 'cured' of autism, but they can learn how to live with it.

- Disorders in the autistic spectrum do not develop because of a child's upbringing, but are present due to predisposition.

- Parents (especially mothers) with autistic children are, out of necessity, very oriented towards their children.

- There are core characteristics and additional characteristics with autistic disorders. Not all characteristics are always present and not all characteristics are always that strong.

- A diagnosis should have a function for the well-being of the person involved and his or her environment.

Focal points regarding attitude

- Autism is not a question of upbringing but of predisposition.

- Having respect for a person also means having respect for the limitations which predisposition puts on this person.

- People with autistic disorders have qualities which are the other side of the coin of their problematic characteristics.

2

Predisposition or environment

When observing problematic behaviour in children, we always wonder where this behaviour comes from. This is an important question. Predisposed behaviour in a child cannot – at least, not easily – be changed into totally different behaviour. The child and its environment must learn to cope with this predisposition. This does not mean that one must resign oneself and despondently endure or accept such behaviour. Once we know that the behaviour is predisposed, it will be possible to see how it can be channeled into more appropriate behaviour. In this way we can help the child to function as well as possible. If the behaviour mainly arises from the environment and is maintained by it – for instance, through upbringing or because the child has experienced a traumatic event – the behaviour can in principle be reoriented and modified into different behaviour that suits the child or his or her potential better.

Development from predisposition and environment

For the development of a child, it is important to know what is within his or her capabilities so that one knows whether the child should be taught to cope with a deficiency or should be stimulated and educated instead. A child with an autistic disorder, for example, has difficulty imagining what goes on in another person's mind; in other words he or she has inadequate *empathic capacity*. Often children with autism can barely understand how people associate with one another. *Evaluating social interaction* is very hard for these children, no matter how intelligent they are. They sometimes have less trouble with mathematics than with understanding why someone says or does something. If we do not know that this is predisposed, we will tend to correct the child whenever he displays socially inappropriate behaviour and does not interact properly with other people. We may become annoyed about the child's behaviour as if he had the choice to behave differently.

If we are aware that such behaviour is predisposed and that the child does not sense how he should behave in particular situations, we will be more inclined to explain things to the child and teach him what is going on and how he could behave. If we start from the assumption that the child does comprehend social relations, we will be more inclined to blame him for not displaying proper conduct, telling him off instead of giving him an explanation.

You tell a toddler a few times that she mustn't kick, that kicking hurts the other child just as it would do if the other child kicked her. You then have to explain this again, for example when the toddler pinches someone. Most children would then have understood that if you hurt someone else it feels the same to them as it would to you, and that it is not right to hurt anyone.

This is not how it works in children with an autistic disorder. No matter how intelligent the child, if this kicking is explained to her in one situation, she often does not yet understand that in principle this goes for all children and also for other situations. Initially, she applies the explanation only to that one child: 'John does not like being kicked, just like I don't like it myself.' However, this does not mean that it is thereby clear to the child that this applies to children in general. One therefore has to explain the same thing to her in relation to Eric, Peter or Omar, until the child understands that 'it hurts boys when I kick them, just like it hurts me when I am kicked'. This may then also have to be explained in relation to girls and adults until she has internalized the abstract rule 'when I kick someone it hurts him or her just like it would hurt me if it were done to me'. If the child then finds that Chris starts to laugh after being kicked, she is utterly confused: does it hurt or does it not hurt? Is it right or is it not right? A child without a contact disorder would in this case form the following abstract rule: if you hurt someone, it bothers him or her but not everyone shows this, some laugh it off. This is a hard rule for a child with a contact disorder because she has to distinguish between just laughing and laughing something off.

An added difficulty with this seemingly straightforward example is that many children with an autistic disorder have a high pain threshold and may not feel any pain when being kicked. Accordingly, they ought to develop the rule: 'I feel no pain when I am kicked, but others do'. It is now becoming clearer how much more difficult it is for an autistic child to develop a correct rule, because what is pain, how does it feel? Children with a contact disorder need extra practice in social contacts, comparable with learning arithmetic when endless series of sums are dished up to teach the child how to add and subtract.

To an important extent, it is predisposition that determines how a child behaves, although this is not always realized in connection with behaviour. When a child is born, we are immediately eager to find out in what way he takes after either parent or either side of the family, but after some time we 'forget' how important predisposition is and very soon we blame the child's behaviour on his upbringing. However, as parents we do know how important predisposition actually is. This we perceive when we have one child and even more so when we have a second child. Right from birth the child shows that he has come into the world with particular qualities. Of course the environment is important; for instance, it makes an enormous difference whether you grow up in times of war or in peacetime; but it is predisposition that determines the boundaries of an individual's possibilities. Upbringing may determine whether a child's potential is used to the full or remains untapped but it cannot bring out something that is not there. The best condition for ensuring optimum development is to enable the child to develop qualities for which he is 'ready' at any given moment in time. If you stimulate and train a child in a skill for which he is not yet ready, it will in principle take him longer to learn and master that skill than if the child starts to develop it only when he is actually ready for it. Premature stimulation may also hamper the development of other skills.

Arnold Gesell (Gesell and Ilg 1949) showed that it is ill-advised to train children in something for which they are not ready. He worked with identical twins whose predisposition, recorded in their genetic material, is in principle exactly the same. He trained one of the twins in motor activities: sitting, crawling, standing, walking, while the other twin was not given such training. The twin that received training did in fact develop these motor skills much faster than the other. After some time, however, the twin without training caught up with the other, and there was no longer any noticeable difference in motor skills. The one that had not been trained, however, had been able to develop the things for which she was ready and as a result displayed a broader development, in more fields than just motor skills. What Gesell is trying to show us is that each child has its own rate of maturation which ought to be respected. We can try to turn our children into child prodigies in a particular field but this will inhibit development in other areas, causing the child to develop less harmoniously as a result.

However, it is not always easy to know what a child is ready for. The developmental psychologist Vygotsky (1962) showed how one can find out. He argued that children had particular potentialities or possibilities which under particular circumstances may develop at a given moment. The possibilities are within what Vygotsky calls the *zone of proximal development*. Within this zone lie the child's potentialities that it cannot yet realize independently. Once a child is ready, a potentiality can be transformed into a skill that can be carried out independently. The skill is then in the *zone of actual development*.

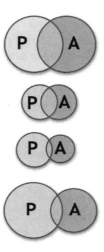

Figure 2.1 Vygotsky's zones of development.

The possibilities that are potentially present in the child lie within the zone of proximal development. The possibilities which the child can perform independently are within the zone of actual development. The overlapping area comprises the possibilities which the child is developing through practice and doing things together with others.

The two circles at the top comprise potentialities (P) which correspond to skills (A). This represents an 'average' child growing up under 'normal' circumstances.

The second set of circles relates to a child whose predisposition covers fewer potentialities (P) which grows up under 'normal' circumstances and proportionately develops fewer skills (A). For instance, a child with autism has less potentialities in the area of social skills.

The third set of circles concerns a child with a disposition with fewer potentialities (P) which grows up under less favourable circumstances and consequently develops fewer skills (A).

The fourth set of circles shows a child, with, in principle, 'normal' potentialities, who grows up under unfavourable circumstances. The skills are not in accordance with the possibilities. This applies, for instance, to neglected or traumatized children. The possibilites are present but cannot be utilized.

The zone of actual development comprises skills which a child can perform independently. A potentiality may develop into a skill in particular through *play, doing things together* and when others *show* how things are done. One of the most important forms is *make-believe play* in which children pretend that a branch is a gun or play at mummies and daddies. Through play the child 'practises' a skill. If, while playing, a child acts out a particular subject, she is ready to actualize the potentiality. If she is not ready for it, the child, even when someone else shows her how it is done, will not easily display the skill. In this case, she will need lengthy training to master the skill. We can observe this principle in operation when the child learns to walk. Walking is a skill potentially present in every child. After some time, the child is ready to learn to walk. With the parents shouting 'bravo', he makes his first steps, waddling like a duck, but if there is something in the corner of the room that a child wants, he will rush towards it on all fours. Only when the child fully masters the art of walking, will he no longer try to speed along on all fours but use his feet instead. Only then will walking have progressed from the zone of proximal development to the zone of actual development.

When a child reaches the age when he could be toilet trained at night, this does not always mean he has matured enough to be ready for it. In general, parents are aware of this and rightly give the child more time to become fully toilet trained. But here, again, there are limits indicating that the child is beginning to deviate from the norm. In this case, the parent can start toilet training with the aid of techniques such as the bed-wetting alarm, which wakes the child as soon as he begins to urinate. The question then is when the child reaches the moment when he requires training. For toilet training, it is important that the child has sufficiently matured before energy can be devoted to training. In line with Vygotsky, it can be argued that if much training is needed the child may not yet have sufficiently matured. It therefore makes sense to explain to the child that a bed-wetting alarm will be used to see if he needs training. If it requires too much effort, the maturation process can be given another chance and training may be resumed at a later stage. It is important to explain this to the child so that he does not lose hope of becoming toilet trained. Hope is one of the most powerful emotions for well-being, for learning, for development and even for healing.

When a child has reached the proper level of maturity, the new behaviour does not always emerge spontaneously. Often there has been habituation as a result of which the undesired behaviour is not necessary but is nevertheless maintained. A clear example of this is stuttering.

Stuttering is a problem of the maturation of the central nervous system. Stuttering is said to be connected with unduly slow coordination of the muscles regulating the vocal cords (Peters and Guitar 1991). The production of a sentence stagnates even though the sentence has already been correctly formulated in the brain. Slowing down behaviour, such as ensuring relaxed breathing or slow speaking, slows the process and helps to prevent or overcome stuttering. When maturation is complete, stuttering often still persists as it has in the meantime become a habit of many years and the child has never been able to develop a normal pattern of communication. This has particular consequences for socio-emotional development. Upon maturation, proper training aimed at strengthening self-confidence and ensuring appropriate language production may be effective to overcome the stutter. Stutterers have to learn an entirely new form of communication, which can to some extent be compared with being on one's own in a country with a totally unfamiliar language. The language of non-stutterers, for instance, has long sentences and no one to help out. No matter how much stutterers would like to stop stuttering, their stuttering behaviour gives them a sense of security and predictability of communication. On reaching the proper level of maturity, stutterers have difficulty letting go of their habits in communicating.

We have said that play, in particular make-believe play, is important in learning skills. In children with autistic disorders, however, capacities for play and imagination are limited. We shall discuss this in more detail in subsequent chapters. More has to be offered, and more frequently, to a child with an autistic disorder than to an average child. We will have to pay more attention to the child's level of social readiness as his or her capacities for social interaction from the zone of proximal development are limited. Since social interaction is of essential importance for human functioning, additional training will have to be provided to teach the child social insight and social skills, even if he or she is not entirely ready for it. In the following chapters, I shall indicate how we can help a child in this respect.

Visible versus non-visible

If a child has a predisposition for something, this certainly does not always means that it is evident from the child's appearance. A child with Down syndrome has a chromosome anomaly that is immediately evident from his or her appearance. The environment responds to this *vis-à-vis* the parent and the child. This means that the need for help is more obviously clear. This is not the case for children with an autistic disorder. Their disorder does not have visible external characteristics. For the parents and the child this may entail an additional burden on upbringing. In order to illustrate this, I have drawn up Table 2.1, comparing a child with Down syndrome and a child with a contact disorder.

Table 2.1 Differences between brain disorder and contact disorder	
Major brain disorder: *Down syndrome*	*Major disturbance:* *Contact disorder*
Abnormal appearance, abnormal functioning	Normal appearance, abnormal functioning
Structural problem: throughout life	Can be confined, with great effort
Behaviour that cannot be directly confused with problems in upbringing, e.g. protruding tongue	Behaviour that can be directly confused with problems in upbringing, e.g. interrupting people
Recognizable as difficult to bring up, a heavy burden	Not directly recognizable as difficult to bring up, more likely to be interpreted as badly brought up
Often various physical disabilities	Often various invisible disorders

To parents of a child with a non-visible disorder, it may be a relief to learn through diagnosis what they have always sensed in the child, namely that there is 'something in the child' that cannot be changed or even modified very much through the upbringing they give. Often, it is less noticeable to other family members that there is something the matter with the child's predisposition. Those who do not live closely with the child frequently have the impression that there are shortcomings in the way the parents bring her up. This is particularly the case when they have to supervise the child for a short while, focusing attention on her. Children who are hyperactive may, for instance, keep quiet for some time. In a new or unusual situations, the deviating behaviour is often less evident. When this happens, many people think that the child's behaviour is due to her upbringing. What is ignored in such cases is that the child's behaviour can be controlled temporarily but that alternative behaviour cannot easily be *automated*. Consequently, the undesirable behaviour re-emerges as soon as the child stops focusing on it. Since it is not possible to focus continuously on specific behaviour at the expense of all other matters requiring attention, the behaviour recurs. This forms the backdrop to the frequent remarks made by the parents: 'Come on, do your best; you can do it if you only try!' What they forget is that the child cannot constantly do her best in one particular respect.

> It is often painful for parents to hear that the aunt with whom the child goes to stay does not see anything wrong with the child's behaviour. It is not long before an accusing finger is pointed at the way the parents bring up the child. Yet, the specific behaviour would inevitably re-emerge while the child was staying at the aunt's place if he were living with her. Even behaviour determined by predisposition moves to the background when a child focuses her concentration upon it. It can in this way be controlled temporarily but the desirable behaviour does not become automated and the undesirable behaviour recurs as soon as attention is relaxed.

For parents, a non-invisible disorder in their child means that not only carers but also the school and their own relatives often wrongly point to the way in which they have been bringing up their child. As the years go by, the parents' powerless isolation gets increasingly worse. The child feels misunderstood. He cannot take the advice of adults seriously because he senses, without being conscious of it, that this is based on misapprehension. An obstinate child can thus in actual fact be a very wise child who ignores advice because he feels that that advice bears no relevance to his problems, the predisposition he has to cope with. The 'arrogant' adult who assumes that he or she knows best and not the child often regards the child that does not heed advice as obstinate and stubborn.

The mother of a boy with a non-visible disorder gratefully felt understood at last when the disorder was diagnosed. Finally her sense of impotence was taken seriously. 'But try and explain this to his grandparents', she sighed. Her words express the loneliness caused by the lack of understanding around her and her lone struggle to help her child.

In addition to the sense of relief brought about by the diagnosis and the reassurance it gives to the family and the environment, the diagnosis also triggers a *mourning process*. While in their heart of hearts the parents knew all along there was something wrong with the child, the diagnosis means that there is no more doubt possible. Their hope of a swift change is being taken away from them and, as mentioned above, hope provides one of the most important reasons to keep people going, motivating them to continue the struggle even in the face of serious, incurable diseases. But, after diagnosis, the child's future and in principle that of the family as a whole looks quite different.

Predisposition is formed by the genetic material, circumstances during pregnancy (an addiction or a metabolic disease but also the amount of stress to which the mother is exposed), and the circumstances surrounding delivery (an oxygen shortage during delivery, for instance, can cause brain damage in the baby). Alongside predisposition and environment, there is a third factor that plays a significant role in the child's development, namely the *maturation of the central nervous system*. This system comprises the brain and the nerve tracts.

Maturation

The maturation of the central nervous system is an important aspect of human development. When we speak of disorders, they are often connected with deviant, retarded or restricted maturation of the central nervous system. As we shall see, maturation is a central issue in autistic children, who have a slowed and often limited maturation of the central nervous system.

The fact is that children are born much too early: the central nervous system takes an additional 25 years to mature fully (Gesell 1965; Tanner 1978; Virgilio 1986). A marked example of this is the *corpus callosum*, a bundle in the centre of the brain, the 'switchboard' of the brain (see Figure 2.2). This organ links all the areas of the brain with one another, right with left and front with back. Between birth and the age of one year, the corpus callosum increases by 42 per cent, with an another 110 per cent increase between one year and 28 years (Ramaekers and Njiokiktien 1991).

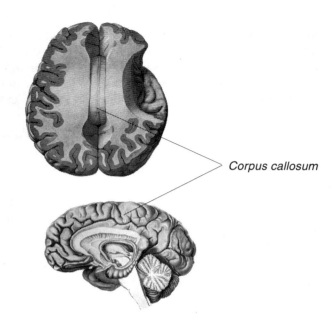

Corpus callosum

Figure 2.2 Cross-section and longitudinal section of the brain (Putz and Pabst 1993). Copyright © Urban und Schwarzenberg Verlag, München. Reproduced with permission from Elsevier.

During maturation the various parts of the brain acquire their specific functions. The brain becomes lateralized, meaning that specific functions develop on the left or right side of the brain. In boys, the right hemisphere will in general develop more strongly than the left while in girls the two hemispheres of the brain develop more equally. Functions such as understanding spatial relations and abstraction are located in the right hemisphere while language functions are more specialized in the left hemisphere. In girls, moreover, the language centres are often located in both hemispheres, ensuring greater availability of language. Below we shall see that this difference in language orientation plays a role in the form which the austistic disorder assumes.

Integration and coordination of the hemispheres increase with maturation, among other things as the result of the growth of the corpus callosum. One of the significant aspects of brain maturation is that connections are formed within the brain (see Figure 2.3). The number of brain cells decreases as links between the cells increase. To an important extent, maturation means the establishment of connections inside the brain.

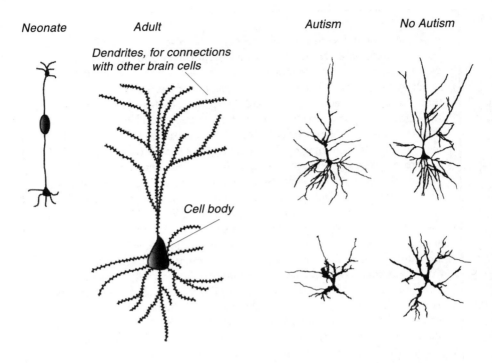

Figure 2.3 Brain cells of neonate and adult (Eliot 1999). Reproduced with permission from Random House.

Figure 2.4 Brain cells of autistic and non-autistic people (Bauman and Kemper 1994). Copyright © Bauman and Kemper. Reproduced with permission from The Johns Hopkins Univeristy Press.

With the increasing maturation of the central nervous system, the nerve tracts leading from and to the brain become thicker and thereby better insulated. Consequently, information can be transmitted more purely to and from the brain, without being disturbed or influenced by other information. The brain structure of children with a disorder within the autistic spectrum deviates from the average. The autistic spectrum includes contact disorders that are characterized, among other things, by a serious inability to evaluate social interaction. They include autism and Asperger's syndrome.

Children with a disorder within the autistic spectrum have a significantly less developed left hemisphere (Bauman and Kemper 1994; Bauman 1996).

It was long assumed that the left and right hemispheres in autistic people would differ greatly from one another. This expectation was connected with the importance of the left hemisphere for language, which may be seriously disrupted in autistic people. The expectation was that the left hemisphere would be significantly less developed than the right one. Post-mortem examination revealed no clear differences in the size of the two hemispheres. New measurement techniques such as magnetic resonance imaging (MRI), positron emission tomography (PET) and magneto-electroencephalography (MEG) have made it possible to map the living brain. Using these techniques, 'photographs' can be taken of the living brain, making it possible to study what the brain looks like when performing various tasks. It is possible to visualize where and how the brain solves mathematical problems and, for instance, where word finding occurs. Accordingly, we can now map differences between individual people and between men and women. One finding has been that in autistic people the two hemispheres show significant differences. The finding that there was no apparent difference in the size of the two hemispheres was due to the fact that in the left hemisphere there are more cells but fewer connections between cells (see Figure 2.4). During maturation, cells die off to make place for connections. In autistic people, the left hemisphere is therefore underdeveloped, more immature (Bauman and Kemper 1994; Bauman 1996).

Nevertheless, brain mapping has not yet advanced sufficiently to display for the individual child whether, and to what extent, his or her brain deviates. Only a strong deviation of brain structure can in neurologic examination be established with certainty through techniques such as MRI scanning. However, differences in brain structure, even if minor, may have a considerable impact on behaviour. Rutter and Schopler (1988) indicate that no great differences have been found in brain structure and that this suggests that there must be subtle differences between the brains of autistic people and those of non-autistic people.

The course and rate of maturation seem to be predisposed to a great extent. As a large part of maturation occurs after birth, moreover, the result of the process will also strongly depend on influence from the environment.

Children who are underfed in the first year run the risk that their central nervous system matures insufficiently without having a chance to make up for this later on. As a result, these children may suffer from disorders which in this case cannot be said to be predisposed as they result from a lengthy process after birth. However, it is an irreversible process that cannot be restored and makes its influence felt throughout life. Nor can it be argued that it is a result of the factor 'environment', although this does play a role. The child faces a structural problem in which maturation of the central nervous system is the decisive factor. Maturation that was potentially normal in the child's predisposition is thus limited by an environmental factor.

The night is presumably important for maturation, in particular *dream sleep, REM sleep*, when the brain is 'cleaned up' (Delfos 2003a). During the first years, but especially the very first year, a large part of sleeping time consists of REM sleep. REM sleep, named after the rapid eye movements occurring behind closed eyelids, is in principle the phase of sleep in which dreaming occurs. The younger the child, the more sleeping time is devoted to dreaming. Babies dream some 50 per cent of their sleeping time, and adults 20 per cent. In premature babies this rises to 80 per cent of sleeping time. Modern theories about dream sleep assume that sleep is necessary to 'sweep clean' the brain, to disentangle meaningless connections formed during the day. Consequently, dream sleep is of crucial importance for the functioning of the brain. This, combined with the large proportion of dream sleep in young children, suggests that dream sleep plays an important role in the maturation of the central nervous system. In the same line of thought, it is thus not surprising that many maturation disorders occur especially at night (*parasomnias*, e.g. sleepwalking, bed wetting, talking during sleep, grinding teeth, restless legs, *pavor nocturnus* – night terrors – stereotypic movements such as head banging and rocking). Getting safely and soundly through the night may well be the best recipe for optimum maturation. The fact is, however, that children who are slow to mature often suffer from sleep problems and have difficulty developing a proper sleep–wake rhythm – *settling* – after birth. Sleep consists of a number of phases (falling asleep, deep sleep, dream sleep, sleep maintenance) of one and a half to two hours on average (see Figure 2.5). Sleep has to continue maturing after birth; in particular the sleep maintenance phase, linking two sleep cycles without waking, still has to be developed. As a result of this, children wake up after one or more sleep cycles and have difficulty falling asleep again. Here, the environment can have a conducive or detrimental effect; conducive in enabling the child to sleep and dream optimally.

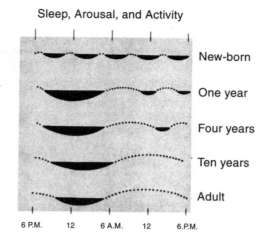

Figure 2.5 Sleep cycles (Morgan 1965). Reproduced with permission from The McGraw-Hill Companies.

Children with a disorder within the autistic spectrum often display sleeping problems: difficulty sleeping (*falling asleep* and *maintaining sleep*) and an excessive need for sleep. The latter applies in particular to children with an autistic disorder combined with an intellectual disability. Since falling asleep and maintaining sleep are difficult, these children cannot adequately convert their need for sleep into sleep, leading to exhaustion. Autistic children have a deviating sleep pattern. They display more discontinuity (*dyssomnias*) in their sleep – disturbed sleep, for instance in the insufficiently matured sleep maintenance phase, and more deviating sleep (parasomnias) such as sleepwalking – than children with an intellectual disability or children without any disorder (Schreck and Mulick 2000). What is conspicuous in autistic children is their disorientation on waking up (Schreck and Mulick 2000). In Chapter 5 we shall see that this is consistent with a poorly developed socioscheme such as is observed in autism. Optimal maturation through the soundest possible sleep is particularly important for autistic children. However, the sleeping problems of children with a maturation disorder make it difficult, and sometimes exhausting, for parents to help their children to sleep soundly through the night.

Sleeping problems in babies are more frequent in those with maturation problems. It is of added importance for them to get a good night's rest. This means that parents are often busy with their child for many nights in a row, causing exhaustion in the parents. Such parents are therefore not helped if professionals ignore this problem and tell them to just let the child cry and not respond. The parents feel perfectly well that the child needs them. It is better to lend support to the parents and build up a network around them to ensure that they themselves can get enough sleep at night, with the family helping out where necessary. The child also needs a sense of security during the night. To the child, a sense of security means knowing that there is help at hand whenever she needs it. The child cries frequently because she doesn't feel well or is hungry but also because she wants to have her parents near. An important aid to creating a sense of security in the child is the smell of the parents. Babies sleeping in the parents' room cry much less. Babies smelling the odour of the amniotic fluid on a cotton bud are comforted more quickly (Varendi *et al.* 1997, 1998). Putting a piece of cloth on which the parents have lain near the baby increases her sense of security and can reduce crying considerably. If the child cries a great deal during the day but not at night, this may be not so much an indication that there is a maturation problem but that she is overexcited during the day and is unable to relax due to lack of sleep.

It is clear from the above that maturation of the central nervous system is of great significance for the child's development. Disturbances in maturation may be innocent in character but may also have substantial consequences. Children with a disorder within the autistic spectrum often display more maturation problems. These relate both to the development of the two hemispheres of the brain and to the maturation of the nervous system and presumably also the maturation of the hormonal system, specifically the part geared to coping with stress.

The *Diagnostic and Statistical Manual of Mental Disorders*, or DSM-IV (APA 1994), the most widely used international classification of mental disorders, relates various disorders to maturation of the central nervous system. In a study (Delfos 2003a) of the references in DSM-IV to problems of the central nervous system taking the form of slowed or limited maturation, a number of disorders were discovered which were termed maturation disorders (Box 2.1).

If we regard autism as deviating and retarded maturation, it will not cause surprise to find that autistic children display these maturation disorders more frequently than non-autistic children. The parasomnias mentioned by Schreck and Mulick (2000) in the sleep pattern of autistic children are also reflected in this list.

Predisposition and individual maturation to a large extent determine the way in which the child experiences the world around him or her. A child's behaviour is determined by the boundaries of his predisposition. If a child does not meet the

---

Box 2.1 Maturation disorders.

- Primary enuresis (bed wetting)

- Primary encopresis (soiling)

- Restless legs

- Involuntary muscular movements

- Tics

- Dyspraxia (coordination problems)

- Grinding of teeth

- Talking during sleep

- Stuttering

- Sleepwalking

- Sleeping with eyes open

- *Pavor nocturnus* (night terror)

- Stereotypic movements: rocking, head banging

- ADHD

- Language development disorder.

---

standards of development of his age category, the question arises: what causes this problem? It may be a *developmental delay* compared with the child's peers. There may be two different causes for this. First, the child may lag behind in his own potential development due to circumstances in his environment. Second, the child may have limited potentialities and therefore fail to develop in a way we would expect at his age. In the latter case, we would prefer to use the term *limited development* rather than the more widely used *developmental delay*. When there is a developmental delay, we are dealing with the fourth set of circles in Figure 2.1; when there is limited development, the second and third sets of circles apply.

Common threads: Basic signs of disorders

When children experience difficulties in their development, there are a number of basic signals indicating this: *anxiety, aggression, hyperactivity* and *psychosomatic complaints*. That a child has problems can also be seen in the course which a development takes that is already under way. For instance, if a child has normal language development and this suddenly stagnates seriously, it may be a pointer to problems. There are even forms of autism (Rett's syndrome and disintegrative disorder) in which there is a loss of skills already acquired, such as language.

In a study of disorders connected with deviating maturation of the central nervous system, the question as to whether there are any common threads characteristic of these problems was also explored (Delfos 2003a). With regard to the way children function, there are two issues that play a crucial role in disorders, i.e. disturbances attributable to the child's predisposition or connected with retarded or limited maturation. They form, as it were, *common threads*, indicating that these *may* be problems determined by predisposition or maturation. We observe these features in an extreme form in children with contact disorders that are part of the autistic spectrum. They are *resistance to change* and *problems concerning empathic capacity* (Delfos 2003a).

Resistance to change does not mean that no new things are embarked upon. The resistance arises when someone else wants a change to the child's activity. An activity that emerges by itself poses no problems, but when the child's own 'programme' is disrupted by an activity demanded by someone else, resistance arises. People who pursue a wide range of activities may likewise suddenly show resistance to change when someone else suggests something.

Change requires a switch and the (quick) processing of new stimuli. Resistance to change is connected with, among other things, the structure of brain hemispheres with mutually very different developments, the corpus callosum and other areas of the brain. A smaller corpus callosum means fewer 'possibilities for switching' from left to right and reciprocally between various areas in the brain. This is one reason why there is more difficulty processing new stimuli. This basic sign of resistance to change can be translated into a *behavioural sign*. The purpose of this is that the presence of the sign provides an indication of the possibility of a predispositional problem. However, it is no proof, because a disorder may occur without this sign, and the sign can be present also when there is no significant disorder.

Resistance to change is related to the difference in the development of the two hemispheres of the brain. If there is a marked difference in the development of the right and left hemispheres, this means that a difference may arise in strength of right-sided and left-sided motor function, resulting in non-smooth motor function. *Left-handedness* may even arise, indicative of a dominant right hemisphere, with the right side of the brain more developed than the left. The left hemisphere coordinates right-sided motor activity and the right hemisphere left-sided motor activity. When there is a difference in development of the two hemispheres there is a greater chance that motor function on the left and right side of the body are not mutually attuned (*left/right coordination*). Accordingly, resistance to change is reflected in the basic sign of *non-smooth motor function*. This is a first sign – though not proof – that we may be dealing with problems attributable to predisposition. If the left and right motor areas differ, there is a greater chance that other parts of the brain have also developed differently in left/right strength. However, the differences may also remain confined to motor function or there may be differences in strength between the two hemispheres without involving problems in motor function. For instance, Geschwind and Behan (1984) indicate that someone with a more weakly developed left hemisphere may well be right-handed, but left-handedness (i.e. a strong right hemisphere, at least in terms of motor function) is certainly an indication that the right side of the brain is more strongly developed than the left.

Non-smooth, non-variable motor function may be indicative of pre-dispositional problems (Hadders-Algra, Klip-Van den Nieuwendijk and Van Eykern 1997). The physical signal of non-smooth motor function is as it were a 'translation' of resistance to change. Children experiencing resistance to change may have problems that are predispositonal in origin – controlled by the brain – and a possible indication of this is non-smooth motor function. We observe this in the difficulty these children often have with left/right coordination, difficulty in learning to button up their coat or lacing their shoes.

Thomas and Chess (1977) have classified children according to their temperament, concluding that there are three types: babies with a *difficult temperament*, those with an *easy temperament* and those *slow to warm up*. Resistance to change is an important element in babies with a difficult temperament. New stimuli are not properly received by these babies and they initially respond by being startled or by rejection. This is also evident in their motor function. Research into motor function in babies shows that in principle they have 'dancing', flowing motor activity. If motor activity is more wooden and jumpy, this may be an indication of disorder (see Figure 2.6). This may serve as a first sign for the early detection of problems, as the study by Hadders-Algra *et al.* (1997) suggests. The study by Hadders-Algra and Groothuis (1999) associates strongly deviating, stiff, wooden motor activity with serious anomalies in the brain. Deviating motor activity that is less pronounced is associated with less serious neurologic anomalies, such as ADHD and aggressive behaviour.

We see this sign of non-smooth motor activity clearly in the autistic spectrum. The motor activity of children within the autistic spectrum is often not smooth but wooden, they sometimes 'flutter' the hands and have a strange gait. Consequently, they often have difficulty mastering such skills as riding a scooter, skating or cycling.

Wing (2001) notes that while wooden motor actions are characteristic of important parts of the autistic spectrum, this is less so for the combination of severe intellectual disability and autism. This is presumably connected with the fact that in those with a severe intellectual disability there is a marked lack of maturation in both the right and the left hemispheres, which may entail less unequal differences in the way motor control is divided between the two. It is one of the differences between the cases described by Kanner (1943) and Asperger (1944). The cases described by Kanner display no major problems in motor function but their gait is

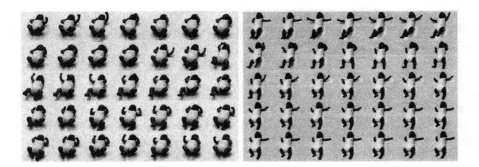

Figure 2.6 Variable and non-variable motor functions (Hadders-Algra et al. 1997). Reproduced with permission from the author and the publisher.

strange, wooden. Asperger mentions wooden motor activity as characteristic of the autistic people with whom he works.

In the next chapter, we shall examine resistance to change in more detail when discussing differences between men and women.

The second common thread is *problems with empathic capacity*. In serious disorders such as autism, empathic capacity is severely restricted, with the child or adult hardly able to imagine what goes on in someone else's mind. One of the main consequences is the difficulty these children have in making friends. Friendship is based on reciprocity and requires empathic capacity in order to build up a mutual relationship. *Difficulty in social interaction with peers* is therefore the translation of problems with empathic capacity. This is a second important sign that there may be problems engendered by predisposition. However, this sign is clearly evident only when children reach nursery school age. In an earlier phase, it may emerge in the form of a lack of *orientation towards the other*. This is already visible in a toddler when he fails to point with his finger when he wants to explain something but instead takes the adult to the relevant location. This is termed *shared attention*; we shall come back to it later. Or it may be visible when a baby fails to share emotions and is more focused on objects than people. We observe this in children with an autistic disorder and it can be demonstrated early using a tool such as the CHAT, the *Checklist for Autism in Toddlers* (Baron-Cohen *et al.* 1996). The two common threads and their translation into basic sign are presented in Table 2.2.

Table 2.2 Basic signs of problems	
Problems	*Translation into behaviour*
Resistance to change	Non-smooth gross and/or fine motor skills
Problematic empathic capacity	Difficulty associating with age-mates

Because they have a brain structure with a less developed left hemisphere, which is where language function is mainly located, children with disorders more frequently have language problems or deviating use of language, for example, using adult-like ways of expressing themselves.

When a child has an important disorder, this is evident in many development tasks, at all ages. One of the most essential tasks is forming *attachments* (Bowlby 1984). Until about the age of three, children are working out a basic scheme for themselves of how people behave towards them, whether their needs are met and whether people can be trusted. This is the formation of an *attachment system*, forging secure, close relationships. The first year and a half are of particular importance for this purpose. A child with an autistic disorder will often have great difficulty in mastering this basic developmental task because it requires the ability to evaluate social interaction. This evaluation of social interaction is a major problem. It means that such children do not easily form a secure attachment or develop trust in the people around them. Later on, they will therefore have extra difficulty in making friends and forging relationships. Often it means that they are strongly focused on only one person, usually the mother, without necessarily being able to maintain a strong *mutual* relationship with that person.

Before discussing the specific features of autistic disorders, we shall first examine a number of general differences between men and women because it will help us to understand autistic disorder. Thereby we shall create a 'normal' framework giving a better insight into deviating behaviour. It will also help us to understand autism better from our own position rather than placing it entirely outside ourselves.

Focal points

- Predisposed behaviour cannot easily be modified.

- A person with an autistic disorder has difficulty evaluating social interaction.

- A help strategy must connect with the source of the problems, whether determined by predispositon/maturation or by the environment.

- Only if there are possibilities within a zone of proximal development can upbringing ensure the realization of a skill, otherwise it cannot.

- We find it difficult to accept predispositional factors in cases where they are not reflected in physical characteristics.

- Bringing up a child with a non-visible disorder is a more burdensome task than bringing up a child with a visible disorder.

- The maturation of the central nervous system is of fundamental importance for development, and continues for many years after birth.

- Sound sleep and proper rest at night are important for the maturation of the central nervous system.

- Children with maturation problems often have sleep problems.

- Children with autism have a maturation problem of the central nervous system.

- Common threads in disorders are resistance to change and problems with emphatic capacity.

- These common threads are translated into the basic signs of non-smooth motor activity and difficulty associating with age-mates.

Focal points regarding attitude

- Respect for a child also means respecting the limits imposed on the child by his or her predispositon.

- The child must be given the opportunity to mature.

Summary

A child's behaviour is determined by his or her predispositon, by factors from the environment and by the maturation of the central nervous system. For optimum development, it is important to start from the development potentialities of the child and to link up with these. To this end, it is necessary to know what are the sources feeding behaviour and which ones play a leading role. For parents and the environment it is important to know that the child's (often difficult) behaviour is not always caused by the upbringing they give him or her but rather by the child's inability and the parents' lack of knowledge of the child, as a result of which their upbringing is not properly attuned to the child. When there are problems that are physically determined without being reflected in physical characteristics, it is often difficult to recognize and acknowledge the predispositional and maturational factors and not to attribute the behaviour to environmental factors, in particular upbringing.

To an important extent, maturation of the central nervous system takes place during the night. Problematic maturation may cause sleep problems. This may explain the fact that children with a disorder connected with maturation of the central nervous system, including the disorders within the autistic spectrum, frequently suffer from sleeping problems. From this point of view, just leaving these children to cry is poor advice; it is better to support the parents and help them in coping with the child at night.

People with a disorder within the autistic spectrum have deviating maturation of the central nervous system, in particular in the formation of connections to and within the left hemisphere of the brain, which is important for language and for putting thoughts and feelings into words.

Basic signs for the presence of disorders with a predispositional source are resistance to change and problems with empathic capacity. These translate into non-smooth motor activity and difficulty interacting with peers, which may be the first signs that there may be problems connected with predisposition or proper maturation.

3

Differences between men and women

Before embarking on a description of what we mean by autistic disorders, it is useful to consider some differences between men and women. The differences play an important role in these disorders and underlie the fact that the number of men with autistic disorders is significantly higher than that of women. The core problem in autistic disorders is *social interaction*, and the fact is that men and women differ considerably in this area.

Gender is an essential conditional factor which to a considerable extent determines the development of the child. This chapter is not intended to describe what *all* men and *all* women are like. Rather, it offers a broad outline, focusing on the 'average' man and the 'average' woman. Men may have female characteristics and women male ones. Nevertheless, when the *entire* range of characteristics in one person is examined, what frequently emerges is a 'male' versus a 'female' structure.

Time and again it proves difficult to speak of the differences between men and women. The inequality of the sexes is often a source of controversy. We have difficulty linking 'unequal' with 'of equal value' and we have a tendency to regard 'unequal' as meaning 'of unequal value'. Since, up to the twenty-first century, emancipation has striven to make men and women not so much of equal *value* but essentially equal, little progress has in actual fact been made in the field of emancipation. While it is true that women have, in particular in the Western world, acquired far more opportunities for development, domestic duties and child care are still mainly shouldered by women, placing a heavier burden on them which may lead some to decide not to have children. Work done by women is still underpaid compared with men and usually has lower status. It would be more sensible to *emancipate by going with the biological stream rather than against it*; in other words, emancipating on the basis of the acceptance and appreciation of the differences between men and women.

Man or woman, XY or XX

An individual's sex is determined by the XX or XY pair of chromosomes, being the female and male pair respectively. In recent years, an increasing number of new techniques have been developed to study cell structure, generating information on the precise nature of predisposition and, in particular, the importance of genetic material. This material is contained in *genes* which are grouped on *chromosomes* within DNA chains. The individual's sex is determined by one of these pairs of chromosomes, namely by the combination XX (woman) or XY (man). In XX, the child receives an X chromosome from the mother and one from the father. In the XY combination, he receives an X chromosome from the mother and a Y chromosome from the father. There are 23 pairs of chromosomes and each pair comprises one chromosome from the father and one from the mother. The genes within these pairs strengthen, mix with or suppress each other. For one characteristic, for instance, it is necessary to have a gene from both parents (in the case of blue eyes) while for other characteristics one gene is sufficient (e.g. for black hair).

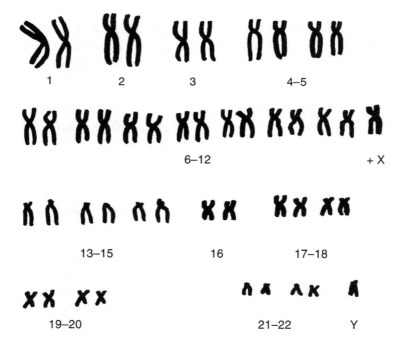

Figure 3.1 The 23 human chromosomes (Passmore and Robson 1973). Reproduced with permission from Blackwell Publishing.

> There are cases in which a chromosome is missing from a pair. Skuse and colleagues (1997) discovered that in Turner's syndrome, where only one X chromosome is present and a second (X or Y) is missing, it does make a difference whether this one X chromosome comes from the mother or the father. People with this syndrome have greater social skills if the X chromosome hails from the father. Accordingly, they assume that the suppression of a gene on the X chromosome is responsible for language disorders and is the cause of developmental disorders such as autism. It would appear that the X chromosome from the father serves to reinforce social skills. In a girl, already possessing an X chromosome from the mother, the X chromosome from the father will strengthen her social skills. In a boy, the X chromosome from the father is missing because he has passed on a Y chromosome to the boy. In boys, therefore, there is no strengthening of social skills through the father.

The role which hereditary predisposition plays in behaviour is becoming clearer thanks to advances in genetics. The XX and XY pairs of chromosomes carry the genetic, hereditary information that generates a range of physical and mental differences between men and women, and these are not confined to visible features.

A number of these differences will be discussed in this chapter on the basis of a bio-psychological model of behavioural problems (Delfos 2004a). Of key importance is the *Geschwind hypothesis* (Geschwind and Behan 1982) according to which the testosterone hormone influences the development of the foetus in the womb, leading to the development of a male or female child.

A high testosterone level during pregnancy has the following consequences:

1. Reduced activity of the immune system. One of the results of this is that in men there is less self-awareness.

2. Inhibition of the left hemisphere of the brain – where language skills are mainly located – with concomitant stimulation of the right hemisphere. In men there is consequently more abstraction and less language orientation and awareness of thoughts and feelings.

3. Higher testosterone level after birth. As a consequence, men are more oriented towards aggression and sexuality.

As the male foetus itself produces testosterone, it is more strongly under the influence of this hormone than the female foetus. Differences between men and women that have particular consequences for disorders such as autism are related to this influence. Appendix V (in electronic form; for access information see p.13) shows schematically and in more detail what influence testosterone has and what this means for autism. At this juncture, suffice it to say that in general men are more strongly influenced by testosterone than women and that in our view the first and second consequences (inhibition of the immune system and difference in hemispheres) play an important role in autism and the third one (testosterone level after birth) is less pronounced.

In developing this model regarding autism, the point of departure is therefore the effect of testosterone on the development of the foetus in the womb. In autism, the effect would be stronger than average.

The 'testosterone finger' appears to present unexpected, strong corroboration of our model. The 2D:4D ratio (index finger: ring finger) of the right hand is an indication of the influence of testosterone in the womb. In women, the ring finger is usually of the same length or shorter than the index finger, in which case the ratio is greater than or equal to 1 (2D:4D≥1). The reverse is usually true in men, with the ring finger longer than the index finger (2D:4D<1) (Manning *et al.* 1998; Manning *et al.* 2000). In autism this difference is even greater, with the ring finger longer than the index finger (Manning *et al.* 2001). This greater influence of testosterone is also observed in top sportsmen (Manning and Taylor 2001) and homosexuals (Robinson and Manning 2000).

We shall limit our focus regarding the consequences of the influence of testosterone on foetal development in the womb to the development of the *self*, the capacity of humans *to empathize with others, linguistic competence, resistance to change, self- reflection* and *capacity for action*. These subjects are significant in understanding how autistic people think and feel.

The self

The first influence of testosterone on foetal development in the womb is the inhibition of the immune system. It takes the form of a restraining effect on the thymus gland, the first building block of the immune system. The thymus plays a role in distinguishing whether substances are 'self' or 'non-self'. This is referred to as the *biological self*, the – unconscious – knowledge that the body has of itself. In men, this biological self is inhibited (Hamilton and Timmons 1990; Damasio 1994, 1999). The biological self presents the first difference between men and women. In women, knowledge about themselves is more strongly developed than in men. The immune system is based on this knowledge, on the biological self. As a consequence of the inhibited biological self in men, their immune system is on average also less strongly developed than in women (Geschwind and Behan 1982, 1984). The immune system checks whether substances are harmful to the body, e.g. a pathogen or bacterium, and proceeds to fight that substance.

It is from the biological self, the unconscious knowledge of one's own body, that human beings possess an *inner wisdom* which they can draw upon to fight deficiencies in the body. Wilkins, Fleischmann and Howard give a striking example of that inner wisdom.

A boy had a great need for salt and did everything to obtain it. He licked the salt off crackers. Whatever his parents did to hide the salt, the child climbed, searched and ate all the salt he could lay his hands on. At the age of three and a half, he was admitted to hospital where he was given a standard diet with normal salt levels. His desire to eat salt was disregarded. After seven days the boy died. Post-mortem examination revealed that he had an anomaly (adrenal deficiency, Addison's disease) obliging him to take up salt externally or die, which indeed turned out to be the cause of death. Until being admitted to hospital, the boy had managed to keep himself alive by taking in extra salt. His body's internal wisdom had shown him what behaviour was necessary (Wilkins, Fleischmann and Howard 1940; Krech, Crutchfield and Ballachey 1962; Gray 1999).

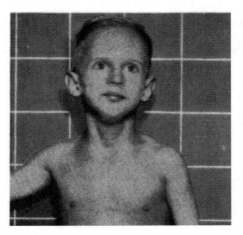

Figure 3.2 The boy who ate salt, aged three and a half. Reproduced from Wilkins et al. (1940) 'Macrogenitosomia precox associated with hyperplasia of the androgenic tissue of the adrenal and death from corticoadrenal insufficiency' in Endocrinology 26, 3, p.387. Copyright © The Endocrine Society. Reproduced with permission.

In this connection, it is interesting to note that children with an autistic disorder often display very limited eating patterns. It often proves hardly possible to make them eat a varied diet. They nevertheless appear to remain surprisingly healthy despite this 'unhealthy' eating pattern (Wing 2001). This is not to say that the desire of autistic children to follow a restricted eating pattern should always be heeded but it may be true that the body's 'wisdom' plays a role here and that there may be less reason for concern than is sometimes thought. In Chapter 10, when discussing resistance to change, we shall take a closer look at eating problems in autistic children. Alongside the body's wisdom, habituation and fear of change play an important part.

Three types of responses of the immune system can be distinguished:

1.   weak response: typical of men

2.   excessive response (autoimmune diseases and allergies): typical of women

3.   immature immune system: typical of (male) children.

In general, men have a weaker immune system than women (Gomez 1991) although the immune system is in fact stronger than we require in a very hygienic environment such as the Western world. Boys can rightly be called the vulnerable sex, even though physically they are often the stronger.

Table 3.1 Gender differences in incidence of disorders (Delfos 2003a)	
Disorders more frequent in boys than girls	*Disorders more frequent in girls than boys*
Enuresis	Anorexia
Encopresis	Bulimia
Pavor nocturnus	Dissociative identity disorder
Sleepwalking	Selective mutism
Talking in sleep	Trichotillomania
Narcolepsy	Self-mutilation
Tics	Phobias
Tourette's syndrome	Migraines
Stereotypical movements	Internalized behavioural disorders
Head banging	Rett's syndrome

Continued on next page

Table 3.1 continued

Disorders more frequent in boys than girls	Disorders more frequent in girls than boys
Aggression	Borderline personality disorder
Compulsive elements	
Language disorders	
Learning disorders	
Dyslexia	
ADHD (Attention deficit hyperactivity disorder)	
Autism	
Asperger's syndrome	
Criminal behaviour	
Asthma	
Schizophrenia	
Abuse of stimulants	
Externalized behavioural disorders	
Stammering	
Disintegrative development disorder	
Pervasive development disorder not otherwise specified (PDD-NOS)	
Multiple complex development disorder (McDD)	

In general, the masculine brain matures more slowly than the female brain. The frequency of hereditary diseases and mental disorders is also greater among boys than girls (Delfos 2003a). Table 3.1 shows gender differences in the prevalence of disorders, based on DSM-IV (APA 1994) and epidemiological research. Most disorders occur more often among boys than girls.

One of the reasons for this is that many anomalies are located on the X chromosome. When there is an 'error' on an X chromosome, it can be 'rectified' by a second X chromosome in the pair XX, a girl. In boys, who have the XY pair, an 'error' on X cannot be rectified because the other in the pair is a Y chromosome. As a result of this and because boys display more risk-taking behaviour during adolescence, and for a number of other reasons, the life expectancy of men is lower than that of women.

Women more frequently display an *overreaction*, an excessive response of the immune system. The principal examples of overreaction are *autoimmune diseases* and *allergies*, affecting women more often than men. Men suffer more frequently from *underreaction*, an insufficiently responsive immune system.

A third possibility, which we see in children, is an *immature immune system* which, due to insufficient maturation, does not yet always respond adequately to the processing of substances inside the body. This we observe more frequently in boys than in girls because boys mature more slowly in all fields. As a result of their immature immune system, boys, and in particular babies up to one year old, more often display the *atopic syndrome* (Geschwind and Behan 1982; Ruwaard, Gijsen and Verkleij 1993; Zeigerand Heller 1995; van Hoogen 1997). The atopic syndrome includes *chronic respiratory diseases* (including *asthma*), *food allergies* such as cow's milk allergy and *atopic eczema* associated with it. Children usually grow out of these allergies. Accordingly, it may be better to speak of a 'not yet fully developed' immune system than of underreaction or overreaction of the immune system. There is no relation between atopic reaction and allergens, nor are there high levels of IgE (Parham 2000). This supports the idea that the atopic syndrome is not an allergic reaction but the result of an immature immune system.

There is a connection between an immature immune system and immaturity of the central nervous system. Temple Grandin (1995a), a gifted autistic woman, assumes that autistic people have an immature central nervous system which may cause them to be *insensitive* (e.g. to pain) and *hypersensitive* to some stimuli (in particular sound and light touch). Asperger (1944) was the first to mention both *hypersensitivity* and *hyposensitivity* in children with an autistic disorder.

There are also differences between men and women in the functioning of the *autonomic nervous system* which responds to danger. It has even been discovered that the difference between them is such that in men who persistently commit criminal offences there is reduced functioning of the autonomic nervous system (Raine 1993; Raine *et al.* 2000). The response from their nervous system may even be too low, as a result of which their body tends to correct itself and seek dangerous situations (Delfos 2004a). In autistic people there is probably also a reduced or delayed response. In autism, this reduced or delayed response is not such that it leads to criminal behaviour or suspense- seeking conduct. Gunilla Gerland (2003), a woman with an autistic disorder but high functioning, indicates in a number of passages of her autobiography that her nervous system often does not work at full strength, as a result of which she hardly perceives stimuli from the environment, or not at all. In the following chapters, we shall explain how this works in people with an autistic disorder.

Because of the connection between maturation of the central nervous system and the immune system, children with disorders more frequently display an inadequate response from a weak or insufficiently matured immune system. For instance, it has been found that children with autism often suffer from a defective response of the immune system (Gent, Heijnen and Treffers 1997). Mesman (2000) found a relation between a high frequency of disease in babies and toddlers and externalizing behavioural problems at a later age. In the meantime, it has been established that disturbances of the immune system are definitely connected with autism (Korvatska *et al.* 2002).

In autism there is often reduced functioning of the immune system. Various researchers have demonstrated this through a lack of T cell and NK cell response in autistic people. As autism can be regarded as the extreme end of the male continuum (Asperger 1944), we would in this disorder expect a more male functioning of the immune system, i.e. reduced immune response, possibly the atopic syndrome, but fewer allergies and autoimmune diseases, and this is indeed a pattern we observe in autistic people (Gent *et al.* 1997).

We have seen that the biological self, a component of the immune system, is less developed in men. The development of the biological self also means that in general women know their body better. They differ in the extent to which they perceive that something is the matter with their body, the extent to which they sense symptoms of a disease, which is referred to as *symptom perception*. This is presumably the reason why women visit their GP more frequently while men in fact ought to do so more frequently as they suffer more often from life-threatening diseases. In general, it is clearer to women where a physical sensation is located while men often have a vaguer idea of this.

Experience has shown that men more often give a vague answer, with vague gestures, when asked where it hurts, whereas women can often indicate this quite accurately. Moreover, men are in general regarded as being 'squeamish'. This is unfounded. They are not more squeamish but

> they experience more pain as a result of the fact that men generally produce fewer endorphins, the body's own painkillers. In order to be prepared for the pain of childbirth, women are in general capable of higher endorphin production than men, and they experience less pain as a result.

As we shall see, in autism we expect to find underdevelopment of the biological self. The fact that such problems may be significant in autism is substantiated by Gunilla Gerland (2003) who in her autobiography mentions that as a child she was hardly aware of bodily sensations. 'Only rudimentary information reached my brain about whether this or that was going on. In fact I had to look at my body to know where I felt something.'

A stronger biological self also means that there is more awareness about who one is, about the *psychological self,* because body and mind cannot be separated (Edelman 1991; Damasio 1994). Damasio, a pupil of Geschwind's, speaks of the *neural self,* a dynamic system of knowledge about oneself that is constantly being updated (Damasio 1994). For instance, becoming angry requires hormone production; no emotion without hormones; body and soul are inseparably linked with one another.

In connection with the development of the biological self, women and men on average differ in the extent to which they know themselves psychologically. Knowing oneself is a necessary condition for learning to understand others. The biological/psychological self develops on the basis of the *me–other differentiation.* Because of the differences between men and women with regard to the biological/ psychological self, the me–other differentiation in men is on average less developed than in women. As we shall see, this also means that women are in general better at imagining what goes on in someone else's mind.

On the basis of a 'self', a 'me', the difference with the 'not-me', the 'other', can be discovered. A less sharply demarcated image of 'self' means that the image of the 'other' will likewise be less distinct and be formed more as a copy of oneself. There is no *cognition* of the identity of the other and therefore often no *recognition* either. Someone with a weak me–other differentiation will easily deny in others feelings he or she does not experience personally. This is not a matter of ill will but rather a lack of imaginative capacity. People who do not know themselves very well will also have difficulty imagining how others feel and think and will find it hard to understand what goes on in another person's mind.

The process by which the self, the 'me', becomes differentiated from the 'other' is called *me–other differentiation* or the process of *individuation* (Mahler 1968). It is a process that starts right after birth, and proper me–other differentiation can therefore already be recognized at an early age.

> Ricky, aged one and a half, was very keen on a television programme intended for very young children. With fascination he watched a scene he liked very much and looked behind him to see if his parents also enjoyed it. As soon as he saw that they were in the room and were also watching, he continued his activity laughing contentedly.

In this situation it is clear that the child already masters a certain degree of me–other differentiation. The child can, while absorbed in the TV programme, imagine that his parents are not in the room and that if they were they might not be watching and enjoying the programme with him. He experiences the other – his parents – as having their own identity doing their own thing, e.g. not being in the room, not watching television or not enjoying themselves, more or less detached from himself.

> We see the non-distinction between 'me' and the 'other' when little children cannot imagine that the world already existed before they were born. The idea that their mother was a child when they themselves did not yet exist appears to them incredible and even unpleasant. Their egocentricity still stands in the way of thinking of an 'other', detached from themselves. As he grows older, the child will be increasingly capable of imagining a world separate from himself.

The development of the 'me' has been discussed by many theoreticians. We generally refer to the development of the *ego*. One of the principal theorists in this field was Freud (1947) who saw the *ego* as a development of the self from the unconscious through confrontation with reality. The *ego* develops in relation to the limits which reality imposes upon the child. Loevinger (1990) has compiled an extensive model of ego development. This development, in nine stages, *ego stages*, from E-1 to E-9, occurs in the child as a result of growing insight into the world around him or her.

E-1 *Presocial stage*: hardly ever occurs; no socially oriented behaviour.

E-2 *Impulsive stage*: follows own needs and wants wishes to be satisfied immediately.

E-3 *Self-protective stage*: understanding of rules, focused on self-interest and wish not to be punished.

E-4 *Conformist stage*: self-interest is identified with that of others, e.g. a group.

E-5 *Self-aware stage*: understanding of personal feelings and thoughts; experiencing deviating behaviour in self and others.

E-6 *Conscientious stage*: responsibility and tolerance *vis-à-vis* own feelings and thoughts.

E-7 *Individualistic stage*: awareness of individual differences and acceptance of differences.

E-8 *Autonomous stage*: oriented towards individual development and social responsibility.

E-9 *Integration stage*: awareness of and responsibility for the place of own individuality within society.

If me–other differentiation remains inadequate, the *other* will be viewed too much as an extension of the *self*. The other is more of an instrument in satisfying one's own wishes than a partner one does and shares things with. Thinking on the basis of a deficient me–other differentiation will tend to be more egocentrically coloured, more self-oriented and less oriented towards empathizing with someone else. *Egocentric* should not be confused with *egoistic*. In egoism one is aware of the effect of one's behaviour on the other and its possible adverse consequences, but one nevertheless opts for it. Someone with egocentric behaviour is not aware of the effect on the other and of possible negative consequences. One needs to possess a certain level of me–other differentiation in order to be able to be egoistic. Asperger (1944) pointed out that autistic children are fundamentally egocentric and act out their wishes without any concern about the effect their behaviour has on others. Egocentricity is not so much self-orientation, nor a lack of interest in the other, but much more a *lack of orientation to the environment* and a lack of imaginative capacity about how the other can play a role in one's own activities, combined with a limited awareness of the other, as we shall see in the next chapter.

The development of self on the basis of me–other differentiation develops differently in group-oriented cultures, such as Asian cultures, than in the West. In group-oriented cultures, the 'me' bears a direct relationship with the family group. Lam (1997) therefore proposes to use the concept of *self in a relational network* for group-oriented cultures.

In psychology, the concept of 'self' is often still viewed as a separate psychological entity. There are various theories about the development of the self. One of the most authoritative theories is Flavell's, which links up with those of Piaget and others. Flavell (1985) speaks of the construction of a self of which the TOM, which he does not mention as such, forms part. TOM stands for *theory of mind*, which is the theory that every human being develops about their own and others' thoughts and feelings. In the following chapters, we shall examine this theory in more detail, as it is of such importance for autism. According to Flavell, children from the age of about two develop a self-image or self-concept which is used as a frame of reference within which to process information about others.

From our point of view, the development of a (neural) self is an ongoing process which begins at conception, with the embryo from the first division keeping track of which division takes place and in which direction this cell division should develop, e.g. stem cells towards developing the heart or brain. The neural self is a comprehensive whole of which we are only aware to a very limited extent from a couple of years after birth.

> The phenomenon that monozygotic twins constitute a symbiotic whole and appear to be aware of each other's existence, even without knowing about each other's existence, is probably connected with this neural self. Cell division in monozygotic twins is different from that in other embryos. While in the 'division-into-human-being programme' a particular direction is determined for the first two groups of cells arising from the first cell right from the very first division, the 'label' attached to the first cell division in monozygotic twins will be 'even though this is the first division, we shall consider the next division as the first division', the point of departure being the development of two human beings instead of one.

Imagining what goes on in another person's mind

The me–other differentiation is of the utmost importance for the development of *empathic capacity*, i.e. the ability to imagine what goes on in someone else's mind. Gillberg (1992) defines empathic capacity as the ability to conceptualize other people's inner worlds and to reflect on their thoughts and feelings.

In order to develop empathic capacity, one has to be able to distinguish oneself from others and to view others as having their own identity, with their own thoughts and feelings. If a child develops inadequate me–other differentiation, she then, and later on as an adult, will have difficulty imagining thoughts and feelings which she does not have herself. Empathizing with another person will then remain confined to feelings one has experienced oneself. Duyndam (2001) argues that empathy is especially a matter of knowledge of one's own feelings. Eisenberg, one of the most prominent researchers in the field of empathy, accordingly defines empathy as the conscious sharing of the perceived emotion of another (Eisenberg and Fabes 1991).

Empathy is often confused with being sensitive. Someone who is not empathic is often wrongly considered insensitive. Empathy means the ability to imagine another person's thoughts and feelings. This does not necessarily mean that one has those feelings oneself and sympathizes with the other. Empathy is most noticeable in sensing and understanding feelings which one has not experienced oneself. Duyndam (2001) points out that it is not a matter of having the same feelings as the other *immediately*, there and then, but of being *potentially* capable of having such feelings. A lack of empathic capacity does not mean that one does not *try* to understand what is going on in the other person's mind. Rather, it means that one does not sense what exactly is going on in the other person and assumes one's own feelings to be present in the other. In this case, instead of empathic capacity or sensing what the other feels, we speak of *projection*, i.e. projecting one's own feelings onto someone else. Placing your own thoughts into someone else is not the same as imagining what is going on in the other person's mind.

A striking example of the phenomenon of projection can be observed in young people with a criminal biological predisposition. They have no problem taking something away that is lying somewhere unsupervised. They do not experience this as a serious offence because in their opinion one does not leave something one considers important unattended. They do not do this themselves. So when something is left unattended, they conclude that the owner does not attach much importance to it and would therefore not mind very much if someone took it away. While young delinquents often make statements to this effect, they are not taken seriously because we cannot imagine they really mean it. No matter how empathic we may be, we also project our feelings onto these young people and can hardly imagine that they mean what they say.

An inability to sense what someone else feels does not mean that one has no feelings oneself. All it means is that the range of feelings with which one can sympathize and empathize remains limited to feelings one knows and experiences oneself. Someone with little empathy can certainly be very sympathetic in the case of feelings he or she has personally experienced.

Empathic capacity is connected with the development of the brain, specifically the left hemisphere. As explained above, empathic capacity is probably related to the X chromosome and the combination of an X chromosome from the mother *and* from the father. On the basis of the fact that the paternal X chromosome enhances sociability, Hrdy (2000) argues that the absence of the paternal X chromosome – which is the case for boys – leads to leaving the home and the group at an earlier stage. As noted above, Skuse and colleagues (1997) found that the paternal X chromosome reinforces social behaviour, as we see in girls, and its absence leads to weakened social behaviour, something we encounter in boys. With regard to empathic capacity, we discern a difference between men and women, with women on average having less difficulty imagining what is going on in another person's mind and actually doing so too.

Since women are on average more oriented towards imagining what goes on in other people's minds, their thinking changes perspective more often: from 'looking at things from one's own position' to 'looking at things from the other's position'. It may well be that one consequence of this orientation in the brain is that women have problems, for instance, with left and right orientation as they immediately wonder from which perspective it is meant to be viewed.

When people look at each other during conversation, they usually look at each other's right eye. They always briefly look at the other's left eye as if to check what is visible in the right eye. Because of the 'emptiness' that is perceived in the left eye, it is more difficult to maintain the glance while looking into each other's left eye than while looking into the right eye. Very soon, there is a need to look away to escape the relative 'emptiness'. When doing a communication exercise on the basis of this fact, women in the group often ask which eye is meant. Men more frequently assume that what is meant is from their own perspective, while women hesitate whether what is meant is from their own perspective or from that of the other person looking at them. This tendency to shift the perspective may well lie at the basis of the many reversals in sense of direction in women. At the opposite end, in autism, shifts in perspective are very hard because autistic individuals have great difficulty imagining what goes on in other people's minds. As we shall see, this is even apparent in speech. In autistic children, for instance, we see this in their difficulty switching between the 'me' and 'you' perspective.

In the male foetus the right hemisphere is stimulated at the expense of the development of the left hemisphere where the me–other differentiation possibly arises from the core of the biological self. In girls the two hemispheres develop more equally. Consequently, men often have a stronger right hemisphere than women and a weaker left hemisphere (Geschwind and Behan 1982, 1984).

If the right hemisphere is more strongly developed than the left, this is often so in various fields. One of the areas where this may become noticeable is motor function, as we saw in the previous chapter. Left/right coordination will tend to be less smooth. Consequently, one indication for a stronger right hemisphere compared with the left is left-handedness.

Since the right hemisphere is on average more strongly developed in men, there are more men who are left-handed than women and there are also more extremely right-handed women than men (Hellige 1993). In autistic people, whose right hemisphere is more strongly developed, we expect to find more left-handed than extremely right-handed individuals. Geschwind and Behan (1984) confirm that in autism there is a higher incidence of left-handedness than in the population at large. One of the individuals which Asperger (1944) mentions in his article on autism, Harro, calls himself 'dreadfully left-handed'. Marc Fleisher, an autistic young man from the excellent BBC documentary *I'm not Stupid* (Fisher 1995), is left-handed. Geschwind and Behan (1982) relate left-handedness with language disorders, e.g. to stammering. Smith, Meyers and Kline (1989) studied the differences between men and women in this regard, finding that left-handed men stammer more frequently than right-handed ones, with, moreover, a substantial difference in frequency.

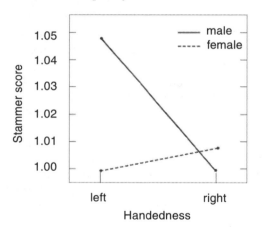

Figure 3.3 Stammering and left-handedness (Smith, Meyers and Kline 1989). Reproduced with permission from Psychology Press.

In women, however, there appears to be the opposite effect, with more right-handed women stammering than left-handed ones. Apart from the fact that more men than women stammer, it was also found that the difference in left/right frequency in women was lower than in men. It was noted that differences in left- and right-handedness in men and women also existed in other respects. Both disorders (stammering) and talents (for mathematics) turned out to be more closely connected with left-handedness in men than in women. It was found that in women the effect of right- or left-handedness was less marked and less important. We shall examine what this means more closely in the next chapter when discussing the various autistic disorders.

The right hemisphere is connected with spatial, abstract thinking and with creativity. In general, these potentialities will be more strongly developed in men. As we noted above, in autism there is a less developed – less matured – left hemisphere. Non-smooth motor activity, however, is not so pronounced if apart from autism there is also a serious intellectual disability, as we discussed in the previous chapter. Wooden motor activity and clumsiness is generally characteristic of people with Asperger's syndrome, the autistic disorder in which there is average to above average – abstract – intelligence.

Another finding is that when people with autistic disorders possess a highly developed skill (one out of ten have a special skill: Wing 2001), or even a talent, this concerns very specific subjects, involving functions that in principle are located in the right hemisphere such as mathematics, music or painting.

The left hemisphere plays an important part in language development. It is therefore not surprising that language disorders are more frequently encountered in boys than in girls (Rutter and Rutter 1993). As many as 60 to 80 per cent of *dyslexics* are male (APA 1994). Different aspects of language are located at different places in the brain. *Finding* words is located in a different place in the brain to *hearing* words. Language production and comprehension is an extensive and complex process in which various parts of the brain have to work together. Back in the nineteenth century, Philippe Broca discovered that a particular area in the left hemisphere is of decisive importance for speech. Possibly of equal importance, however, is the fact that the left hemisphere holds the capacity for expressing thoughts and feelings in words, i.e. awareness of one's own feelings (Hamilton and Timmons 1990). In fact, the development of the biological self into the neural self goes hand in hand with the development of awareness. A person with a strongly developed left hemisphere is strongly oriented towards feelings, putting these feelings into words and expressing them; which in effect is something we observe more strongly in women, whose left hemisphere is on average more strongly developed compared with the right, than in men.

Recognizing that the left hemisphere is less developed in people within the autistic spectrum, we are less surprised to find that they have language disorders or strange uses of language because of the importance of the left hemisphere for language. At the same time, a weaker left hemisphere means less awareness of one's own feelings. People with a disorder within the autistic spectrum are therefore lagging behind on two counts, having more difficulty recognizing their own feelings and also more problems putting them into words than people without an autistic disorder.

> Describing this problem, Richard Lansdown (in Peeters 1996), an autistic adult, notes that he sometimes takes beta blockers to suppress the physical symptoms of anxiety, and although he can now tell people that something is bothering him, he still cannot do this at the moment itself.

A less developed left hemisphere does not mean that within the autistic spectrum there is always weaker language function. One of the disorders on the autistic spectrum is Asperger's syndrome. The fact is that apart from autistic features this syndrome is characterized by 'normal' language development. Nevertheless, it is in general not completely normal. The language used often appears somewhat 'archaic' and pronunciation has been called affected, pedantic. The words used suggest, sometimes wrongly, a high level of intelligence. Instead of a weak language function, children and adults with Asperger's syndrome often produce an unstoppable flood of words. However, expressing thoughts and feelings in words is problematic and this tends to stem the flow. Someone with an autistic disorder may, for instance, be perfectly aware that he or she feels something but may be quite unable to express it in words.

> The amazing flood of words that may occur in people with Asperger's syndrome is connected, among other things, with the incapacity to imagine what goes on in other people's minds and the concomitant inability to take turns in conversation. A child with a disorder within the autistic spectrum says what she wants to say and rarely checks whether the other person can and wants to listen to it. Furthermore, people with autism often have problems picking up the thread of their story and therefore wish to prevent being interrupted.

The consequence of the difficulty for autistic people to put their thoughts into words is that, when they are capable of speech, they tend to give greater attention and care to the way they express their feelings. In doing so, they often give verbal expression to their feelings in astute, poetic and original ways, as we shall see in subsequent chapters. In order to do so, however, others must give them the chance to complete this process of searching for words.

As a result of the disparity in language development and the difference in focus on thoughts and feelings, there are in general considerable differences in communication among men and women (Tannen 1990). This difference in language functioning may cause tension between partners of different sexes. With regard to expressing feelings, the difference in language functioning in men and women is often perceived as painful. Women are strongly oriented towards this activity whereas men often give the impression that they would rather avoid it, although it would be more accurate to say that men are 'less capable' of it.

In people with an autistic disorder, empathic capacity is weakly developed; they seem to live in a world of their own without much awareness of the people around them. I should like to recall that Hans Asperger has said that the brain structure of autistic people is as it were extremely masculine. It is not surprising in fact that significantly more men than women have an autistic disorder. In general, four times as many boys as girls have an autistic disorder, and in the case of Asperger's syndrome there are reported to be six to ten times as many boys as girls (Wing 2001). When in the following chapter we shall discuss the various forms of autistic disorders, we will take a closer look at differences in prevalence in autistic disorders and examine the idea propounded by Asperger (1944) that autism in women possibly assumes a different form than in men.

The difference between men and women as regards empathy has a biological, evolutionary origin. Examining the original roles of men and women from the viewpoint of evolution, we see that the difference in empathic capacity is necessary. In principle, a woman has to be able to bring another being into the world. This other being, the baby, is helpless for a considerable period of time and the woman can provide the food – breastfeeding – needed to keep the child alive. As she puts another being into the world, she clearly has to be able to empathize with another person and understand the other's needs and thoughts. The mother's empathy is therefore a necessary condition for the survival of the child in particular and the species in general. While the woman is looking after the child, she is not in a position to protect the nest. This is therefore originally the man's role. This means that a man has to be capable of aggression to protect the nest. In order to be able to be aggressive, he must, however, not have too much empathic capacity as this would inhibit his aggressive behaviour. When a man puts himself into another's shoes, his aggression in principle diminishes. Indeed, research has shown that aggression in men in general diminishes when their victim shows signs of pain or suffering (Kaplan and Sadock 1995). The fact is, however, that the need for aggression has been enormously reduced in our society. Security is now to a large extent assured by society as a whole and no longer by the 'head of the family'. As a result, aggression has increasingly become a bad thing rather than something good. Whereas in the past someone who dared to go out and fight was judged positively, nowadays there is more appreciation for someone who deliberates and discusses things. From an evolutionary point of view, a lack of empathy is therefore necessary for men. As soon as another demand is made on a human being, nature responds to this. This is why a man whose wife is pregnant produces more 'care hormones', making him more oriented towards looking after his pregnant wife (Storey *et al.* 2000).

It appears that men are better able than women to judge signs of danger and anger (Eisenberg, Murphy and Shepard 1997). This research places our thinking about the empathic capacity in men and women in a different light. While it is said that women tend to be more empathic than men, this appears to be valid only for a particular part of what we should like to call the empathic spectrum. There is a difference in *empathic capacity* between men and women. It appears that male brains are quicker and better at receiving signs of danger while women are better at evaluating feelings in others.

This difference in empathic capacity has certain consequences for the way in which men and women on average seek security and attachment. A women will be more inclined to seek emotional attachment in interpersonal contact where she can imagine what goes on in the other person's mind. A man will tend to seek his security much more in social prestige as it is there that he recognizes dangers.

The differences in empathic capacity (imagining what goes on in other people's minds as against recording signs of danger emitted by others) which have developed in the course of evolution probably also have consequences for the way *memory* works. The role of women requires a strong *short-term memory* (what does the child need right now?) whereas a man needs a better *long-term memory* (what was the course of the seasons and what was connected with it?). This is borne out by research carried out by Herlitz, Nilsson and Bäckman (1997) who found that women did have a significantly better short-term memory than men. In autistic people, in whom we encounter a more male structure, we sometimes find a phenomenally strong long-term memory. In many cases, they are able flawlessly to recall details from their youth but they are often quite unable to remember an appointment made a week earlier. People with an autistic disorder often have a spectacular memory for storing facts, a good *rote memory*, while memory for making connections between facts is very weak.

There is also a difference between men and women in the way memory stores emotional elements. In men, the right *amygdala* (small structures in the brain which play a role in signalling danger) play an important part in remembering emotional events but in women this is a task for the left amygdala (Cahill *et al.* 2001). In people with an autistic disorder, we find that the amygdala work differently than in non-autistic people. The amygdala in people with an autistic disorder are underdeveloped (Howard *et al.* 2000). One result of this may be their poor ability to recognize faces and facial expressions (Baron-Cohen and Hammer 1997; Tantam 1997). We shall see that danger signalling is better developed in autistic people than the signalling of positive emotions. This may also be connected with a subtle difference in the development of the two hemispheres.

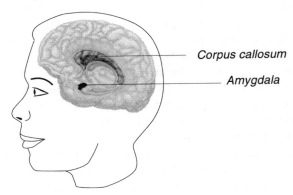

Figure 3.4 Amygdala and corpus callosum (Kalat 1998). Reproduced with permission.

The lack of empathic capacity which we encounter to an extreme degree in people with an autistic disorder is counterbalanced by an inability to *manipulate* the other person and a general tendency to face the other much more openly and sincerely. In general, people with an autistic disorder are much more open and sincere in everyday life. Consequently, it is highly exceptional for people with an autistic disorder to display criminal behaviour (Ghaziuddin, Tsai and Ghaziuddin 1991; Attwood 1998).

Moral development

The difference in me–other differentiation and empathic capacity has particular consequences for moral development which evolves as the child comes up against boundaries in trying to realize its wishes and desires. Imagining what goes on in another person's mind is of essential importance in taking account of the boundaries of others.

Moral development depends on a number of factors, including upbringing, culture and intellectual potentialities but also on gender. As in many other areas, moral development also reveals differences between men and women. There are various levels of moral development. Moral values can be measured, for instance, by fairness or care for others. Men are more oriented towards *competition and fairness* while women are more focused on *care for others and cooperation* (Damon 1988). This difference depends partly on differences in me–other differentiation and accordingly the tendency towards more egocentric or more empathic thinking.

Moral thinking is connected with the way in which people judge good and bad, their attitude towards their fellow human beings and the way they deal with others. Egocentricity and empathy are an area of tension in this context. The tendency of girls to be more oriented towards care for the other reflects their greater empathy while the focusing of boys on competition and fairness reflects their greater *capacity for action*. We shall see that testosterone supports a stronger capacity for action in men. However, for moral development and its expression in behaviour, orientation towards the other is also necessary, i.e. an awareness of what something means to the other. Moral development is based on *ego development* which evolves more rapidly in girls than in boys (Cohn 1991). Westenberg *et al.* (2001) report that, measured by the ZALC (a sentence completion test for ego development), girls can be ahead of boys by up to four years in ego development. The difference is greatest at age 15–17 but by the age of 25 the ego development gap between men and women has closed. The Minnesota studies of monozygotic twins have shown that 50 per cent of the difference in ego development between boys and girls is genetically determined (Newman, Tellegen and Bouchard 1998). Damon (1988) indicates that women's moral orientation (care for others and cooperation with others) is in fact evidence of a further and more highly developed moral awareness in women than in men who are more focused on fairness and competition.

The difference in the nature of moral development is also encountered in connection with *lying*. It appears that men more often lie for egoistic purposes whereas women more frequently lie so as not to hurt someone's feelings, telling 'white lies' (Vrij 1998).

Resistance to change

Another difference between men and women that is relevant in understanding autistic disorders is *resistance to change*. Here, too, brain structure plays an important role. In Chapter 2, I mentioned in this connection the importance of the development of both hemispheres and that of the corpus callosum. The *corpus callosum* together with the *hypothalamus* constitutes the communication centre of the brain; in the previous chapter, we referred to it simply as the 'switchboard' of the brain.

Research has shown that there are differences between men and women with regard to the corpus callosum. In women, it is larger on average than in men (see e.g. Burke and Yeo 1994). This applies in particular to the posterior part of the corpus, the *splenium*.

The size of the corpus callosum depends on the number of 'connections'. Conduction of various stimuli entering the two hemispheres – e.g. auditory (hearing), tactile (feeling) and visual (seeing) – is faster and more effective with a larger corpus callosum. Moreover, the fact is that sensory stimuli are more quickly received in women's brains than in men's (Dennen 1992).

In men, the size of the corpus callosum decreases more rapidly with age than in women. The larger size of their corpus callosum probably means that in women's brains all kinds of information, various stimuli entering the brain, can be coordinated more quickly than in men and new information, including changes, is more readily processed. If the brain is capable of processing a large number of stimuli, it is easier to cope with a change. It will also be easier to do several things simultaneously. Combining multiple activities tends to be easier for women than for men who are more inclined to focus on a single subject for longer. A smaller corpus callosum may therefore be connected with resistance to change. On average, resistance to change is greater in men than in women and increases with age.

> The differences in the size of the corpus callosum in men and women are reflected in the fact that men in general show a tendency and ability to focus for a long time on one activity, one subject, while women are more able to focus on several activities simultaneously and are better at multitasking. It is thought that the corpus callosum is responsible for what Darwin has called female intuition: 'quick information processing' which leads to 'quick knowledge'. However, scientists have not yet established whether this is truly the case. New techniques such as MRI scanning also entail new problems. Nevertheless, the existence of such differences is further borne out by recent findings concerning differences in the corpus callosum in disorders that are more prevalent among men than women, such as autism and ADHD.

In light of the relation between brain structure and the processing of stimuli, it is understandable that children with ADHD (attention deficit hyperactivity disorder) – children who are easily distracted and do not process stimuli efficiently – have a corpus callosum of below average size (e.g. Hynd *et al.* 1991; Semrud-Clikeman *et al.* 1994). It is not surprising that in autistic children, who are strongly resistant to change and often respond negatively to new stimuli, it has been discovered that their corpus callosum is likewise smaller than average (Egaas, Courchesne and Saitoh 1995; Piven *et al.* 1997, 1999; Goldberg, Szatmari and Nahmias 1999). Moreover, it has also been found that the corpus callosum in people with Asperger's syndrome, which is regarded as a milder form of autism, is larger than in people who are deeply autistic (Lincoln *et al.* 1998).

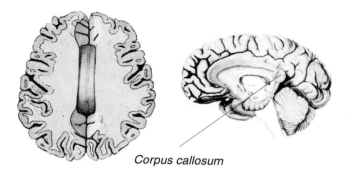

Corpus callosum

Figure 3.5 Longitudinal section of the brain of a person with Asperger's syndrome (Lincoln et al. 1998). Reproduced with permission from Springer.

Research into the processing of stimuli in autistic people has revealed a difference with non-autistic people. The stimulus enters the brain just as quickly, it is perceived just as quickly (*orientation reflex*) but in the brain of autistic people the subsequent phase, when thinking is switched on, runs more slowly, with the signals proceeding through the brain at a slower pace (Frith 1989). It appears that on average men have a less strongly responding autonomic nervous system, causing stimuli to be processed by the brain more slowly (Delfos 2004a). Martijn Dekker (2001) notes that in the literature on autism he has not found any reference to the fact that people with an autistic disorder have problems combining various activities. His own experience and those of the autistic people with whom he is in contact through his Internet site *Independent Living* show that this is a serious handicap in everyday life.

Self-reflection

On the basis of the elements described above (biological/psychological/neural self, left hemisphere with its language orientation and awareness of processes, empathy and corpus callosum), there are reasons to assume that there is a difference in *self-reflection* between men and women. Self-reflection involves examining the self, in particular behaviour and underlying motives. While self-reflection may be regarded as an essential component of human existence, it is an activity that is not developed equally in everyone. In various disorders, including autism, there is even very deficient self-reflection. By deficient, we do not mean reduced or less developed self-reflection but self-reflection that is not 'rounded off' into 'knowing' and 'feeling'. The extensive activity with regard to self-reflection which some people with an autistic disorder engage in, especially people with Asperger's syndrome, does not lead to well-considered insight, but rather to a hypothesis or *educated guess*.

In these people, self-reflection cannot find fertile ground or link up with what in Chapter 5 we will call the socioscheme.

Clear me–other differentiation is a prerequisite for self-reflection. To be able to think about yourself, i.e. to engage in self-reflection, you must be able to distinguish your own 'me' from 'others'. As self-reflection means reflecting upon yourself, it requires taking some distance from the self. Self-reflection proceeds on the basis of a self-image and is also the continuous source for correcting the self-image.

For self-reflection to be successful, it is necessary to recognize the self, have knowledge of the self, have a developed me–other differentiation and proper language functioning. Self-reflection is a form of language behaviour without necessarily having to be expressed in speech.

A less developed biological/psychological self, as generally encountered in men, will inhibit the development of self-reflection. Self-reflection exists by the grace of speech or at least inner speech, which has been termed *egocentric* or *inner language* (Vygotsky 1978). Since putting thoughts and feelings into words is an activity that on average is less developed in men, it will also inhibit self-reflection, though this may very well occur alongside considerable language skills in other fields.

The corpus callosum also plays a part in self-reflection. In order to be able to think about yourself and feel what goes on inside, it is necessary to lay links between the various components that play a role in self-reflection: facts, emotions and memories. The corpus callosum, the 'communication centre' in the brain, assists in establishing these connections.

The differences in development – left hemisphere, corpus callosum and biological/psychological self – stimulate self-reflection in women. As a result of their *menstrual cycle*, moreover, women are as it were 'trained' in examining their own physical and mental state. The menstrual cycle can cause considerable fluctuations in their state of mind. Around the time of ovulation, this state of mind may be highly positive and just before or after menstruation it may trigger a depressive or aggressive mood (Delfos 1993). Behavioural and psychiatric disturbances in women may fluctuate as a result of this hormonal oscillation (Kaplan and Sadock 1995) and the problems which women's lifecycle (pregnancy, childbirth, nursing, menopause) entails (Moffaert and Finoulst 2001).

As women's functioning is subject to these fluctuations, they often shift to a mood in which they wonder what is happening to them. It is as though their body constantly urges them to examine what is going on, regularly leading to the conclusion that the state of mind is connected with the menstrual cycle.

Although women often find it hard to admit this, their partners tend to be aware that they are about to have their periods. To them, the woman's depressive or aggressive behaviour is a sign that menstruation is imminent. The emotional cycle runs parallel with the hormonal cycle (Delfos 1993). During the cycle, a 'manic' and a 'depressive' phase seems to emerge in tandem with fluctuation in hormone production during the menstrual cycle.

Women have an advantage in engaging in self-reflection with regard to brain structure, whereas men have an advantage in coping with danger and fear.

Capacity for action, anxiety and aggression

There are many other differences between men and women and these are not only connected with brain structure but also, for instance, with hormone balance. *Hormones* have an important effect on human behaviour. They are the 'messenger substances' of the body. There are significant hormonal differences between men and women. *Testosterone* is called the male hormone because it occurs at much higher levels in men than in women. Men have a more stable and higher testosterone level than women. On average, the testosterone content in men's blood plasma is nine times that of women (Bernards and Bouman 1993). Testosterone diminishes with age (Dabbs 1990). It is also affected by the seasons but less so than by age. Women have significantly more oestrogen in the blood and it plays a role in the menstrual cycle.

Each hormone serves many different functions. Testosterone is, among other things, connected with reproduction and growth but also with aggression (Taylor *et al.* 2000). In general, the higher the testosterone level in humans, and in animal species, the more aggression is displayed (Dabbs, Hopper and Jurkovic 1990; Dennen 1992; Taylor *et al.* 2000). This relation is less clear during adolescence as in this case aggression is also strongly fed by environmental factors (Halpern *et al.* 1993a, 1993b; Constantino *et al.* 1993).

Testosterone can also be produced under the influence of particular activities. Conflicts are a trigger for testosterone production but also particular professions such as politics and the theatre cause an increase in testosterone production (Dabbs 1992).

Aggression is often viewed as a negative form of behaviour. The fact is, however, that it is a behaviour which may be necessary for survival and which in a less intensive form involves a person's *capacity for action*. The high level of testosterone in men ensures that in general they are more capable of such action in the face of danger than women are. Testosterone is the hormone ensuring the capacity to act. 'Action, not words' is an expression that pertains more to men than women whereas 'express your feelings' seems to be woman's domain. Because of their capacity for action, men tend to be more practically involved in solving a problem whereas women prefer to talk it over.

At a high testosterone level, people will, in difficult situations and when faced with danger, tend to *act* or display aggression. A low testosterone level, however, will be linked with *helplessness*, fear and a tendency to appeal to others for help. It is also true that men are better able than women to evaluate signs of danger and anger (Eisenberg *et al.* 1997), as we saw above.

When faced with danger, adrenergic hormones are produced in the body, triggering the *fight or flight response* (Selye 1976). Here, 'danger' means anything causing stress, for example, someone threatening you, losing someone dear to you or even having a negative thought. When perceiving danger, men are more inclined to 'fight' and women more to 'flight', but even more often the woman is paralysed with fear and quite unable to take action. In Chapter 11, when discussing fear, we shall examine in more detail the differences in action in the face of danger between men and women.

The adrenergic hormones such as adrenalin which, for example, causes an increase in heartbeat, make activity possible. The capacity for action supported by testosterone makes it possible to carry out that activity. A harmonious balance of adrenalin and testosterone – there are many more hormones involved but for now we shall leave them out of consideration so as not to make things unnecessarily complicated – therefore enables action. Too much testosterone will stimulate *aggression* while too little will often be associated with incapacity to act and with apathy and *depression* (Delfos 2004a). If the balance tips to one side – too much testosterone – aggression may result; if it tips to the other side – too little testosterone – it may lead to anxiety and depression. To ensure that action can be taken when danger looms, there ought to be a balance between, in particular, testosterone and adrenalin. Given these facts, it is no surprise that aggression disorders are more prevalent among men and anxiety disorders more among women. When considering anxiety and obsession (in Chapter 11), we shall analyse this more closely and present an outline relating anxiety to aggression and depression.

Gender differences and upbringing

When we speak of capacity for action in the face of danger or of spatial thinking, we find that men appear to have the upper hand; when we speak of expressing and examining a state of mind and of empathy, it appears that women are in the lead. There are far more differences but those referred to here are significant in connection with autistic disorders. Generally speaking, women are more language-oriented and have greater empathy, their bodies fight disease with greater intensity, but they display less capacity for action in the face of danger. They struggle with anxiety more often than men. On the other hand, men are in general more spatially oriented, are more creative, more capable of action, less language-oriented, less able to express thoughts and feelings, and physically more aggressive. They are more effective in coping with fear in that they take action sooner, thereby reducing anxiety. There are also differences in moral development. Women more often apply moral values reflecting care for others and cooperation; men more frequently adopt fairness and competition as moral standards. Moreover, women will in general be more capable of self-reflection than men. Men will show a greater tendency to remain focused on one single subject whereas women will be more able to combine several activities simultaneously.

Differences between men and women are not confined to differences arising from predisposition. Differences are also influenced by *socialization*, upbringing of boys and girls by family and society. Upbringing often links up with the differences that are predispositional and in this way the differences between men and women are further enhanced by socialization. Current emancipation of women has shown that socialization in the last centuries and the concomitant repression of women gave rise to exaggerated differences between men and women. Women and men appear to be more similar than used to be thought. It is also true that they are more different than was assumed at the beginning of the wave of emancipation (Delfos 2004b). The fact that men and women have also literally grown closer in physical height shows that we lean more and more on psychological elements and less on physical ones. Consequently, there is now more fertile ground for emancipation than ever before.

The differences between men and women have particular consequences for their functioning in society. Whichever disorder we consider, it will always have different consequences in boys than in girls. The consequences of a disorder are invariably judged by social functioning. A male child will, because of his predisposition, move towards a fundamentally different future to a female child, and this will often be further emphasized by socialization.

Schematic presentation

To end this chapter, we sum up the influence of high testosterone on foetal development in the womb in Table 3.2.

For men there is greater testosterone influence on the foetus in the womb than for women. In people with autism this influence is even stronger in that the immune system is inhibited; the right hemisphere of the brain is stimulated at the expense of the left; the level of testosterone after birth is, however, lower than average and the autonomic nervous system is inhibited.

Table 3.2 Influences of high testosterone in the womb	
A. Inhibition of the immune system (see also Table 5.5)	• Biological/psychological/neural self inhibited • Limited fight against disease
B. Stimulation of right hemisphere at expense of the left (see also Table 5.5)	• Limited language orientation, in particular thoughts and feelings • More abstract, technical, spatial and creative intelligence • Limited awareness of feelings and thoughts
C. Lower than average testosterone level after birth	• Less aggression-oriented • Less sexually oriented, fertility problems
D. Lower/slower responding automatic nervous system	• Response to danger: more fear than aggression; slowly subsiding • Compensation through sensory response

Consequences for autism

The differences between men and women discussed in this chapter have particular consequences for autism. Following Hans Asperger, we can say, and will show in the following chapters, that in autism there is a more male brain structure with all that this entails.

Focal points

- Men and women differ considerably in their social interaction.
- Human self-knowledge is biologically and psychologically contained within a neural system of constant information processing.
- Humans have an inner wisdom which to an important extent controls behaviour.
- The immune system has not yet fully matured at birth.
- Children with a disorder are more likely to have the atopic syndrome: airway problems, food allergy and eczema.
- On average, men have a less developed me–other differentiation than women.

- Autistic disorders go hand in hand with a more male brain structure.

- Autistic people have a deficient me–other differentiation.

- Autistic people have a deficient empathic capacity.

- Autism usually goes hand in hand with deviating language development.

- Autistic people have stronger resistance to change.

- Autistic people have difficulty with self-reflection.

- Men and women differ strongly in the way they deal with danger, with men more inclined to take action and women to refrain from action.

- Men more often have aggression disorders, women more often depression disorders.

- Socialization tends to enhance the predispositional differences between men and women.

Focal points regarding attitude

- Predisposition is important: it is the foundation of everything.

- Men and women are different in predisposition, which has particular consequences for their behaviour.

- Respecting the primary role of predisposition means recognizing the biological differences between men and women.

- Autistic people suffer from egocentricity rather than egoism.

Summary

Differences between men and women are not confined to what is visible. There is a fundamental difference in brain structure which controls behaviour. Men and women are essentially different; for instance, in their empathic capacity and the extent to which they are able to correctly evaluate social interaction. The differences start in the womb with the XX or XY pair of chromosomes. The male XY pair of chromosomes causes an increase in the production of the testosterone hormone. A high testosterone level inhibits the – language-oriented – left hemisphere, stimulates the right hemisphere, reduces the workings of the immune system, and leads to a higher testosterone level after birth. As a result, women generally have a stronger me–other differentiation, are more language- and empathy-oriented, fight disease with more intensity, and display less inclination to take action in the face of danger. They more frequently have to cope with anxiety and depression. In contrast, men are in general more oriented towards abstract and spatial thinking, are more creative, take action when faced with danger, are less language-oriented, less able to express their thoughts and feelings into words, and physically more aggressive. There are also differences in moral development. Women more frequently apply moral values that reflect care for others and cooperation while men adhere more to fairness and competition as moral standards. As women are oriented towards language and are more capable of expressing their feelings and thoughts, they tend to be better at self-reflection than men.

Bearing these differences in mind, we will have to emancipate in the direction of the biological stream rather than against it if we wish to give people optimum chances for self-development. Although socialization is often viewed as the principal source of differences, it probably – in an exaggerated way – only continues upon fundamental differences already existing. Socializing boys into boisterous and assertive behaviour links up with their tendency towards taking action under the influence of testosterone. Socializing girls towards care for others links up with their empathic capacity.

Generally speaking, autistic people have a brain structure that is more male in nature. Their language problems, reduced empathic capacity and problems evaluating social interaction are examples of phenomena connected with this.

4

Autistic disorders

The core concept in autistic disorders is difficulty in evaluating and understanding *social interaction*. Autistic people experience difficulties with this in a way that is not commensurate with their intellectual capacity in other fields. In other words, the extent to which difficulty is experienced in evaluating social interaction does correspond to what we would expect on the basis of the child's intelligence, no matter how limited it is. This lack of insight into social interaction is all the more noticeable if the child has sufficient intellectual potential, or even if he comes across as intelligent. In children with an intellectual disability it is often more difficult to recognize autism, as the lack of ability to evaluate social interaction is sometimes wrongly attributed to their intellectual disability. Other autistic characteristics, such as stereotyped behaviour, rituals or hypersensitivity to stimuli, are in this case more evident.

Apart from genetic predisposition, autism may also be caused by rubella infection while the foetus is in the womb and by some brain disorders (phenylketonuria, hydrocephalus and particular forms of meningitis). There also appears to be an increased risk of autism if there is fragile X syndrome, a chromosome disorder involving a fragile site on the X chromosome. Autism also occurs more frequently in children of mothers addicted to alcohol. The severity of the disorder is related to the degree of exposure to alcohol during growth in the womb (Aronson, Hagberg and Gillberg 1997). Autism occurs in all cultures and presents the same picture in all cultures.

There are various forms of autistic or contact disorders, classified into various diagnoses in an autistic spectrum as pervasive developmental disorders. This means a disorder that is present from early youth or manifests itself after some time and continues into adulthood, in which the person's general functioning is seriously hampered because it penetrates into all lines of development (intellectual, social/emotional, physical and motor). As autism is a developmental disorder, behaviour varies, depending on the person's age and mental capacity. The common thread is deficient *empathic capacity*. Since this is something that also occurs in disorders other than autism, Gillberg (1992) even proposes a new term for all different autistic disorders and the forms connected with them: *empathy disorders*.

The different forms

The most serious form of autistic disorder is *autism*, also known as *Kanner's autism* or *classic autism*. This term is used for the form showing the features which Leo Kanner (1943) listed in his description of autism. The principal characteristics are extreme social isolation (*aloneness*), the urge to keep everything unchanged (*sameness*), a fascination with particular objects and deficient use of language as a means of communication.

Autism is at the extreme end of what is called the *autistic spectrum* (Wing 1998), the whole range of disorders with autistic characteristics. In addition to autism, it includes *Rett's syndrome, disintegrative disorder, Asperger's syndrome* (named after Hans Asperger) and *PDD-NOS*, also known as *atypical autism* (WHO 1992). Many people with an autistic disorder also have a serious intellectual disability (until recently it was thought that about three-quarters of autistic people also had an intellectual disability but currently it is assumed to be one-quarter; see Figure 4.5). For autistic people with an IQ above 85 the expression *high functioning autism* (HFA) is therefore used. However, cases like that of Birger Sellin (1995) show that their intelligence cannot be measured by the usual methods. Because of his behaviour, which came across as clearly intellectually deficient, and his total silence, no one suspected that he had actually been reading the books he had been leafing through from the age of five. The fact that Birger Sellin could read and write was discovered because his mother used the *facilitated communication* (FC) method in which the autistic person's forearm is lightly supported by another person, communicating encouragement and support. While it is not easy to achieve success with this method (Mostert 2001), in Birger Sellin's case it worked very well. The measured intellectual disability proved to be incorrect and, quite to the contrary, the boy turned out to be highly gifted. Difficulties in social interaction and the fact of being withdrawn often makes it harder to measure intelligence in autistic people.

It is not always easy to distinguish the various forms of autism, except for Rett's syndrome and disintegrative disorder which are distinct from the other autistic disorders in that they involve the disappearance of skills that were previously present. Some researchers take the view that the forms of autism are so different that no clear single cause can be discerned (Gillberg 1992). My assumption is that the cause of the various forms is not the same but that within the various forms brain development is such that me–other differentiation is affected or damaged. This leads to a specific pattern of behaviour which has serious consequences for social intercourse and entails certain types of behaviour. Accordingly, my position is that the problem with social interaction is the core problem of the autism disorder, in line with Kanner (1943) and Asperger (1944), and that the other aspects are subordinate to it. The theory of *central coherence* (Frith 1989, 2003) is based on the view that the problems of social interaction are the result of other deficiencies, e.g. in language functioning. Damasio and Maurer (1978) likewise abandoned the primacy of social interaction and developed a model for the neurological structure of autism based on a number of aspects of autism (motor function, language and communication, attention and perception, rituals and compulsions). They based their model on a comparison of the behaviour of people with an autistic disorder with that of people with brain damage. In this model, the idea of a deficiency in dopamine transport in the brain plays a significant role. In the meantime, studies on the theory of mind (Baron-Cohen 1989) have given social interaction a more central position again. Frith (1997a) indicates that the problem with social interaction is not the result of defective language but quite the contrary: defective social interaction affects language development.

In addition to the autistic disorders, there are a number of related diagnoses: *multiple complex developmental disorder* (McDD), *non-verbal learning disability* (NLD), *visual thinking* and *hyperlexia*. For a description of the various diagnoses and the criteria used, see Appendix I. In the present chapter, I shall give only a brief outline. Table 4.1 lists the various diagnoses.

Table 4.1 Autistic and related disorders	
Autistic disorders *PDD (pervasive developmental disorders)*	*Related disorders*
Autism (Kanner's autism) HFA (high functioning autism) Asperger's syndrome PDD-NOS (pervasive developmental disorder – not otherwise specified) Rett's syndrome Disintegrative disorder	Alexithymia McDD (multiple complex developmental disorder) NLD (non-verbal learning disability) Hyperlexia Visual thinking

The diagnosis of autism is based exclusively on behavioural characteristics. 'Ticking off' items on the diagnostic list of DSM-IV (APA 1994) is one of the main tools in determining autism. However, DSM-IV is first and foremost a statistical measure, i.e. characteristics are outlined that often occur concurrently. Such a context says nothing about the importance of characteristics nor about their cause or whether they are interrelated.

Vermeulen (1999a) notes that the diagnosis of autism demands a great deal of creativity and flexibility from diagnosticians. He takes the view that diagnosis has to be multidisciplinary, with observations in various day-to-day situations at home, school and work. Disorders within the autistic spectrum are mainly diagnosed from symptoms as described in DSM-IV (APA 1994) and ICD-10 (WHO 1992) and cannot (yet) be measured medically with full objectivity. The fact is that the diagnosis cannot be reliably made before the age of two, and 30 months is taken as a guideline. Gillberg, Nordin and Ehlers (1996) indicate that signs of autism can be established at 18 months. Conversations with parents and observations of behaviour can be informative between 18 and 24 months. However, diagnosis is not possible any earlier than about 30 months. For Asperger's syndrome, it is often even later. This is because early signs can also be indicative of other disorders, e.g. serious learning disorders. In fact, children with learning disorders seem to show more deviations at the age of 12 months than children with autism (Happé 1998). At 18 months, children with an autistic disorder display problems in social development without any clear problems in other fields. Nevertheless, there are indications that children with an autistic disorder show subtle deviations already at a very early stage (Happé 1998).

According to DSM-IV (APA 1994 – see Box 4.1), the diagnosis of autism – Kanner's autism – comprises 12 features, of which at least six are required for a diagnosis of autism. Of these criteria, at least two should come under A (social interaction), one under B (impairment in verbal and non-verbal communication) and one under C (restricted repetitive and stereotyped patterns of behaviour, activities and interests). In PDD-NOS, there are three (or more) of these criteria, with at least one under A. As the DSM list covers all criteria for autism, the list in Box 4.1 is also included in Appendix I.

PDD-NOS stands for *pervasive developmental disorder – not otherwise specified*. The addition NOS is meant to indicate that the problems are not covered by the description of other pervasive disorders. It is not a clearly demarcated syndrome of characteristics but is used for cases in which only a number of features of autism occur. One characteristic of PDD-NOS is that the use of language in not strongly deviant and evaluation of social interaction is not as severely impaired as in the other diagnoses within the autism spectrum. In PDD-NOS, aggression problems are more frequent than in other autistic disorders. It still frequently happens that people are diagnosed with PDD-NOS who in fact ought to be diagnosed as having Asperger's syndrome. Since DSM-IV does not provide guidelines on how many criteria and which ones should be present in order to be able to identify a case as PDD-NOS, there is a considerable risk that this diagnosis is made where there is no or hardly any autistic behaviour. For a diagnosis of PDD-NOS, there should at least

---

Box 4.1 Criteria for autism according to DSM-IV (APA 1994).
Reproduced with permission.

A. Social interaction

1. Marked impairment in the use of multiple non-verbal behaviours such as eye-to-eye gaze, facial expression and gestures to regulate social interaction;

2. Failure to develop relationships appropriate to age;

3. Lack of spontaneous seeking to share enjoyment, interests or achievements with other people;

4. Lack of social or emotional reciprocity. An autistic person seems to be unaware of the existence of other people's feelings; he or she associates with others as if they were objects.

B. Impairment in verbal and non-verbal communication

1. Delay in the development of verbal communication, without attempts to compensate through e.g. gestures; sometimes absence of verbal communication;

2. In individuals with adequate speech, marked impairment in the ability to initiate or sustain a conversation with others;

3. Strange use of contents or form of language, e.g. *echolalia, stereotyped speech, repetition, switching personal pronouns* and *idiosyncratic language.*

4. Lack of imaginative and varied play.

C. Restricted repetitive and stereotyped patterns of behaviour, activities and interests

1. Preoccupation with one or more stereotyped patterns of behaviour;

2. Strong adherence to specific, non-functional rituals or routines;

3. Stereotyped, repetitive body movements;

4. Persistent preoccupation with parts of objects.

---

be three features, one of which is in the social interaction category. In the past, the term *autistiform behaviour* was customary. This term was in fact more transparent as it was clear that there was no autism but behaviour similar to it. Looking at the DSM-IV list in Box 4.1, it is clear, for instance, that the features mentioned under A also occur in neglected children and children with attachment problems. In particular A2 (failure to develop relationships appropriate to age) is behaviour which we observe in children with various problems (neglect, attachment problems, traumatic experiences). A3 (lack of spontaneous seeking to share enjoyment, interests or achievements with other people) also occurs frequently in these children. Accordingly, sound diagnosis requires not only knowledge but also experience. This experience is necessary to be able to distinguish the bafflement of an autistic child in associating with her peers from the distrust of a child with attachment problems. With regard to A3, a distinction should be made as to whether the child fails to share her interests with others because of autism or as a result of neglect. An autistic child does not know that another child does not think, know or feel the same and is sometimes totally unaware of the other. A neglected child, however, is aware of the other but does not expect anything from the other and does not believe that the other could possibly be interested in him or her. These examples clearly show how difficult it is to diagnose PDD-NOS in particular.

Asperger's syndrome (a term first used by Lorna Wing in 1981) is character-ized in particular by impairment in evaluating social interaction, normal and often above average intelligence, and undisturbed and undelayed language development. Language development within the autistic spectrum is related to intelligence (Nordin and Gillberg 1998). Frequent characteristics of people with Asperger's syndrome are awkward motor activity (left/right coordination and eye/hand coordination) and deviating interests. These two features, however, occur throughout the autistic spectrum and in many other developmental disorders (Ghaziuddin and Butler 1998).

It is not always possible to make a sharp distinction between the various forms in the autistic spectrum and it is rare for children to display all the features to a serious degree. Some researchers, for instance, argue that there is hardly any difference between HFA and Asperger's syndrome (Schopler, Mesibov and Kunce 1998; Vermeulen 1999a). If one abandons the criterion of delayed language development, the differences between HFA and Asperger's syndrome in fact also disappear. Moreover, children who at first sight show signs more indicative of HFA appear later on to be more consistent with the criteria of Asperger's syndrome. Baron-Cohen *et al.* (1997) note that there are subtle differences in 'reading' other people's thoughts in individuals with HFA compared with those with Asperger's syndrome. The language use of people with Asperger's syndrome may appear overly polite and sound rather elderly. In this respect, it may differ from HFA (Ghaziuddin and Gerstein 1996).

Wing (1998) argues that for helping and treating people with an autistic disorder it is of no relevance whether their syndrome is autism, HFA or Asperger's. She remarks that the more the intelligence levels correspond, the more differences between children with different diagnoses disappear. Information on the quality of social interaction and the level of verbal and non-verbal expression is of greater significance for therapy than the categorization of cases into different diagnoses of autism or autistic characteristic. Wing mentions the following major criteria of Asperger's syndrome which differ to HFA: no marked lag in development of cognitive skills, in language or motor development, and the presence of awkwardness.

The distinction between 'autistic spectrum' and 'autistic features' is likewise not always perfectly clear.

Apart from the disorders of the autistic spectrum, there are a number of related conditions in which contact disorders occur frequently but are not regarded as a core problem. One of these, non-verbal learning disability or NLD, arose from the field of neuro-psychology. In NLD the core facet is an important disparity between language development and abstract development. This is reflected in the difference between verbal and performal skills in an IQ test. There is said to be a significantly higher verbal intelligence quotient (VIQ) than performal intelligence quotient (PIQ). We encounter the same thing in many people with Asperger's syndrome. Children with NLD may have very good language development and at the same time lag considerably behind in abstract thinking. Often they learn language suddenly, as if by themselves, talk easily, and frequently produce a flood of words that is difficult to stem; or they may be late in language development. The abstract side, for instance the capacity for arithmetic, however, is very slow to develop. Volkmar and Klin (1998) argue that some people with Asperger's syndrome also show the characteristics of NLD, which according to them is not the case in people with HFA. On the other hand, in Asperger's syndrome we also see the opposite picture, low VIQ and high PIQ.

There are also diagnoses which concern partial aspects, e.g. hyperlexia (the unstoppable flow of words) in children with high verbal capacity. Another diagnosis is visual thinking, where the way in which the individual thinks, namely in images rather than words, is viewed as the core of the problem. It is said that Einstein was a visual thinker and that he showed signs of Asperger's syndrome (Grandin 1988).

In the mean time, there is a new syndrome that is being investigated, namely multiple complex developmental disorder or McDD (Buitelaar and van der Gaag 1998). This diagnosis has a number of features in common with autistic disorders and some with schizophrenic disorders. The emphasis is on the schizophrenic features, namely disturbances in *affect*; in particular anxiety and aggression. In McDD, moreover, there is also problematic social functioning and thought disorders. It is related to what used to be called *borderline disorder* (Lafeber 1984) at a time when autism was classified under psychotic disorders. Nowadays, 'borderline' means something quite different (Delfos 2001a) and borderline disorder does not include autistic characteristics. It is now a disorder with strong mood shifts. In McDD, a number of autistic features are combined with psychotic features.

Frith (1992) writes that the same problems in conceptualizing someone else's thoughts and feelings may lie at the basis of autism and schizophrenia.

Charles contracted meningitis as a six-month-old baby. As he grew older, he increasingly showed signs of autism. He was more and more withdrawn, didn't want to go to school and eventually didn't want to leave the house. In his early twenties, he developed a serious psychosis. The good-natured, rather quiet Charles lost his self-control and became aggressive towards his mother with whom he normally had an excellent relationship. In this psychotic phase, he was admitted to hospital, received medication and did everything to return home as soon as possible.

He returned home but then nothing could persuade him to leave the house at all. After two years, there was a recurrence of psychosis. He was extremely anxious. Under therapy, his anxiety diminished somewhat and he managed to take some rest, sleeping for a short while. On waking up, he was seized by an all-pervasive anxiety. He did not say a word, uttered no sound, his eyes expressed indescribable fear. With devoted care and reassurance, he slowly returned to reality after a couple of hours. Suddenly he passionately exclaimed: 'I know it again, I know it again, this is a chair and that's a table, that's the sound of a dog barking.' Once recovered, he said that he had lost all language and had been terribly afraid. It appeared that due to the psychotic condition he had ended up in a state of aphasia, seeming like a six-month-old child without language.

It may be argued that disorders in the autistic spectrum are characterized above all by a developmental picture that occurs in very young children, which comes across as disturbed and strange as it is totally inconsistent with the person's age and potentialities. In McDD there is a fundamentally disturbed picture which does not seem like an immature young child; there is a deviant, more psychotic picture.

Annette was a vivacious nine-year-old. Her mother was very worried about her. Annette had many conflicts at school and did not understand why this was so. In fact she was very sensitive and caring but at times she could be overcome by great excitement. When this happened, her head was very 'hot' inside. Once, when her group at school went swimming, she refused to go into the water because her head was very hot and she was afraid the other children would burn if she jumped into the water.

> Even though she functioned quite reasonably at school, psychotic elements became apparent with increasing frequency. At the age of ten, she once cried out in despair: 'If the screaming in my head doesn't go away, I will commit suicide one day!'

In McDD, the prognosis is not clear. There is a possibility that the child will grow out of it or that the problems will develop into an autistic or schizophrenic disorder.

Social and emotional development

Since social interaction is of fundamental importance in disorders within the autistic spectrum, social and emotional development may give an indication of what Gillberg (1992) has termed *the empathy disorders*. The first building block of this process is ego development.

Piaget (1972) was among the first to study the way in which the self, the ego, develops. He designed an experiment in which the transition from 'egocentric' to 'empathic' could be investigated.

> Piaget studied experimentally how egocentricity can be measured in a child. In the experiment, he seated a child at a small table. In front of it was a small pile of sand; at the other side of the table there was a doll also on a chair, with a lower pile of sand in front of it, and at yet another side of the table there was no one but there was also a small pile. Piaget (1972) asked the child which pile was in front of the doll. Up to a certain age, the child mentioned the pile it had in front of itself, and only after the child no longer thought in strongly egocentric terms was it able to name the correct pile.

Mapping social development is currently receiving a great deal of attention. Traditionally there have been methods involving projective tests – such as the *children's apperception test* (CAT), *thematic apperception test* (TAT) and *Columbus* – in which children have to tell a story on the basis of pictures. The underlying theory behind projection tests is that the child's own history and emotions are projected into the story. In the case of children with Asperger's syndrome, it sometimes happens that

Figure 4.1 Piaget's experiment concerning egocentricity (Harris 1998). Reproduced with permission.

Harry seriously devoted himself to the task of describing the cards of the Columbus test. There was not a trace of tension, only strong concentration. He described all details in the pictures as extensively as he could. He did not describe a single relationship between the people or any connections between the objects depicted. The picture he saw he described in minute detail.

this objective is not achieved because the child primarily enumerates the details she sees in the picture.

A child or adult who gives such a description is not necessarily someone who does not wish to reveal his or her thoughts and feelings or someone who is insensitive but possibly someone with a disorder within the autistic spectrum who first and foremost pays attention to the details of a picture. Another form of projective diagnostics is the interpretation of drawings.

A disadvantage of projective tests is that the results can be interpreted in various ways. Moreover, projective tests are not specifically intended to record a child's social and emotional development but rather to obtain an overall picture of the child's personality and detect problems in his life or past history.

Figure 4.2 Columbus test, card 1 (Langeveld 1969). Reproduced with permission from Swets and Zeitlinger.

Theory of mind tests, or TOM tests, are more specifically focused on social and emotional development. These tests examine theory of mind: the ideas someone has about his or her own thoughts and feelings and those of others. The best-known one is the Sally-Ann test which we shall discuss in the next chapter (Frith 1989). A TOM test developed and studied in the Netherlands is that designed by Pim Steerneman (Steerneman, Meesters and Muris 2000). This test examines to what extent a child is able to imagine what goes on in someone else's mind. We shall discuss theory of mind in more detail in the following chapters.

Another method for mapping out social and emotional development is the investigation of *ego development*, the development of self-awareness. Treffers and Westenberg (1997) developed the Dutch version of the tool which Loevinger (1990) designed on the basis of her ego development theory, which is known as *the sentence completion test* or SCT. The Dutch version, known as ZALC (which stands for *sentence completion list for social and emotional development curium*), makes it possible to obtain an estimation of ego development and an indication of the level of moral development. It consists of the beginning of a sentence which has to be completed, for instance: *My mother and I...* The level of social and emotional development is measured through the nature of the answer, judging whether it shows reciprocity and insight into transience and in the process of establishing relationships. *My mother and I get on well now* gets a different score than it would without *now* or if the words *with each other* were added. Although it seems to be highly dependent on the

Figure 4.3 TOM test (Steerneman et al. 2000). Reproduced with permission from the author.

subject's language level, this is in fact not the case. If one is able to express oneself in language, the level is expressed quite stably across sentences. Other sample sentences are: *If a child never wants to do things in the group… / What I like about myself is that… / School…* Westenberg, Cohn and Blasi (1998) have further developed this tool.

Sparrow, Balla and Cicchetti adapted the *Vineland social maturity scale* (1984), developed by Doll, which can produce an overall picture of 'social maturity'. The following areas are mapped out through this test: communication (receptive, expressive, written language), daily skills (personal, domestic, social), socialization (interpersonal relations, play and leisure, social skills) and motor skills (coarse and fine motor activity).

Classification of autistic children

There is no sharply demarcated picture of *the* autistic person, as there are major differences in individual problems, for example in language ability and intelligence. Each child, moreover, has his own character and predisposition which may generate a wide variety of behaviour in various areas; and each child grows up in a unique environment which is in constant interaction with his predisposition. What makes it even harder to recognize autism clearly is the fact that there are often more problems than autism alone. For instance, there is often *comorbidity* (concurrence of various disorders). A group in which autistic characteristics or autistic features often occur is children with *deficits in attention, motor control, and perception* (DAMP). This group also includes children with *attention deficit hyperactivity disorder* (ADHD). Autism is also quite frequently combined with *Tourette's syndrome*, which involves multiple tics, usually motor *and* verbal tics. Autistic characteristics are particularly prevalent in children with severe intellectual disability. Many autistic people, in particular those with low intelligence (Gillberg and Ehlers 1998), also have epileptic seizures which arise during adolescence, with about 30 to 40 per cent developing epilepsy before the age of 30 (Volkmar and Nelson 1990). Kars (1996) recommends making an electroencephalogram (EEG) because it also enables detection of aspecific anomalies which may clarify some behavioural disorders. It should be noted that behavioural problems that occur in autistic children correspond in many respects with those in children with other developmental disorders (Wing 2001). However, the difference remains that the behaviour of children with autism appears 'strange' and 'naïve'.

Wing (2001; Wing and Gould 1979) distinguishes three types of children with an autistic disorder: *aloof and indifferent, passive accepting* and *active but odd* (see Figure 4.4). To these she adds *stilted and overformal* for adolescents and adults with good intelligence (Wing 2001).

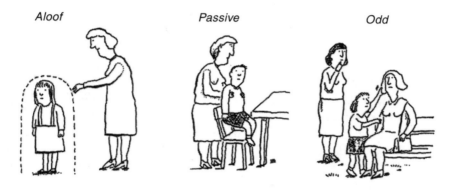

Figure 4.4 Three types of children with autistic disorder, according to Wing (Happé 1998). Reproduced with permission.

Aloof autistic children are extremely withdrawn and live as it were in isolation from others, behind a glass pane. This form is characteristic of Kanner's autism. In such children, there is virtually no reciprocity in contact with others and there are very limited cognitive potentialities. As a result of their seriously restricted intellectual capacities, their autistic disorder is often not recognized. Passive autistic children do not seek contact actively but undergo contact stoically. They also show impairment of reciprocity in contact and they clearly suffer from communicative problems. The third group, consisting of children with an autistic disorder whose behaviour is active but odd, has the best cognitive potentialities and the highest intelligence. Their intelligence may range from normal to above average. There are characteristics often encountered in Asperger's syndrome. The autistic children in this group may strongly claim attention. Here, again, there are problems in reciprocity but these children tend to be unable to join in rather than having an impaired need for reciprocity in contact with others. Stilted and overformal children are often found among those with Asperger's syndrome; they have above average intelligence. In their case, there is often no or late diagnosis. People around them describe them as eccentric, bizarre, egoistic and weird (Vermeulen 1999a).

Prevalence of autistic disorders

The prevalence of autism differs according to diagnosis. Kanner's autism is the most frequently diagnosed form, and many who have this also have a severe intellectual disability. Until recently, epidemiological studies showed that 70 to 80 per cent of autistic people were intellectually disabled. However, researchers such as Chakrabarti and Fombonne (2001) and Baird and colleagues (2000) report that the figure is only 25 to 30 per cent or 40 per cent. For the creation of the image of autism, it does make a difference whether most autistic people are severely mentally handicapped or of normal and above average intelligence. Figure 4.5 illustrates this difference. Of people with an intellectual disability, only 25 per cent have an autistic disorder.

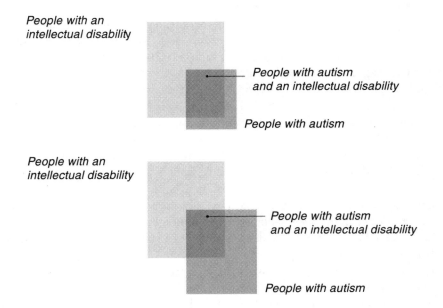

Figure 4.5 Graphic representation of people with an intellectual disability and people with autism.

In Kanner's autism, one out of four or five children never learns to speak (Wing 2001). The number of autistic children was reported to be 2 to 3 per 10,000 to 16,000, depending on different definitions (Wing 2001). Haveman and Reijnders (2002) reviewed the prevalence of autism in the period from 1966 to 2001. They discovered that there had been a significant rise in prevalence in epidemiological studies after the publication of DSM-IV and ICD-10. They corrected the studies for age range, publications and size of the sample population, concluding that there had been a substantial increase from 1966. They found a prevalence of over 16 per 10,000. The criteria and studies had become more precise and Haveman and Reijnders therefore assumed that there had been systematic underestimation in the past. In the Emanuel Miller Memorial Lecture, Gillberg (1992) pointed out that there was no increase in diagnosis of Kanner's autism, but a rise in HFA and Asperger's syndrome. This he attributed, among other things, to the interest that had developed in the subject.

The milder forms of autism are often not recognized in childhood but only when people have become adults, and even then it regularly happens that autism is not recognized as such. Adults with Asperger's syndrome are often labelled 'odd', having a 'one-track mind', 'egoistic' and 'eccentric' by people around them. As for the prevalence of Asperger's syndrome, the figure is estimated to be 36 per 10,000 children, and for the autistic spectrum as a whole 58 per 10,000, i.e. approximately 6 per 1000 children (Hill and Frith 2003). Views differ about the prevalence of autistic disorders in men and women. Wing (2001) mentions a 4:1 ratio for autism in general. Attwood (1998) mentions 10:1 for boys versus girls, but focuses on Asperger's syndrome in particular. The higher the intelligence, the higher the ratio of men in relation to women. Gifted people with Asperger's syndrome include hardly any women. In their review, Hill and Frith (2003) mention a ratio of about 3:1 with regard to the entire autistic spectrum. Uta Frith (1989), in the second edition of her classic book (published in 2003), reports a 15:1 ratio for Asperger's syndrome. The high prevalence of men and women with an autistic disorder combined with intellectual disability suggests an organic cause (Frith 1989). We see a similar phenomenon in such disorders as Down syndrome and in children with infantile encephalopathy. While there are significantly more boys than girls with these disorders, the ratio drops dramatically with decreasing intelligence.

It may well be that too little attention is given to the gender-specific aspect of autism. Asperger (1944) noted that not only do boys more frequently display autism than girls, but also that in girls the syndrome is not as marked. He had the impression that autism in women became more marked with age as if autism became full blown only as women grew older. I have not found any studies reporting differences in the nature of autism between men and women as Asperger did, but in my own experience I have encountered a similar picture in respect of women of normal or above average intelligence. In women with autism, there is more often a severe intellectual disability. While in normally gifted people the man: woman ratio is as much as 10:1, in autistic people with an intellectual disability it is closer to 4:1. Rutter, Hussain Tuma and Lann (1988) report that autism patterns in boys and girls may well be different, calling for more research to investigate this aspect.

The adult autistic women I have seen myself appear incapacitated in a wide field, with general impotence, whereas in men the disorder seems to be more focused on the specific area of social interaction.

While it is certainly not possible to base any scientific conclusions upon general autobiographies, it is instructive in this regard to read autobiographies of people with an autistic disorder. It is clear from Gunilla Gerland's (2003) autobiography that she is inept in a wide range of social activities, from crossing the road to understanding someone else's attitude towards herself, although this would not be expected in the light of her overall development. On the other hand, she has major talents. Her autobiography is a book with literary qualities. The fact that in the course of her life her functioning has steadily improved does not seem to be the result of growth from within but of consciously trying to remember and continuing to apply what she has learnt about social intercourse. If we compare this with Birger Sellin (1995), who is very severely disabled socially because he cannot speak, we see definite personal growth over the years. He has gained insight that is not only based on knowledge but on growth from within, despite the fact that his behaviour still comes across as deeply autistic. Birger Sellin seems to be more a 'normal' human being imprisoned in 'abnormal' functioning, whereas Gunilla Gerland seems to be more an 'abnormal' human functioning 'normally'.

It would seem that women's functioning shows more of a downward trend as they grow older. In men with Asperger's syndrome, an upward trend is more frequent, with individual functioning improving as they mature and acquire more knowledge about social interaction and life in society. In this context, it is interesting to mention the only form of autism which, as far as we know, almost exclusively occurs in women, namely Rett's syndrome. In women, we see a sharper downward trend in development, starting with normal development for a couple of months or one or two years, followed by a loss of the skills acquired and the concomitant emergence of autism.

In Veerle Beel's (2000) book, which in my opinion does little justice to autism – quite the contrary – the last chapter concerns a married couple in which the wife is autistic, again showing a picture of a normally gifted but in some ways seriously disabled woman. These opposite and crossing lines of development remind us of what we discussed in the previous chapter in connection with stammering and left- and right-handedness, where Smith, Meyers and Kline (1989) discerned similar gender-specific crossing lines in stammering and mathematical talent.

In this connection, Hans Asperger (1944) makes a particularly intriguing remark. He says that he assumes that men and women differ in *the way they inherit*. Since we always speak of heredity in an undifferentiated manner, this may well be a visionary observation in the field of genetics, with regard to inheriting genes. It may well be that in autistic women there is more often a cerebral disintegrative process and in autistic men a progressively restorative progress.

In his Emanuel Miller Memorial Lecture, Gillberg (1992) posits four causes of autism:

1. autism occurring in the family (8.5%)

2. autism connected with a medical condition, e.g. fragile X syndrome (37%)

3. autism with non-specific brain dysfunction and without familial history of a medical condition (46%)

4. autism with familial history and without brain dysfunction (8.5%).

Early detection

While in the past it was thought that autism could only be diagnosed at a later stage, we now know that the child can show symptoms of autism at an early stage. It should be added that this applies much more strongly to Kanner's autism than to Asperger's syndrome, which is recognized only much later. As one of the features of Asperger's syndrome, some researchers therefore use as a criterion the later age at which Asperger's syndrome manifests itself compared with Kanner's autism.

Various diagnostic tools have been developed for early detection of autism. I have already mentioned Baron-Cohen's *CHAT*. With the aid of CHAT, autistic characteristics in children can be discerned from the age of 18 months. On the basis of research into early detection, various tools have been and are being developed. Another scale is the *AUTI-R* scale (Berckelaer-Onnes and Hoekman 1991) which has been developed and standardized for children with autistic disorder without intellectual disability. It is standardized in comparison with three other groups, i.e. children with severe hearing loss, children with an intellectual disability without autism, and children without disability. Aarons and Gittens (2000) have compiled a list of characteristics that can be discerned from the age of 18 months:

- little interest in peers or inadequate association with peers

- language is not used as a means of communication

- limited play with repetitive character

- unusual interests

- impairment in interpreting events

- no shared attention with others for objects

- the child is described as 'odd', 'moody' or 'extremely stubborn'

- strongly attached to one parent.

In the meantime, scales are being developed worldwide to diagnose autism at an early stage. The Dutch Autisme Team Gelderland (2000) finalized their *ATG questionnaire* in 2001. It is a very extensive list of questions designed to record medical information concerning pregnancy and the child, cognitive development, sensory development, motor development, social development, speech/language/communication development, identity development, play development, ritual behaviour, resistance to change and problematic behaviour.

In intelligence testing as part of diagnostics, attention is paid to VIQ/PIQ ratio and constructing a story (discovering a logical structure in a concatenation of events). In two important intelligence tests, the *Wechsler Intelligence Scale for Children* (WISC) and the *Wechsler Adult Intelligence Scale* (WAIS), people with an autistic disorder score poorly in story construction. The idea is to compose a logical story on the basis of a number of separate cards which together make up a kind of comic strip. Children with Asperger's syndrome have great difficulty with this task. They place the cards in random order and do not know how to turn them into a logical story. For these children, establishing causal links is considerably simpler with regard to laws of physics (If it rains, you get wet) than with regard to social interaction (Because I do this, he does that). In another component of the test, doing jigsaw puzzles, the same children may get a very high score because they have a very good eye for detail, as we shall see in the next chapter.

Verpoorten, Noens and Berckelaer-Onnes (1999/2001) are developing the *Comvoor* test. Comvoor (which in Dutch stands for communication precursors) is an experimental tool to highlight indicators of supportive communication. It involves tactually and/or visually perceivable information at various levels of abstraction. The target group consists of people with an autistic spectrum disorder who do not communicate verbally or do so only poorly.

Within the framework of the influential *TEACCH* programme (treatment and education of autistic and related communication handicapped children), the *PEP* (Psychoeducational Profile) test (Schopler and Reichler 1979) was designed specially for autistic children. As these children could not be studied through the usual tests, the PEP test was developed specifically for children between the ages of one and twelve. For adolescents and adults, the *AAPEP* test has been compiled (Mesibov *et al.* 1988).

Now that I have outlined the various diagnoses, the time has come to go to the heart of the matter and describe the nature of the problems in autistic disorders.

Focal points

- The core problem in autistic disorders is difficulty evaluating social interaction combined with impaired empathic capacity.

- There are various terms used for autistic and related disorders: pervasive disorders, contact disorders, disorders within the autistic spectrum, a-spectrum, empathy disorders, autism-related disorders.

- The various forms of autistic disorders are as follows: autism, HFA, Rett's syndrome, disintegrative disorder, Asperger's syndrome and PDD-NOS as closely related to autism.

- DSM-IV mentions 12 criteria of autistic disorder, six of which have to be present for diagnosis of autism; for PDD-NOS, only three have to be present.

- There is a 'precursor' to autism and schizophrenia: McDD (multiple complex developmental disorder).

- There are syndromes in which a number of features of autism are present but in which these are not the principal ones: NLD, hyperlexia and visual thinking.

- The difference between the various forms of autistic disorders cannot always be clearly demarcated.

- Asperger's syndrome is a 'milder' form of autism in which language development is intact and intelligence is normal to above average.

Focal points regarding attitude

- Awareness that the child lacks knowledge about social interaction.

- Awareness that the child has various levels of development for various subjects.

- Awareness that it is not possible to make a clear diagnosis as to whether there is autism.

Summary

There are various causes of autism, among which genetic predisposition is the most important one. A second important source is diseases, such as particular forms of meningitis. Difficulty in evaluating social interaction is used as the core concept for autistic disorders. Other important factors are information processing, eye for detail, sensory sensitivity and rate of development. The various disorders within the autistic spectrum are described on the basis of behavioural characteristics, expressed in lists of characteristics as published in DSM-IV. The autistic spectrum ranges from the most severe form of autism, known as Kanner's autism, to PDD-NOS in which only some autistic features are present. In McDD some aspects of autism are incorporated together with psychotic aspects, which form the most important features. Autistic disorders are much more frequent in men than in women, except for Rett's syndrome which is almost exclusively found in women. There are related disorders such as NLD, hyperlexia and visual thinking. Four types of autistic people can be distinguished, from extremely withdrawn and passive, to demanding or very formal in contact with others. These are connected with level of intelligence.

5

The core of the problem

In order to understand autism, various subjects are central. When making a diagnosis, researchers such as Frith, Happé and Wing start from the fact that there has to be at least the *triad* of characteristics: qualitative problems in the field of *social interaction*, of *communication* and of *imagination*. With autism, social contact is the central point.

Social interaction

Most characteristic of the problem of disorders within the autistic spectrum, reflecting the first point of the triad, is difficulty in assessing social interaction. A child with a disorder in the autistic spectrum has a lot of trouble with understanding what others are thinking and what the impact of his or her own behaviour is on the people around him or her. The reason why this is difficult for the child is, among other things, because he or she finds it difficult to recognize and put into words his or her own feelings. In other words, poor knowledge of the self makes knowing another person a struggle, as I explained in Chapter 3. This characteristic can be observed most clearly with people who have Asperger's syndrome. We assume that this most characterizing problem with social interaction is also the core of the problem. That is to say that we assume that other characteristics of information processing, such as an incorrect understanding of time and space or eye for detail, are connected with the core problems but are in the background. We place this within the framework of the development of a *socioscheme*. At a later point we will discuss this in more detail. This is different from the general starting point that assumes that processing information inadequately is the core of the problem. Although researchers proceeding from the theory of *central coherence* indicate that inadequate social functioning may be characteristic, they assume, however, that this is only one example of information processing which is not functioning properly. They explain this recurring symptom as caused by the fact that processing such complex social information constitutes an extra problem (Wing 2001). We assume that there is a failure in information processing in very specific areas which are connected with the development of social interaction, and not so much that the social interaction is an example of the failure which also takes place in all other areas.

The world for children with Asperger's syndrome and the other autistic disorders is full of people who show all sorts of incomprehensible behaviours. In order to understand behaviour, the autistic child has two possibilities: first *knowing* the behaviour through his or her own experience or trying to *figure out* the behaviour. They cannot often 'sense' behaviour as the average person can. 'Sensing' is probably developed by being oriented towards oneself-in-relation-to-the-other from birth. The autistic child is, however, more self-oriented: proceeding from himself and not so much oriented towards himself in relation to the other, as a result of which he does not learn and store a lot of knowledge and experience about himself with regard to the other or about others in general. Developing the me–other differentiation is of great importance here. This development will be discussed further in Chapter 7.

Assessing social interaction is directly connected with the extent to which one can put oneself in someone else's shoes, the *empathic ability*. People with a disorder within the autistic spectrum have enormous difficulty in imagining what goes on in other people's minds. They find it hard to imagine a different way of thinking, feeling and experiencing to what they know themselves or have experienced. 'You must have been in Africa to know what it is' certainly applies to them.

> Maria received the news that a friend of hers had died. It made her sad. When her son Jordan, aged 11, came home he saw that his mother was crying. His mother explained that she was sad because a friend of hers had died. 'Do I know him?' Jordan asked. 'No', his mother replied. 'Oh, then I don't have to be sad', he replied and went on with his business.

In the course of their lives they are, however, capable of compensating for their lack of empathy with their intellect. Because of their life experience and their practice in making abstractions as they grow up, they can imagine a wider scale of human existence than their own restricted world. Because of their difficulty with sensing and sympathizing with others, people with Asperger's syndrome are often seen as unfeeling or insensitive. This does them an injustice.

Unfeeling or being 'stuck'

People who have experienced the anxiety of an autistic person, their struggle to keep their head psychologically above water and the affection that they often show, know that they are not insensitive or confrontational, but that they lack the ability to imagine what other people are thinking and they are often preoccupied and fully engrossed by their own problems. Autistic people often feel caught in an emotional wave which washes over them.

Going to primary school, for example, can be a terrifying experience. The appeal made on social interaction is very high there, especially amongst children's peers. The 'attack' on an autistic child's nervous system can sometimes already be enormous regarding the sudden quantity of sound and movement generated by all those children at school. In addition, autistic children are often the object of bullying because of their conspicuous behaviour. Because of their panic they can be very forceful and ignore the interests of others.

> 'If you force me to go to school again tomorrow, I will run away!' shouts the ten-year-old, desperate Charles. He is in a panic when he has to go to school. His desperate mother makes an all-out effort to try to get him to go to school. Charles hardly even dares to leave the house, so his threat is empty: he wouldn't even dare to run away. He just does not know any more how he can reach his mother. Even though his mother, during that time still without any help, is at an utter loss, she takes his cry for help seriously and no longer forces him to go to school.

Because autistic children are less oriented towards their environment, they will sooner 'express' emotions than 'share' them. Many emotions expressed by autistic children have a negative nature and are therefore more easily picked up by the people around them. Positive emotions are not shared so much and are therefore noticed less; also, because with positive emotions the child does not make any demands on the people around him and their peace is not disturbed. A clear example of such an emotion is, for example, the pleasant high, the *hypnotic trance* into which autistic children sometimes send themselves, into which they can withdraw into themselves. It will only be noticed when the positive emotion is strongly opposite to that which one would expect. This happens, for example, when a beatific smile passes over the child's face when actually she has hurt herself badly.

The autistic child's range of feelings is less wide with many feelings developing a lot later than what we are used to with non-autistic children, and sometimes not at all. Some autistic children's feelings will develop much more strongly than those of non-autistic children, for example, the feeling of estrangement, being a stranger in a strange world. A number of feelings develop more slowly or inadequately with autistic people. This relates to feelings which are connected with interpretations of other people's behaviour and feelings which arise from interaction with others. Shame, for example, is an emotion which has a close relation with the people around one. Anxiety or anger, on the other hand, can exist without having a relation with other people. Many emotions develop and deepen with interaction with the environment. Because this interaction with the environment is less strong with autistic people, the emotional development is deviant. Also, controlling and suppressing feelings is normally strongly dependent on the environment. Because autistic people have less contact with their environment this regulation system also works less strongly. They often express their emotions with full force, especially as a child, and this often poses big problems for the parents and educators.

Theories regarding autism

Even though social interaction is the core of the problem, this does not mean that this is the most noticeable symptom of autism. Often, the way of talking, the non-smooth motor system or the intrusive, obsessive interest in certain subjects such as dinosaurs, flags, trains or maps, are more noticeable.

There are three important psychological theories in the field of autism (Bailey, Phillips and Rutter 1996; Berckelaer-Onnes 1999). The first focuses on the awareness of someone else's feelings and thoughts, the *theory of mind* (TOM) (Premack and Woodruff 1978; Leslie 1987; Baron-Cohen 1989). TOM is the inner theory which everyone develops with respect to how people think and feel. This, with autistic people, is supposed to be inadequately developed. The second theory is the theory of *(weak) central coherence* (CC) (Frith 1989, 2003; Frith and Happé 1994). This theory assumes that with autistic people, giving a meaning to the collected information does not reach central coherence – unity – and is not given an unambiguous meaning. The weak central coherence, or *disengagement*, causes them to remain stuck on details. Part-observation, *fragmented observation*, takes place, and these fragments are not formed into a coherent unity that connects the loose fragments with each other.

The third theory, the *planning and executive function* (EF) (Ozonoff, Pennington and Rogers 1991; Pennington and Ozonoff 1996), pays attention to the problem of planning and organizing. The obsessions of autistic people and their resistance to change are explained in this theory as being due to a lack of ability to plan.

Table 5.1 shows the three most important theories and their core aspects together.

Table 5.1 The three most important theories and their core aspects		
Theory	*Abbreviation*	*Core aspect*
Theory of mind	TOM	Difficulty with social interaction
Central coherence	CC	Attention to details and difficulty in forming them into a whole
Planning and executive function	EF	Difficulties with planning, resistance to change, repetitive behaviour

The three theories in themselves each explain an important aspect of autism, but do not give a comprehensive explanation of all the aspects of autism (Bailey *et al.* 1996).

Baron-Cohen (2003) proposes a theory of differences between men and women, with the *empathizing-systemizing brain* (ES), and he positions autism, as does Hans Asperger (1944), as the extreme male brain.

Frith (1989, 2003) indicates that the theories have shortcomings and that a model regarding autism should in fact be about self-awareness. This is the central point of the model that is presented in this book and of which the socioscheme is the central concept.

The model in this book in fact contains the three theories and other research findings. All theories and findings are placed in the socioscheme. At a biological level the starting point is the development of the *neural self* and the forming of *awareness*; at a psychological level it is the forming of the socioscheme.

Theory of mind (TOM)

Wing (1988) mentioned three areas which have a problematic character in the case of autism, called the triad: social behaviour, communication and imagination. The theory of the TOM explains all three phenomena, starting from an underlying variable called *mentalizing*. It concerns the ability to make representations or visualizations. In social behaviour this is related to imagining your own and another person's thoughts and feelings: the forming of a theory of mind. Communication follows on from that and, moreover, requires one to be able to make a representation of the symbolic value of language, because a word refers to a concept. The lack of imagination is also connected with this, and we see this demonstrated most obviously in autism by the absence of make-believe play, in other words, the capacity to imagine that something represents something completely different – pretending, for example, that a box is a boat. In the psychological explanation of autistic disorders TOM plays an important role. This concept was first used by Premack and Woodruff in 1978 and has been elaborated on by researchers such as Baron-Cohen, Wing, Frith and Happé. Everyone develops a TOM in relation to their own thoughts and feelings and those of other people. TOM is about what other people are like and what intentions and plans they have, and we use this to attempt to understand and predict behaviour. TOM is the tool with which social interaction can be interpreted and directed. It is developed using empathy, putting oneself in someone else's shoes. This is what autistic people find so difficult, and their TOM is therefore inadequate.

> One of the more familiar tests with which to examine the TOM is the Sally-Ann test, developed by Uta Frith (1989). It concerns two children. Sally has a basket and Ann has a box. Sally puts a marble in her basket and leaves. While Sally is gone, Ann takes the marble out of the basket and puts it in the box. The question is: where will Sally look for the marble when she returns? In order to be able to answer the question correctly, you have to put yourself in Sally's place. She does not know that the marble has been taken away during her absence and the right answer should therefore be that Sally will look for the marble in her basket. Children who have Asperger's syndrome will generally say that Sally will look for the marble in the box, because after all that is where it is. Despite the necessity for change of perspective 20 per cent of the autistic children do give the right answer (Vermeulen 1999a). Most, however, only give the right answer when they are older and more experienced. Children without an autistic disorder generally do not have any difficulty answering this question correctly.

Usually at the age of around four, children realize that other people have thoughts and feelings that direct their behaviour. In the diagnostics of children with an autistic disorder, tests are used to examine whether children do have this realization (Happé 1998). When we look at research into the intellectual development and abilities of children, however, we may wonder whether this age is indeed correct. It seems more likely that at this age it is a combination of consciousness-raising and linguistic communication. Adults often make the mistake of thinking that children only understand something when they can put it into words. Research into communicating with children shows that many of the abilities of children remain unknown and unused because adults communicate within a linguistic framework which children have not yet mastered sufficiently. Moreover, when children are

This is Sally

This is Ann

Sally has a basket

Ann has a box

Sally has a marble. She puts the marble in her basket

Sally goes outside for a walk

Ann takes the marble out of the basket and puts it in her box

Sally returns

She wants to play with her marble

Where will Sally look for her marble?

Figure 5.1 The Sally-Ann test (Frith 1996). Reproduced with permission.

interviewed the conversation frameworks are not made clear enough, causing children often to show behaviour which is adjusted to adults. In this way the children's own point of view does not come into its own (Delfos 2000).

In the TOM is a wealth of often 'subconscious' knowledge of how other people think and feel. In everyone's TOM there is, among other things, the *recognition of emotion*, the degree to which we can place emotions displayed by another person. This recognition of emotion is inadequate with autistic people. In order to develop a TOM it is necessary to have an understanding of mental states like opinions, knowledge, ignorance. People with autism have difficulty in forming a picture of mental states (Baron-Cohen 1990). The TOM has proven to be a fruitful theory for the development of understanding autistic thinking, but it is not capable of offering explanations of, for example, repetitive movements or the way that these children look at their hands while turning them as if fascinated by them. I am of the opinion that the TOM is one link in the socioscheme.

The TOM is especially powerful for explaining the social behaviour of people with autism; many other aspects, however, remain unexplained. Happé (1998) indicates that the triad also does not give an explanation for a number of aspects that often occur with autism: the restricted interests, obsessive need for sameness, specific areas of skills, 'idiot savant' skills, excellent memory for facts, rote memory, preoccupation with parts of objects, memory for sentences, memory for associated items, echolalia, pattern recognition, puzzle skills, sorting faces by emotions, and being able to recognize faces upside down. A number of these elements are explained by the theory of central coherence.

Central coherence (CC)

Wing (1988) indicates that the TOM fails to explain an important aspect of autism, notably the inability to select experiences and to make these into a coherent story. This given can, however, be placed within the theory of central coherence (CC). It offers an explanation for the sharp 'eye for detail' often existing with autistic people or for the excellent score achieved for the hidden figures test. The starting point of CC is that there is a dysfunction of the part of the brain that forms a coherent picture out of various details. The difficulty with recognizing faces (Baron-Cohen and Hammer 1997) is part of that. Children with an autistic disorder have difficulty connecting various aspects of an emotion (facial expression, movement, voice) together (Hobson 1993). CC theory takes this limitation in the ability to reach a coherent, integrated image and explains autistic people's problem of social interaction as being an inability to convert the various details of the social interaction into a coherent social image which can steer social behaviour. This integration proves, however, to be problematic, especially in the field of social stimuli. Objects are often recognized more easily than people. This means that the problems play a lesser part in the field of information processing in general, but play a greater part in the field of social interaction. Another indication of this is that Rieffe, Meerum Terwogt and Stockman (2000) showed that normally gifted autistic children do have a TOM, but don't use it in everyday situations.

One of the problems with the CC theory is that the concept of a dysfunction in the brain is a static one, and it seems that when autistic children grow older, clear developments in forming coherences and forming unities based on details can occur. Autistic people *are* capable of facial recognition, often at a later stage and often in a delayed manner. Moreover, details can only be detected from a whole image.

Combining details to make a meaningful entity takes time. The details, the fragments, are put together in the brain to form a coherent entirety. This is the process of CC. When the formation of CC is delayed, this will take more time to do. It means that the information processing in the brains of autistic people goes differently. We can state three subjects where there are differences. First, autistic people focus less strongly on people than non-autistic people do. Because of this, 'people-subjects' will be processed less quickly than 'object-subjects'. A second difference is the degree to which various subjects can be processed simultaneously and in connection with each other, which in computer terms we call 'multitasking'. Autistic people, as we saw in Chapter 3, are better at concentrating on one subject and find it more difficult to process more than one subject at the same time. A third difference is the need to process information accurately and without mistakes. This requires more time and may produce quantity at the expense of quality. As a result of these different factors, the speed of processing can be slower. Research into processes which test these CC processes shows that there is a difference between autistic and non-autistic people (Frith 1989, 2003).

Information processing both in nature and pace forms the core of the CC theory. Followers of this theory tend, however, to regard autistic thinking as being too mechanical. The emphasis is sometimes too often on 'not-being able to' instead of the interest, the focus and the pace. Baron-Cohen (2000) emphasizes that it is more about thinking differently than about a deficit. Thinking differently is, however, not an insensitive, not-understanding thinking, but a different focus, a different field of interest. Baron-Cohen states that we do regard a neighbour who is autistic as someone who has a disability, because he has a problem in the field of social interaction; but that we do not regard people who are strongly empathetic as people with a handicap, because they are weak in the fields of technology and mathematics. Baron-Cohen (2003) developed the E-S theory. He starts from an empathic brain structure (E-brain) or a systemizing brain structure (S-brain). Women would more often have an E-brain and men an S-brain. In the case of autism it would be an S-brain, a systematizing brain structure. The E-S theory does not explain all aspects of autism, it only stresses the point Asperger (1944) made that autism reflects the extreme male brain.

The theory of CC can explain a part of the phenomena concerning autism, but not sufficiently. In EF theory, attention is focused on different problems that occur with autism, notably regulating and organizing behaviour.

Planning and executive function (EF)

People with autism have a resistance to change but also a difficulty in regulating their behaviour. Their repetitive behaviour can be strongly obsessive. Both the planning and the controlling of their behaviour may cause problems. The TOM and CC theories cannot explain these aspects sufficiently. The power of the explanation of the theory of the 'planning and executive function' (EF) lies particularly in the field of the organization of behaviour in people with autism.

The executive function is the ability to hold on to an appropriate unity, a set of coherent problem-solving activities, for a purpose. This unity comprises one or more of the following elements:

1.   the intention to control a reaction or to postpone it to a more appropriate time

2.   a strategic plan for a series of actions

3.   a mental image of a task, including the storage in the memory of the relevant facts and the desired target state in the future.

Typical EFs are being able to change a set of problem-solving activities; being able to hold on to that set; having no loss of control when disturbed in some way; being able to control behaviour; being able to integrate elements over time and space; planning and having a working memory (Pennington and Ozonoff 1996).

EF is concerned with central regulation processes, that is to say at brain level. The theory of EF has been developed from the knowledge of people who have a frontal lesion. A problem with this is that a lesion is a completely different, significantly less static problem than a maturation or a deviant or variant functioning of the brain. Also, with EF, just as with the CC and to a lesser extent the TOM, the idea of a more static form of dysfunction plays a part, instead of a delayed, deviant, inadequate or variant development. Autistic people can carry out many complex activities where EF plays a part, especially when they are able to do it at their own pace. Their problem does not usually concern a total inability but more the pace at which it can be carried out. Hardly any attention is paid to that in scientific research.

A nice example of neglecting the pace problem is in the research done by Didden, Palmen and Arts (2002). They researched the effectiveness of a training conducted with youngsters with HFA/Asperger's syndrome. Their intention was to encourage the youngsters to ask their coaches more questions. The tight research design included a period of five seconds, given to the youngsters to ask a question, before the word 'Stop' would sound. The amount of questions asked increased. The question is, however, whether this was because of the training or because of the five seconds of silence, giving the youngsters the chance to ask their questions at their own pace. The group leaders appeared to experience it as an 'eye-opener', first giving them the chance to say something within five seconds and then realizing that they were too quick to offer help.

EF assumes a dysfunction and places the accent on the frontal lobe of the brain. Possibly not enough attention has been paid to people with autism actually being able to carry out complex activities. In an experimental situation there is also the problem of the amount of time involved.

Slower information processing can lead to a sharper image, but when this process is tested at an early stage, the impression may arise that it concerns inability. Another problem is that the theory of EF cannot explain many aspects of autism. It can explain the lack of imagination much better than the special interests, the frontal lobe better than the deviant amygdala. In addition, research shows that the functioning of the autistic brain is not focally deviant but shows more of a complete pattern (Bailey *et al.* 1996).

The theory of EF is a general psychological function theory that already has a very long tradition. As far as understanding deviant behaviour is concerned this theory has been especially fruitful for understanding ADHD, specifically, the inability to control behaviour. It is so fruitful because it offers an explanation of a core behaviour of ADHD, notably the mixture of hyperactive and impulsive behaviour and the inability to concentrate, which is connected with it.

The problem of EF as an explanation of autism is that it is not an explanatory model with regard to autism, but a general model of behaviour. The CC came into existence as a model starting from one aspect of autism, namely the problem with forming central coherences. The fact that the model also has a general validity for explanation of behaviour was an additional phenomenon; the point of EF is that it concerns a general theory that can be applied to autism.

EF relates to a set of related explanations of how behaviour is regulated and organized. The model examines the 'how' rather than the 'why'. The importance of EF for autism is that research has shown that with autistic people many EFs are a problem; planning behaviour and adhering to it often create big problems. The resistance to changes which we see with autistic people can be explained using the theory of the EF: as an inability to complete a change of set, an inability to imagine a different situation and an inability to curb a ongoing activity. In this way we can understand repetitive behaviour proceeding from the EF as a lack of ability to curb behaviour. Autistic people's problems with TOM are explained by EF theory as proceeding from a lack of ability to form mental images in general. The fact that people with autism are indeed able to build up a TOM over years is not explained by the EF theory. Even more difficult to explain with this theory is the fact that autistic people are able to imagine, for example, other people's mental states but these usually do not concur with reality. Autistic people are also extra sensitive to experiencing stress with other people, notably their mothers (Wing 1996). What they have is therefore more a deviant way of imagining than an inability.

The power of the theory of EF lies in the fact that it puts the finger on the way in which information processing could function with autistic people, the 'how'.

The theory of EF is oriented towards the output, while the theory of CC is more oriented towards the input. The theory of EF places the lack of orientation in time and space in the context of an integrative problem. This is strongly associated with the idea of CC, but EF places this partly at a higher and partly on the same level of integration as the CC.

The socioscheme in relation to other theories

The three authoritative theories in the field of autism (TOM, CC, EF) each explains one aspect of autism in particular. Bailey *et al.* (1996) indicate that research does not support these theories sufficiently and that they only explain a part of autism. One of the weaknesses of the three theories is that, according to them, they do not offer an explanation for the fact that autism is characterized by delays in development instead of a dysfunctional development. Bailey *et al.* indicate that there is a need for a comprehensive concept. TOM (Leslie 1987; Baron-Cohen 1990) explains in particular the inadequate social interaction. The theory of CC (Frith 1989) offers an explanation for the attention to detail and the difficulty with distinguishing main issues from side issues. The EF theory (Pennington and Ozonoff 1996) offers an explanation for the resistance to change and the repetitive behaviours. All three theories have as a perspective for autism a dysfunction of the brain. Baron-Cohen's (2003) model (E-S) explains elements of autistic behaviour in a more coherent whole than the other theories, but does not touch the core of autism as such, the self-awareness Uta Frith (1989) spoke about. However, his model comes closest to the socioscheme. Baron-Cohen proposes that Geschwind was right – in retrospect – when he spoke about testosterone and the right hemisphere, but he does not develop his E-S model from the testosterone hypothesis as the model of the socioscheme does.

The theory of the socioscheme does not regard autism so much as a dysfunction, but as a variant of development. What the other theories all pass over is the essence of the story, *being withdrawn into oneself,* which was exactly the reason why Leo Kanner and Hans Asperger gave it the name *autism.* The theory of the socioscheme therefore takes the little orientation and non-automized orientation towards people as the core of the problem, and an inadequate me–other differentiation as its spearhead. Scientific research showed that no specific dysfunction could be found in the brain, but it did show a general deviant image (Bailey *et al.* 1996), something we would also expect with the theory of the socioscheme. The socioscheme explains the system of behaviours as a specific development and thus can do justice to the positive qualities and not only focus on the problematic sides of autism. Research-wise the theory of the socioscheme predicts different behaviour in various fields to the three mentioned theories. See Appendix IV (in electronic form; for access information see p.13). In addition, it offers an explanation for the comprehensive anxiety that so often characterizes people with autism and the many other aspects which can play a part in autism.

The socioscheme

Frith (1989) indicates that 'being aware' and knowing yourself as the basis on which you learn to know the other, are of great importance for autism, but also states that she cannot make a connection with the theory of CC or of TOM and leaves this subject touched upon, but undiscussed. In the second (2003) edition, Frith pays more extensive attention to this subject and even mentions the *homunculus*, an old concept that fell from favour, the 'little man' who had all knowledge of mankind. She indicates that knowledge of the self is an important subject with autism and that deviations can be expected regarding non-autistic people. She does not elaborate on this idea.

In the model presented in this book it is especially the knowing of yourself, the me–other differentiation, which is a spearhead.

In Chapter 3 we indicated that empathy develops following on from the me–other differentiation and that this lags behind in the case of a brain with a less developed left hemisphere, as is the case with autistic people. We could call this a lack of inner grip, inner structure. The way a human being functions comes from a number of basic inner blueprints. The 'little boy with the salt' in Chapter 3 is an example of that. The *body blueprint* (Sacks 1984) is another example of that. It is one of the building blocks which we called the *neural self* (Damasio 1994) in Chapter 3. This body blueprint, a 'map of the body', is constantly updated. Every body part has, or rather forms, an area in the brain. This area disappears when the body part is amputated or when the information cannot be transported to the brain because the sensory tract concerned has been cut through. When the sensory tract between hand and brain is cut, there is, for example, no area of the hand in the body blueprint in the brain; even though in reality that hand does exist. The hand is then not experienced as 'own' and a sense of estrangement arises with respect to a part of the 'own' body. A disorder of the body blueprint goes together with fundamental estrangement and anxiety.

This fundamental blueprint of who one is, namely of one's own body, can be underdeveloped with autistic children, causing them sometimes to be surprised even as a pre-schooler that they have a hand and that that hand is attached to their own body. Babies can play with their hands for a long time and admire them for hours: it is a normal development phenomenon. Autistic children can still do this for a long time, long after they should have outgrown that phase. They look, as if mesmerized, at their hands and move their hands in front of their eyes. This is different from the fluttering of hands autistic children do when excited. The body blueprint is a building block of the total scheme, the socioscheme. The body blueprint is one of the parts of the 'me'. The realization of the 'me' is the first building block on which the realization of the 'not-me' can develop. The 'not-me' initially is everything, both object and human. Only following on from the realization of the 'not-me' does the distinction between human and object develop, the realization of the other person. Gunilla Gerland (2003) describes in her autobiography that she had the same set-up when drawing people as she had for houses: 'For me the difference between people and houses wasn't clear.' We can see with autistic children that this realization does not develop well. Babies are quick to learn to make a distinction between people and objects; with autistic children this develops very slowly and people often feel treated like an object by autistic children. The distinction between 'object' and 'human' is not made sufficiently by these children.

> An adult asks the autistic boy Jamie, aged four, to get the ball which he is holding over his head. Jamie complies with the assignment, but an unpleasant feeling is conjured up in the adult. Because of the way in which Jamie deals with him he feels like an object instead of a human being. Jamie uses him as a stepladder to climb up to the ball.

The unpleasant feeling that Jamie in this example – without being aware of it – conjured up, has to do with the fact that Jamie did not treat the person in this example differently from the object. People expect that children of his age treat human beings differently and with more attention than they do an object. The way in which children with autism do this differs essentially from the way in which someone with antisocial problems (from attachment problem to psychopathy) does this. A person with antisocial problems will use another person as an instrument for his own needs. He is to a certain extent aware of the other, but does not take the other into consideration. An autistic child is insufficiently aware of the other and does not intentionally use the other as an instrument. When growing older this awareness does grow, especially with children with normal intelligence, and subsequently the other person is taken into consideration.

Because of a limited orientation towards people problems arise with the development of emotional contact, empathy, emotions and when learning to assess social interaction. Because of her limited interaction with the environment the autistic child gets little information about other people's emotions and how to respond to them. Wing (2001) states that with autism it may be a question, at an even lower level than the TOM, of a disturbance of the congenital system that takes care of a differentiated awarding of emotional value to the various sorts of experiences.

Our model takes as a starting point disturbance at a deeper level, namely the socioscheme with its me–other differentiation, where making the difference between 'me' and 'other' and the awarding of *meaning* to 'person' and 'object' can develop.

Because of the limited orientation towards people, *facial recognition* is not well developed. Emotional facial recognition is limited (Baron-Cohen and Hammer 1997; Tantam 1997). Children with an autistic disorder have difficulty with connecting the various aspects of an emotion (facial expression, movement, voice) (Hobson 1993). The weak integration of the brain and aspects such as a less strongly developed corpus callosum (see Chapter 3) probably also play a part here. This integration is, however, specifically problematic in the field of social stimuli. Objects are recognized better than human beings.

According to the theory of the socioscheme, the reason for the problem with facial recognition is that it requires focusing on other people, interest in the other, orientation towards the other and a continuous process of awareness of the presence of others. It is precisely that capacity that develops slowly in people with autism, according to the theory of the socioscheme, and it is characteristic that orientation towards people is not automized. It is, however, not a static given and matures over the years, no matter how slow this maturation can sometimes be. Rieffe *et al.*'s (2000) research concerning autistic children having a TOM but not applying it in the appropriate situations can be explained in this context. The information is available in the TOM, but autistic children do not convert it into behaviour. For that to happen, an awareness of the other is necessary, an orientation towards the other, and this orientation towards people should to a certain extent be automized, natural.

Van der Geest (2001) shows that no differences can be pointed out between autistic children and non-autistic children in the way in which they look and fixate, nor the way in which they 'scan' people and objects. This is contrary to what is expected from the theory of the (weak) CC. Van der Geest and colleagues (2002) suspect that the difference in looking is not connected with the nature of the visual stimuli and the integration of stimuli, but with factors in the social interaction, which is, in terms of the theory of the socioscheme, a lack of orientation towards the other. Another problem with the theory of the (weak) CC with regard to facial recognition is that autistic people actually recognize objects, or even more likely, certain details and can even give them a lot, and sometimes an obsessive, amount of attention.

The forming of the 'me' in relation to the 'other' creates a scheme with which the 'me' is placed in the world. This is done in a physical sense, through the perception of the borders of the body, proceeding from the biological self; but also in a psychological sense by means of, among other things, *time* and *space*. The socioscheme can be seen as a comprehensive 'me placed in the world'. A person forms a blueprint of who she is, how she stands in the world and how she stands in relation to the people around her. *The socioscheme comprehends the conscious and subconscious knowledge of oneself, how one stands in the world and how one stands in relation to others.*

Table 5.2 represents the most important aspects of the socioscheme.

Table 5.2 The socioscheme	
The 'me' placed in the world	
In a physical sense	*In a psychological sense*
Body scheme	Me–other differentiation
Body boundaries	Self-image
Body functioning	Sense of space
	Sense of time
	Social insight
	Empathy
	TOM
	Social functioning

The theory of the socioscheme, as we will see, places the lack of orientation in time and space in the context of, among other things, a motivational problem in the sense of a lack of focus on persons and of a non-automatic orientation towards people. In the case of *regressive autism*, where developed skills are lost again, the age at which the regression starts – in the first two years – is such that the not-egocentric thinking is still strongly underdeveloped. The nature of the autism in the case of regressive autism will, however, be different than that with autism that is slowly manifesting itself, comparable to the loss of a sense versus the not-functioning of the sense following on from the predisposition.

Also, the resistance to change and the problems with the planning of behaviour should be placed in an interactional context, according to the theory of the socioscheme. The resistance to change, for example, is one against changes from outside. The autistic person can keep on generating new behaviour and new activities proceeding from himself, even come to renewal and creativity. The resistance only exists when the activity is imposed by another person and the autistic person's own activity is interrupted or when the activity is stopped and another person imposes a different activity. Breaking through plans from the outside meets resistance; breaking through plans from within is only a problem if the activity has reached an obsessive stage.

The socioscheme and the me–other differentiation

The socioscheme comprises a large diversity of subjects from which we can understand autism. From the biological-psychological-neural self the me–other differentiation is formed and following on from that the self-image.

The me–other differentiation is a process that continues one's whole life long, from the subconscious recognizing of the 'me' to the realization of 'me' versus 'not-me' and 'object' versus 'human being'. Developmental tasks in me–other differentiation are:

1.   me versus not-me

2.   not-me: object versus human

3.   attachment

4.   familiar versus strange

5.   developing an attachment system

6.   strange: good versus bad

7.   social interaction: building a theory of mind

Mahler (1968) wrote of *separation* (breaking loose) and *individuation* (becoming an individual) as two phases in the individuation process of the child. This process takes place in various phases. In Table 5.3 the various phases of this process are represented. With autistic children this individuation process can go very slowly and remnants from previous phases remain active for a long period of time.

Table 5.3 Individuation process according to Mahler (1968)		
Age (months)	*Stage*	*Description*
5–10	Differentiation	Person separation between baby and mother
10–16	Practice	Development of attachment to mother
16–24	Approach	Strongly focused on presence of mother, afraid of strangers
24–36	Consolidation	Confirmation of individuation; the child becomes more able to function apart from the mother, but the mother remains as a safe base: *emotional object constancy*

In Chapter 7 we will discuss the me–other differentiation and the meaning thereof for children with autism in more detail.

The socioscheme and time and space

As human beings we stand fundamentally in relation to the other. In the life related to the other person 'time' and 'space' are being formed. These concepts are in close relation to the world around us and the people with whom we live in particular. In fact, they exist by the grace of the other, of the human not-me. The human being becomes aware of time because the other restricts his activity. There also exists an intuitive time experience which people experience by the physical signs of time, such as the setting sun. This realization of time is a *lived-through time*, not an *experienced* time with *awareness* of time. It is especially the realization of the self in relation to time in the surrounding world which causes problems for the autistic person. This is also broader than just being in contact with people. Without the presence of people, time can also be experienced by thinking of the other; for example, in an hour the neighbour will drop by. When growing up, the realization, the awareness, of the other becomes more and more clear and the infinite feeling of time decreases.

An autistic child has little realization of the other, of the effect of himself on the other or of the other on himself. He lives from a fundamentally egocentric perspective. The autistic child is the centre of the world and is little aware of the other, thus, he is little aware of time. Time becomes clear by the confrontation with the other.

With the autistic child there is not enough coherent, logical inner structure (Wing 2001) based on which a situation can be understood and predicted. This applies both to the aspects of social interaction and to time or space. This inner structure is interpreted as a 'social body blueprint', and therefore I introduced the concept of socioscheme. The socioscheme comprises the conscious and subconscious recognition of oneself, how one stands in the world and how one stands in relation to other people. One of the elements which is comprised in the relation with the other is time. Without people around you, you do not experience time. Time and also space are experienced by the grace of the people amongst whom you live. You become aware of time because you do not live in a vacuum, but stand in relation to others: time is up, you should have got dressed, the bus is coming to pick you up, it has become dark and your parents want you to go to sleep, in ten minutes your husband will come home, you have half an hour so you can still… The older people become, the more they are aware of their relation to others and the restrictions of their own activities that this entails. When becoming older, one gains more knowledge and a deeper insight arises in oneself. You start to understand the world around you better. You are becoming more and more aware of how you stand in relation to another person. When becoming older we therefore experience the feeling that time passes more and more quickly.

> Most people have for a minute a, passing, experience of having lost contact with time. For a moment you think that you're 35 instead of 45; you quickly realize that you made a mistake and wonder what you did during the last ten years and immediately the socioscheme fills with reality. Or for a minute you don't know who you are on the phone, you cannot think of your own name or you find it strange to be in your own body. Such experiences show how alienating that can be. As if one were standing on the edge of a ravine.

An autistic child, due to their *egocentric perspective*, has little realization of time. They live in a time-free world and keep being taken by surprise that there appears to be time which restricts what they do and want. The child is usually not aware of the people around them. The child is totally engrossed in their activity and 'forgets' the time, but also where they are. That awareness only arises when the world around them forms a structural part of their life.

In order to improve the problem of time realization with an autistic child, a clock can be hung up near the child and it is indicated where the hands will be when a certain activity is over. This helps the child to stay somewhat aware of his environment. The problem will, however, only really be solved when the child is taught to experience time in relation to the other. And it is not only important with respect to time that the child remains orientated towards the people around him; it also applies to all subjects for social interaction.

What applies to time also applies to experiencing space. Autistic children often 'clumsily' walk into things. They knock things over because they do not pay attention to the world around them. They also have difficulty in keeping enough distance when having contact and stand too close (Attwood 1998). Everyone has a kind of 'territory' around them and feel uncomfortable when another person comes too close without being asked. Gunilla Gerland (2003) describes these experiences which cause her to be unable to assess the distance which separates her from, for example, an approaching vehicle, causing her difficulty when crossing the street well into her adulthood.

Gunilla Gerland (2003) writes in her autobiography that well into adulthood she had difficulty placing herself 'in the world'. 'I often just bumped into someone or suddenly stood still because I could not estimate the distance to the other person. [...] Now I can estimate speed and distance and I assume that partly because of the improvement of that ability I am less clumsy now. It is easier now to feel how my body relates to the environment.'

The relation of oneself to the other develops inadequately or is delayed with children with an autistic disorder. The world is experienced from a fundamentally *egocentric perspective.*

When Joe was three years old, he became scared when he was riding a tricycle on a road where at the end of it a goal was painted on a wall. He saw the goal becoming bigger and bigger. He thought that the goal was coming towards him. He did not realize that it was he who was moving and not the wall. As adults we can still see a remnant of this way of thinking. We see the same kind of effect when we are sitting in a stationary train and the train next to us is leaving. We tend to think that we ourselves started moving and that the other train is standing still.

The autistic child does not often put herself in the other person's place and the whole thinking is therefore directed egocentrically. This means that autistic people encounter problems with perspective changes, which we discussed in Chapter 3. One of the many consequences thereof is that they may have difficulty with the use of 'me' and 'you'.

When we are addressed with 'you', for example, 'Do you want to do that?', we know that we have to change perspective. The 'you' that the other person says is our 'me'. With children with an autistic disorder this change in perspective is often not carried out, which is also the case with very young children. They keep thinking taking themselves as a starting point and do not turn the perspective around. We can therefore see this problem of perspective change with the autistic child, who has trouble with using the me and you forms correctly. The 'you form' used by the other is copied 'indiscriminately' and not translated into a 'me form': 'You should not do that any more', as a comment by the mother to the autistic child, is received by the child as 'You should not do that any more', instead of 'I should not do that any more'.

This egocentric perspective decreases as one becomes older because the realization of both time and space becomes more and more registered in the consciousness. In order to orientate oneself in a room the same applies as to time, one has to be aware of the not-me and of the other person. When people, normally speaking, enter a room they first examine it for people and then for objects. The human being is obviously the main subject. For babies this is not so obvious, this distinction has to be built up following on from the me–other differentiation. We will see in Chapter 7 that for children with an autistic disorder this happens with some difficulty and at best is very delayed.

As well as the realization of time and space, memory also plays an important part in social contact.

Memory

Little is known as yet about the exact working of the memory. A lot of neurological research has gone into its working, but for now this has resulted in more questions than answers. There is a beginning of insight. The idea that the memory saves and keeps everything correctly and in its original shape has been superseded; that seems to be technically impossible, cells die and are renewed. The question is what *does* happen. Modern insights make a reasonable case for the fact that the memory is a constant process, where data keeps getting re-processed. It is possible that an event is stored as a whole and when a similar event occurs only the deviant part is remembered and added stack-wise to the previous memory.

Although the development of knowledge in the field of the memory keeps requiring changes in classifications and concepts, some concepts are still used. This applies, for example, to the classification of memory into the *sensory memory*, the *short-term* or *working memory* and the *long-term memory*. The sensory memory is there for sensory experiences that are saved for a short time (unless they are transported to the working memory). In the working memory information is kept for a short period. The long-term memory is there for information which is kept for a long time.

Research, for example by Meltzoff (1985, 1988a, 1988b) and Rovee-Collier and Gerhardstein (1997), shows that children can remember things that happened in their earliest childhood. Remembering is even a matter of course; how else can a baby become worried if his mother leaves the room? Research by Varendi, Porter and Winberg (1997) clarifies how far this goes: the baby is comforted when he smells the amniotic fluid put on a cotton bud. The baby can only recognize his 'own' amniotic fluid by means of his memory. The baby has a memory already at a very early age. Learning can only be through the memory and probably starts in the womb. At the same time we hardly have any memories of our earliest childhood; that goes for both pleasant and unpleasant experiences (Schachtel 1973).

Generally the memory for what happened a long time ago remains more intact than the short-term memory. The short-term memory seems to be strongly dependent on the maturation of the central nervous system after birth. It is therefore not surprising that we see a strong, sometimes phenomenally strong, long-term memory and a weaker short-term or working memory in people with an autistic disorder (Boucher 1981; Attwood 1998; Wing 2001).

> Gunilla Gerland (2003) expresses the importance of the working memory when she states: 'Other people seem to have such a memory, good or bad, somewhere in their body. As if they just know where they put something, without having to think that they put it exactly there.'

Gunilla Gerland's example shows that her socioscheme functions inadequately. It fails to update undertaken activities sufficiently, causing an incomplete picture to be formed and everyday things not to seem natural, as they are for non-autistic people. Farrant, Blades and Boucher (1999) discovered that children with an autistic disorder were only badly able to assess how long they would need to learn something by heart. They were badly able to indicate when they had learned something sufficiently and could reproduce it.

I have already stated that in men and women we can expect differences between long-term and short-term memories, and in people with Asperger's syndrome we can expect a more masculine structure (Chapter 3). Moreover, strategies that enable one to remember also play an important role for the memory in the short term. With autistic children these strategies are developed more by themselves. Their learning strategies are different from those of other children because they do not develop their learning strategies from contact, nor from what they learn at school. As we will see later on this can result in learning disorders. These children often have strategies which are too limited. The development of the short-term memory and the working memory are limited even more because of that. Renner, Klinger and Klinger (2000) discovered that people with an autistic disorder only remembered the end of a list when doing memory assignments and not the beginning *and* the end, as non-autistic people did. They suggest that people with an autistic disorder use different strategies to call up things from the memory to non-autistic people. They do not use categories to organize facts or to remember them better (Bowler, Matthews and Gardiner 1997), it is as if they only store facts. 'Remembering' goes automatically, without being based on a strategy. This form of remembering can be seen with young children. Berversdorf and Hughes (2000) indicate that facts are not remembered within a context, but as loose data. They indicate that neurally this can be expected in the brain, because the brain cells of autistic people in certain areas (for example the hippocampus) show fewer branches and less connections with each other.

Memory strategies are only developed after about the age of seven (Flavell 1985). Children with an autistic disorder can sometimes have impressive amounts of facts in their memory, without ever trying to remember these. They can 'store' whole books as a collection of facts, even without understanding what they read.

Apart from the memory strategies the degree of personal involvement also influences memory. Children, for example, remember events in which they were involved better than events which involved their peers (Millward *et al.* 2000). Because children with an autistic disorder have a delayed (social) development and are less oriented towards social contact, this applies to them even more.

The memory is also sensitive to the nature of an event. According to Bower (1981) events during which the emotional charge corresponds to the emotional experience of the person at that moment (*emotional congruence*) are remembered relatively well. This applies in particular to positive experiences. In general these are remembered better than negative ones. We can already see this characteristic with babies who are younger than two months and who can remember things, and definitely remember the pleasant things (Rovee-Collier and Fagan 1981; Sullivan 1982).

For the development of the socioscheme the memory is important, because new elements are placed and tested, with respect to old elements in the memory. An inadequate or an egocentric directed memory is therefore an extra hindrance for the development of an extensive socioscheme.

The socioscheme and identity

In the same way as the body blueprint, which we regard as part of the socioscheme, the socioscheme as a whole keeps being updated. The state of affairs as far as age, health, intelligence, popularity, parental love and so on are concerned are constantly updated. When a physician asks someone who has been unconscious for a while the question 'what is your name?', he makes an appeal to the essential activity of the socioscheme, because the person's name is the foundation of his or her own identity. The experience of not knowing what your name is can be compared with not being able to feel your own hand. Autistic children have more difficulty orientating themselves when waking up (Schreck and Mulick 2000), as if the socioscheme were slowly filling up when they awaken.

Experiencing one's own identity is difficult with an inadequate socioscheme, as is the case with autism. Typical is the description of Bender (1947) of what in her time were still called 'schizophrenic' children. The term 'autism' had not yet been established. Lauretta Bender describes the same problems as Kanner, but more elaborately, and including more children than only autistic children. She declares the lack of awareness and realization of identity as the essential problem:

> The significant problems are identity, body image and body function problems, object relationship and interpersonal relationship both in the family and the larger world, orientation in time and space, meaning of language and, finally, the problem of anxiety. The disturbance in identification processes; that is, difficulties in identifying one's self and thereby relating to the rest of the world, is the essential psychological problem. (Bender 1947)

The socioscheme is a complex comprehensive unity. The self-image is part thereof, but also one's age, opinion about oneself and one's appearance, perception of one's health, and one's TOM. All elements of the socioscheme exist as entities of thinking and feeling of the self in relation to the other. We compare our perception of our own health to that of others and probably against a basic knowledge about how a body should be (see the little boy with the salt from Chapter 3). We know our age because it is an important part of our identity and people around us adjust their attitude to that. We have an image of ourselves as seen through the eyes of others.

We can assume that autistic people's socioscheme is not much developed. Because the me–other differentiation is limited and the autistic child experiences himself as more apart from others than in relation to others, the scheme is not updated much with information about how the child stands in relation to that other, what the other thinks about him, what is expected by others or how the other will act in a certain situation. Vermeulen (1999b) states that the autistic person does not experience himself much as a 'thread' of his life; there is too little 'self'.

The socioscheme and theory of mind

The TOM is part of the socioscheme. Building up an idea of what other people are thinking makes their behaviour more predictable and makes it possible to assess what will happen to us, in relation to the other. Autistic children probably start a lot later, and more inadequately, with building up a TOM than other children do on average (Happé 1998). In the most favourable case they will build this up better by 'thinking' than by 'feeling', by means of 'ratio' rather than by means of 'intuition'. Two reasons can be mentioned for that. First, our starting point is that children with an autistic disorder following on from a weak left hemisphere have not much awareness of their thoughts and feelings and know their own 'me' insufficiently. Because of this they miss a calibration point based on which they can assess the other. The second reason is that when they are ready to consider the other, they are in a time period when thinking and language are dominant over feeling. As a result thereof they form their TOM more by thinking than by feeling. Bottroff (1999) makes a distinction between a *hot* TOM, formed based on feeling, and a *cold* TOM, formed based on rational knowledge, a 'thought-out' theory.

> Martin is appreciated for his enormous wealth of knowledge. This is seen as one of his very strong sides. He himself knows full well that this strength serves to compensate for his lack of sensing.

An exception in developing 'sensing' is a negative feeling in the other. Autistic children are often remarkably sharp in being able to notice subtle signs of negative feelings in other people (Wing 2001). This is surprising because autistic children are supposed to be bad at sensing emotions in other people. In order to understand this we have to go back to Hans Asperger's statement, which was that the brain structure of autistic people is more masculine, and to Chapter 3, when we discussed the *empathic ability,* placed within an *empathic spectrum.* There is a difference in the empathic ability of men and women. The male brain proves able to sense signs of danger better than women (Eisenberg, Murphy and Shepard 1997), as we saw in Chapter 3. Women, on the other hand, are better able to assess other feelings in other people. If we think of autistic disorders being features of more 'masculine' brains, we can place this ability to notice negative feelings. The orientation towards negative feelings can be found in the drawings of young children with an autistic disorder. The scenes they draw are often full of danger, warlike and bloody (see Figure 5.2).

The *amygdala* play an important part in detecting danger. The information enters the amygdala and there it is 'decided' what will be passed on to the consciousness because of its importance.

Damage to the amygdala can result in a very sociable personality (Damasio 1999), which does not detect signs of danger, fear or excitement and therefore does not show any aggressive behaviour. Research by Baron-Cohen and others (1999) indeed confirms earlier research into the deviant functioning of the amygdala with autistic people.

The importance of the amygdala in detecting danger becomes visible when they are removed. Then the Kluver-Bucy syndrome arises, which is characterized by an abnormal lack of fear and aggression (Buck and Ginsburg 1997).

Figure 5.2 Goose with exploding tummy (Bettelheim 1997). Reproduced with permission from Simon & Schuster, Inc.

In this way the outside world becomes more threatening to autistic people, the negative signs come through more strongly than the positive ones. A large part of what goes on in the outside world is, however, not based on negative feelings or danger. Autistic children are insecure because they do not know how other people think and feel and will behave; thus autistic children who can talk will react by asking numerous questions. They want to know what is going to happen minute by minute. Once they get an answer they subsequently want to know what will happen later. Once we know this and understand it better, we will not be so quick to think the child is whining, but rather that she is insecure and frightened. That affects our attitude and the way in which we coach the child. When something does not happen, this means to the autistic child not only that the activity does not take place, but also – and *this* is what makes her insecure – that she does not know what will happen instead. When we tell the child that something will not happen the child ends up in a state of fear and falls into a void, often expressing this by aggression and resistance. This is not so much because the child wants the original activity to happen at all costs – sometimes this is even less attractive to the child – but mainly because she wants the world to remain a clear, orderly and predictable place. This also means that it is better to tell a child what *will* happen than what will not, or, in any case, first what *will* and then what *will not* happen.

When one does not have one's own inner structure in which it is expressed how one stands in relation to other people, literally and figuratively, this can lead to strong feelings of estrangement and to intense anxiety. This is what we keep seeing with autistic people. Anxiety and estrangement are important emotions with autistic people. In children this anxiety will often be expressed in (hyper) activity and problem behaviour. We will discuss this in more detail in Chapters 11 (anxiety) and 12 (aggression).

By way of a summary, the process of one of the most important building blocks of the socioscheme, the me–other differentiation, is described in Table 5.4, with the steps following on from that in the differentiation process together with some of its effects. In the course of the next chapters these elements will become more clear when we discuss them within the context of the behaviour connected with them and the way in which autistic people can be helped with them.

Table 5.4 Me–other differentiation as a building block for the socioscheme	
Me–other differentiation → me awareness → not-me awareness → other awareness	
Ability to get into the other's mind	Awareness of other's existence
	Awareness of other's presence
	Orientation towards other
Social knowledge → social insight → social skills	Capacity for reciprocity in contact
	Ability to play with others
	Ability to take others into account
	Ability to make friends
	Ability to mobilize help
Sense of time	Capacity not to be taken by surprise by time
	Ability to complete tasks
	Ability to take account of others
	Ability to plan
Sense of space	Ability to orientate in a space
	Capacity not to bump into everything

Social interaction is of great, if not vital, importance for people. When one has a disorder where assessing social interaction is a problem, life will be difficult and often even terrifying. Because of the difficulty with assessing it is not clear what the behaviour of the other person means, but it is also difficult to know what kind of behaviour towards the other is correct. Assessing the meaning of information entering the brain becomes laborious: what is important, what not? The eye for detail, the sometimes obsessive interest in detail which autistic people can have, is possibly connected hereto.

Eye for detail

With the disorders within the autistic spectrum a number of characteristics are inextricably related to the disorder; inadequate social behaviour, for example. Within that main characteristics and deviant characteristics can be distinguished (see Appendix I). Apart from these characteristics there are a number that occur often, but are not inextricably connected with the disorder, and characteristics that occur proceeding from the situation in which the child with the disorder grows up and which we can call *situation specific*.

I have already stated that the inadequacy in assessing social interaction is the core problem of people within the autistic spectrum. We call this the *core characteristic*, also because this characteristic in particular hinders the social functioning enormously. If we take the brain as a starting point, information processing may be indicated as a core problem instead of inadequate empathy. Deviant information processing is inextricably connected with the autistic spectrum. One of the most striking things with that is, especially in people with Asperger's syndrome, the sharp 'eye for detail'. It makes them very good in some tasks, such as making puzzles or recognizing hidden figures. They find it easy to divide large geometrical figures into smaller parts (Frith 1989, 2003). Some people with an autistic disorder, Kees Momma being one of them, are able to draw unbelievably accurately (see Figure 10.1). When they see a building, they absorb the details exactly without specifically paying attention to it, so that they can represent it later without any problem and do so accurately. A non-autistic person has to hear, time after time at drawing lessons, the phrase 'drawing is looking', whereas for autistic people it goes without saying. Baron-Cohen and Hammer (1997) discovered that the parents of children with autistic disorders were also good in recognizing hidden figures and also weak when assessing eye expressions, which forms further support for the idea of autism being hereditary.

Information processing by people within the autistic spectrum does not seem to go the same way as with average people. Making a difference between essentials and detail is less strong, or obviously slower.

John, for some time now a student at university, has to plough through many books when studying for his examination. Despite his intelligence, he has a great deal of difficulty in distinguishing between main issues and side issues. To create order he underlines all the important things and consequently his books are completely covered in underlined text. In books which are written badly John completely loses track because he then also misses out on the framework used by good writers.

Details are important, and even more so when the outline is not clear. The 'material' is stored, based on details from which an outline can be formed. Subjects with different values, main issues and side issues, all are treated the same. The side issues are therefore given a lot of attention which in the eyes of others is disproportionate.

In the respectful, informative BBC documentary *I'm not Stupid* (Fisher 1995), about Asperger's syndrome, Francesca Happé explains that a child with Asperger's syndrome who crosses the street may not notice the policeman he sees as a whole entity, but can immediately focus his attention on a detail like the button on the policeman's jacket.

We can also see this way of approaching things with very young children. A child who is given presents on his first birthday will often be enthusiastic about and fascinated by the wrapping paper and put the present aside. He still lacks the knowledge that the content is more important than the packaging. In this way wrapping paper and content are on the same level for him. Both are just as attractive.

Jack, in his early forties, always wants to talk about everything he has experienced in therapy. He always brings a little piece of paper with his experiences written down on it. He also wants to relate as many experiences as possible in the hope that the therapist can make a logical whole of it, create order out of it, extracting out the main issues and therefore placing the experiences in a useful context for him. His experience with the therapist teaches him that an abundance of detail is not necessary, but he finds it hard to suppress the urge to talk about it.

With John, in his late twenties, something similar happens in therapy. He wants to talk about all the details surrounding an event because he thinks that the therapist cannot form a picture if she does not grasp all the details he possesses. He has no idea what the main issues are and how things relate. When he realizes that the brain of this therapist works differently from his own, he starts working more efficiently and asks where he should start from, whether he should give more details or whether the therapist has already formed a picture, and asks her how these abstractions have been formed.

Because of the difficulty of distinguishing main from side issues and reaching a transcending image, autistic people may run the risk of staying close to the details and as a result of this sometimes take things too literally, as we may also see with children at the stage when the transcending form of thinking has not yet been sufficiently developed (Piaget 1972). In her inaugural speech Berckelaer-Onnes (1992) expressed her respect for the special qualities connected with literal thinking:

> I share their [the parents of autistic children] love for these children: they have something so pure, so touching; lying, manipulating, plotting and the like are not part of their social activities: *They live to the letter.*

The theory of CC argues that literal thinking is a way of thinking that cannot transcend details and thus is stuck to details without reaching a transcendent image. Yet really what it is about is communication between autistic and non-autistic people concerning their perception of the environment. In view of, among other things, their inadequate social skills, communicating with autistic people requires extra skills. When communicating with children, adults make many mistakes of interpretation and often do not link up to the 'language' of the child (Delfos 2000). Apart from the possibility that autistic people think literally, there is also the risk that non-autistic people take the statements of autistic people too literally.

Because the differentiation between objects starts slowly, the distinction between human and not-human is also not experienced at different levels: a vacuum cleaner and a visitor can be on the same value level for a child with an autistic disorder. People then come across as being things. This can be interpreted as being insensitive and people can sometimes be deeply offended by statements made by the child. An autistic child can have a totally different form of attaching value regarding people and things to non-autistic people. This attachment does not only take place verbally, but also non-verbally. It can already be observed in eye contact. A difference in value attachment becomes clear through eye contact. It is possible that that is one of the first signs by which parents and others may notice early on that the child is different and it is often referred to as being 'strange', rather than 'troublesome' or 'difficult'. The terms 'different' and 'odd' especially express the difference of the contact. The eye contact is often experienced as unusual: not a contact, but a look or a stare. People with an autistic disorder seem to 'study' rather than 'take in'. They think. Gunilla Gerland (2003) describes that her thinking always follows her actions and feelings. This exact studying is maybe also the reason why people with an autistic disorder can often amazingly reach the essence of something and often distinguish kitsch from art accurately, as Asperger (1944) indicated.

How does this story end?

A   B

Figure 5.3 Cartoon of a man on the phone (Vermeulen 2000a). Reproduced with permission from the author.

Peter Vermeulen (2000a) gives the example of a cartoon (see Figure 5.3) in which an angry screaming man is on the telephone. The question posed is which picture is the correct ending of the story. Autistic people choose the answer where not only the emotion is the thread of the story. They examine the cartoon carefully and include in their answer the 'detail' of the clock on the wall, giving the course of time. Vermeulen suggests that autistic people do not find the emotion important and therefore come to a 'wrong' answer. But the opposite is true. More thorough study of all aspects of the story clarifies that the clock is a decisive factor. Chronologically only one answer is correct, even if the emotion displayed in the picture is less plausible. Our experience is that further study sometimes shows that the autistic person has a deeper and better thought-out, though slower, insight than the non-autistic one.

'Studying' and paying attention to some details more than others often causes children with an autistic disorder to express their emotions differently, and also experience different emotions. Research by Ricks and Wing (1975) shows, for example, that parents of autistic toddlers recognize better the statements made by their children when they hear a tape recording with statements made by various toddlers regarding an emotion, than parents of non-autistic toddlers. The statements of autistic toddlers are clearly 'different', 'odd'. Parents experience the 'oddness' of their child in many subtle traits.

Making *eye contact* is an activity that transcends looking. *Looking* makes the other thing, or person, an object (Sartre 1943/1971). Eye contact makes the other person a subject. An exchange takes place. Looking, consisting of registering the visual stimuli and thinking about what is being seen, is supplemented by the eye contact with an *exchange*. In Chapter 8, when we examine social skills, we will discuss in more detail the nature and meaning of eye contact for people with an autistic disorder.

A baby is busy during its first weeks with processing all the information that reaches him. Looking consists then mainly in processing information, there is hardly any eye contact. The baby's socioscheme is too limited to be used as a basis for placing new impressions. According to the way in which the environment reacts to his needs, the baby places certain images, sounds and smells as belonging to the pleasantness of fulfilling his needs. The baby learns to make a distinction between the 'me' that has certain needs and the 'other' that knows how to satisfy those needs. Because of the importance of his needs the patterns which together take care of the satisfaction of these needs, 'people', become separated from the other things that can be seen, heard, felt or smelt. In the eyes of the baby this can be found in the sense of recognition and satisfaction when looking at his care givers: the beginnings of eye contact. During the period that this eye contact is developing, it will not yet occur everywhere and with everyone. The basic schemes of the child still have to be worked out. We can see that at the moment when the very young baby is taken outside and his look expresses looking without having eye contact. We walk through the woods and the baby makes us become part of the picture he is looking at, the trees and the sky. Filled with new impressions, the baby's eyes do not express a familiarity with us when we are among the trees, while when we are at home they would.

With a child with an autistic disorder this process of looking and putting a meaning to things goes on for a longer period of time. The child keeps looking and thinking, without the reciprocity of recognition and especially without expressing the meaning and value of recognition. The human being is not automatically allocated the highest importance and in this way a totally different classification of main and side issues arises to that of non-autistic children. We saw this earlier in the example of Jamie and the ball on page 117. All objects are perceived as being much more at the same value level. Details become very important, because they form the parts for creating order in the chaos of information which is not naturally classified into priorities because it cannot yet be linked up to structures which are present in the socioscheme. Allocating value to various objects does not follow the usual path with autistic children (Wing 2001).

We see this difference also in the normal development of babies. Male babies tend to look more at objects and female babies more at faces (Connellan *et al.* 2001). This difference disappears after some time. With autistic children it probably takes longer to disappear. More 'object value' is allocated to 'faces' and putting a meaning to something by distinguishing between human and object takes place only later, sometimes so inadequately that it is hardly recognized.

Kees Momma (1996), an autistic man who wrote an autobiography, describes how he could look at the handle of a door for a very long time and how he only became aware of his mother when he was two years old.

The difference in the nature of the information processing of the objects that the child looks at, means that a child with Asperger's syndrome may be seen as being insensitive and heartless. Details can become very important and can stand in the way of normal functioning. It is not unusual, for example, for a child from the autistic spectrum to have an aversion to another person because he has a physical disability. The deviation from what is familiar in that case inspires aversion. The child may come across as being very blunt, without realizing what effect her statement has on someone else.

> Eric did not want to play with Margaret because she walked with a leg brace. Not because he found it scary, but because he had an aversion to it.
> After his first day at school Walter said: 'I'm not going back there because they have snotty noses.'

What can be a minor detail for a child without an autistic disorder can be as important to a child with Asperger as a character trait such as 'being nice', and can therefore become a reason to reject another person, or be more easily ready to ignore that person.

The eye for detail is possibly a way in which the mind of a child with a disorder within the autistic spectrum compensates for the absence of the ability to assess social interaction. The interaction as a whole is not understood properly, but by paying profound attention to detail it may be possible for the child to examine what the interaction as a whole means. A disability in social interaction is a serious disability. The fact that compensation is needed is obvious when we realize that social interaction is essential for human functioning. A lack of social interaction can easily conjure up a lot of anxiety. Here we can see a similarity with the reaction to traumatic experiences. A traumatic experience is incomprehensible; later we pay attention to all kinds of details involving the event. Only after we have processed the event and have given it a place and therefore also more or less understand what has happened to us, do the details move into the background and the outlines remain. Asperger (1944) was of the opinion that it is a matter of strong compensatory characteristics, such as an eye for detail, which can sometimes help the person with an autistic disorder perform very well socially.

The eye for detail also makes it possible for a child with Asperger's syndrome to notice things that other people overlook. This characteristic ensures that as an adult they are sometimes very good in tasks where details have to be discerned, in aviation or informatics, for example.

In the theory of CC the attention to detail is explained as being a result of the inability to form a meaningful unity and the inability to generalize from details

(Frith 1997a; Vermeulen 1999b). Autistic people are assumed to get stuck in details. Vermeulen (1999b) compares the thinking of autistic people to a computer. All details are at the same level, and the computer cannot bring them together into a meaningful unity. Frith (1989, 2003) sees a variety of behaviours (rigidity, resistance to changes, stereotype behaviour, rituals) as arising from one problem, namely the limited urge to CC, unity. The highest form of thinking includes the need to give meaning and this is very inadequate in people with an autistic disorder, according to Frith. In this way there is no link between the mutual details and a higher meaning which can bring the details to a coherent unity. There exists a *disconnection* between the details and a central meaning.

Vermeulen (1999b) formulates this as the tendency to go into details because the meaning of the unity passes by the autistic person. In the next chapters we will see that the attention to detail is rather a result than a cause of the behaviour of autistic people and that the various behaviours have different causes and also other purposes, notably stress management.

Although bringing everything together to become a logical unity is definitely important in the functioning of autistic people, it does not seem to be a comprehensive explanation principle. Happé indicated back in 1994 that this theory is applied in a too generalizing manner. The starting point for the theory of CC is that everything around the autistic person is observed in detail, not as coherent, meaningful unities. They are supposed to have a fragmented observation, built up from loose pieces and not as a unit. However, there are arguments that the observation pattern of autistic people cannot be only fragmented. First, the lack of CC does not apply to all subjects. Children with Asperger's syndrome are often master computer users. In front of a computer they are excellently able to distinguish main from side issues. Some of the more intelligent people with Asperger's syndrome show a talent for mathematics. This requires a very methodological mind where the distinction between main and side issues is very important. Another example is that children with an autistic disorder are able to recognize people when they see them in different circumstances and in different clothes. The attention to detail is therefore not the same at every moment, for every subject or at every age. The attention to detail increases when the situation is unclear (this goes for all people, by the way). We can see this same process when people have had a traumatic experience. A characteristic of a traumatic event is that it appears to us as being improbable. The result is that after a traumatic experience people pay an enormous amount of attention to details which later prove to be unimportant (Delfos 1999a, 2001b, 2003a).

The theory of CC suggests that the autistic mind tries to start building up a unity from the details and cannot achieve this because the person does not see the unity. This is not the case. It is rather a question of zooming in on a detail of the picture. The unity has been noticed, but the deeper meaning of that unity is not understood. By zooming in on details an attempt is made to understand their relation to the unity. The selection of those details is dependent on the degree of insight. When there is a lack of insight it is possible that completely unimportant details are chosen for further investigation. When people around them who, because of their insight, know that something is an unimportant detail, and are not interested in it, the autistic person will not take them seriously. He feels like he is not being taken seriously in his search for the meaning. Only when the other person is able to link up and place the detail in the unity, thus differentiating its meaning, will the autistic person feel that he is taken seriously.

The attention that autistic people have for detail becomes most striking when they are dealing with social interaction. Details of clothes suddenly become more important than another person's self. The autistic mind diligently searches the details hoping to give a meaning to the unity. The theory of the socioscheme assumes that because of the inadequate socioscheme a fundamental problem in the social interaction will arise. In view of the importance of social interaction for the human being and the lack of understanding which the autistic person often encounters, we see that her attention to detail is an attempt to research what the importance of a specific detail has for the unity. Details are given attention so the autistic person can examine what the main point and what the side issues are. In this way the socioscheme is enlarged. This applies to subjects at interpersonal level, but not so much to other subjects. Distinguishing the main and side issues of a computer programme is often easier for autistic people than with the subject of interpersonal contact. The opposite probably applies to strongly empathic people. Autistic people's development of the thinking process causes them to keep thinking in an associative way instead of a causal way for a longer period of time. This can also be the reason why some details are given more than average attention. In addition, the interest in details can fulfil a function in combating anxiety, which so often bothers autistic people, because it has a hypnotic effect.

When the importance of the various details is unclear a word may be formed to do justice to all details, which is why many autistic people have the surprisingly idiosyncratic use of language that characterizes the syndrome. Moreover, their limited orientation towards the other and limited awareness of the other are responsible for the fact that they feel the need less strongly for what one could call a *shared vocabulary*. A porcelain statuette of a cat with zebra stripes is called a 'zebra cat' by a five-year-old autistic girl (Derks 2002). We often see the phenomenon with autistic people. Vermeulen (2002a) describes a similar example and interprets the phenomenon of a 'cow cat' (a drawing of a cat with a cow print) as the inability to place details in a context; autistic people do not know whether it is a cow or a cat. But if we use the socioscheme theory, we do not so much expect an inadequate observation but an inadequate or idiosyncratic interpretation in a social sense. Asking the girl more questions reveals that she had the right perception but wanted to give that which was unusual in the object a name of its own. She said that a cat could not have zebra stripes, that it was a statuette, not real, and that that was the only reason she called it a zebra cat. It was clear to her that it concerned a cat – the grammatical order alone already makes that clear (zebra cat and not cat zebra) – but she was affected by the fact the cat was depicted in an atypical way: 'Cats don't have stripes like a zebra', she said. This rather indicates the difficulty of understanding why such a picture is made, the amazement about a fantasy that isn't hers, than a weak central coherence. The problem, if it could be called that, is more in the field of the interpretation of behaviour than of the coherence of observation, and in autistic people's lack of a need for a shared vocabulary.

The theory of the socioscheme assumes that social interaction is of great importance to human functioning and that with a problem in that area other functions can be overdeveloped as compensation. Analogous to the blind person whose hearing develops more, the senses with autism may possibly develop more strongly in order to reel in the necessary information as much as possible. All details will be given equal attention and are examined for their ability to distinguish main issues and side issues. This may cause the problem that the details disproportionately remain important, but it also allows one to form a deeper and more correct realization of the subject. Jumping to conclusions is a mistake which probably will be made less quickly by autistic than by non-autistic people.

Frith (1997a) indicates that the problem of CC is not so much an inability, because autistic children in some situations can and in others cannot generalize things. Frith states that it is maybe not so much the ability to reach central coherence, but the *urge* to do it. This may possibly be absent because the child does not always feel the need to generalize, or does not get to generalizing because she is absorbed in all the details.

In addition, in order to compose a unity, one must have sufficient knowledge, and observations have to be interpreted in frameworks. Children prove, for example, to function better in conversation when the conversation has a framework of what is expected from them and how the conversation will be held is made clear to them (Delfos 2000). The same probably applies to observation. When it is clear to children that people perform plays and dress up, these transformations will have less impact on them. It has to be clear to them that people do these things and why they do them. The meaning of a uniform goes further than just a garment. In order to grant a meaning, knowledge is necessary. If one cannot give a meaning to the unity, one looks to the details for a hold to construct a meaning.

Apart from the need to understand the unity by means of details, attention to details also has a completely different function. Just as examining details can lead to insight into the unity, attention to details when we already understand the unity can lead to a more profound insight. This is often what we see with (autistic) people with a more than average intelligence. The depth of their insight in certain areas surprises the non-autistic person, and is often beyond his comprehension.

Sensory experiences

Children with an autistic disorder usually examine objects for a long time via their touch and sense of taste. Babies and toddlers also examine a subject thoroughly by means of their mouth. When the child develops, she moves on to other forms of examination where looking becomes very important. Children within the autistic spectrum can to a greater or lesser degree examine objects for a long time by means of their mouth or fingers. An autistic pre-schooler may suddenly lick the central heating or rub a piece of clothing between her fingers in order to feel it. The senses of children within the autistic spectrum can be very sensitive. Rimland indicates that with approximately 40 per cent of children with an autistic disorder, there is oversensitivity of one of the senses (Rimland 1990). Sometimes there is oversensitivity to light, even to the extent of making sunglasses necessary. Strip lighting, a computer or television can affect them strongly.

Sam, 24, is autistic and has an intellectual impairment. He is oversensitive to sounds. He wanted very much to be with his father in the shed when he was doing little jobs. Every time his father was sawing Sam would get very upset. The sound overwhelmed him so much that he tried to cover his ears just to be able to be with his father. The family experimented with ear plugs and a walkman with music on in order to exclude the sounds of the band saw, so that Sam could stay when his father was working.

Some children cannot tolerate certain pieces of clothing, because they feel as if they grate roughly on their skin, while for other people they seem to be made of a rather soft fabric. There can be an oversensitivity to sound, causing some noises to sound like thunderclaps in their ears (Grandin 1995b). In a beautiful documentary *Look at My World*, about three autistic children, what oversensitivity means for a child is represented. We see a little boy sitting in class with all the sounds around him amplified. The scraping of a chair, sucking on a pen, the door closing: the sounds are deafening and in this way the viewer realizes why such a boy is distracted all the time. Instead of an unmotivated child, we suddenly realize that the child is prone to exhaustion because of the continuous stream of loud sound. Temple Grandin even indicates that a lot of unmanageable behaviour can be connected to (the fear of) painful sounds. The sensitivity of the senses does not, however, always mean pain; a touch can also be overwhelming and confusing. Bettison (1997) indicates that an improvement in autistic behaviour arises when children with an autistic disorder and an oversensitivity to sounds are trained in sounds (Stehli 1995). Temple Grandin (1995b) describes how difficult it is to approach sounds in various ways. She does not manage to exclude background noises without excluding *all* sounds. It is as if she only has a general 'on-off button', making it very difficult to listen to something without being overwhelmed by all surrounding noises. The necessity to exclude sounds is felt even more strongly by her because they are perceived as being so loud that it hurts.

It is possible that sensitivity of a certain sense is not the same every day. It probably has to do with an overload of the nervous tracts, or maybe rather an immaturity of the nervous tracts, causing everything to be perceived as being louder. We can see these temporary changes, which are probably supported hormonally, when women during a pregnancy suddenly are oversensitive to certain smells. An indication that it is immaturity of the nervous system that causes oversensitivity is that it usually decreases with age.

We have already seen that people within the autistic spectrum have a limited maturation of the central nervous system, in the sense of a significantly less strongly developed left hemisphere of the brain compared to the right hemisphere. Also, the nerve tracts can have a less strongly developed maturation. During maturation after birth the nerve tracts thicken causing a better insulation of the signals to be transported. If this does not happen enough then an overload can arise causing an interference to the various stimuli. The child can easily become overstimulated. The easiest way to understand this is when we consider being overstressed. This is in fact nothing else but the nervous system being over-stimulated. Every form of stimulus seems to be one too many at a certain point. We notice in fact the first signs of being overstressed when sounds that usually do not bother us start bothering us. When we have 'too much on our mind' we also notice we have difficulty in paying attention, concentrating, and even that our loaded nervous system cannot process certain sounds at that moment. With people within the autistic spectrum this can be a chronic problem, due to the immaturity of the nerve tracts or a temporary oversensitivity caused by stress, tension or anxiety.

Kees Momma (1996) writes about this oversensitivity to sounds which lasted till late in his adult life.

> At the moment I still have trouble with kitchen sounds, like the clattering of plates or a spoon that is dropped on a saucer. Although everyone tries their best to do everything as carefully as possible, the over sensitivity has become stronger because of that.

But as with all things, problems also have their positive aspects. A sharply adjusted system of sound processing can also mean a perfect pitch and produce an excellent piano tuner.

Use of language

The second point of the triad, *communication*, is problematic for autistic children. I already mentioned the eye contact that often needs a longer time to develop from 'looking' to 'exchange'. A second – autistic – characteristic which makes communication difficult, is the limited reciprocity in contact due to inadequate empathy. Autistic children find that the symbolic function in communication is laborious, especially when we talk about the more severe forms which are combined with an intellectual disability. Using the index finger in order to point something out is often not done by autistic children, but they will take you by the hand and lead you to the object. When children at the age of eighteen months still do not point at something to make something clear to their mother, this can be an indication that there could be an autistic disorder (Wing 2001). Children with an autistic disorder share less with others. Shared attention, for example by pointing at something or coming to show something, occurs less in children with autism. They communicate what goes on inside them less to others. They express their feelings, but often not with the intention of making these clear to the others. It is more about the expression itself than about making the feelings known to someone else.

The communication problem proves to be poignant in that area which is so important: language. We have already discussed earlier the own-formed language of autistic children, the idiosyncratic language, what we called *shared vocabulary*. That this is part of a wider communication problem rather than being a specific language problem is clear, because it is not only the spoken language, but also the sign language of an autistic child which is underdeveloped (Wing 2001).

Interpreting gestures also causes a lot of problems for people with an autistic disorder. Peeters (1996) observed that gestures are usually about expressing feelings, and so the use of gestures creates extra problems for autistic people trying to understand the feelings of another person.

The development of language is often delayed, although with Asperger's syndrome and PDD-NOS there is hardly any delay. The language function in children within the autistic spectrum is not normal in general. In most serious forms of autism, there is a totally disturbed development of language resulting sometimes in no or a limited use of language. Elisabeth and Niko Tinbergen (1985) assumed that autistic children did not *want* or *dare* to speak, due to a deep-rooted fear. This idea can be found back with Birger Sellin, the young man with autism who, after a period of severe illness, has not spoken since the age of two. Years later he learned to communicate by means of a computer. He wrote: '...talking is too valuable and...I am unworthy of being able to speak' (Sellin 1995).

Problems with language, by the way, are not only an obstacle for people with autism disorders in communication, but also an obstacle to structuring the world around themselves. Language is an instrument used to create order in the world (Vygotsky 1962). Thinking out loud, as young children do, serves to guide and structure behaviour ('Now I put the block in'). Children with an autistic disorder can think out loud for much longer periods than children normally do.

Producing and understanding language can cause problems. Many people with an autistic disorder struggle with an *expressive language disorder*. This disorder lies in the field of the production of language. Characteristic are word-finding problems, long pauses in sentences, leaving out small words or certain sounds, making grammatical errors and making short sentences. The use of language is, as a result, not fluent.

One of the frequently occurring problems for people with an autistic disorder is taking language too literally. The question 'Can you get up?' will be answered with 'Yes', but because the question is understood too literally, the action is not carried out. The child feels that she has answered the question correctly, as a questioning of her abilities and not as a request to get up.

> Bob, aged seven, has a few autistic traits.
> 'Bob, you should not always jump to conclusions.'
> 'I'm not jumping at all.'

As with so many other aspects of autism we also see this behaviour in young children up to a certain age. In the case of people with autism this lasts much longer and with serious forms of autism is permanent. Atypical forms of language development are also found which can go on into adulthood; for example *echolalia*, the repeating of words which were spoken by someone else. Vermeulen (1999b) indicates that people with an autistic disorder are more oriented towards the form than towards the content of the language. The result is, among other things, that they have difficulty with the correct interpretation of stresses. A simple sentence such as 'I can't come home', can have three totally different meanings depending on which word the stress is on and thus can send three different messages to the listener.

Words that give a vague indication, for instance, 'sometimes', 'often', maybe tomorrow', can confuse autistic people. Their tendency to take things literally flounders on these words which neither have a clear nor a literal meaning. Berckelaer-Onnes (1992) calls this 'living to the letter'. When there is a difference between a verbal and a non-verbal expression, people with an autistic disorder often have a problem with that. Ambiguities, polite phrases, manipulations, false modesty, over-assertive behaviour, under-assertive behaviour or shyness all are expressions with which someone with an autistic disorder has difficulty. These expressions consist of double messages and often also messages that at one level are completely opposite to another level, a difference between verbal and non-verbal.

This is not only a question of taking things literally, but also and especially a question of thinking more purely and not tending to read things into something. Autistic people therefore often sigh: 'Why don't you just say what you mean?' People with Asperger's syndrome will not easily consciously charm someone, try to impress or keep something a secret. They will also not easily recognize such behaviour within other people (Tantam 1997). People with an autistic disorder will also not try to hurt someone's feelings. When they do, it will hardly ever be done intentionally. They are, on the contrary, excessively oriented towards doing things properly and in the way that they should be done (Frith 1997b).

People with Asperger's syndrome use language correctly, but often in a deviant way. The language is often 'old men's talk'; children with Asperger's syndrome frequently seem to be precocious. The language can also have a somewhat formal character and thereby give the impression of sophistication or distance.

Alec had been fascinated by the labels on bottles and jars since he was a pre-schooler. He acquired an enormous vocabulary consisting of strange and unusual words. For example, when he was young he used Latin words, the meaning of which he did not know. His pronunciation was affected and when communicating Alec spoke in the third person for years. 'When one experiences that a grandfather passes away, it may be possible that as a result one has to contend with problems.' For the listener it was not at all clear whose grandfather had died, when this had happened or what exactly was the problem. Later it proved that Alec's own grandfather had died, that his family was very sad because of their loss and that Alec wanted to talk about this phenomenon in order to understand it better.

The formal, businesslike use of language can give the wrong impression to the listener. People with Asperger's syndrome often use few emotive words in their expressions. Their statements can therefore come across as businesslike and cool. Non-autistic people, completely unjustly, think that the absence of emotive words points to a lack of emotions. The emotions are definitely there, but the tendency to and ease of expressing them are missing. For the non-autistic person it is important to let go of the idea that there is a connection between having emotions and expressing those emotions in words. For autistic people it is important to realize that the listener needs information about the emotions.

These are the youngsters and adults whom Wing (2001) calls 'stiff and formalistic'. Their use of language often comes across as poetic and seems to express great sophistication. Attwood (1998) indicates that some people with

Asperger's syndrome tend to speak in the third person. The use of language arises from within themselves and has not been stimulated or taught by their upbringing. This only becomes clear when it is noticed that nobody in the environment of the child or the youngster speaks like that.

Hugo spoke in a very refined manner, even affected. At secondary school he was an outsider. Everyone felt that he was 'different'. The teacher was curious to meet Hugo's parents at the parents' evening. She expected them to be very civilized and educated. This was not the case. They were ordinary people and their son did not resemble them at all. They had no idea where he got his way of speaking and manners from.

People with PDD-NOS and with Asperger's syndrome can display an enormous flood of words, also called hyperlexia. They are unstoppable and do not know the proper way to alternate with others in order to have a good dialogue. They easily lapse into monologue. Because they are not so good at putting themselves in someone else's place they tend to project their own thoughts and feelings on their conversation partner, causing the conversation to become unilateral. They appear stubborn and pigheaded in the way in which they hold on to their own train of thoughts. Asperger (1944) describes the irresistible need to make the other person party to the subject that caused the interest. Having no idea of what other people are thinking causes autistic children to feel treated unjustly, when their conversation partner shows boredom and frustration, while their conversation partner has no idea why they should feel aggrieved. Autistic children often have a very strong sense of justice and in this we see again the strong masculine brain structure (see Chapter 3, moral development).

The use of language can come across as very impersonal and detached. Sometimes no names are mentioned when people are being discussed.

At the end of his adolescence, Alec was very busy trying to make contact with girls. He spoke to his therapist extensively about what happened when he was making contact. No names were ever mentioned, which made it not always that easy for the therapist to follow the story. The therapist was a bit hesitant to ask him for the girl's name because she was under the impression that Alec, by not naming names, was trying to keep some privacy. She therefore interpreted it that he was concealing names instead of just not mentioning them. When she asked him whether he wanted to say the girl's name, he reacted in a surprised way: 'You don't know her, so her name is not important to you.' The therapist replied that in her memory all facts about that girl would be grouped around her name and that if he would speak about her she could, as it were, open that 'drawer' in her brain. Alec looked interested and had no problem mentioning the name; ever since he has always mentioned a name when speaking of someone. This little intervention proved to make the communication significantly easier. With a small intervention Alec's communication with the world around him became a lot more normal.

Children with Asperger's syndrome can be very attentive and express themselves politely, sometimes even going over the top. The somewhat more formal language and the social rules of politeness make it easier for them to know what to do and how to deal with someone. Nevertheless, the use of language is such that one wonders where they could have learned these utterances, especially because they are used in situations where these communication styles are less common.

Joe, aged three, said to a peer who did something which pleased him: 'You will probably grow up to be a Lady.'

It seems that both the phrasing and the use of words in autistic children are drawn from primitive sources, the protolanguage used by poets. Another 'prehistoric thing' is the interest in dinosaurs, which often occurs and sometimes seems to come from a *collective consciousness* in which *archetypes* are stored, as Jung (1975) put it.

Children with Asperger's syndrome often think deeply about human interaction. This enables them to come up with surprising new concepts.

The living situation with his mother was no longer bearable for the 17-year-old Alec, so another solution was looked for. He went to have a look in a community for youngsters. When talking about this Alec strikingly called this way of living 'thrown-together living'. He called people who lived in blocks of flats 'stackable people'. This characteristic of Alec enabled him to write beautiful poems.

In autistic people's language a lot of *neologism* occurs: a completely new, original way of looking at things. Their contemplative way of thinking is expressed by this means. Combined with their eye for detail this can lead to fascinating literary products when there is also a literary talent, as is the case with Gunilla Gerland (2003).

Again, we can use the language development of young children to show in an exaggerated way what happens with children with an autistic disorder. Babies and toddlers initially do not see language as a form of communication but as a toy. Making sounds gives pleasure and listening to sounds can make them roar with laughter. They copy and mimic sounds, reminding one of the echolalia of autistic people. This plays a part in the process of mastering language and especially communication. Also the forming of neologisms is seen often with young children in their attempts to convert understanding into words while their vocabulary is not adequate enough.

To conclude this subject I list a number of verbal communication problems:

- delayed or no language development

- problems with language production

- problems with understanding language

- problems with the symbolic function of language

- deviant use of voice, monotonous and too loud or too soft

- wrong impression given due to precocious language

- detached language

- businesslike words used more than emotive words

- stiff and formal use of language

- flood of words

- interrupting

- badly tuned to conversation partners

- projection of own thoughts and feelings on the other

- taking literally what the other person is saying

- having problems when there is a difference between verbal and non-verbal expression

- wrong use of stress

- wrong interpretation of use of stress

- more oriented towards the form than the content of the language
- feeling of being unjustly treated
- repeating what has been said (echolalia)
- neologisms.

Striking interests

The third point in the triad of characteristics of autistic disorders is the *imagination*. Fantasizing by children with an autistic disorder is unusual. Imaginative play in particular is often missing.

Make-believe occurs in three ways (Leslie 1987). The first is using one object to represent something else, for example, using a broom as a horse. Parents teach their children this game when they imitate the sound of a horn while pressing on the baby's nose. The second form is changing the composition of an object; for example, pretending to lift heavy weights while using empty boxes. This element is in the game where parents pretend to grab their child and make scary noises. The third form is imaginative play; for example, playing at being a doctor. Parents teach their children this when they copy the other parent: 'And what will Daddy do when he comes home?'

This form of playing is of great importance in order to understand what goes on in other people's minds and for practising skills that go along with various social roles. In daily play children practise various roles. Vygotsky (1978) stated that with the help of playing the child develops skills and learns what her role in certain situations should be. Behaviour, especially social behaviour, can be lifted in this way from the *zone of proximal development* to the *zone of actual development* (see Chapter 2 about Vygotsky). Normally a child is interested in what kind of attitude she has to adopt and therefore likes to play this out in a game. The child prefers to play out these situations together with others because one's role in social life is always related to that of another. Playing shop, playing school, playing house, all are ways of mastering social interaction. The child extends her TOM by means of imaginative play.

Just how important this aspect of social interaction is can be seen, for example, when playing school. Children are less concerned in playing out their subjects from school – arithmetic or language – than they are practising social rules (Elbers 1991). They like to play the part of a strict teacher who tells them what the rules are and how children should behave in class, giving out severe punishments and scant rewards. Children in their play are more strict than their most severe teacher. In fact, when playing school children are finding out how authority and obedience works, an enormously important aspect of social functioning. Autistic children are not ready for this game until years later than their peers are.

When internally, as with the autistic child, there is insufficient orientation towards the other person and therefore little interest in that other person, the child will not occupy himself with such games. He will also have little knowledge that can be used in these games. In this way the development of the TOM will increasingly lag behind. The autistic child directs his interest to subjects other than social contacts. The interest of autistic children is a result of a situation of not-understanding: it is often directed at subjects where they can try to fathom something thoroughly. With children with a more than average intelligence, subjects connected with the question as to how everything came into existence are very popular. Astronomy, archaeology, ancient times and notably dinosaurs, which appeal strongly to the imagination, can catch the interest of the child with Asperger's syndrome.

Joe was very young when he taught himself how to read. Being highly gifted enabled him to study books on astronomy. He was very lonely. He did not manage to go to school and playing with other children was a big problem. But Joe had created his own world in which comets played an important role. One of the comets was his friend and he conjured him up when he was lying in bed and feeling sad.

Technical subjects that pertain to how something works and of which it is possible to get a complete overview – unlike social interaction – are also favourites. In addition, technical subjects are related more to the right hemisphere of the brain which is developed more strongly than the left one. Trains are a favourite subject. Perhaps with trains it is the special combination of technique, methodical control and the hypnotic, tranquil and rhythmic sound (that reminds one of the rocking and head banging of the autistic child) that is a reason for the attraction. Travelling in the car, buggy, train and even on the bike are regarded as being pleasant by children with an autistic disorder, at least if they are not afraid of the movement and of their destination. The rhythmic movements and the regular, hypnotizing sound of the train give a pleasant sensation. One of the problems of babies and toddlers with autistic disorders is that they have difficulty getting themselves to sleep, especially those without an intellectual disability. They develop all sorts of techniques to soothe themselves to sleep, including rocking and head banging. The trains and the car take over this activity and for children who are not yet able to get themselves to fall asleep, going for a ride in the buggy works as a sleep-inducer. For most children after about four months it suffices for them to be able to put their fingers in their mouth, or to be able to hold a pacifier in their mouth, in order to soothe themselves to sleep. Some children have this problem for a longer period of time and children with an autistic disorder can have long-term problems with sleeping.

The interest in trains is possibly connected with this hypnotizing effect. But also town and country planning, with its exact figuring out of where and how people live in a city, can become a fascination.

Robert, aged 12, spent a lot of his time making maps. On white A4 typing paper he kept designing a part of an enormous city. Everything had its place: the houses, shopping centres, schools, footpaths, residential areas, plants, rivers. He stuck the sheets of paper together with sticky tape. Through the years it had become so large that even he had never seen the whole city spread out. He drew it off the top of his head, where all the details were stored. The pieces of paper were stuck together in groups and by now there were various bundles. We organized the use of a gym in order for him to finally assemble his amazing production. He walked through the gym delighted putting the pieces of his city together which, by the way, fitted together perfectly.

People with autism can be totally absorbed in their interests. The attempt to force these interests on others occurs specifically with people with Asperger's syndrome (Gillberg 1997). This goes together with their strong orientation towards social contact compared to persons with classic autism.

Obsessive behaviour and rituals

Autistic children show many stereotypical behaviours. There is a lot of repetition in their behaviour and it often takes on obsessive forms. With the help of rituals they create order in their world and they cannot bear any disturbance of this order. An autistic child can rant and rave, become aggressive or panic when he or she is forced to break off from the ritual. According to Frith (1989) stereotypical behaviours can arise and continue because a mechanism of *switching off* at the highest level of central cohesion is missing. The desperation which the autistic child displays when he or she is obstructed in certain forms of behaviour makes one suspect that there is a different meaning hiding behind the stereotypical behaviours and obsessions.

It is possible that when this behaviour is disturbed an underlying fear within the child is exposed. We will see in Chapters 11 and 12 how these problems are connected with the autistic structure. The stereotypical, repetitive and obsessive behaviours offer a possibility for the child to keep the unknown, and therefore also frightening, world under control. Movement is also an excellent way of decreasing anxiety, as we will see in Chapter 11. That such behaviours are more about taking action than about the subject itself, we see in the fact that autistic people have more *compulsions* (obsessional acts) than *obsessions* (Gillberg 1992). Unlike people with OCD (obsessive-compulsive disorder) autistic people never have *just* obsessions, these are always accompanied by compulsions: the acts are central (McDougle 1998).

People with autistic disorders have obsessions and compulsions such as repeatedly organizing things, the need for symmetry, repeatedly telling or asking, touching or drumming their fingers on the table. They do not have the characteristic OCD obsessions with aggression, sexuality and cleaning (McDougle 1998).

We can see that anxiety plays an important role because obsessive-compulsive behaviours increase when the child (the same applies to adults) is anxious or under pressure (Frith 1989).

Actions which recur in daily practice are very open to becoming rituals; for example, taking showers for a long time, performing rituals when going to sleep or reading newspapers.

Derek could not be dissuaded from reading the paper. He could not bear it if he was behind with reading papers and when they piled up he became tense. It was unthinkable that he would skip reading those papers or throw them away. The birth of his daughter, however, interfered with this activity enormously. He was very tense about that and it was a huge victory for him when, after some time, he was able to throw the newspapers away unread.

With girls in particular, making themselves look pretty, especially by combing their hair, is a favourite ritual. Also, organizing everything in the room, putting everything exactly in the same place, can magically take hold of an autistic person. At the same time the chaos created is often so vast, that he cannot find the way out of it any more and has no idea as to how to get rid of that enormous amount of mess. His room can become over-organized or, on the contrary, chaotic, depending on his ability to sort out the mess. Eating is also open to rituals. With these subjects the resistance to change, which we will discuss in Chapter 10, also plays a role.

Learning disorders and going to school

Children with a disorder within the autistic spectrum may have to contend with *learning disorders*. With people who have the Kanner form the language function is often disturbed to such an extent that there is often no linguistic communication. Temple Grandin, an autistic woman who has become world famous because of her inventions in the field of dealing with cattle, writes about her incapacity to speak when she was three years old. While she understood everything she heard around her, she was aware that the only way she could make something clear was by screaming (Grandin 1995b).

Because with a lot of people an autistic disorder is combined with an intellectual disability, there is no normal possibility for them to learn. This includes every field, not only language development.

With children with Asperger's syndrome or PDD-NOS various learning disorders can occur. In Chapter 3 we showed that these can be related to the unbalanced development of both hemispheres of the brain. These can be temporary if maturation progresses sufficiently and there is an adequate amount of stimulation at the right moment. Children with Asperger's syndrome often have a disharmonious intelligence profile, as we have already seen. The relation VIQ/PIQ is out of balance. They are sometimes very linguistically skilled but fail in arithmetic, or *vice versa*. The profile may also change in the course of time and areas can be developed further whereas earlier there was doubt whether that would happen.

There are two areas in particular that can cause learning disorders in children with Asperger's syndrome and PDD-NOS. These are language and writing. The language development of children with Asperger's syndrome can be deviant in different ways, both strikingly strong and early and strikingly weak and late. Almost 50 per cent of children with Asperger's syndrome have slow language development, but can speak fluently when they are five years old (Gillberg 1989). Language development takes place in highly intelligent children with Asperger's syndrome at a very young age (they may even come across as precocious); often they can read and write at an early age.

A second area of learning disorders that definitely occurs with Asperger's syndrome is writing disorder, or dys(ortho)graphia, in which control of the fine motor system and eye–hand coordination is impaired, affecting the ability to write. Hamstra-Bletz and Bie (1985) mapped the specific way of writing of people with dysgraphia. This disorder is characterized by a writing pattern with a barely legible, chaotic picture. Writing takes a lot of time and is laborious, without becoming regular. When writing in block letters the legibility improves. A device for children with writing disorders is being developed (Delfos, in preparation).

Writing requires a fluent motor system; this is not in keeping with the often wooden motor system of children with Asperger's syndrome. Writing is often difficult for them and frustrates them. Encouraging them to write should be balanced with awareness that a good handwriting style will probably never be developed. The current possibilities with computers can help children with this disorder to develop their language skills further without becoming too frustrated by their writing problems.

A general problem for children with Asperger's syndrome and PDD-NOS is their limited readiness for school as far as carrying out tasks and dealing with peers is concerned compared to their cognitive maturity. Their resistance to carrying out the allocated tasks and to conforming to a normal school pattern can have such consequences that the child cannot be maintained at school. Their autistic characteristics mean that they find it hard to conform to their teacher's wishes. They cannot easily be influenced by means of punishment and reward, and often refuse to interrupt their own inner programme. Also their lack of orientation in time and space makes going to school difficult. On the other hand, they can be obedient almost as a reflex (Asperger 1944), and they find it pleasant when they are offered structure.

Being so poorly orientated towards their environment also causes them to be less open to learning techniques offered to them. They can therefore put their teachers on the wrong track. The teacher at one point thinks that the child has understood a certain method for reaching solutions and expects that he will apply this to other problems. After some time the child develops his own solution strategy. When it proves that this strategy is not the right one for further problems in that area, he is stranded. The teacher therefore has to examine what strategy the child has developed himself for solving problems.

An instruction given by the teacher to the class as a whole often does not reach children with an autistic disorder. It has to be pointed out to them separately that the instruction also applies to them.

Educating children with an autistic disorder asks a lot of teachers. In giving help to children with an autistic disorder teachers have to be able to 'turn off' their emotions and not become angry or try to be loved (Asperger 1944).

Special education is not yet tuned in enough to these children. Specific care aimed at these children is necessary. Williams (1995) wrote a very useful and respectful guide for teachers which can be found on the Internet (see Appendix II, listing Internet sites with recommendations for teachers, and Appendix IIa in particular where a summary of Williams' article can be found).

Especially for children with Asperger's syndrome combined with a more than average intelligence, going to school causes enormous problems. There is no type of school specifically adjusted to their needs. They get stuck in regular education because they cannot conform properly to the school structure, which takes as a starting point the assumption that the child can to a certain extent be considerate of other people. In special primary schools and special education there are more children with low to very low intelligence, and highly intelligent children with Asperger's syndrome do not have any link with their peers there or in mainstream schools, not even in the cognitive field, which is strong with them. Cognitively they are ahead of their peers and in other areas they are behind. This requires a school that is able to give help to the child on a broad basis, so that the child can be with young children and cognitively go along with older children. In the coming chapters we will discuss these problems further.

Kunce and Mesibov (1998) and colleagues developed the TEACCH programme (Treatment and Education of Autistic and related Communication handicapped Children) for the education of children with autism. In this programme education is built up step by step and adapted to the specific child. In a regular school situation this is, however, hardly ever feasible. We do, however, see more and more schools that have a special class for children with an autistic disorder. Education should be specifically aimed at the child. The TEACCH programme therefore begins with, as the first step, becoming acquainted with autism and what autism means. Understanding from within is of great importance. Vermeulen (2000b) wrote a workbook for people with Asperger's syndrome to help them understand themselves. There is also a book for young children in which autism is explained (Delfos 2003c). Understanding autistic people is important. Peeters (1996) shows how important that is: if you cannot build up a positive atmosphere in upbringing and education, you'd better not start with it. However, working out a positive approach for people who are so different is not that simple.

In the box below the six steps of the TEACCH programme are put together. In order to tune the education programme to the specific child one observes for the purpose of social interaction the following behaviours:

- *proximity* (being close to someone, looking at someone)

- *dealing with objects and body* (motor system problems, understanding use of an object – like a glass)

- *reacting socially* (response to smiling, response to contact initiatives by others, shaking hands)

- *taking social initiative* (inviting shared attention)

- *socially unacceptable behaviour* (aggression, (self-) mutilation)

- *resistance to change* (resistance to unannounced new activity).

Box 5.1 TEACCH: Steps in education for autistic people (Kunce and Mesibov 1998).

Step 1   Understanding autism

Step 2   Understanding the unique child by carefully establishing abilities and inabilities

Step 3   Increasing predictability and understanding for the child by fixed routines and schemes

Step 4   Giving clear instruction and expectations in order to enlarge understanding of the child

Step 5   Structuring and giving tasks

Step 6   Motivating pupils by using their special interests

To conclude this chapter we present the most important elements of autism in Table 5.5, which is partly an elaboration of Table 3.2. We will limit ourselves to two main influences on the development of autistic traits: A, the inhibition of the immune system, and B, the stimulation of the right hemisphere at the expense of the left one.

The elements in Table 5.5 are under the section which applies best to each of them, but there is a mutual connection. In the next chapters various elements from the table will be elaborated on.

With this we round off the first part of the book, *What is it?* In the second part, *What can you do about it?*, we will go into the ways in which the child, the parents and adolescents and adults with autism can be helped. Here more behaviour patterns will be discussed and behaviour will be examined in more detail.

Focal points

- The triad of problems in autism comprises problems in the fields of social contact, of communication and of imagination.

- People form a theory of mind (TOM) – a theory about how people think and feel.

- Children with an autistic disorder develop a less wide range of feelings.

- Children with autism are less oriented towards sharing attention, not out of indifference, but out of being less 'in the world'.

Table 5.5 Influences of high testosterone in the womb on the immune system and development of the right hemisphere

The first two influences in detail	
A. Inhibition of the immune system	
I. Biological/psychological/ neural self	• Limitation/delay in me–other differentiation • Limitation of self-image development • Limitation of identity development • Impaired empathic capacity • Impaired sense of time • Impaired sense of space • Limited TOM • Difficulty with planning activities • Difficulty with (evaluation) of social interaction • Imposing rather than requesting help.
II. Fighting diseases	• Atopic syndrome • Weaker fight against disease.
B. Stimulation of the right hemisphere at the expense of the left	• Putting thoughts, feelings into words • Abstract/spatial/technical focus • Resistance to change • Learning disorders • Non-fluent motor system • Savant talents • Long-term memory stronger than short-term memory • Filing based on facts more than on coherence

- People with autism can hardly take into consideration feelings that they do not know themselves.

- People develop a *socioscheme*, a scheme about themselves, how they stand in the world and in relation to the people around them. Some aspects thereof are the body blueprint, the TOM, the realization of time and the realization of space.

- Children with an autistic disorder have difficulty developing an extensive socioscheme.

- Realization of time and space arises from the realization of the relation to the other.

- An eye for detail with autistic people may be a compensation for the difficulty with assessing social interaction.

- Eye contact develops from looking to exchanging.

- Sensory stimuli can affect autistic people particularly strongly.

- Language development or the use of language by children with an autistic disorder is atypical or unusual.

- Children with an autistic disorder have difficulty with imaginative play, while this form of playing is of great importance for developing social insight and social skills.

- With children with an autistic disorder obsessive behaviour and rituals occur regularly.

- Learning disorders, including language and writing disorders, often occur with children with an autistic disorder.

- The TEACCH programme has as its basis understanding autism, and learning to know the specific child in order to later link up to the child and his or her interests.

Focal points regarding attitude

- Respect.
- Warmth.
- Patience.

- Help should have as its first starting point understanding the disorder.

- It must be understood that the sensory experiences of autistic children can be stronger.

Summary

What connects autistic disorders are the problems with social interaction. The three most important theories in the field of autism are the theory of mind, the theory of central coherence and the theory of planning and executive function. Researchers in the TOM use a triad of characteristics of autism: problems in the field of social contact, of communication and imagination. The starting point of the model of this book is the absence of the me–other differentiation and, based on that, an inadequate empathic ability.

The model presented in this chapter is that of the socioscheme. In order to clarify the activity of forming an image of oneself, of the world, of others and of oneself in relation to others, the concept of the socioscheme was introduced. This scheme also includes the realization of time and space, which both derive their meaning from the person in relation to the other. The TOM – acknowledging thoughts, feeling and intentions to oneself and others – is part of this scheme. The characteristics occurring with disorders within the autistic spectrum, such as deviant interests and obsessive behaviour, sensory experiences, learning disorders or resistance to change, get an integrated place in the model as derivative problems.

Part 2

What can you do about it?

6

Before and after diagnosis

Diagnosis of the autistic spectrum with its various syndromes has become increasingly established in recent years. Some ten years ago, the focus was almost completely on the serious form of autism, Kanner's autism, and its combination with intellectual disability. In the past few years, milder forms, such as Asperger's syndrome and PDD-NOS, have also come to the fore. Research into these is in full progress. The issues involved are becoming steadily clearer. The differences between various syndromes are not always very distinct and that between a syndrome and 'normal with autistic features' has become vague. The increased interest in autism and the fact that a disorder within the autistic spectrum cannot always be sharply demarcated give rise to the risk of incorrect diagnosis. In the past, the situation was quite the opposite as the disorder was not recognized at all.

As a result of the variety of terms that has evolved, there is also the risk that a range of problems indicative of autism proper is euphemistically referred to as *PDD-NOS* or *atypical autism*, in order to soften the impact.

The disorder, but not the diagnosis

As the diagnosis has started to receive more serious attention only in recent years, many adults have not been diagnosed.

Since the age of 16, Martin had known that he was different. He didn't know how and why he deviated but he did know that he was always an outsider. During his student years, he asked his fellow students despairingly what was wrong with the way he behaved. They couldn't tell him: 'If you don't know that, it cannot be explained', was how they put it. He had been looking for help since the age of 16, going from individual therapy to relational therapy. He tried the regional institute for mental welfare and then turned to various alternative forms of therapy. 'When I was 30,' Martin pointed out, 'I managed to explain my problem to the mental welfare institute, though with a great deal of difficulty: "I don't know myself. Whenever I try to get to know myself, I come up against a large grey area inside. That's why I'm here: to get to know that grey area." No one understood what I was trying to explain and it didn't get me anywhere.' He continued his search because the messages he was getting ('show yourself for once', 'express yourself', 'don't escape', 'don't be so lazy', 'don't be so rational') in no way corresponded to what he was feeling and experiencing. He was in his forties, with two divorces behind him and five children, when he ended up with a new therapist and at last heard that the diagnosis was 'Asperger's syndrome'. It was a shock, a confrontation and a huge relief: all the pieces of the puzzle finally fitted together. From that moment on, he was on surer ground about what he had to learn, what knowledge he had to acquire, what were his weak spots and what his strong points. After some time, he was able to explain to those dear to him what made him tick. It made it much easier to get on with each other.

Martin's sister is deeply autistic, with Kanner's autism. It is in fact surprising that Martin has had to wait more than 40 years before becoming aware that he has the same disorder as his sister, though in a very mild form. Happé (1998) noted that when someone in a family is autistic (with Kanner's autism), there is a greater chance of other autistic disorders, such as Asperger's syndrome, being present in other members of the family. It may well be that the child with the milder autistic disorder appears virtually normal compared with the child with the more serious form, with the result that the problems of the child with the milder form remain in the shadow. It is also possible that the latter's behaviour is construed as imitative behaviour rather than similar predisposition.

The problems of people of normal or above average intelligence are often not clear to those around them. In some cases the problem is recognized right away, while in others it may take months, or things may become clear to their partner only when they are living together (Vermeulen 1999b).

A child with an autistic disorder feels that he deviates from the people around him. In general, deviating from the majority gives rise to a feeling of inferiority. But deviating from the majority in, say, mathematics is of a different magnitude to deviating in social interaction. When someone 'deviates socially', he or she may develop a feeling of being inferior as a human being. Moreover, a child with an autistic disorder will not be able to understand why he is always the odd one out in social situations. Without the diagnosis, the child does not know what the problem is and how he could do something about it. As a result, the child may feel increasingly helpless; as puberty approaches, depressive feelings often grow steadily stronger.

It should be clear from the above that a – correct – diagnosis can help not only the parents or therapists but also, and especially, the people concerned themselves. Gunilla Gerland (2000) stresses that it is in particular the people themselves who need to receive information in the course of the diagnostic process.

In the second half of the twentieth century increasing emphasis was placed on upbringing. Children with an autistic disorder were often regarded as badly brought up. Therapists tended to blame the parents. For some time, it was Bruno Bettelheim (1967) in particular who propagated the view that autism was a disorder caused by the parents. Annabel Stehli (1995) described the feelings of guilt, the loneliness and the burden of shame she felt as a parent of an autistic child; at the same time, she felt that Bettelheim was wrong.

Figure 6.1 Bruno Bettelheim (Bettelheim 1967). Reproduced with permission from Simon & Schuster, Inc.

Many parents who have now reached middle age and older are weighed down by this feeling of guilt. To make matters worse, their grown-up child fails to find his place in community. No matter how hard they have tried, the child has not been helped. Quite the contrary, because of the wrong diagnosis the child has been wrongly dealt with. The child, now an adult, also plays with the idea that it was because of her upbringing that she cannot cope. For parents it is very difficult, after so many years of a lack of understanding, to break away from this way of thinking. They had always been blamed as the cause of their child's behaviour; now it suddenly appears that there is no question of blame.

Irving is nearly 30 years old. When he was little, his father left because he could not bear his son's behaviour and blamed Irving's mother. His mother is extremely vulnerable after all the blame and guilt which the medical and educational advice centre, psychiatrists, psychologists, social workers and her husband heaped on her. Yet she has to look after her child and she is all alone in this. Caring for her son is almost too much for her. His furious outbursts terrify her. The house is full of damaged spots which she tries to hide by covering them with pictures. She is concerned about his loneliness and distress, and often her worries keep her awake at night. She is tired of looking after Irving and worrying about him. The situation has escalated to the point that it is not easy to find professional help for him. Even the psychiatrist at the autism care centre to which he has been referred can hardly get through to him. Irving and his mother are left with the result of years of failing services.

If it proves possible in the future to diagnose autism by investigating chromosomes, the neutrality of the role played by the parents and child may be enhanced. One of the highly problematic aspects of late diagnosis is that the parents – and the child – face the situation alone. Raising a child with an autistic disorder is a difficult task, putting an immense strain on the parents' relationship. Upbringing based on the usual strategies for raising a child is doomed to fail and the father and mother tend to blame each other for this. They disagree about how the child ought to be brought up. The mother tends to be strongly supportive of the child to try and reduce his anxiety whereas the father is eager to impose a strict structure and mete out punishment so as to control the child's behaviour. If professionals point to upbringing as the cause of the problem, the pressure on the family gets (even) greater, further increasing the strain on the couple's relationship. Without being able to provide figures to substantiate this claim, I have the impression that after some time many mothers end up having to cope on their own because the father leaves. The fact is, moreover, that this often involves sons who have inherited their predisposition through their father. As Hans Asperger (1944) pointed out, many fathers of children with autism have autistic features themselves, without suffering from autism as such. Bringing up the child together with the mother may well become even more difficult as a result, in particular if the condition has not been diagnosed in the father. If it has, it may in fact be beneficial to the family if the father shares particular characteristics with his child as he is in a better position to recognize the child's behaviour, explain it to others and see things in their proper context. Gillberg and Ehlers (1998) note that parents with poor empathy probably have more difficulty bringing up their children with an autistic disorder. On the other hand, they point out that such parents recognize themselves more readily in the child and therefore establish closer contact with him. In my experience, fathers with autistic features or with Asperger's syndrome in fact often have a highly empathic partner, ensuring that both necessary qualities are present in the upbringing. The wide difference between the partners, however, may exert strong pressure on their relationship, as a result of which it may not continue long enough for them to be able to bring up the children jointly.

Although – empathic – mothers of autistic children often try to understand their child, they frequently fail. They may be able to alleviate the child's anxiety to some extent but often do not know sufficiently what to do to teach the child to cope in social contexts.

> Alec, who was 23 at the time, and his mother, were shown separately the instructive film *I'm not Stupid* (Fisher 1995), which deals with Asperger's syndrome. Alec's reaction was: 'I assume that for my mother there will be the joy of recognition.' The mother's first reaction to the film was: 'I had no idea that he had to work so hard, had to think to carry on a conversation, and now I understand why he always interrupts me.'

Autistic problems may also be caused by meningitis which often occurs when the child is about six months old. However, it is not certain whether the autistic disorder is caused by the meningitis or whether a child with an autistic disorder is more susceptible to contract meningitis at that stage.

> Charles contracted meningitis at the age of six months. Fortunately, the doctor got there in time and he was given the necessary treatment in hospital. The doctor established that he had not sustained damage from the illness. Charles's mother therefore concluded that he would grow up normally. However, it soon became clear that Charles had autistic and psychotic features (multiple complex developmental disorder, or McDD). It is not probable that the autism could be attributed to the

meningitis because Charles had already shown signs of being different as a baby. Already at that time, his motor activity had been quite deviant. He would stiffen up when someone touched him and when he was startled by noise.

Parents quite early sense that there is something wrong with their child. They feel that she is 'different', 'strange', 'odd'. Sometimes they go from one practitioner to another to get an answer to their question of what is wrong with their child. When at last they find out that their child has an autistic disorder, they feel relief. Finally it's clear. But then they enter a *mourning process*. They have a sense of *relief* because they finally have an answer, because they feel that the answer is correct, because their feelings of guilt can now dissipate as it is not their fault the child is acting this way, and because it now becomes clear how the child can be helped. The parents are *mourning* because they would prefer their child not to have an autistic disorder, they feel grief and sometimes bitterness about the time lost for their child and because their dreams about the future now evaporate. And then they become anxious and worried about the child's future.

The earlier the diagnosis is made, the sooner the parents and child, but also the school and others around the parents and child, can learn to deal with the problem. Various tests have been developed to detect autism at an early stage. One of the main tests is the CHAT, developed by Baron-Cohen (Baron-Cohen *et al.* 1996), which can be administered from the age of 18 months. It consists of two parts. The first comprises nine questions to the parents, including some about the child's desire to be whirled around, playing with other children and pointing with the finger. The second part consists of questions about observations by the doctor or therapist and covers making eye contact, make-believe play and motor skills (Aarons and Gittens 2000).

Now that our knowledge about the autistic spectrum has expanded, more children with these problems will be diagnosed as such. But there is also a risk that the diagnosis is made when there is in fact no autistic disorder.

The diagnosis, but not the disorder

Increasing interest in a particular disorder always goes hand in hand with instances of wrong diagnosis. In the case of the autistic spectrum, this concerns in particular the milder forms: Asperger's syndrome and PDD-NOS. Kanner's autism encompasses so many criteria that there is less chance of erroneous diagnosis. Nevertheless, failure to recognize Kanner's autism remains a problem if other disorders are present at the same time, such as intellectual disability. The milder forms have the same autistic characteristics but to a lesser degree. These disorders do not require as many characteristics to be present to warrant diagnosis.

In autism there is behaviour which to a greater or lesser extent is present in everyone. When the wrong diagnosis is made, attention is usually focused in particular on unmanageable behaviour: fits of temper, rituals and poor contact with peers. The core of autism, however, is a poor ability to evaluate social interaction. In the faulty diagnosis, poor evaluation ability is sometimes confused with failure to take account of others: egocentric versus egoistic. But an autistic child is in principle prepared to take account of others. People with Asperger's syndrome can be very considerate if they know what another person needs and if it is within their reach to try and meet this need. However, the problem is that the child's capacity for knowing what the other is thinking and what the other needs is impaired. When an autistic child refuses to take account of others, this is often connected with a disturbance of his or her own 'programme', provoking too much anxiety. This situation can evoke a great deal of resistance in an autistic person.

Non-autistic children, i.e. children who *are* capable of sensing what another feels, may because of circumstances not be prepared to take account of the other person. This is *egoistic* rather than *egocentric* behaviour. A child with an autistic disorder may *seem* egoistic and insensitive but in fact he or she is not.

A child without an autistic disorder who, egoistically, does not take account of another may do so for various reasons. Important factors are frustration and anxiety. Children may, as a result of what they go through, sustain frustration and anxiety and subsequently express this in hyperactive, anxious or aggressive behaviour. For instance, children involved in a divorce may become quite unmanageable, in particular during the first two years. Often there is a worrying downturn in performance at school (Worden 1996). Children who have been sexually abused may become aggressive or withdrawn, depending on their age and other factors (Delfos 1994, 2001b). These instances involve environmental factors more than predisposition, as is the case in autistic disorders. There may also be a combination (*comorbidity*) of various problems – e.g. ADHD or fear of failure – with an autistic disorder. The symptoms of neglect may also be confused with those of autism. Quasi-autistic behaviour has been reported in an extensive study among Romanian adopted children. Rutter and colleagues (1999) used the term *quasi-autistic pattern* while Hoksbergen and colleagues (2002) speak of *institutional autism*. The Romanian children appeared to have been seriously neglected in orphanages, leading to behaviour that is more serious than what we observe in *insecure attachment* (Bowlby 1984). Their self-orientation, with a great deal of *stereotyped behaviour*, is suggestive of autism; but it appears that after having spent some time in a properly caring adoptive family such behaviour recedes and eventually disappears. Any serious lag in language development is caught up. These children do not display the strong anxiety frequently found in autistic children.

Rather, there is apathy; which indeed is not surprising for children who have learned that little help and support is to be expected from other people.

In children the various diagnoses are more difficult to distinguish than in adults. Adult behaviour shows more variety. Active behaviour, as we shall see in Chapter 11, is a way of reducing anxiety. The same (hyper)active behaviour can therefore arise from a range of sources, from anxiety to ADHD.

The anxiety associated with the autistic spectrum probably arises as the world appears so strange and incomprehensible to autistic people and because others are always making demands on them, making them anxious. In children with ADHD the anxiety may result from an immature hormonal system combined with anxiety-enhancing environmental factors (Delfos 2004a).

While active, aggressive and obsessive behaviours may perhaps be the most striking features of a disorder within the autistic spectrum, the common thread is an impaired capacity to evaluate social interaction. These children are structurally 'off the mark' in their contact with people. This happens not only in one situation but throughout: at school, at home, wherever they happen to be. As a result, they fail to establish any rapport with their peers, not because they disrupt play, as is often the case for children with ADHD, but because they constantly get it wrong in their contact with others. As Martin's fellow students indicated, it is difficult to put it into words; the child's behaviour is not exactly wrong, undesirable or inappropriate, but constantly 'off the mark'.

Since we, as parents, are so strongly focused on the small number of offspring we have and are eager to get the most out of them, with actually less educational effort than parents in the past, it may well be that we are less tolerant of deviations from an ideal image we have in our minds. Because of this, a child may end up with a label, not because she has a disorder but because she does not meet the expectations of the people around her. Moreover, autistic characteristics – such as a poor sense of what is going on in other people's thoughts, rigid patterns of behaviour and a one-track mind – are normal features of many people who certainly do not have autism.

Accordingly, it is advisable to have a disorder in the autistic spectrum diagnosed by people who, in addition to their particular knowledge, have extensive experience with the autistic spectrum. Experience is an important source of knowledge over and above the diagnostic criteria and tests.

A child who is wrongly diagnosed with a disorder in the autistic spectrum when, for instance, there is an environmental factor present, is bound to be given the wrong care. He will be stigmatized by the diagnosis. The parents and the child will not make proper efforts to ensure normal development but will assume an attitude of dependence on outside help, on therapists and other professionals. A wrong diagnosis may seriously harm the normal development which the child is potentially capable of. Attention will be focused on his behaviour whereas it ought to be directed to the environmental factor. The child will feel misunderstood. The advice given will not be consistent with the child's own experience and will often – quite rightly – not be heeded. The child's trust in adults will be shaken as a result.

In the following chapters I shall outline the various aspects of the autistic disorder and indicate how upbringing, school and professional care can respond to it, starting with me–other differentiation.

Focal points

- Asperger's syndrome and PDD-NOS regularly occur in adults without being diagnosed.

- An accusing finger is often pointed at parents of a child whose autistic disorder has not been diagnosed.

- People with an autistic disorder are certainly capable of having relationships and getting married.

- Couples where one has empathic qualities and the other does not may have an advantage when raising a child with an autistic disorder.

- Parents who have an ideal image of their children in mind run the risk of finding their child deviant although he is in fact normal.

- The considerable interest in autism may lead to faulty diagnosis.

- Hyperactive and troublesome behaviour in children may be a symptom of a disorder but may also be a sign that the child has a problem somewhere. It may also be the result of a failure in upbringing.

Focal points regarding attitude

- Autistic features occur not only in autistic people but are also widespread among non-autistic people.

- It is necessary to acknowledge the burden on parents of an autistic child.

- A critical examination of children's upbringing and behaviour is necessary to prevent faulty diagnosis.

Summary

Diagnosis of one of the disorders in the autistic spectrum has important consequences for the child's development and his life as an adult. Parents sometimes have to go on a long search before finally finding out what is wrong with their child and before it is clear what makes their child so different from others. For a long time, parents were considered as the source of the problem. Following a long period of emphasis on the impact of upbringing, there is now a growing awareness of predisposition and heredity as the causes of autistic disorders. Once they have heard the diagnosis, parents may feel relief that it is not their fault the child behaves unusually. This is followed by a period of mourning and grief as parents would prefer their child not to have an autistic disorder. They may also feel grief because the real problem was discovered so late.

Nowadays autistic disorders are more frequently diagnosed in the early years. Many adults with autistic spectrum disorders suffer from a lack of understanding from those around them and also from themselves *vis-à-vis* their environment, as they are viewed as 'ordinary' people whereas in fact they have an autistic disorder.

Another consequence of the increasing interest in disorders within the autistic spectrum is a higher frequency of faulty diagnosis: the diagnosis is made but the disorder is not there. The cause may be excessive attention on the child's behaviour alone and the growing demands which parents nowadays make on their children. A child who is wrongly diagnosed will receive the wrong type of care, which may seriously harm his (potentially) normal development. Moreover, an autistic disorder may coincide with other disorders, further complicating the picture.

7

Stimulating me–other differentiation and empathy

To provide guidance for working with children with an autistic disorder and their parents, Rutter (1985) lists a number of general objectives:

1. Ensuring that the family can cope.

2. Objectives focused on the child:

   - stimulating its development

   - attenuating specific behavioural problems

   - removing non-specific behavioural problems.

When we turn our attention to how children and adults with an autistic disorder can be helped, we should realize that it requires insight, empathy and a different way of looking at things. Children with an autistic disorder must be helped and guided to cope with their social disability and develop their qualities. There is no other way. While autistic disorders have a significant predispositional component, there is no medication to cure the disorder (Happé 1998). Autism is too extensive and interwoven with all human behaviour to be covered by medication: there is no medicine to stimulate maturation, no pill to develop empathy. Nevertheless, there are medicines for various symptoms suffered by some autistic people. Anti-psychotic and anti-depressive drugs and benzodiazepines, for instance, are used to treat hyperactivity, aggressiveness, self-mutilation, emotional outbursts, stereo-typed behaviour, sleep problems, anxiety, negativism and social withdrawal. In addition to the side effects and the risks when these medicines are used at an age when children are still in full development, children with autism are also at risk of suffering the opposite effect, as we shall see in the next chapter when discussing the response to anaesthetics. The fact remains that there is no medication for the core of the problem: me–other differentiation. The first requirement in trying to help people with an autistic disorder is therefore acquiring an insight ensuring that upbringing and care can meet the autistic person's needs.

We have highlighted impaired me–other differentiation as the core of the problem of the autistic spectrum. When autistic disorder is combined with intellectual disability, it makes the possibilities of learning to distinguish between oneself and others more problematic. In Asperger's syndrome and PDD-NOS, intelligence and language ability are normal in principle and can therefore be used to reinforce me–other differentiation. The child himself uses this intelligence and language in an effort to overcome the anxiety evoked by the world around him.

Inadequate me–other differentiation and symbiosis

Egocentricity is connected with limited me–other differentiation: no adequate distinction is made between 'me' and 'not me'. The process of me–other differentiation continues throughout life, with the main development taking place in the first few years. The ego stages posited by Loevinger (1990) make it clear how limited ego development is in children with an autistic disorder. They remain in the initial stages of *pre-social behaviour* and *impulsive behaviour* for much longer than the average child.

The following example illustrates limited me–other differentiation. If Tom, described in the example, had been three years old, we would have found his behaviour normal, but at seven it is a cause for concern.

Seven-year-old Tom was having make-up applied to his face. He fell silent with pride when he looked at himself in the hand mirror; he looked so wonderful. He then handed the mirror to the play therapist to have himself admired: 'Look!' Tom was unaware that only her own image was visible in the mirror. What's more, as he did not see himself while being made up, he also assumed that the therapist could not see him either. Tom did not realize that the therapist just had to look at him in order to see him. In any case, she was the one who had made him up and had therefore been involved in the whole process. The fact that Tom could not (or could hardly) understand what went on in the other person's mind limited his insight to his own perspective.

Predispositional factors may hamper me–other differentiation and consequently also empathic capacity. A less developed left hemisphere of the brain may play a causal role in egocentrically oriented persons. However, *environmental factors* may also play a part in inhibiting the development of empathic capacity or its application. A mother who does not let go of her child, hardly leaving him any scope for independent thinking and constantly filling in his thoughts, will hamper the development of me–other differentiation. In the most serious case, we speak of a *symbiotic relationship*, with mother and child appearing unable to function independently from one another. In this case, the mother is anxiously focused on the child and the child dares not undertake anything without her nor does he feel free to do anything without her approval. He lets his behaviour be determined entirely by the mother. The child's thinking and feeling are overwhelmed by the mother's thoughts and feelings. He does not learn to make a distinction between himself and the mother, which is a first building block for achieving me–other differentiation. As a result, the child does not learn properly to understand what goes on in other people's minds as he feels, and has in fact become, much too dependent to be able to do so. Overall, the child makes a very dependent and anxious impression.

This problem is different from deficient me–other differentiation which is caused by predisposition and plays a role in autism. Poor me–other differentiation determined by predisposition is not, in principle, combined with strong, anxious focusing on the mother. When it is a bit older, the child appears to function independently from the mother unless there is a problem for which he needs her. The child sometimes undertakes things as it were *too* autonomously; and he may even appear to function in complete detachment from the environment and be highly egocentric. A child with poor me–other differentiation often seems to be unaware of what is happening around him. He does not pay much attention to what other people do. It is only when the other person frustrates his wishes that the child appears to become aware of the other person. At such moments, the child makes demands on the other person, often the mother, in order to get what he wants, according to his own norms and in his own way. A solution different from his own is unwelcome and is refused. Accordingly, the other person's role is limited to implementing the solutions thought up by the child. On the whole, the child therefore does not make an anxious impression, even though there is certainly a feeling of anxiety. The anxiety, however, is confined to specific situations such as a deviation from a proposed plan.

In a symbiotic relationship, the mother needs the child for herself. The mother penetrates the child's identity as she wants completely to appropriate the child. When, however, there is poor me–other differentiation, the reverse situation occurs: the child badly needs the mother. In this case, it is important for the mother to find a balance between teaching the child things and giving him sufficient scope to develop independently. A child with an autistic disorder claims the mother for himself, but in a symbiotic relationship the mother claims the child for herself. Since the development of a child with an autistic disorder does not follow the same rate in all areas, it is much more difficult for the parents to find a balance between helping and letting go than with a child without the disorder. Some areas develop quickly and others slowly, and others again follow a normal rate of development. Sexual development is a clear example of this. In a child with an autistic disorder, biological maturation does not deviate from the norm; first menstruation occurs at an average age for girls. However, the psychological, relationship side of sexuality lags years behind biological maturation.

For the parents and carers of a child with an autistic disorder, seeking a balance between dependence and independence is therefore far more difficult. Because of her – justified – concern for the child, the mother is strongly focused on the child and keeps adults who do not understand her child and give the wrong advice at a distance. This is why the relationship between mother and child was in the past (but sometimes still today) wrongly characterized as symbiotic. This applied, for instance, to the relationship which Irving's mother had with her son (in Chapter 6): their relationship was termed 'symbiotic' because it was assumed Irving's behaviour was due to upbringing and not to predisposition.

Delayed development

Examining the problems of autism, we find that there is delayed development in particular areas. We have already noted that some autistic people have an intellectual disability alongside their autism. The extent to which they lag behind in development is even greater and covers far more areas, often making it impossible for them to cope on their own even when they have reached adulthood.

The slow development is apparent in various fields. For instance, children with autism rarely engage in fantasy games but often really enjoy games toddlers play, long after they have moved beyond the toddler stage. We have already noted that there is limited maturation of the central nervous system or, depending on the form and severity of the autism, a part of the central nervous system.

It is useful to bear this in mind when we speak of helping children with an autistic disorder. Autistic children with normal or above average intelligence also develop extremely slowly and with limitations in particular areas. This applies especially to the development of social evaluation and contact. It is as though part of the development runs more slowly, like a film in extreme slow motion, while development in other fields moves ahead at a normal or above average pace. In some fields, the development of the first two years in a child with an autistic disorder may extend over many years. The idea of delayed development comes from Baron-Cohen (1989). Research such as that by James and Barry (1980) has confirmed the idea of delayed development at a psycho-physiological level. One argument in support of the idea of delayed development is that not a single autistic child passes the TOM test successfully at the normal calendar age. Since the child develops very slowly in particular areas, its development will become deviant when in terms of age it is ready for this development. Age-adequate and age-inadequate elements will become intermingled, which may sometimes give rise to a bizarre pattern of behaviour.

One of the main forms of learning is make-believe play. During childhood, this is a very common way of learning social rules. At primary-school level, role play of all kinds is quite usual. By playing mummies and daddies, a child practises upbringing and its effects. Playing school is an excellent way of learning to deal with authority. A parent who watches children playing school and takes things too literally would be inclined to go to the school and bring the traumatizing teacher to account. But the child is not in fact imitating the teacher but, through play, examines how authority is exercised, how it works, how people obey, and explores the boundaries. In other words, such play is of fundamental importance for social adjustment. A child or young person with Asperger's syndrome is often ready for such play only years later. Instead of at the age of eight, such a person is sometimes ready for it only at age 17. At that age, the chance that he or she will have an opportunity to play such a game in the peer group is extremely small. For him or her, playing school would be age-adequate play. But he or she would rather be expected to begin experimenting, mix with girls or boys, go dating. However, these examples are age-inadequate forms of behaviour for him or her. As a result, a deviating development, undesirable for the person concerned, is set in motion. Playing school at the age of 17, no matter how much fun it seems, is perceived as inappropriate. If 'playing school' takes the form of a form of a piece of theatre, it is more acceptable. All this person basically wants is 'to practise social behaviour' and he or she looks for ways to do so, looks for legitimization.

Once we realize that a child has restricted development, we know that our normal way of upbringing will fall short of its target. Children with an autistic disorder display behaviour in some areas which we normally encounter in very young children, and sometimes only in babies.

Typically autistic behaviour is a common thread right from birth. As the child grows older, it may assume other forms; head-banging as a baby and toddler, for instance, may grow into fidgeting when the child is of primary-school age.

As growing up means further maturation, it is possible that autism manifests itself more seriously in the first few years than in subsequent development. As we saw in Chapter 4, it is consequently difficult to distinguish between Kanner's autism and Asperger's syndrome. In the early years, there may appear to be the more profound form of autism – Kanner's autism – while in the following years the pattern may seem to right itself and suggest the milder form of autism, i.e. Asperger's syndrome. The older the children, the greater the differences between those with various forms of autistic disorder. This is partly due to predisposition, to the rate of maturation, but partly also to upbringing, help and experience. As we have pointed out earlier, the central nervous system takes about 25 years to mature. In the beginning the differences are therefore less than after a couple of years when the maturation process has been able to evolve. Only then it will become clear how problematic the person's maturation is and which areas are impaired.

Our usual method of upbringing entails the expectation that the child, once she is ready for a particular skill, will quickly master it with our help. We encourage the child, show her a few times how it is done, and soon she does it by herself.

Without being aware of it, we have 'virtual statistics' in our heads on the basis of which we judge the behaviour of children and others. Parts of these 'statistics' are probably innate, instinctive, while other parts are formed through what we learn during our lives. These statistics are the reason why parents feel quite early on that their child deviates, that there is something the matter with the child, long before specialists are able to establish the diagnosis of autistic disorder. The parent's socioscheme indicates that there is something going on. A child with an autistic disorder does not comply with a number of these statistics in our heads, in particular those concerning social contact, reciprocity in contact and sensing what is going on in other people's minds. If we wish to help a child with an autistic disorder, we will have to let go of these statistics. A child with an autistic disorder will master some skills only much later or not at all. It will often also take much longer to master these skills, and only when the child is *ready* for it. The learning process is therefore not only *delayed* in some areas but it also proceeds *at a slower pace*. Another factor to be borne in mind is that training the child in the skill will not easily lead to automated behaviour (Asperger 1944). The learned behaviour will usually not become automated at all. The child will have difficulty displaying the learned behaviour spontaneously, without stimulation or pressure. In other words, we will have to educate a child with an autistic disorder with more patience and over a longer period. We should also have less expectation that the child will naturally assimilate what she has learnt and carry it out independently. The following example serves to illustrate what this means in practice.

Peter, aged seven, attended a normal primary school but there were doubts whether he would manage there. He was an awfully nice boy but he was 'different' and at school the children responded to this. The psychiatric centre's provisional diagnosis was non-verbal learning disability (NLD), and possibly eventually Asperger's syndrome. A re-examination after one year confirmed Asperger's syndrome. Peter's mother reported that he displayed obsessive behaviour. This she had concluded from the fact that he kept on asking the same question: 'Who is stronger, the lion or the tiger?' He repeated this question with all kinds of animals, for instance: 'Who is stronger, the snake or the lizard?' The question is whether this is in fact obsessive behaviour or if his questions concealed a developmental task which the child was struggling with.

Peter is a boy and at primary school boys tend to establish a physical pecking order. They fight with each other to determine who is the strongest. As a boy, you have to know what you are up against, whom you challenge and whom you don't, which challenge you take up and which one you don't. When people see two boys together, they can in general say intuitively who would win in a fight. For this purpose, we refer to our TOM, we consult the information stored in our theory of mind. We are not or hardly aware of the criteria we use in this connection, e.g. a boy's height, whether he exudes assertiveness, etc. – we 'sense' it. Peter did not sense this and therefore used thinking in order to figure out who was the strongest. He used various animals for this who represent the various criteria, the lion's strength, the snake's speed, the elephant's size. This led him to a number of questions which all centred around the same subject: how can you see who is going to win, how do you know whether you can take someone on?

His mother did not know what lay at the basis of his questions and Peter was unable to formulate the right question. At his age, boys already know a great deal about fighting and strength and they also know how to figure out who is the strongest. Peter was not only a bit late, he would also need more time to master this; if indeed he would ever master it, as there were aspects to power and strength which he had not learnt, not figured out, did not know, because he did not sense them.

It is not for nothing that I have chosen the example of Peter who is trying to figure out how power relationships work in the playground. Autistic children are often boys, certainly in the case of Asperger's syndrome and PDD-NOS, and for boys physical behaviour is important. It is particularly important at primary school. Children with an autistic disorder often have awkward motor activity, in particular those with Asperger's syndrome. Their being different is often clear sooner to their peers than to diagnosticians. Unfortunately, the peer group tends to take it out on them, and children with Asperger's syndrome and PDD-NOS are therefore often bullied at primary school. This makes it all the more important for them to figure out the social rules although it is this that is so hard for them to do. Peter badly needed his mother and his teacher to find out how to get on with his peers.

As young children tend to do, youngsters and adults with an autistic disorder often take things too literally. In language development in young children, we see that as they acquire more knowledge of language they also become more aware of the multiple meaning of words. This development extends over more years for children with an autistic disorder. We find it endearing when young children interpret statements literally. In older children, we find it odd. Endearment gives way to surprise or even annoyance and we consider their reaction 'dumb'.

For people with an autistic disorder, but also for people with autistic features, it is difficult to distinguish between 'real' and 'acted'.

Derek was delighted with the birth of his daughter. He was mad about her and she loved playing with her dad. When she was two years old, she once said to him: 'I shoot you dead.' Derek was shocked: how could she say that? He was quite unable to place his daughter's remark in her age phase and interpreted her statement literally.

As a result of difficulty distinguishing between 'real' and 'pretend', fights often get out of hand. During the fight, the other child may accidentally hit a bit too hard. Children with an autistic disorder do not see this as a mistake but as a signal that 'inflicting pain' also forms part of the game. The difference between a mock fight and a real fight is not always clear to them. Not only do they interpret words literally but often situations too.

As a result of this difficulty in interpreting things, young people with Asperger's syndrome often find 'comprehension' at school very hard. In such exercises, the pupils have to 'interpret' the text, they have to rise above the literal meaning (Delfos 2002d). Vermeulen (2002b) stresses the importance for schools of paying attention to communication and ensuring that the linguistic message comes across as it is meant and that it is not taken literally.

When we examine the example of Peter, we see that the child needs more explanation to perform properly the activity of 'fighting in the school playground'.

> Michael was a mild-mannered boy of nine. He had never yet had a fight. He saw around him that boys fought and he understood that it was a way of being part of the group. He found this strange and unpleasant, but being an outsider and not belonging to the group was much more unpleasant. So Michael started a fight with one his friends. The others stood around them. After some time he pulled himself free and ran away. When he came home, he started sobbing desperately: 'How do you know that the fight is over? What do you have to do to get it over with?'

Asperger (1944) indicates that because of their awkwardness children with this disorder also more often hurt others unintentionally during rough play.

A strange world

Children with Asperger's syndrome and PDD-NOS appear so 'ordinary' that they are treated as if they were not different and are usually at a regular school. They are aware of being different and desperately try to be one of the group. They are often excluded by their peers. They try to find out why they are excluded and spend a lot of time trying to figure how social interaction works in order to master this skill. Their egocentric perspective gives them a completely different view of interaction to the way it works in reality.

> Five-year-old Joe had a wonderful time at play during therapy. His mother came to collect him and full of enthusiasm he ran out of the therapist's house onto the pavement. He nearly bumped into a child walking past with a passer-by. Nearly, because the passer-by prevented the collision with his child by stopping Joe with his hand. As a result, Joe ended up in the bushes. He was totally upset and shocked and cried terribly. When his mother asked why he was in such a panic, it became clear that Joe thought that the man had deliberately given him a push so that he had ended up in the bushes. His fundamentally egocentric perspective prevented him from perceiving the effects of his behaviour on others. The man's behaviour was experienced as the starting point, without any connection to his own behaviour. Joe therefore understood the man's behaviour as a deliberate act aimed at him, for which there was no cause in his own behaviour. It came completely out of the blue.

> Viewed from this perspective, it was very frightening indeed to believe that there were people walking about who just push you into the bushes for no reason at all.

The egocentric perspective may lead to strange thoughts, similar to psychotic thinking. In psychotic thinking, however, contact with reality is severely impaired; in other words, thinking is not consistent with reality in that something is sensorially perceived that is not there, for example, one hears a voice that is not there. In Joe's example, there is a problem in *interpreting* the situation whereas in psychotic thinking there is a fundamentally different *perception*. Autistic people make many errors of interpretation in social interaction; psychotic people suffer from disturbed perception. An autistic person's thoughts may seem psychotic but are in fact not so. The problem is their fundamentally egocentric perspective.

> Jack, aged 25, liked driving his car. He drove well and enjoyed it but was very annoyed by traffic lights. Whenever they turned red when he was approaching, he was convinced that the light was deliberately switched to red to annoy him. Even though he had passed his driving test with flying colours and was very intelligent, he had no notion that the traffic situation was regulated independently of road users. He just could not imagine that the system went beyond individual road users. To him it was unimaginable that the traffic situation was not specifically geared to him. Due to his egocentric perspective, he felt personally hurt went the light switched to red.

Children with an autistic disorder constantly find that other people have a completely different view of the world than they have. As adults, they become even more keenly aware of this, causing them a great deal of suffering.

> Martin, Peter's father, was a grown man of 40, with a family of three. His earlier relationship, from which two children had been born, had broken down. He had his own business and was fairly successful. He had always felt different; in his marriage he was cruelly confronted with his limitations. Not so much from inside; he was aware of his own

limitations only through the other. His wife had enormous difficulty with the fact that for Martin it was so hard to understand what others were feeling. Martin was aware that he was sometimes excluded from communication. He was often in a situation in which a number of people carrying on a conversation clearly understood each other and looked at each other in a way that made it obvious that everything was clear between them. He could see this going on, without understanding why this should be. 'That's the moment that I feel utter despair. The others understand each other and I remain an outsider.'

To autistic people, social interaction means thinking hard, being hardly able to communicate naturally, and not 'sensing' swiftly what others think and feel. It is therefore not surprising that this makes them angry or causes them to anxiously withdraw within themselves.

Sensing or learning the rules

The process of 'sensing' has always intrigued scientists, but the puzzle is far from being solved. 'Sensing' means that we know things without such knowledge being arrived at through a process of conscious thought. Often, we are unable to explain afterwards why we know. This knowledge is probably partly based on very early neural pathways in the brain. We see this happening in language. A child assimilates language actively though unconsciously. She does not consciously know the rules of grammar but still says 'I sleeped', perfectly conjugated; nobody has taught the child this. When she hears it should be 'I slept', the child realizes that the conjugation is an exception to the rule and from then on she will correctly conjugate the verb. Subsequently, the child even applies the rule to other verbs where this is appropriate.

All over the world, linguists are trying to reveal the underlying grammar of languages. For a linguist, this is more difficult than for a child who, when still a toddler, forms the underlying grammatical structure of a language by herself, and even of two or three languages if she is exposed to them. It is from this self-conceived grammatical structure that the child can produce 'I sleeped'. When the same child has grown up, she will rarely learn to speak a new language fluently unless she happens to have an exceptional talent for languages. During early youth, the brain is ready for establishing links between brain cells for language. Later on, these links can still be formed but only with great effort, and they will rarely be fluent. This 'fluency' of language can be compared with sensing.

In earliest youth, a number of basic principles are formed, meaning that particular areas of the brain are developed. If particular areas of the brain mature more slowly, such as important parts of the left hemisphere in autistic people, skills in which the left hemisphere plays a role will develop more slowly or defectively. As we have seen, the left hemisphere accommodates an important part of language function and the expression of thoughts and feelings into words. However, the corpus callosum and other parts of the brain also play a role. It may well be that the basis for sensing is formed during earliest youth. This applies to various subjects. One 'senses' that a particular sentence is not correct in English, one 'senses' that the differences in height between the steps of a flight of stairs are too small, and one 'senses' that someone in unhappy. It means that the knowledge becomes 'fluent' and 'natural' if it gets a chance to develop in the right period. If this is not the case, it will have to develop through thinking and training and will not easily become 'fluent'.

> Charles had a very limited repertoire of words to express feelings. If you asked him 'How are things?' he would say, for instance, 'I'm all right'. This statement could cover a whole range of feelings. Charles never expressed strong feelings, even if he was experiencing them. The phrase 'all right' could mean 'I feel OK but I'm not very happy', or 'I feel great and I've had a wonderful day'. His vocabulary was also limited for negative emotions. During therapy, attention was therefore given to finding appropriate words to accompany the emotions he experienced.

In general, knowing oneself and recognizing emotions are difficult for people with an autistic disorder. Remember the example of Martin in Chapter 6, who expressed this lack of self-knowledge so aptly when he told his therapist: 'I don't know myself. Whenever I try to get to know myself, I come up against a large grey area inside. That's why I'm here: to get to know that grey area.' With these words, Martin expresses the fact that there is an area of himself he does not know and at the same time he shows that he is aware of it. Francesca Happé (1997), in her analysis of autobiographical writings of autistic people, concludes that a degree of self-awareness is an indication for a more promising course, a more favourable prognosis, than if there is no (conscious) awareness at all. Years later, Martin said: 'I've learnt to know my own emotional world by exploring the emotions of others.' What Martin was referring to is in fact the process parents go through with their children. On the basis of her child's behaviour, even just a simple glance, the mother gives expression to the child's feeling: 'You're tired, aren't you, it's been such an exciting day. Come, let mummy tuck you in nicely and tell you a story.' In no time the mother gives voice to what the child feels, lays a link with the cause of the feeling and suggests a solution. Children with an autistic disorder have a strong need for such 'lessons' from their environment.

People with Asperger's syndrome are often told that they are too rational and do not show their feelings, as if it were a deliberate act by the autistic person *vis-à-vis* the other. Martin accurately expressed the lack of understanding of those around him when he said: 'They say that I'm rational, that I should express my feelings, but they want me to look there where I'm blind.'

The sphere of social interaction goes one step further than feeling what is wrong with oneself. Sensing social interaction is underdeveloped in autistic people. We already see this difference between men and women. With regards to the relation between 'fluent' knowledge and maturation, we expect women to have more 'fluent' knowledge than men because boys mature more slowly than girls. Autistic people do not only have a retarded but also a limited maturation of the central nervous system. Accordingly, when we speak of stimulating me–other differentiation, it will be a matter of learning rather than developing. The younger the child, the better the possibilities for stimulating the me–other differentiation by stimulating the development of the brain. The older the child, the more it will be a matter of existing potentialities in the brain.

Developmental tasks

At every age, there are new tasks for children, youngsters and also adults to master. For a child with an autistic disorder, tasks in the field of social contact are, time and again, at every stage of life, a heavy burden. The task itself is not heavy as such but becomes heavy because the people around the child are developing at a different pace and have expectations of the child that he is unable to meet. Although the number of skills increases with age, *social anxiety*, the uncertainty about functioning properly in the community, greatly increases in the meantime.

We can expect a child with an autistic disorder to master development tasks in the social sphere at a later stage and assimilate them at a slower pace. Moreover, the learning process will not always end in proper mastery of the skill. This means that we can help a child with autism at every level, even as a baby. However, the problem is that because of the above-mentioned 30 months' guideline, we cannot yet diagnose a baby as autistic. To most parents, however, it is clear before that time that there is something the matter with their child. Often their concerns fall on deaf ears in their environment and they try to reassure themselves by telling themselves that there is nothing seriously wrong and that things are bound to be all right in the end. If research will one day make it possible to diagnose autistic spectrum at an early age, in babies, it will also become clear what kind of help is most appropriate for the baby. Until that time, we shall have to derive it from our knowledge of developmental psychology.

Schopler and Mesibov (1988) outline how social interaction develops in children with an autistic disorder. However, they almost exclusively point to what the child is not occupied with and is not capable of, resulting in an enumeration instead of a clear view of autism.

In developmental psychology, we refer to developmental tasks which a child should fulfil. These tasks lie in various fields. In connection with autism, our focus is on the field of me–other differentiation and that of social and emotional development. The stages in the development of me–other differentiation are listed in Chapter 5 (page 130).

Flavell (1985) describes how, for a child, discovering himself as a physical object and as a human among humans are the first tasks he has to perform in me–other differentiation. We shall consider the tasks listed above one by one, starting with babies. As a baby, it will certainly not be clear whether the child has an autistic disorder, but it is meaningful to indicate the development task and see what a child needs. This is important because the same principle arises for the autistic child at a later stage, possibly at a stage in which autism has already been diagnosed so that appropriate help can be provided at that time. If such help is offered earlier, it may well have a preventive effect. As a general rule, we could say that we ought to determine a child's position with regard to a particular subject and then examine the situation in the way appropriate for that stage of development. This may mean that we deal with a toddler as if he were a baby for some subjects and as a toddler for others. It is not possible to indicate ideal ages because each child develops at his own rate. All we can do is describe a 'normal' development and use this as a reference to evaluate the child's mental age in relation to each subject. In order to obtain an indication of a child's mental age with regard to particular behaviour, any behaviour that is deviant, that causes surprise, can be taken as a point of departure. If we try to view this behaviour as normal and link it with an age, we shall discover the state of development with regard to that subject: *this behaviour is normal at age...* We will thus not only obtain the child's stage of mental development but employ the techniques to help that we usually offer a child of the corresponding calendar age with regard to that subject. This is borne out by the example of the 17-year-old boy who needs to play school. We should also bear in mind that each child has her own predisposition which sets her personal boundaries and should be respected.

Respect for a child also means respecting the boundaries imposed upon the child by his or her predisposition.

A pre-schooler with the developmental task of a baby

It is important to realize that a child with an autistic disorder may take years achieving the social development which is normally completed in the first year of life. In the social sphere, me–other differentiation is a baby's and pre-schooler's first developmental task on the basis of which the child can develop attachment (Bowlby 1984). A baby comes into the world helpless and must as it were immediately make efforts to ensure that he is fed, helped and protected. For this purpose, the baby's primary behavioural tool is *crying*, protesting. This sound signals to the baby's environment that there is something wrong and that the baby needs something. The baby has a *grasp reflex* enabling him to grab hold of something when he is at risk of falling. These two basic ways of making something clear persist for longer in autistic children. A child with an autistic disorder will for a much longer period use crying or screaming rather than words, or grab or cling to someone, in order to make it clear that there is something the matter.

In order to mobilize help, it is important for the baby to distinguish between 'me' and 'not me'. To a large extent, this is done through the senses. In Chapter 5, when we discussed the example of walking in the woods (p.136), I described the process a baby goes through in learning to distinguish between 'me' and 'not me' and between 'human' and 'non-human' or 'object'. This distinction is of considerable importance as it is a human which the baby has to mobilize for help and not the things around him. For this process, the baby needs his senses and we find that all the senses are pressed into service. The sense of vision will often rise to prominence in acquiring information only much later. In autistic children, we find that the senses that provide information about the environment are often employed with greater intensity. It is as if in this regard there is already compensation in acquiring as much information as possible so that the weakly developed me–other differentiation can still be achieved.

A baby links images, smells and sounds together into a pattern which he recognizes as forming part of the satisfaction of his needs. These patterns become increasingly clear and familiar to the baby: people, mother and father. The baby perceives that they are separate from himself and becomes aware that he must keep them close at hand to secure their help when needed. To this end, the baby develops behaviour which he copies from the persons he wishes to keep near: *smiling, holding* and, after some time, *babbling.* The baby learns to use smiles to keep adults near and associates this with satisfaction of his needs. The satisfaction of needs gives the baby a pleasant sensation and this pleasant sensation is gradually associated with the person satisfying his needs. As a result, his smile eventually becomes a genuine expression of pleasure and contentment and not just a movement of the mouth copied from adults. Close observation of the baby reveals the transition from copied grimacing to copied smiling to thinking smiles and eventually from directed smiles to spontaneous smiling.

Even this basic communication is impaired in a child with an autistic disorder. Satisfaction of needs seems to be detached from the person ensuring it. Because of her limited me–other differentiation, the child is hardly aware of the fact that the other person is detached from herself and of the effect which her behaviour has on the other person. It impedes reciprocity of contact and this develops more slowly than in other children. Kees Momma (1996) clearly describes this in his autobiography.

> When, around the age of two, I had discovered my mother, I felt safe and secure with her. But to her I was a mystery: a child which reacted quite differently or not at all to every approach.

By establishing a mutual relationship, a child learns to take account of the other. Learning to take account of someone else happens primarily to keep the other 'on friendly terms' as the person who satisfies the child's needs. This linkage of *egocentric behaviour* (I want that) with – healthy – *egoistic-manipulative behaviour* (I do this in order to get what I want) is soon learnt by the baby. It leads to awareness of the extent to which and the way in which another person plays a part in fulfilling his own wishes. In a child with an autistic disorder, this awareness does not develop properly. As a result, carers are often for a long time felt to be more interchangeable to the child. It therefore takes much longer for autistic children to establish a mutual relationship than for non-autistic children. In profoundly autistic children, this sometimes never develops properly at all. Sigman and her colleagues (1984, 1986) discovered that children with an autistic disorder do in fact develop attachment with the mother but express it in a completely different way. One of the most striking findings was that they sought little *shared attention*; for instance, they rarely showed toys to their mother and rarely smiled at her. Even though they did show a reaction when the mother left (the 'distress situation' in the study) and were content when she returned, they did not take any initiative to establish contact, to share attention. This is in fact the first stage of the development of attachment, *response to distress* – 'attachment' in the purest sense of the term (Bowlby 1984) – and the next stage, *forming a relationship*, is still underdeveloped.

In its pure form, attachment is forming a scheme of *what people do when you are in distress*. On the basis of research into attachment, Ainsworth and colleagues (1978) arrived at four different types of attachment: *secure attachment* and three forms of *insecure attachment*. These four forms can be converted to the associated scheme with regard to aid in distress. The different types of attachment and the associated styles of upbringing by parents (Ainsworth) and the schemes which children form (Delfos) have been brought together in Table 7.1. The different types of attachment exist in practice but also mixed forms.

Table 7.1 Attachment and its translation into schemes

Style of upbringing (Ainsworth)	Type of attachment (Ainsworth)	Scheme formed by the child (Delfos)
Consistently responsive: Always responding to the child's needs and distress	Secure	In principle you can count on people when you are in distress
Consistently unresponsive: Not responding to the child's needs, neglect	Insecure: anxious-avoidant	You cannot count on people when you are in distress. You must involve as many people as possible but not establish profound contact with a person because that is not effective, that person may leave you and then you have nothing
Responsive to own wish: Responding to the child according to one's own needs, needing the child for oneself	Insecure: anxious-resistant	You cannot count on people when you are in distress, on the contrary, then they even expect something from you
Inconsistently responsive: Sometimes responding and sometimes not responding to the child's needs. Frequent in psychiatric problems e.g. parents with psychotic episodes	Insecure: disorganized	There is no way of predicting people's behaviour when you are in distress; sometimes they help you, then they turn their back on you, then again they expect something from you

Table 7.1 makes it clear that attachment is strongly connected with orientation towards human beings, something which may evolve only much later in children with autism. This means that forming attachment may develop later and more slowly in children with autism.

The absence or deficiency of a mutual relationship also means that the child does not properly make the link between her own pleasant behaviour and behaviour which she wishes to bring about in the other. The child does not experience herself in relation to the other and consequently does not make a link between herself, her own need, the other's behaviour and the other as a person. This means that the child does not learn properly that she must display behaviour that the other finds pleasant in order to get a response from the other. She lags behind in developing smiling and laughing. Nor does she learn what behaviour the other likes. In an infantile way, a child with an autistic disorder remains somewhat linearly focused on satisfaction of her needs without placing this in the context of the person providing it.

The first way to ensure that needs are satisfied is to cry and scream. As, certainly in young children, needs have to be satisfied to prevent them from falling ill or even dying, a child with an autistic disorder will run the risk of making a link between negative behaviour and satisfaction of needs: crying, screaming, protesting. This is the behaviour we observe in a child with an autistic disorder who, even though he has moved beyond the baby stage, still goes on whining and nagging to gets his way. The idea of trying to get what you want in a more subtle manner, by giving the other what she wants, is inadequately developed in these children. In Chapter 10 we shall discuss the formation of behaviour and ways of channelling undesired behaviour in the right direction.

In order to bring about the connection child–satisfaction of needs–pleasant feeling–carer, which may engender reciprocity and contact, it is important that this connection be clearly established. This is done by the carer responding to the child's need, ensuring that the child sees the carer during satisfaction of the need, smiling and verbalizing the contact – in fact doing what people always do in contact with a baby. For autistic children, this will have to be maintained for longer to give them a chance to make the satisfaction-of-need–caring link and develop attachment. At a later stage, when the child is a pre-schooler or toddler, we are no longer inclined to do this although the child with an autistic disorder still needs it.

When we seek eye contact with babies, however, we should be aware that this is very tiring and exciting for them, increasing their heart rate. It is therefore necessary to look away briefly so that the baby can calm down (Field 1981). A parent who does not respect this makes the baby restless, overexcited. The question is whether eye contact as a sensory perception is even more intense for a baby with an autistic disorder than for a non-autistic baby. We will discuss the meaning and intensity of eye contact for autistic people in Chapter 8. In principle, we consider it important to follow the child, offering brief and frequent eye contact, for instance when eating, without forcing it on the child. Because of the intensity of eye contact, it may perhaps be advisable to involve other senses too, such as touch and voice. One possibility is to establish a link between receiving food and touch.

Forming attachment is a reciprocal process. For parents of autistic children, it is often difficult to continue to muster attachment behaviour towards their child because, from the baby stage, they have often felt rejected and have the impression that they cannot establish good contact with their child. Parents with an intellectually disabled child therefore often have more difficulty attaching to the child (Riksen-Walraven 1994). Parents of a child with a serious physical or intellectual disability have to go through a mourning process in response to the problem. The future they envisaged for their child requires adjustment. Forging attachment is hampered by the process of mourning. Parents of an autistic child may well feel constantly rejected because the child hardly ever seeks (eye) contact, if at all. In this case, the attachment process is impeded by feelings of hurt, uncertainty and anxiety in the parents.

Most adults find it strange to behave towards their child in a way that does not fit in with the child's calendar age. It seems strange to speak in a sing-song voice to a child of primary school age, or to coo, whisper in his ears or kiss him in the neck. Autistic children often love silly sounds, romping about and music. Most adults find it easy to display attachment behaviour with babies and thus link up with the child, although they do so more exuberantly when there is no one else around to see or hear them. It is all the more difficult to link up with a five- or eight-year-old child who in fact still needs such attachment behaviour or is only just ready for it. Adults often fail to see that the autistic child actually needs this. People who have no understanding of what autism is all about soon find the child childish and reject and try to cure her of such behaviour. In Chapter 10, when discussing resistance to change, we shall examine the problems of learning and unlearning behaviour and consider why this has less chance of success in autistic children.

Children with an autistic disorder often have to be stimulated towards interaction in a way that is different from what we are used to and have come to expect. Dawson and Lewey (1989) discovered that they can more readily be stimulated into interaction when their behaviour is imitated. Their interest is kindled by seeing their own behaviour in others.

As we have tried to illustrate through the example of Peter and his questions about strength and speed, a child with an autistic disorder needs examples in the field of social contact for longer and in greater numbers in order to attain a particular level in the social sphere which will, nevertheless, be lower than that of his peers. Whether with regard to coping with change or social contact, a child with an autistic disorder has a *different developmental pace* compared with other children. When a child is ready for a particular developmental subject, she will develop it in interaction with the environment. However, the subjects prevailing in the environment at that time will be adequate for the autistic child's *calendar age* but not for her *mental age*. This slower pace problem entails not only delayed development in particular areas but also steady deviation from the usual development. When a child of about five becomes aware of the existence of people around him, he will not be able to process this insight at the level of his mental age because a five-year-old is in fact expected to be making friends. Forging friendships, which is consistent with the calendar age of five, will then take a form that appears strange to the environment; calendar age and mental age will get mixed up and may lead to strongly deviant behaviour.

A baby establishes contact on the basis of an incipient insight into itself in relation to others. For a baby with an autistic disorder this will therefore be more difficult to achieve. It means that the parent will have to invest more and for longer in order to bring it about. It is important to stimulate the establishment of contact but it is also important to respect the individuality of the child's development and not to force anything through for which the child is not ready. As a general rule, one could say that the things one wishes to teach to the child should be done *frequently* rather than *protractedly*. It is inadvisable to try to achieve an objective in a few attempts. Children, especially autistic children, feel uncomfortable if they are overburdened. Children also dislike failing. It often leads to stagnation of the learning process and to outbursts of bad temper. By repeatedly making brief attempts, the child will not so easily feel overburdened and will remain interested. Learning to make contact with a baby with an autistic disorder is probably not fundamentally different from making contact with a non-autistic baby. Rather, it is a more prolonged process which can often only be embarked upon later and one in which the child does not attain the level normally expected in children without an autistic disorder.

Strange and familiar

The next important developmental task in the sphere of social interaction is to distinguish between familiar and strange. Most babies perceive, around the age of eight months, who are the familiar figures in their environment who look after them. They form an attachment to these people and then become reserved towards others. *Fear of strangers* develops and the child becomes *shy of other people*. A child with an autistic disorder will have more difficulty distinguishing between 'familiar' and 'strange'. For a fairly long time, the child will often remain indifferent towards the person looking after him. The example of Kees Momma who discovered his mother at around the age of two shows that this is not so much a matter of indifference as of delayed learning. Once an autistic child makes this distinction, and this will in principle be much later than at eight months, the phase of undifferentiated shyness *vis-à-vis* unknown and less known people which a baby enters at eight months, will probably last longer.

A child who begins distinguishing between familiar and strange clings to the normal carers and is inimical towards others. When a child is eight months to one and a half years old, people do not experience this as a major problem and in fact find it quite touching that the child is so strongly focused on familiar people. To the parents it is even a sign that they are important to their child, and as a result they feel closer to him. This reinforces the parents' attachment *vis-à-vis* the child. It also means that if the child does not go through this stage at that age, this makes it easier for the parents to deal with the child – the child is not choosy about who looks after him – but they may possibly feel less special, less important, causing their attachment to the child to be more difficult. If the child is shy of other people at the age of two, three or older, this is not recognized as such by most people. The child keeps others at a distance, probably no longer cries like a baby, but expresses his fear of strangers by being blatantly unfriendly. Others often view him as rude and impolite rather than shy of strangers and anxious. The result may be that parents are then regarded as poor educators who have not taught their child the elementary rules of propriety.

As in the previous developmental task, the child will have to be taught that unknown does not necessarily mean unsafe and that these unknown people can, and even should, also be approached in a friendly manner. The reassurance given to a baby, allowing her to find a safe haven with mother and from that position explore the world, should also be offered to these children.

Compared with the baby, the parents of a child with an autistic disorder such as Asperger's syndrome and PDD-NOS have the advantage that the child develops linguistically more or less normally. Consequently, they can use language to explain things. In doing so, however, they need to bear in mind that the child needs more examples in order to arrive at an abstraction because he lacks an inner structure, a sufficiently differentiated socioscheme, to which the statements can be related. The abstractions are needed as a frame of reference within which to evaluate experiences, for otherwise they remain at the level of performing a 'trick', as we shall see in Chapter 8 when dicussing social skills.

Let us recall the example from Chapter 2 (p.32) about hitting, kicking and pinching. A child with an autistic disorder needs more and regular explanations, with more examples. An added problem is that the expectations of the people around the child are different. Because of the child's age, they expect that she can and will sense things which she is certainly not yet ready to do. People can be completely taken aback by the child's behaviour. An autistic child may suddenly address complete strangers and animatedly talk about her experiences. It is important to let the child know that adults do not understand, do not expect her behaviour and, therefore, have certain expectations *vis-à-vis* the child which she cannot meet. This explanation may ensure that the child is less concerned about other people's expectations.

Michael was four and a half when the Dutch feast of St Nicholas was celebrated in his grandpa's company. He showed no fear of Black Peter, St Nicholas's black servant, who therefore began to chat with Michael. He talked with him about the presents and about school. Michael was friendly and opened up to him. Black Peter, who was used to dealing with children who were afraid of him, kneeled down next to Michael and talked about the presents. Then he put his arm around Michael to have their picture taken together. Michael could not bear being touched, stiffened like a board and screamed out loud the moment Black Peter put him arm around him. His mother rushed towards him, explaining what was happening, telling Michael that Black Peter liked him and did not know that he did not like being touched. If Black Peter had known this, he would certainly not have touched him.

Michael took good notice of this explanation, as became clear a few months later. One day, Michael and his mother met the neighbour's wife on their way home. They had never had any contact with her but now she walked along with them, talking and chatting, and then she unsuspectingly took Michael by the hand. To his mother's surprise, Michael let her and this time did not react. After the neighbour had gone in, Michael said: 'Isn't it strange that she just grabbed my hand, I think she doesn't know that she can't do that.' And he was right. The little boy who used to get a serious panic attack when touched had learnt to show an adequate response. Even though he found it very unpleasant to be taken by the hand, he assumed that the neighbour was unaware of this and this was enough to control his panic.

Just as with eye contact, autistic children are often sensitive to other stimuli, such as touch and sound. When touched, some children with an autistic disorder may turn as stiff as a board, a physical attempt to ward off the other person. We can see the beginning of this in babies. Charles (in Chapter 6), for instance, did this even before he contracted meningitis. Children with an autistic disorder can vary considerably in the extent to which they tolerate being touched. For instance, they may not like holding hands during a walk but may enjoy romping about. They often find a slight touch unpleasant and rougher ones pleasant (Wing 2001). As babies, they may like being swaddled but get into a complete panic when being held tightly.

This, too, should be dealt with carefully and regularly. It seems that massage may be helpful for children with a sensitive skin. Research by Field (1995, 1996) has shown that massaging children has a calming effect, stimulates the immune system, diminishes pain and encourages growth. Getting used to sounds helps to reduce hypersensitivity to auditory stimuli (e.g. Grandin 1995b).

Mothers and fathers repeatedly explain things to their baby and pre-school child and verbalize things, and this remains necessary in the social sphere for toddlers and primary school children with Asperger's syndrome and PDD-NOS.

When giving an explanation, one should realize that the child does not always understand things the way they are meant. While this applies to all communication, what we know intuitively about ages and understanding of language often does not apply to a child with an autistic disorder. Such a child will continue to take language literally for much longer. The funny language mistakes typical of three- to four-year-olds often persist for much longer in children with autism. Often they even produce language constructions on the basis of their understanding. Mistakes that produce *neologisms* are quite frequent in children between the ages of three and four. If the child in the following example had been ten instead of three and a half, it would have been not merely endearing but rather odd or, at best, evidence of a creative mind.

> Myra, aged three and a half, was very fond of Anna, who led her play group, and just couldn't wait to see her again after the holidays. She asked her mother: 'How many nights do I have to sleep backwards to see Anna again?'

Adults generally find it difficult to communicate with children (Delfos 2000), and when a child does not respond in a way that is adequate for his age, most adults have no idea how to deal with him. In the next chapter we shall examine communication and the conditions for communication more closely.

Strangers: Good and bad

Once the child has learnt that there is 'strange' and 'familiar' and that strangers should also be approached in a friendly manner and may be safe, he also has to learn that this does not apply to everyone. In this respect, the autistic child lags behind considerably compared with other children. Wing (2001) points out that when an autistic child learns that he should be friendly to strangers, he may apply this to all strangers. As a result, the child will show excessively friendly behaviour towards total strangers in the street. People do not always appreciate this and sometimes it is inadvisable to be too open towards strangers anyway. The child will then have to be taught that he cannot behave in such a friendly manner towards *all* strangers. Children with an autistic disorder can learn this, without reverting to unfriendly behaviour towards every stranger (Wing 2001). However, the learning process takes time.

A child without an autistic disorder has a whole range of information about how she stands in relation to others. For instance, she has already stored how crying and smiling elicit a particular response in the parents. In children with an autistic disorder, it is possible that this has passed them by. Already at quite a young age, children have a clear insight into causal links (Aguiar and Bailargeon 1999; Delfos 2000). While playing at the crèche, at neighbours', and relatives' houses, the child will have gained rich experience about how people may behave. This also includes less positive and frankly negative experiences, and the child has learnt to connect this with her own behaviour and with characteristics of the people around it. The child is building up a theory of mind, TOM, as part of her socioscheme.

In an autistic child, the construction of a TOM is much more cumbersome. Me–other differentiation is less developed and the child perceives himself as a separate entity rather than in relation to others. Others are components in his life rather than separate beings with their own thoughts and feelings. A child with an autistic disorder will therefore need more help and input from the outside about how a theory of mind can be built up. Since this TOM is more based on external opinion than on internal feelings and perceptions, it will be less sophisticated. Exceptions confirm the rule, but to an autistic child the exception obliterates the rule, removing the solid ground from which one understands how things work. Nevertheless, learning how things work in the world seems to be the only way. Eventually the baby and the pre-schooler will also learn this, primarily through external information and subsequently by connecting their own experience to that information. Here, again, the principle is: better to do it often and briefly than to give a long explanation a couple of times.

On the basis of the theory of mind, the child will learn the features of someone who can be trusted and those of someone who cannot. Given the fact that adults also have problems with this and can quite often be surprised by the behaviour of those closest to them, it is clear that this is a particularly difficult task to master for an autistic child. Her primary response will be black and white. Accordingly, her attitude will initially be indifferent and then negative *vis-à-vis* anyone who is not her direct carer. When she learns that strangers may also be trusted and have to be approached in a friendly manner, the child will then be positive towards all strangers. Reserve and control, a wait-and-see attitude, is something an autistic child has to learn after she has learnt friendly behaviour towards strangers. As this is a development which the child goes through in an ever-deepening awareness of how things work in the world, she will in principle not revert to her earlier behaviour of assuming a negative attitude towards strangers but begin to combine friendliness with reserve.

It is also possible that the child is not rude and unfriendly but generally withdrawn and anxious. This is often the case with girls. Here, too, it is important to adopt an approach of helping the child develop an adequate TOM. When a child is withdrawn, the problem is that she does not confront the environment very much, making it less obvious that she is failing to interpret social interaction properly. In this case, it is of particular importance to pay attention to the way in which the child perceives the world around her and to help her in further developing her TOM.

What is important when a child is forming an adequate TOM is to inculcate that there are always exceptions, that social life cannot be categorized into black and white and also that it is not possible to know and understand everything. As the rich nuances in social intercourse among people cannot be distilled into simple abstractions, evaluating social interaction will always remain a formidable task for people with an autistic disorder. For an autistic child, it is therefore important that he knows that he can rely on the judgment of people already familiar to him. *Ego help*, in the form of people whose opinion is reliable, may play an important supporting role in the development of autistic people. This part is primarily played by the parents but it is important that the child learns to extend this to several trusted adults, making him less dependent on the parents' presence.

Social intercourse

While we indicated above how important it is to link up with the baby's needs, it is of equal importance to teach the child that her needs cannot and will not always be satisfied. As she grows up, the child becomes aware that her needs cannot always be satisfied. This leads to *frustration*. The child responds to this frustration with anxiety, distress or anger, partly depending on the child's nature. Being able to cope with frustration, *frustration tolerance*, and to *delay satisfaction* are important instruments in living together with other people. The satisfaction of a need is often crossed by the other person. There appears to be a connection between postponement of satisfaction of needs and later school performance and social success. Children who learn at a young age to postpone satisfying their needs have a better chance of sound development. For children with an autistic disorder, postponement of needs is a difficult task as the child has difficulty thinking in terms of time and place. Their defective social insight also makes it difficult to defer satisfaction of a need in the expectation that it is bound to be satisfied later on. It is important to teach this to the child. In doing so, however, one has to bear in mind that postponing satisfaction of needs can be learnt only if it is focused on subjects that are not of major importance and the child has developed sufficient confidence in the people around him (Gesell and Ilg 1949). In autistic children, this will usually be somewhat later, possibly two to three years later. For example, it is not advisable to teach deferment of satisfying the craving for food in babies who are breast- or bottle-fed.

Frustration tolerance is of great importance in social intercourse. Learning social interaction is the next development task. It requires *social skills*. It encompasses compliance with rules of politeness but also, and in particular, taking account of others. This task is again more complex than the previous one, me–other differentiation and distinguishing people from objects and from one another. Each subsequent task is built upon the previous one. If a previous task is not adequately mastered, we know that little can be expected from the next one.

Focal points

- The self-orientation of autistic people is connected with limited me–other differentiation.

- A child with an autistic disorder is strongly focused on the mother; in a symbiotic relationship, the mother clings to the child.

- A child with an autistic disorder may take years to attain the social development which is normally rounded off in the first year of life.

- The older the children, the greater the differences between them.

- The development of autistic children is not only delayed, it also evolves more slowly.

- As mental age and calendar age become entangled, development is not only delayed but also deviant.

- Children with an autistic disorder need more examples of a particular subject in order to attain the proper abstraction with regard to it.

- Children with an autistic disorder have a fundamentally egocentric perspective.

- Children with an autistic disorder have to work things out instead of sensing them.

- In the emotional sphere, children from birth have to achieve a number of development tasks: distinguishing me/not me, human/object, strange/familiar, attachment, strangers good and bad, and social interaction.

- Building up frustration tolerance is important if one is to be able to live with other people.

Focal points regarding attitude

- Again: respect for a child also means respect for the limits imposed on the child by his or her predisposition.

- Link up with the child's mental age.

- Better to explain something often and briefly and allow the child to experience things, rather than once and at length.

Summary

Defective me–other differentiation is the point of departure for understanding a disorder within the autistic spectrum. Defective me–other differentiation is fundamentally different from a symbiotic relationship between mother and child. In the former case, the child needs the mother when he has a problem and is at the same time able to function quite independently from her. In a symbiotic relationship, the mother needs the child and the child does not dare to function separately from the mother.

As an autistic child's development is not only later but also slower, these children will, at a later stage than their peers, require more and more frequent explanations about social interaction. Due to their egocentric perspective, they have quite a different outlook on social interaction than others.

In the emotional sphere, children have to achieve a number of development tasks from birth: distinguishing me/not me, human/object, strange/familiar, attachment, 'good' and 'bad' strangers, and social interaction. Children with an autistic disorder take significantly longer mastering these tasks, years instead of months. Particularly in the case of children of normal intelligence – which is the case with children with Asperger's syndrome and PDD-NOS – it is hard to realize that they may take years achieving the social development of the first year of life.

8

Social skills

The greatest problem concerning a child with an autistic disorder is the way in which he or she interacts with others. Some autistic children are extremely withdrawn and appear to live completely in a world of their own, while others are socially awkward and always seem to make the wrong remark at the wrong moment or feel that they are always treated unfairly in contact with people, causing them to have outbursts of bad temper. The first form (*withdrawn*) occurs frequently in Kanner's autism, the second (*socially awkward*) is frequent in Asperger's syndrome and the third (*angry outbursts*) occurs more often in PDD-NOS. However, all three occur throughout the autistic spectrum because, as we have already pointed out, the line of demarcation is not always easy to draw.

Children with an autistic disorder do not adequately master *social skills*. The fact is that these are skills that cannot simply be taught. Social skill ought to evolve from *social insight*, which is lacking in autistic children to varying degrees. Because of hampered me–other differentiation, these children have problems imagining what goes on in other people's minds and because of this they are unable properly to acquire social insight.

Social skills or 'tricks'

It is important to teach social skills to children with an autistic disorder. However, if such skills are not based on social insight, they are mere 'tricks'. The child knows the skill and can use it but lacks the ability to judge when it ought to be applied.

> The mother of eight-year-old Steve was constantly faced with the fact that the people around her just did not understand why she was worried about Steve. Consequently, she felt she was all alone. At first, Steve gave the impression of being a friendly, clever boy. But he was very lonely, had no friends, no playmates. His mother was eager to enable

him to gain experience in social contact, but every attempt ended in failure. Eventually she enrolled Steve in a club for handicrafts. She warned the instructor that Steve was socially a bit awkward and that things might sometimes be difficult. After the first time, the instructor remarked that she had no idea what the mother had meant. Everything had gone smoothly. Steve was friendly, cheerful and made jokes. But after the second time, things became clear. Steve did exactly as he had done the first time, saying the same things and making the same jokes. Only now it was no longer applicable and his jokes were misplaced.

To children with an autistic disorder, social behaviour is never something obvious. In particular, people with Asperger's syndrome feel the need to be part of the group but just cannot figure out how they should behave in social contact. They feel like a blind-folded child playing 'pin the tail on the donkey' who pins the tail on the belly instead of in the right place.

Out of a desire to be part of it and make friends, an autistic person tries to behave in a way that he or she thinks is a proper response to other children and is expected by them. *Adjusting to the situation* is usually outside the range of possibilities as this implies being able to imagine what goes on in the other children's minds and from that position understand what they wish the autistic child to do. Instead, autistic people are always trying hard, without being rewarded for their efforts with successful social contact.

When the therapist asked Jerome, in his early thirties, whether he was trying very hard and had always done so, he burst into tears, sobbing uncontrollably. After some time, he explained that he had always tried so hard but in spite of this he had always been bullied and had never been part of the group.

When reading the first version of this book, Martin was deeply touched by Jerome's remark. Martin had also tried the best he could, without much success. He saw the same thing in his seven-year-old son Peter.

For non-autistic children, the information which carers impart concerning social interaction in general links up with the insight they have already developed themselves. This insight is not based only on what the child experiences in direct contact. The child also registers the things around him or her and learns about relationships which people have with one another.

If we want children to acquire good social skills, we should bear in mind that they do not only learn the words we teach them but also our screaming and swearing when we lose our temper; not only the caress they receive but also the smack they see someone give and receive. Parents are always taken aback when the child's first words include the bad ones that were not meant for his ears. The child also learns from the quarrels he witnesses between his parents. We are often unaware of this, in particular when children cannot speak properly yet, but when we see their anguished expression we realize that they are perfectly aware when something is seriously wrong. When Birger Sellin (1995) could communicate through a computer, he indicated that in all those years when people were convinced that he was intellectually disabled he was startled by all kinds of things people said, convinced that he could not hear or understand them.

It is therefore advisable to keep babies and pre-schoolers away from conflicts between other people. This will not always be possible; after all, parents are only human. When children start applying that anger, it is useful to teach them not only that they should not do so but also that the parents themselves were wrong doing it. In this way, the child learns that this is not a desirable way of behaving in contact with others but that one does not always have enough peace and self-control to behave in an ideal manner. Parents are human beings and cannot always be 'super parents'. In general, children eventually understand that parents are susceptible to various moods and may have all kinds of worries, sometimes causing them to display undesirable and unintended behaviour. Children with an autistic disorder, however, do not adequately perceive the nuance between 'chosen' and 'uncontrolled' behaviour in others. The different forms of conduct are placed at the same level and serve as a possible guideline for the child's own behaviour. For autistic children, it is therefore important to receive an explanation for the behaviour of the parents and other people around them. This places a heavy burden on the parents because it means that they have to face their own negative behaviour. They have to acknowledge that they should not have displayed such behaviour and subsequently have the self-control and maturity to recognize the mistake and explain it to the child. These are psychological processes that demand the utmost from people. Normally parents can be confident that children will sense these things, that they do not always have to be perfect parents. Obviously, it is not always possible for parents to give their autistic child an insight in their own functioning. The appeal to engage in self-examination is exhausting and infringes upon a profound sense of privacy.

Awareness of the child's thinking and the limitations of his insight into social situations will help parents to provide him with the necessary information. If the parents do not understand the child, they will have more difficulty discussing their own behaviour. They are also more likely to be provoked into negative conduct because they perceive the child's behaviour as intentionally aimed against themselves rather than as socially impaired behaviour. However, even if the parents do have this insight and are fully prepared to do what is best for the child, they easily get 'burnt out' by the attention the child demands from them. It seems as if autistic children invade their carers' brains. Parents of an autistic child never have a 'day off' in their brain. Not only does the child make enormous demands on their attention but, as a result of his behaviour, his lack of 'sensing', he also imposes upon the parents feelings and thoughts they would prefer not to have. As a child with autism cannot always sense or understand what is going on in the parent, the parent is sometimes forced to rise above his or her own feeling of powerlessness in order to help the child. For instance, when a parent comes home from work in a bad mood, is dejected or upset and as a result snarls at the child, the child with an autistic disorder will often be quite unable to understand why. While a non-autistic child senses that it had better keep away from the parent for a bit until the mood blows over, an autistic child will demand the parent's attention and need an explanation. The parent is forced to rise above his or her negative feeling and open up to the child. This is exactly the situation that leads to burn-out. This term *burn-out* has been around for a very long time to describe the behaviour of parents with autistic children. The total physical and especially psychological availability that an autistic child can demand can lead to burn-out.

Children learn about how contact works by having contact with others, but also the contact between people around them shows them how contact works, long before they are able to express this in language. This can be observed very early on in children without a contact disorder.

Max was a year and four months old when he went on a visit to the woman next door. Her son was there with his wife and their three-month-old baby. Max was crazy about the baby. He did not know the baby's parents so it was exciting and fun at the same time. Two weeks later, he again went to visit. The telephone rang. The woman answered the phone. 'Daddy', Max said happily. His mother explained that it was often his daddy who was on the phone and that this was why Max thought it was his daddy. Thereupon the woman interrupted her telephone conversation and said to Max: 'No, it's not Daddy, it's Alice, who you saw some time ago when she was visiting here', and she resumed her conversation. Max pottered about a bit and looked at the woman saying emphatically: 'Baba'. His language was too limited to explain: 'I know who you have on the phone, it's Alice, the mother of the baby who was visiting here the other day.' Max mastered only a few words but knew perfectly well how to choose the one word to make himself clear. This shows the beginnings of Max's capacity to understand what goes on in another person's mind.

A child with an autistic disorder is strongly self-oriented and, as we saw in the previous chapter, misses important information in the earliest developmental stage. She has been unable naturally to build up a theory of mind and her *socioscheme* is largely based on her own perceptions and experiences and is very limited as a result. The child's social knowledge is restricted and bears little or no relation to an underlying social insight. Consequently, the child lacks a socially adequate inner structure on the basis of which she could interpret and evaluate social behaviour. She needs thought to legitimize social behaviour.

Michael went to primary school. After a year, he was due to move on to another school. In the meantime, it had become clear that he faced a number of problems at school, but his teacher was not attuned to his behaviour. She did not manage to make him do things and join in with the others. She wanted to avoid conflict and Michael remained friendly but imperturbable in the face of every task. The teacher's solution was to leave him to his own devices and let him get on with it, allowing him to play with Lego and giving up her attempts to get him involved with the class. Michael's mother was eager that at the new school he should be involved. She explained to the new teacher that Michael was actually very amenable provided that it was explained to him what something was for. If he did not get an explanation, he would refuse. The teacher applied this knowledge and after some time she told the mother that it was a bit surprising to have such a child in the class but that he was indeed quite amenable and he did things quicker and better than the others once he had been given an explanation. She gave the example of putting the chairs on the table. Up to then, the teacher had always told the children at the end of the day: 'Put your chair on the table.' But Michael had refused to do so. Then she had remembered the mother's remark and explained to Michael that the chairs had to be put on the table so that the cleaners could clean under the tables and the floor would again be nice and clean for the following day. As a result of this explanation, Michael did what he was asked and even encouraged the other children, explaining why they should do so too. Suddenly Michael had changed from an obstinate boy to an amenable child who had a positive influence on the others in the class.

Children with an autistic disorder do not easily follow ordinary practices or authority. This is connected with their defective me–other differentiation, making them rather unsusceptible to appreciation or disapproval by others. Resistance to complying with authority or common practices also occurs in gifted children who like analysing what things are for and are not prepared to just blindly accept things.

Eye contact

Eye contact is important for social contact. To an autistic child, this is certainly not easy. Eye contact is a non-verbal exchange of feelings and thoughts. Through eye contact, mutual contact is established. To a large extent, reading of non-verbal communication takes place through 'reading' of the eyes. It is not for nothing that poets have long referred to the eyes as the 'mirror of the soul'. In Chapter 3 I described how this reading works in practice with the right and left eyes. Making eye contact also means more information. Like so much information, this information can come across with great intensity in autistic people. Birger Sellin (1995) writes:

> ...a loving glance has a tremendous impact without words [...] once a woman looked at me lovingly, that was so beautiful, I often think back on it with delight and will never forget it, but many glances are so difficult to bear and lead to unforgettable grief.

John struggled with the intensity of eye contact. He wanted to learn to make 'ordinary' eye contact, not so intense. He felt that eye contact often went together with an infatuated feeling, as if you wanted to do all sorts of things with the other person.

These statements on the intensity of eye contact reminds us of research carried out by Field (1981) to which we referred in Chapter 7, which shows that for babies eye contact is very exciting and causes an increase in heart beat.

Research by Baron-Cohen, Wheelwright and Jolliffe (1997) shows that people with an autistic disorder have considerably more difficulty reading facial expressions and in particular find it very hard to 'read' the eyes but also to send messages with their eyes. Tantam (1997) even argues that Asperger's syndrome is caused by an innate lack of *gaze reflex* for social situations, resulting in impaired *joint attention*. We can place Tantam's ideas in the framework of the development of me–other differentiation and of the distinction between 'human' and 'object'. We recall what was mentioned in Chapter 5, namely that baby boys look longer at objects than at people, compared with baby girls. At the level of normal development, we thus already see a difference in response to social stimuli between boys and girls. Here we are once again reminded of Hans Asperger's (1944) statement that autistic structure can be viewed as an extremely male brain structure.

Eye contact has a set of social codes. Looking each other in the eye is – often wrongly – interpreted as a sign of sincerity. On the other hand, looking at someone for too long is impolite. In many cultures, and certainly in Arabic cultures such as that of the Moroccans, it is a sign of a lack of respect if a child looks into an adult's eyes during conversation. In this situation, eye contact is not appreciated. In contrast, eye contact in Western cultures is appreciated and a lack of it is often construed as a sign of anxiety, evasion or lack of interest. Making or not making eye contact is therefore not without ambiguity.

This cultural difference may well be connected with the value assigned to respect and honesty. Respect is highly valued in non-Western cultures. In upbringing, for instance, authority is based on the child's respect for the parents. Reading emotions in the eyes would perhaps affect respect. In most non-Western cultures, *automatic respect* plays an important part. In Western cultures, this automatic respect has largely been lost and respect is now something that has to be earned. This makes it less necessary to lower the eyes. Looking the other in the eyes is in fact conducive to examining whether respect is merited; the eyes are examined, among other things, for sincerity.

Eye contact demands concentration and may therefore be interrupted in order to enhance concentration. However, it may also be avoided to prevent the other person from seeing something in one's eyes or to avoid seeing something in the other's eyes. Segar (1997), a young man with Asperger's syndrome, has written a 'survival guide' for fellow sufferers. It includes an attempt to describe rules for eye contact.

> Eye contact is hard to get right because it is hard to tell whether you are giving someone too much eye contact or too little when they are talking to you. While people are not talking and when you are not talking to them, it is often best not to look at them. This is because people can usually see that you are looking at them out of the corner of their eyes and this may make them feel uncomfortable, in which case they might talk about you behind your back. To control your gaze might be difficult for you but it is by no means impossible. When you point at someone while speaking about them to someone else, this may seem impolite when they notice it. When you quarrel with someone while making eye contact, this may come across as very aggressive. Try not to point at people – it will help you to avoid difficulties. When you are talking to someone or they are talking to you, you are expected to look at them, bearing in mind the following guidelines: to look at someone for less than one third of the time may be communicating that either you are shy (if you keep looking down) or you are dishonest (if you keep looking to the side). To look at someone for the whole time, giving steady and unbroken eye contact, can mean one of two things. Either you are challenging them (the aggressive gaze) or you fancy them (the intimate gaze). However, in other cultures (Mediterranean Europe), it can also symbolise companionship. For someone with autism it can be very difficult because

first we have to be sure that it is appropriate. Also fixed eye contact can forcefully distract us when we try to talk. (Segar 1997)

Non-autistic children often also look for situations in which adults cannot look at them and are themselves occupied with something (doing the dishes or driving a car) in order to broach an important subject. In such situations, it is easier for the child to concentrate on her own words and she will not be affected by the intensity of the adult's eye contact which usually strongly focuses on the child when she brings up a problem (Delfos 2000).

Concentration is focused more inwardly when the eyes are averted and thinking is not interrupted by the other's verbal or non-verbal activity. When a person is thinking, he or she is more inwardly focused and usually averts the eyes. This often means that the person looks obliquely upwards.

It is often said of children with an autistic disorder that they avoid eye contact. It is in fact not so much avoidance (Frith 1989) as turning away the eyes in order to concentrate. As in many other respects, it is clear also in this case that autistic children display a great deal of behaviour which is appropriate for a younger age. Social interaction, in particular its verbal aspects, demands great efforts from a young child, and the child therefore has to concentrate strongly on this communication in order to understand the interaction and join in. To this end, the child looks away and thinks. As we have noted above, the intensity in the gaze of adults can distract children away from understanding interaction.

Social interaction is all the more demanding for children with an autistic disorder. If they are to understand, follow and join in the interaction, their concentration will have to be optimal. To achieve this, they reduce eye contact to be able to think about the contact with stronger concentration (Wing 1992; Baron-Cohen *et al.* 1995). Their eyes are turned inward and lose depth. What they often do is to turn inward upon themselves to think about the social demand which contact makes on them.

Roger, a five-year-old boy with a contact disorder, spent large parts of a conversation looking obliquely upwards. The teacher thought he was evading eye contact and asked him why he was always looking up during conversation. More competently than any expert could have explained it, the boy expressed with perfect clarity what he was doing: 'That is to read inside my head.' Children with a contact disorder have difficulty understanding social interaction and depend on figuring it out by thinking about it. Quite rightly, therefore, this child said that he 'read' the information available in his brain.

Attwood (1998) reported that you could see children with Asperger's syndrome thinking about giving an answer to a question where other children would reply spontaneously. With advancing knowledge and the increase in complexity of the socioscheme, insight into how to respond in particular situations increases as well. Yet subtle social situations will always baffle people with Asperger's syndrome.

Not making eye contact may give the impression that contact is being avoided, that there is no interest; but it may also give the impression that attention is focused on something completely different.

Martin was talking to his therapist about the breakdown of his marriage. In the meantime, he looked fixedly over the therapist's shoulder. She looked around to see what he was looking at, in a reflex as people tend to do. She saw nothing and asked Martin what was the matter. 'Nothing', he said, 'this is something that people are always asking, what I'm looking at, but there's nothing'. 'But you were looking so intensely', the therapist responded, and Martin explained: 'Behind you the net curtains are hanging in folds and through them I see a chimney pot and I'm trying to get the chimney pot into one of the folds. Then I have a quieter image and I can concentrate better, because what we're discussing is so important.' Rather than showing a lack of interest and focusing on something else, Martin was clearly making an effort to concentrate better. From then on, the two changed places so that Martin faced a white wall with a quieter image.

Asperger (1944) reports that in the more than 200 cases of autistic disorder that he dealt with, this special gaze was invariably present.

In some people, this turning inward and thinking does in fact look as if they are 'scanning' their brain. The eyes move very rapidly from left to right. This 'reading in the head' may mean that all kinds of areas of the brain, left and right, are searched for information. It may possibly also lie at the basis of *rapid eye movements* (REM) which occur behind closed eyelids during dream sleep when many images are linked up to one another, often giving rise to weird dreams.

'Eye vibrations', rapid eye movements, were very striking when Alec was a child and adolescent. It was one of the reasons why making eye contact was virtually impossible. As he grew older, this scanning diminished until it was hardly noticeable as his knowledge of social contact increased at the same time and became readily accessible, obvious knowledge to him.

For a person with an autistic disorder, thinking about social interaction is a major part of communication. In fact, it ought to get a place during interaction. Normally, we are used to asking people after an important conversation to think over what has been said. In people with an autistic disorder, this should happen much more often *during* conversation.

> Despite being in his forties, Martin still had difficulty registering and understanding all the information imparted in interaction. He had always tried very hard to follow everything and always found this exhausting. He once said: 'It's not a question of not being able to receive the information but needing more time for it. The other person doesn't give you this extra time and then the moment has passed and you have to focus on something else again.'
>
> From the moment he knew that this was connected with his autistic disorder, he felt freer to interrupt conversations and insert a short break to think it over.
>
> The result was that the quality of his conversations improved enormously. The problem in interaction proved to be much more a problem of speed than one of content. The change of pace, interspersed with breaks for thinking, considerably enhanced the quality of his discourse.

Research done by Yirmiya and colleagues (1989, 1992) shows how important pace and thinking is for autistic people. In their studies, children were asked a number of questions after viewing video recordings in which emotions were expressed. Autistic children did not perform any worse in judging emotion but they did need significantly more time to arrive at their answers and showed higher concentration than the non-autistic children.

Martijn Dekker (2001), a young man with Asperger's syndrome, notes that communicating by e-mail is an ideal form of communication for people with an autistic disorder who are able to use e-mail. Contact can be established which in a face-to-face meeting would hardly be possible if at all because people with an autistic disorder would be hampered by their communication deficiency. The great advantage of e-mail is that the *speed problem* is absent. It is possible to read at one's own pace, and think, feel and respond whenever one is ready for it. Get-togethers of people with an autistic disorder also go much more smoothly if all of them pretend to be e-mailing, with the breaks for thinking to which Martin referred in the example above.

Since defective eye contact plays a role in enhancing concentration, no attempt should be made to remedy this by insisting that the child looks the other person in the eye during conversation. This is because the result could be that the quality of the contact immediately diminishes because the child is less able to follow the interaction due to reduced concentration. On the one hand, this means that the child should be respected and aided in this regard; for example, more interaction could take place in situations in which there is no need for the child to look at anyone, such as during walks or car trips, or simply by respecting the child's need not to look at you during conversation. On the other hand, it should be explained to the child what a lack of eye contact means to other people, so that at particular moments he or she may choose to establish eye contact to improve contact quality. The child has to learn that eye contact also serves to structure a conversation. For instance, eye contact indicates that conversation can begin or that somebody wants to say something. One could say that in a conversation eye contact serves to insert non-verbal punctuation marks.

In Segar's book (1997) we see that he always gives a reason for behaviour, motivating the reader to display the behaviour. This is in fact what we witnessed in the example of Michael and his teacher in connection with putting chairs on the tables. Getting explanations is important for all children, but it is of even greater importance to children with autism because they cannot sense situations by themselves. While for a child with a non-autistic disorder the explanation provides words for his feelings, to the child with an autistic disorder the explanation means that a feeling can be vented, recognized and put into the socioscheme as new knowledge. For a child with an autistic disorder, understanding what is going on is one of the few ways of overcoming the anxiety *vis-à-vis* this strange world. Kees Momma (1996) stresses that the explanations his mother patiently, respectfully and warmly provided him with throughout his life had been of decisive importance for him in learning to cope with his autism.

Ronald lagged behind considerably in all developmental tasks. Each new task cost him a huge amount of time and effort. People were invariably taken aback by the seriousness of his behaviour. A developmental task such as focusing the eyes, for instance, took him a very long time. But also his muscles developed more slowly, causing concern that he might never be able to walk. His parents guided him through each and every task with a great deal of attention and devotion. Learning to talk was perhaps the most spectacular achievement. Ronald's mother was very verbal. 'I am an enormous chatterbox, I never stop talking to him all day', she said. 'I think that in spite of everything he has learnt a great deal as a result and he is beginning to talk.' His father was mad about him and spent a lot of time every day, at quiet moments, intensively practising talking with him. A less verbal mother and a different father would probably not have achieved as much with Ronald as they had.

A child with an autistic disorder is greatly helped by knowing that he has to make eye contact every now and then in order to maintain contact with other people. At particular moments in a conversation, such as the beginning or the end of some-thing said by the child or the other person, eye contact is easier to establish. Eye contact while speaking could give the child more information about the meaning of what is being said. But children are not yet able to process that flood of informa-tion. Because they are less focused on others, children with an autistic disorder have little experience of the fact that there is so much additional information that can be acquired non-verbally through eye contact.

For Martin, following interaction was often more than he could handle. He indicated that a great deal just escaped him. He was greatly focused on the words that were spoken but he had never given much attention to non-verbal messages. Unlike words, he did not consider them as facts and he tended to ignore them at least on the conscious level. It helped him to learn that non-verbal signals could just like other signals be treated as facts and contribute towards understanding interaction. Armed with this knowledge, he began to focus more on non-verbal signals in conversation.

Lack of contact orientation

Children with an autistic disorder are less orientated towards other people. They are often self-sufficient. This ought to be respected as such and social contact should certainly not be forced upon them. Yet, all opportunities should be seized to establish and expand social contact.

> Michael could spend hours just sitting on the floor in his room with his back against the wall, staring in front of him, with occasional rocking movements. He would seem quite ordinary, not unhappy or sad. Also, at his grandmother's, he could withdraw and just sit on the floor for a while. His parents just let him be but every now and then his mother or father would come and sit next to him on the floor. His mother would ask, 'What are you looking at?' and he would answer, 'Nothing'. She would then sit down next to him and tell him about the figures she saw in the picture on the wall opposite, saying how nice it was just to sit there together.

Lack of interest in contact is not a problem in itself. Someone who's introspective need not necessarily be unhappy. Using our average standards, we judge someone like that to be lonely, which does not mean that this is how that person experiences it. We must take care not to apply our standards to people with an autistic disorder. An autistic woman once said: 'I don't need friends as much as people who meet me half way.'

The weaker focus on contact is connected with the way in which people with an autistic disorder approach subjects. Let us recall the example of Jamie in Chapter 5.

> An adult holds a ball above his head and asks four-year-old Jamie to get the ball. Jamie carries out the task, but his action makes the adult feel uncomfortable. Because of the way Jamie behaves towards him, he feels like an object instead of a human being. Jamie is using him as a ladder to climb to the ball.

What is happening in this example is that Jamie is classifying subjects differently from children without an autistic disorder. Jamie sees the ball as the central subject and all other subjects as subordinate to it and this is also how he approaches the adult. Children without an autistic disorder will always view the human being as the central subject and experience everything else as subordinate to this. When there is a subject with which someone is occupied and that occupation is interrupted by someone else, who asks the first person to do something else, the result is a conflict of interests, involving two subjects that are coordinate. In autistic people, this conflict develops more slowly; and in children with Kanner's autism it often does not emerge at all. Coping with a task requires total concentration which, for children with an autistic disorder, can be mustered only by assigning a completely central position to the subject and excluding all other influences. As a result, children with an autistic disorder are less evidently involved with people in their environment and much more with the subjects demanding their attention. This gives rise to the impression that they are not interested in others and instead are more self-oriented because of a lack of feeling, whereas in fact it is for them a necessary condition to be able to cope with everyday life. It is not Jamie's intention to evoke an uncomfortable feeling in the adult, he is in fact utterly unaware that there is something the matter. It is the adult who senses infallibly that Jamie would approach him differently if he realized that he was a human being and not a ladder. It is the adult who interprets Jamie's behaviour as well considered rather than unconscious.

In therapy, John learnt that people with an autistic disorder do not automatically rank 'human' higher than 'non-human' and that this could lead to unintended problems in communication. He applied this at work. When he had started his job, his basic assumption had been that everything had to be done in a way that was best for the company. He had been surprised to find that he was not being appreciated at work despite his great devotion and the many questions he asked to be able to do better. He did his work as best he could and felt responsible for the money he earned. He discovered, however, that his work was far more appreciated if he put less energy into it, asked fewer questions and invested more energy in building up a relationship with his colleagues.

Because of their greater self-orientation, autistic people have less need spontaneously to share their experiences with others. Important events may happen in their lives without them involving or even just telling others about it.

This non-sharing may lead to unexpected situations. Victor, aged five, lived in a children's home and seemed to be an intelligent boy. He liked looking at books. As it was assumed that he couldn't read yet, this 'reading' of books was seen as just pretending, enabling him to withdraw from what was happening in the group. He displayed little activity at school, and in fact spent most of his time in the corner with building blocks. One day, when Victor and his group were at summer camp, they all went shopping together at a large supermarket. The children, all aged between four and eight, were very noisy and the leader of the group told them to make less noise. 'Children have to be quiet', she said, 'look, that's what it says on the sign over there'. 'No', said Victor with perfect calm, 'it says: save for the most beautiful crystal'. The fact is that Victor could read, he had taught himself and no one around him had any idea because he never shared what he was doing with anyone. The books he had been looking at turned out not to be a pretext to withdraw from the group, as the leader had thought: he was actually reading them.

It is often very difficult for parents to cope with the child's lack of contact orientation. Focusing on contact shows that somebody is interested in you and, by implication – as people interpret it – that you are worthwhile as a human being. Consequently, a lack of contact orientation produces the opposite effect, giving the impression that the other is indifferent and uninterested. Parents often interpret the child's lack of interest in them as a negative judgement by the child of them as people. When a child is not focused on the parents, they often perceive this as a rejection of them as human beings. This interpretation seems all the more obvious when the parents find that even in times of distress the child does not always turn to them. A well-known example of this is *pain*. Children with an autistic disorder often show little reaction to pain, sometimes seeming quite unemotional. This is hard for the parents because they have to be particularly on their guard in case there is something wrong with the child.

Michael's mother had learnt to react immediately if Michael called out 'Mummy' in a soft, quiet, rather thin voice. Once she had found Michael with his hand bleeding after he had cut himself on a glass and he had merely quietly cried out 'Mummy'.

As yet, we know little about the details of this process of little response to pain. Some assume that it has to do with a lack of capacity to put feelings into words (Wing 2001). However, the example of Michael shows that there could be something else going on. The thin voice suggests a trance-like state in which Michael probably finds himself as a result of what happened. It may well be that people with an autistic disorder also feel less pain because their body produces more pain-killers by itself, the body's own *endorphins*, causing them to enter a trance-like state.

There are indications of endorphin hyperfunction – overproduction – in autistic people (Gillberg, Terenius and Lönnerholm 1985; Gillberg 1992).

We frequently observe *self-mutilation* in autistic children, in particular if the disorder is combined with an intellectual disability. The strange thing is that this does not cause them discomfort, in fact they seem to like the feeling. It may well be that in these children the self-mutilation serves to stimulate production of endorphins, which causes a pleasurable feeling, a pleasant rush.

Children with an autistic disorder often also show an atypical response to painkillers and opiates. Some children need not be anaesthetized and feel no pain during surgery while others cannot be anaesthetized and anaesthetics and sedatives put them in a cheerful mood (Wing 2001).

We assume that children with an autistic disorder create situations themselves which produce extra endorphins. They do this, for instance, by looking into the light but especially through activities involving an element of repetition which may cause a *hypnotic trance*, such as head banging and rocking to and fro. The trance is visible in their eyes. The children seem to be in a world of their own, closed off from the people around them. Everyone is familiar with these forms of behaviour, which are stimulated by practising yoga, for instance. In a child with an autistic disorder, however, we see this happening frequently and especially longer and later than just the usual behaviour in the baby stage. Grandin (1995b) reports in her autobiography that it costs her a lot of effort to remain focused on the world around her. She easily slips into a state in which she is closed off from the outside world and has narrowed consciousness. Gunilla Gerland also states that she likes withdrawing within herself:

> I spent a lot of time within myself. It was as though I was in my own world, screened off from all the rest. But there was no world there inside me. It was more a kind of zero state, a neither-nor. It was a state of having being emptied without being empty or filled without being full. (Gerland 2003)

Here Gerland formulates the emptiness within her. It is reminiscent of the 'grey area' to which Martin referred (Chapter 6) and which we may relate to the limited development of the (neural) self, a limited knowledge of one's own self.

In Chapter 11 we shall come back to this self-hypnotic behaviour. What is necessary for the young child becomes something to the older child and adult that causes them to be too closed off from the world around them and to lose contact where contact is necessary.

The fact that the child seems to have so little need for the parents, even when he is in pain, can give them the feeling of being unimportant and exchangeable. There are nevertheless many moments when the child shows that he badly needs his parents. He turns to the parent because he knows that that is where he gets support, security, knowledge and certainty, and help in difficult situations. The bond with the parent is there but does not always materialize in the usual way. As the child lives in a strange and often frightening world, he is in fact strongly focused on the parents or carers and keenly assimilates information about them. Children with an autistic disorder can therefore, to the surprise of the people around them, flawlessly register tension in their carers. This is why they are often also keenly aware of weaknesses in others. They seem to register these negative signals better than positive ones. Viewed from Asperger's assertion that autistic brains have a more male structure, it is interesting to recall the research by Eisenberg *et al.* (1997) who discovered that men are much better than women at perceiving signs of anger and danger. It is possible, therefore, that the capacity of autistic people to receive negative signals is also connected with their brain structure, which is deemed to be more male and therefore more oriented towards perceiving danger. Wing (2001) indicates that children with an autistic disorder are very sensitive to signs of stress in the mother. According to Vermeulen (2000a), parents of autistic children have the impression that their children are very sensitive to negative signals, but in fact this is not a special capacity but a reflexive reaction and behaviour that is communicated and evoked by parents. However, if we take Eisenberg's study seriously and also the views of Asperger himself, we have to conclude that the parents are probably right and that autistic children are particularly sensitive to negative signals. In the same context, we can include the findings of Sigman's study, mentioned by Frith (1989): children with an autistic disorder spend more time expressing negative than positive emotions.

Once parents are more aware that the child has a general lack of contact focus, they will be better able to interpret his behaviour and find it less upsetting. But the fact remains that it is still difficult to relate to the child if there is no basis of mutually experienced contact. The conditions for contact seem to be too unilaterally on the child's side. Consequently, the parent misses the contact when he or she wishes to initiate it and finds that the child doesn't want it. This may cause the parent to feel used when the child needs and enforces contact.

The fact that autistic people are focused on themselves also affects the way they experience *privacy*. The need for privacy in people with Asperger's syndrome can be very strong. It is fed from two sources. The first is that they have less need to share their experiences with others. We also see this in the normal differences between men and women, for instance in the way in which men and women react after something important has happened. Men often have a need to reflect upon this by themselves whereas women usually feel the need to share it with others and get in touch with their friends to be able to share their inner stirrings (Taylor *et al.* 2000). The second source of the need for privacy is that *non-privacy* means contact, which is something that requires a lot from people with an autistic disorder. The contact overwhelms them and they cannot simultaneously process the information.

This leads to the strange situation that they need distance from the contact in order to know how the contact feels. This is very annoying for partners of people with an autistic disorder because they really want to know their partner's views. They also want to share their views but their partner in fact needs distance in order to discover the feeling. For people with an autistic disorder or autistic features, it is also very difficult to experience something the moment it happens. Only when the visitors have gone does it become clear that it was a nice evening.

Both Jack (early forties) and Alec (late twenties) were in a meaningful relationship. They both had Asperger's syndrome and often experienced the same things. They both frequently needed to withdraw within themselves to feel what they thought of something. This was why both of them were quite worried about the prospect of living together with their partner. Sylvia wanted to live with Alec and carefully asked him how he felt about it but came up against resistance on his part. Joanna wanted to move in with Jack but Jack strongly resisted it. Joanna always felt this as a rejection because her wish to live with him had grown out of her love for Jack. Consequently, she could not interpret Jack's behaviour as anything other than a lack of love for her, and she was completely devastated by this. To Jack this was incomprehensible because his need for privacy had nothing to do with his feelings for Joanna.

Communication

For people with an autistic disorder, communication is not easy. It makes a difference in what situation the communication takes place. A group of people means an overwhelming amount of communicative information that has to be processed. In a group, someone with an autistic disorder will therefore look for an opportunity to keep aloof.

The author discussed with Alec which situations involving him could be used in this book. A number of examples were considered including the neologism of 'thrown-together living'. When he was asked whether he could indicate what was important to him, so that the book would be less dependent on the author's perspective, he replied: 'Groups! My loathing of groups in any size or form. It doesn't matter how small or large it is. I believe my choice of the words "thrown-together living" adequately expresses the dislike I feel about groups.'

Although contact with others may be a formidable task for people with an autistic disorder, they do feel the need for contact. Martin, for example, strongly longs for a group he can be part of.

The longing for contact is even stronger in people with Asperger's syndrome or PDD-NOS because contact seems so much within easy reach. They try very hard to communicate. As they grow up, increasingly it is made clear to them that communication does not run smoothly. Their need for knowledge about this is therefore considerable, unless their experience has been so negative that they anxiously withdraw from contact. In therapy this means that they wish to make sensible use of their time, often turning up to the appointment with a clear list of items to be discussed. Moreover, they are used to the fact that their working memory, their short-term memory, does not function well and know that they could easily lose important information. For people with Asperger features, the need to make optimum use of therapeutic counselling is even stronger because they feel that the gap in their contact with people around them is so narrow that it is bridgeable given proper dedication.

John, in his late twenties, wanted to get the most out of his therapy sessions. He meticulously prepared every appointment and always turned up with a list of points he wished to discuss. He even figured out for himself how to discuss each item and provided extensive information which he believed the therapist needed to be able to arrive at an answer. During the holiday period, a number of weeks passed between two appointments. The therapist greeted him with the words: 'Hello John, long time no see. How are things?' John answered, smiling: 'Well, that's three subjects. I in fact assumed that you would ask how things are because you do that all the time, and I've prepared that question. So let's first do that subject.' He took out his notes and started reading what he had thought out about how he was doing.

Often, contacts do not run smoothly and may lead to a great deal of distress, in particular if the condition has not been diagnosed. There is a great lack of understanding on the part of parents and partners and much anxiety and sense of failure in those struggling with the condition, without people around them being aware of it. As a result, serious conflicts may arise.

Ken had had a serious conflict with his daughter who had been living on her own for some time. He did not understand her and the professional counsellor whose help he had sought was not sure how to deal with this slightly strange girl. Ken regretted his outburst and phoned his daughter to tell her that he was concerned that he had gone too far, asking her if she would like to pop round. To his utter surprise, she replied: 'I first have to think about that.' Ken was deeply hurt and felt rejected. Some time later, when the possibility of Asperger's syndrome was mentioned, he remembered this occurrence and for the first time began to understand his child: in such an important interaction, she first had to think before responding. It was not rejection, she just could not follow his pace.

Communication serves a number of functions:

1.   asking for something

2.   inviting attention

3.   refusing

4.   making remarks to share attention

5.   providing information

6.   asking for information

7.   expressing emotion (Peeters 1996).

For people with an autistic disorder, it is in particular functions 4 to 7 that are problematic because these are more oriented to sharing attention and feelings.

Since communication is so difficult for people with an autistic disorder, they need to get an explanation of *conversational frameworks*, i.e. the purposes and rules of conversations. An interview follows quite different rules from a spontaneous chat with someone you meet in the street. Children still have little knowledge of the rules underlying discourse. It appears that children do significantly better in conversations if the conversational frameworks are explained to them (Elbers 1991). This applies even more so to autistic people. 'Conversational framework' means the nature and purposes of a conversation. In a police interrogation, it is necessary to know that the conversation is used as part of a judicial process, that the intention is to speak the truth and not make things up. In a therapy session, the purpose is to discuss problems; the discussion is covered by professional secrecy and will not be divulged to others without consent, and if any untruths are told this means that the help will be inadequate as it is based on wrong information.

In a book about conducting conversations with children (Delfos 2000), I emphasized that it is important to adjust to the child's mental age and bear in mind that this mental age is not the same for all subjects. A number of communicative conditions are listed for conversations with children, as summarized below. These are at least as important for children with an autistic disorder as for other children.

1. Lower yourself to the same (eye) level as the child.

2. Look at the child while you speak.

3. Alternate making and not making eye contact with the child while you speak.

4. Make sure the child feels at ease.

5. Listen to what the child says.

6. Use examples to show the child that what he or she says has an effect.

7. Tell the child that he or she should tell you what he or she thinks or wants because otherwise you will not know this.

8. Try combining playing and talking.

9. Indicate that you are breaking off the conversation and will resume it later if you notice the child is losing interest.

10. When you have had a difficult conversation, give the child the chance to recover.

In addition to these communicative conditions, *metacommunication* – commmunicating about communication – is of considerable importance. We are metacommunicating, for instance, when we say: 'Why do you look so surprised when I say that?' Or: 'When you talk to me when I'm on the phone, I can't listen to you.' The metacommunicative conditions are listed below.

These lists give the impression – wrongly – that conversations have to be strongly verbal in nature; a non-verbal form of communication is particularly important with young children.

1. Make the purpose of the conversation clear.

2. Let the child know what your intentions are.

3. Let the child know that you need feedback.

4. Let the child know that he or she may keep silent.

5. Try to describe what you feel and follow your feeling.

6. Ask the child for his or her opinion of the conversation.

7. Make metacommunication a fixed part of your communication.

Metacommunication is important for children with an autistic disorder because they have little knowledge of social interaction and therefore sense things much less in conversations. They often are not really aware of what is going on in the other person's mind during communication. Communication requires adjustment to the other's mental age, from the form of metacommunication to questioning techniques (e.g. young children ask questions in a *spatial* rather than a *temporal* framework, i.e. 'where' instead of 'when') (Delfos 2000).

> Martin said he had no idea how the contacts he ended up in went wrong: 'Suddenly, without me being aware of it, something went wrong again. I myself don't notice that I deviate. But suddenly I'm out of it again, at least that's what I find out afterwards. Then I want to understand how it came about, but that means that I have to look exactly in the area where I'm blind.'

Some rules, such as *taking turns in a conversation*, are not applied by children with an autistic disorder and this makes it difficult to carry on a real conversation, a dialogue rather than a monologue. This applies in particular to children with Asperger's syndrome and PDD-NOS who in principle have normal language development. Taking turns means having some insight into the impact which words have on the other person, sensing that the other wishes to say something and perceiving through non-verbal signals that the other wishes to say something. When someone starts talking in the middle of the other's sentence or interrupts them, this may be impolite but it may also be a spontaneous and welcome act emphasizing the reciprocity of the conversation. For people with an autistic disorder, this distinction is not always easy to make. When they are speaking, they think that it is important for the other to know all the details of their line of reasoning or the minutiae of an event, and they may launch into a lengthy monologue. Having different opinions is a nuance that is difficult to grasp for people with Asperger's syndrome, and they seem therefore eager to convince the other person that they are right. The listener, however, feels submerged by the flood of words and begins to lose interest in the conversation. Reflecting on content fades into the background and eventually all that is left is the wish that the autistic person stop talking.

A problem of a completely different order in communication with people with an autistic disorder is their voice. Their *prosody*, the sound of what they say, may be unpleasant to others. Their voice is often loud or, on the contrary, too soft and their delivery may be very monotonous.

The fact that an autistic person has limited empathic capacity does not mean that he or she does not think about other people. The thoughts and feelings that are ascribed to other people are often incorrect because of their restricted theory of mind. When a child with an autistic disorder does think about the other person, he believes that he knows what the other thinks and is unaware that it may be wide of the mark. The child ascribes feelings to the other and appears insensitive to the other's protestations about this. 'You cannot decide how I feel, only I can, only I know', Michael's mother cried out in despair when once again she got entangled in her son's verbal violence, convinced as he was that he knew what his mother felt. It is important to teach the child the pluriformity of truth.

It is difficult for everyone, convinced as we all are that we are right, to nevertheless be open to other perspectives. The belief of being right may be fed by a limited view of the truth or by another perspective without being aware that it is only a limited truth. Colour-blindness tests such as Ishihara's (1957) seem a useful way to illustrate the pluriform nature of truth. In this test, pictures are shown with dots of different colours and intensities. The arrangement of the dots forms the pattern of a figure. For instance, there are various strong and soft red and purple dots between strong and soft green dots. The arrangement of the dots in the picture may conjure up different images, depending on the predisposition of the person looking at them. For example, all the red and purple dots may form a figure 8 but only the strong-coloured red and green dots together form a 3. If you are red–green colour-blind, you do not see the difference between red and green, but do see the intensity of the colour, and therefore are able to see the figure 3 made up of the strong coloured red and green dots. The colour-blind person who sees a 3 or a person who is not colour-blind who sees an 8 both feel that what they see is the truth. Both are right, and yet their truth depends on the information at their disposal.

In addition to their need to present their own point of view and line of reasoning and their lack of awareness that the other person wants to do so too, people with an autistic disorder are also at a disadvantage because the other person's statements may cause them to lose the thread of their own arguments. This is mainly because the other person is not predictable to autistic people as a result of their limited socioscheme. The other person's remarks are therefore unexpected to the autistic person, causing confusion. As a result, people with Asperger's syndrome may seem overly forceful in their eagerness to give their own opinion, leaving little scope for their listener. The thought process may likewise be affected in this communication whereas in normal communication the other's contribution may be a useful complement. A condition for being a complement, however, is that the other's remarks can immediately be fitted in with one's own argumentation. People with Asperger's syndrome often have difficulty incorporating the new 'detail', the other's contribution, into their own line of reasoning. Another factor is memory. People with an autistic disorder have a weaker short-term memory than average (see also Chapter 5). Accordingly, they easily lose the thread after an interruption and are very keen to stick to their own story. For the same reason, they tend to interrupt other people as they are concerned about forgetting what they were going to say. Once they have started to speak, they seem unstoppable.

Ceaseless argumentation in conversation is quite striking in people with Asperger's syndrome (Wing 2001). Their single-minded argumentation is often a virtual monologue. They are eager to convince the other person and also want to have the last word.

The difficulty imaging what goes on in another person's mind also has advantages. Communication is slower but often much more precise, purer and more sincere than with someone without an autistic disorder. A person with an autistic disorder can often say things the way they are, without value judgement and without wishing to hurt the other. This is what we see happening in young children when they exclaim with surprise: 'Doesn't that woman have a big nose!' This we perceive as characteristic of little children, but children are soon deemed to understand that such statements are not acceptable and are considered inappropriate.

> Bob, aged seven, uninhibitedly walked up to a group of boys and asked them: 'Is it true that you steal bikes?'

We see the same thing when autistic children repeat behaviour that is unpleasant for another. The child is, as it were, trying to understand what the other's response is and why. To the other, it may come across as mean and heartless. We see this in an innocent form when a child shouts 'Boo!' to make someone jump. A child with an autistic disorder may even laugh heartily when someone else feels dreadfully unhappy, if the child does not know this emotion. In order to understand the other's behaviour, the autistic child may time and again elicit the behaviour. While the other may experience this as bullying (Vermeulen 2000a), the child is in fact trying to catch up cognitively and emotionally.

From the behaviour of adults children learn what is and what is not appropriate. They lose their spontaneity to say things purely, without ulterior motive. Autistic people retain this spontaneity, sometimes referred to as naïeveté, for much longer. They continue making such remarks for longer, and because of their calendar age this is perceived as inappropriate. The difficulty imagining what goes on in someone else's mind leads to the retention of this spontaneity and also means that autistic people are rarely manipulative because you have to be able to get into someone else's mind before you can manipulate him or her.

Like Alec in the example in Chapter 5, Martin preferred not to use names in therapy sessions. 'It is not good to name names, that's gossiping', he said. Surprised, the therapist asked him to explain himself. 'If you use names, it can be traced', he explained. The therapist suspected that Martin had quite different ideas about gossiping than she had, and she asked him to explain what gossiping meant to him. He explained that gossiping meant that you said something about another person that was damaging to him and that this damage was prevented by not mentioning the person's name. The therapist added that according to her one of the most important elements of gossiping was that by saying bad things about someone else you praised yourself at the other's expense. Martin's wife, smiling contentedly, nodded at this explanation. Martin was dumbfounded: 'But surely you don't feel great when you put someone else down?' Very briefly the therapist and Martin's wife had a brief glimpse of the much purer world of autistic people.

Autistic children who understand deceptions in the TOM test appear to be dishonest more often and lie more frequently (Happé 1998). As it is not easy for children with an autistic disorder to imagine what someone else thinks or feels, they try to influence the other's behaviour through *sabotage* rather than through *deceit*. Sabotage directly influences the other's behaviour, for example, by obstructing someone else; deceit plays on the other's mental state and manipulates the other into the desired behaviour without his or her being aware of it (Vermeulen 1999b, 2000a).

The meaning of language

Language is of fundamental importance to people. They explain things to each other through language. The problem is that we lean so heavily on language that we are put out when language is not used. For children who have difficulty speaking, it is therefore important to help them look for words.

Samuel, 24, has an expressive language disorder. It went undiagnosed for a long time, partly because his paucity of language was attributed to intellectual disability. It was also apparent that he had an autistic disorder. However, his intellectual abilities proved greater than had initially been thought. It was wrong to attribute his language limitations to his intellectual disability. It was decided to link up with the sounds he produced spontaneously and choose words that could directly communicate his opinion about something. In this way, Samuel learnt to say 'all right' (all-o-wight) when he agreed with something and 'not all right' when he did not.

For some time, Samuel would at regular intervals put his hand to his head. However, he did not have headaches. With the help of dolls and gestures and sparse use of words, an attempt was made to find a way of helping him to indicate what was going on in his head. He felt a pressure in his head. In order to prevent epileptic seizures, it was important to find words and gestures to be able to communicate with him about this.

The problem of communication, in particular verbal communication, has led to the use of *pictograms*, in which situations are depicted with the aid of photos and drawings (see Figure 8.1). Specific communication through pictograms is conducive in particular for children and adults with a limited capacity for verbal communication due to intellectual disability or expressive language disorder. By pointing at a picture, it is possible to communicate something in cases where language is lacking. However, working with pictograms can also be useful for children who are able to communicate verbally. For instance, a daily schedule of activities can be visualized on a wall panel with pictograms at home or at school. At school, this is important in particular for autistic children in order to attenuate their uncertainty about what is going to happen next. In Chapter 10, when discussing resistance to change, we shall see that this resistance is largely connected with the unpredictability of what is going to happen. A panel with pictograms illustrating what will happen that day is useful, making the day's events visible and predictable (see Figure 8.1).

The use of language includes references to the other's experience. Language has a fundamentally referring function: a word itself has no meaning, it only carries meaning because it refers to something else. Many words refer to objects. In general, their meaning is clear although the same object may have a wide range of different external shapes and forms. Things become more difficult with words that do not refer to a concrete object. Some of these can be quite clear but may have different emotional values (*connotations*) associated with the word.

A simple word such as 'red' appears to be clear and not open to multiple interpretation. When asking people about this, however, it appears that everyone has his own associations with the term. Some perceive 'red' as a warm colour, others as aggressive or obtrusive. Yet others associate it with a lack of money or with blood. Depending on your association with the colour, you attach meaning to a subject involving the colour. When a child comes to school in a red sweater knitted by her mother, one teacher will have a very different impression and feeling from another. One will find it warm, the other a bit obtrusive.

The problem gets worse with words directly referring to feelings. The range of interpretations in this case is as great as the number of people involved. To people with an autistic disorder, the range remains limited to their own feelings and those they have learnt about over the years. The rate at which language develops from about three words at the age of one to 2000 at the age of five clearly shows how much information is processed through language. And 2000 words are not 2000 meanings but a multiple thereof. Meanings that are associated with the capacity to understand what goes on in somebody else's mind – for example, words denoting emotions which autistic people do not know themselves or activities in which they themselves do not take part – will be less easily understood by children with an autistic disorder and less easily find a place in their vocabulary. Consequently, these children will lag behind in development and the gap will widen over time. The language spectrum will increase but words and meanings may be less embedded in the socioscheme which, although it expands, still lags considerably behind that of non-autistic children. In this way, language and its meanings become an important issue and a focus of attention, even an obsession.

During supper, Steve just could not stop correcting the language mistakes his little brother made. His mother had explained to him that his brother was learning the language and could not yet master it properly, and that it was not right to tease him about it. Steve, who with his above average intelligence understood this perfectly, still did not stop obstinately correcting his brother's mistakes.

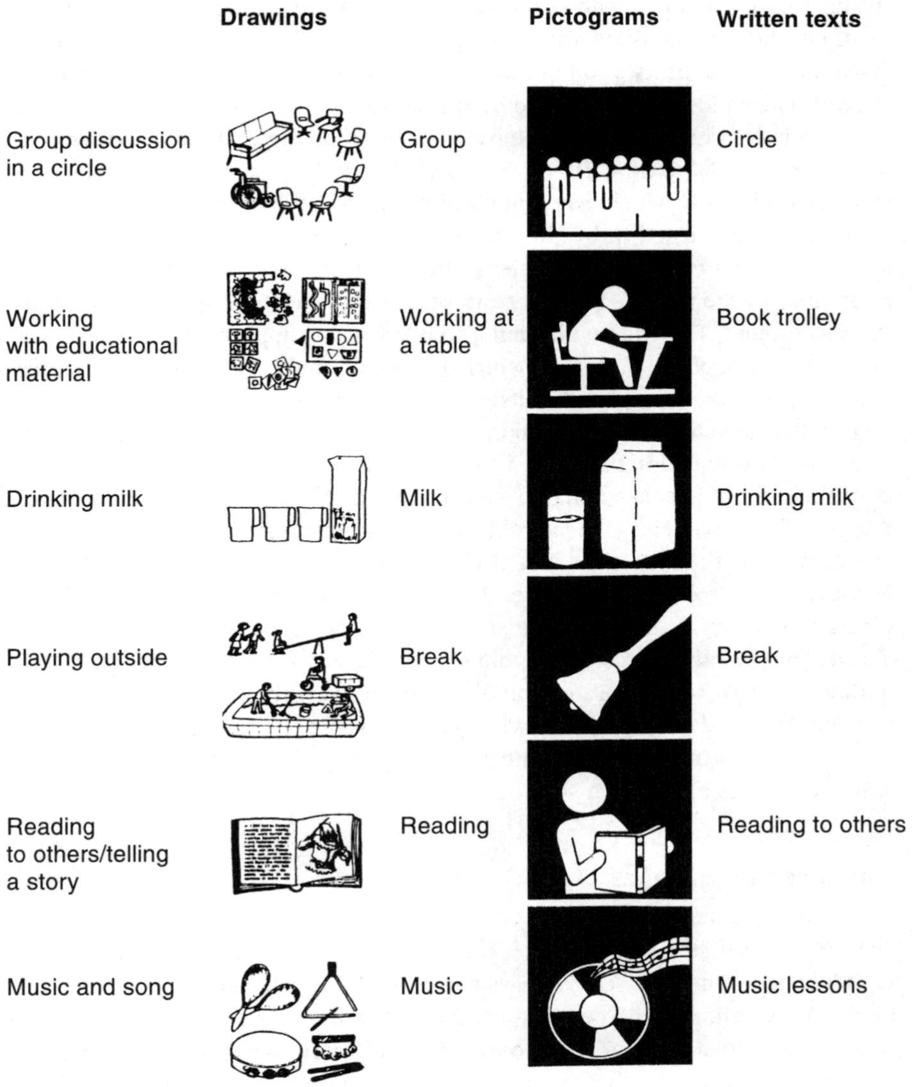

Drawings	Pictograms	Written texts
Group discussion in a circle	Group	Circle
Working with educational material	Working at a table	Book trolley
Drinking milk	Milk	Drinking milk
Playing outside	Break	Break
Reading to others/telling a story	Reading	Reading to others
Music and song	Music	Music lessons

Figure 8.1 Morning curriculum at the PI school for intellectually disabled children in Duivendrecht, the Netherlands, using drawings, pictograms or words (Fenenga 1993). Reproduced with permission from the Paedological Institute Amsterdam.

The main language problem for a child with an autistic disorder is that words can have both a literal and non-literal meaning. When listening to young children we often enjoy the funny situations that arise as a result. Selma Fraiberg (1959) has given a wonderful description of how language can develop in the child's *magical thinking*. The child may be afraid to disappear down a drain as long as she has no idea of relative size and does not know that she is too big to disappear down the hole. Because of her still defective knowledge of language, a child may take remarks too literally which may cause feelings of anxiety. For instance, she may be scared of being sucked in by the vacuum cleaner because she has heard that it hoovers up 'everything'. As toddlers, children learn *metonymic thinking*, which means that a word refers to another concept. Taking statements literally moves into the background. The child understands that 'having a cuppa' means 'drinking tea (or coffee)'. *Metaphoric thinking*, in which a concept is replaced by another concept that represents the relevant subject symbolically, becomes possible only at a later stage, when abstract symbolic thinking emerges. This development is often much slower in autistic children. By the time the average child is discovering that not everything should be taken literally, the autistic child is still right in the middle of this period. Consequently, when problems arise in communication, it is advisable to investigate whether the child has perhaps understood something too literally. However, apart from the labyrinth of the many meanings of what is being said, the greatest problem to people with an autistic disorder is what is not said, as Vermeulen (1999b) has so aptly pointed out. Refer to the list on p.148 for an outline of verbal communication problems in people with an autistic disorder.

The factors described above will cause problems for most children with an autistic disorder in associating with their peers at primary school, in particular when the others make jokes.

The meaning of jokes

Children's command of language becomes more sophisticated at primary school level. Not only do they learn to apply the rules of grammar, they also learn to 'play' with language. The child learns to get away from the literal meaning of words and begins to experiment with connections and symbolism. The many jokes arising in this period ('When is a door not a door?' [When it's ajar]; 'What kind of rooms have no walls?' [Mushrooms]) that are passed on from generation to generation show the emerging capacity to get away from the literal meaning of language and connect subjects that at first sight do not seem to have anything to do with each other. Children love showing off their newly acquired skills.

From many jokes typical of the primary-school period, children with an autistic disorder learn that they are expected to display a language skill which they do not yet possess. This expectation arises because they appear to be functioning normally in other aspects of language. Consequently, children with an autistic disorder can easily become the butt of teasing and bullying. They do not understand the jokes, which make clear who is 'in' and who is 'out', those who do and those who do not form part of the group. The child with an autistic disorder increasingly finds that she remains an outsider. The more the child experiences that she is not part of the group, the greater the chance that she will be teased and bullied.

Cracking jokes is also an exercise in manipulating people. By telling jokes, the child tries to get others – especially adults – to fall into the trap. The child soon discovers that he can get the better of the adult as long as he tells jokes that the adult has not heard. Adults are likewise attached to a number of meanings, and jokes appeal to an unusual meaning. In order to be able to be successful at making jokes, it is therefore necessary to go through a development in which one not only can detach oneself from the literal meaning of language but also acquire the capacity of imagining what goes on in another's mind and guessing what he or she will think. Moreover, the other person is deceived not only verbally but also non-verbally. Telling a joke means putting on a performance that is based on an evaluation of how the other thinks and feels. And it is this that poses problems to a child with an autistic disorder whereas children without the disorder can thoroughly enjoy it.

Eight-year-old Dave told a joke. 'There was this man who had 100 ping-pong balls and he put all of them into the boot of his car. Then a car crashed into the back of his car and the boot opened and all the balls fell out. The man went looking for them and in the end found 99 balls.' In the meantime, the listener noticed that Dave was trying very hard to tell this complicated joke correctly. He interspersed his story with asides such as: 'How did it go again, oh yes, then he had an accident.' At the point where the 99 balls had been found, Dave gave up. He forgot how the joke ended and what the punchline was, and he did not want to think about it any more. He then started a new joke about two people facing each other across a table in a pub. One was smoking, though this was forbidden, and the other pointed this out. When the smoker did not respond, the other got angrier and angrier and threatened to pull the cigarette out of the smoker's mouth and throw it away. As there was still no response, the threat was carried out. The cigarette was pulled out of the smoker's mouth and thrown out of the window. Then a little doggy ran after it and Dave said: 'What did the dog have in its mouth when it came back?' 'A cigarette', the listener said obligingly. 'No', Dave said triumphantly, 'the ping-pong ball!'

Through jokes a child tries out his or her power over the other, particularly over adults. The telling of jokes increases in the period at primary school but lying also becomes more sophisticated. In order to lie successfully, you have to be able to imagine what goes on in another person's mind. One has to be able to guess how the other person thinks in order to know when and how a truth should be concealed if an untruth is to be accepted. Autism involves an extreme form of hampered me–other differentiation. To a lesser extent, this also occurs in other disorders, where the consequences are, however, quite different. *Externalized behaviour disorder, psychopathy* and *antisocial personality* involve reduced me–other differentiation, reduced empathy (Delfos 2004a). This me–other differentiation, however, is not so weakly developed in people with psychopathic disorders and there is therefore a certain capacity to imagine what goes on in another person's mind. The most important motivation of people with psychopathic disorders is their own interests, which they may pursue by manipulation and lying. The aim is to get another to do something against his will and to make sure one is not caught in the pursuit of negative and criminal activities. It is this very focus on self-interest with regard to negative subjects that makes these people highly aware of what is going on in other people's minds in connection with their focus of interest. It is a misleading quality which is sometimes mistaken for empathic capacity. Indeed, therapists adopt a cautious approach with such people, making sure not to unduly strengthen their awareness of what goes on in other people's minds as it would only make them more skilful in pursuing their criminal behaviour. This, however, does not apply to autistic people.

A child with an autistic disorder will stand out because of her greater purity than the average child; she is utterly and totally honest. When an autistic child is confronted with her own inabilities, it is useful to place these in the framework of this quality. It will to some extent restore the child's self-image and enable her to view an occurrence in perspective. Also for the adults around the child it is important to remember the child's positive qualities so as not to get caught up in the problematic aspects.

It is in particular during the primary-school period that a child with an autistic disorder loses contact and is rejected by the group because he does not understand jokes. It is socially undesirable not to understand jokes or not be able to bear them. Even adults tend to laugh and pretend they understand a joke rather than admitting in company that they are the only one who does not understand the joke. If they themselves are the butt of the joke, they find it is better to pretend to laugh than get angry and show that they feel hurt. A child who does not understand all these nuances is soon made to feel this, as early as the first classes at primary school.

To a child with Asperger's syndrome or PDD-NOS, it is important that one explains how jokes work and what the intention is. Infantile jokes often have no effect on adults when they are prepared for them. While children with an autistic disorder want to join in cracking jokes in order to be part of the group, their jokes often have no affinity with the other children's world and the other children therefore often are not aware that it is a joke.

Peter, aged seven, went to a new school. He came home dejected. 'I'm not going to school any more, all the children tease me', he said. His mother tried hard to find out what had happened and it appeared that Peter had done his utmost to make contact with the kids at the new school. He had made all kinds of jokes but no one had laughed about them. To Peter there was no other explanation than that they deliberately did not laugh. He could not imagine that someone else did not like his jokes or did not get them. He therefore interpreted the fact that they did not laugh as a deliberate choice directed against him. This he perceived as bullying.

A joke can be explained, but when this is necessary the joke is no longer funny. You cannot teach a child that is not ready for it to understand or tell jokes. The most that can be achieved in the meantime is to teach the child to respond in a particular way when someone else tells a joke and teach him not to worry too much about it. This is not easy for the child because he often does not understand what the joke is, frequently relates the laughter to himself and has the feeling that the others laugh at him. This is why it is necessary that the child very early on learns the difference between 'laughing at someone' and just 'laughing'.

Other people's limits

At primary-school age, children take a great leap forward in motor development, in particular between the ages of four and eight. Children love playing outside and being physically active, from climbing to cycling. They begin to learn the *social codes*, such as the difference between 'real fighting', 'pretend fighting' and 'sport'.

Five-year-old Tom worked off his aggression about the pain he had sustained in judo on four-year-old Bill. 'Tom, you should not keep Bill down in that hold, he doesn't know how to defend himself because he does not learn judo and you do, you'll hurt him like that. Judo is a form of self-defence, not a way to hurt others' scolded his mother. 'That's not true', Tom replied with indignation, 'I always get hurt a lot at judo'.

At his age, Tom's response is usual and normal, but about two years later he ought to know these differences. Children who, because of their predisposition, have difficulty with social contact often also have wooden motor activity, and this applies in particular to children with Asperger's syndrome. Serious problems in social contact often go hand in hand with *non-smooth motor activity*. Consequently, such children lag behind in forging balanced social contact. From about the age of four, moreover, it becomes increasingly important to join in with motor activities. This applies more strongly to boys than to girls because boys are more focused on jointly undertaking physical activities. Children who experience difficulty in social interaction and are awkward in their motor activity will therefore lag behind in making contacts and will tend to be excluded by other children. Where this is the case, consideration could be given to giving autistic children *physiotherapy*. It should be borne in mind, however, that maturation cannot be forced. If the child is not ready for it, it makes little sense to try to teach her particular skills through intense training. It could lead to the child feeling she is failing, and this is not conducive to her self-image. Training is useful on a limited scale, in accordance with the child's own wishes, and with a specific objective that is achievable in the short term. Physiotherapy aimed at improving motor function could be helpful if it can improve the way the child associates with her peers. Through ball games such as throwing and catching, parents can help the child improve her motor activity.

Through physical games and sport, a child learns to deal with a physical dimension of me–other differentiation, namely the other's physical boundaries. Children can discover these limits through sport and games and learn to respect them. Sport and games are possible ways for children with an autistic disorder to deepen their me–other differentiation. However, in sport and games it is necessary to take account of the other through understanding what goes on in the other's mind. This goes further than just taking account of someone. Since children with an autistic disorder do not sense when and how they can take account of the other, they can do so only if they have learnt it for a particular situation. As social interaction is difficult for such children, team sports involving a great deal of interaction will cause more problems than individual sports. Stimulating the child to take part in individual sports with clear rules of engagement can help him to take account of others and learn to deal with others' boundaries.

It should be clearly borne in mind, however, that children with an autistic disorder do not lack respect for others' limits. Respecting another's limits is possible only when the limits are clear. Only when the child has learnt to sense these limits will he be able to respect them. As soon as an autistic child gains an insight into how to deal with others, he will adjust his behaviour towards them, unless this conflicts with his own programme because that would cause anxiety. Sensing the other's limits is based on the capacity to imagine what goes on in the other's mind, an awareness of the effect that one's behaviour has on the other.

Hoffman (1984) points out that when the educator draws the child's attention to the effects his actions have on the feelings of another person, the child learns to understand others better. Through the insight the child acquires into another's feelings, his empathic capacity can be stimulated. This *inductive approach* can eventually lead to *prosocial behaviour* (Hoffman 1984; Krevans and Gibbs 1996). The inductive approach is necessary for children with an autistic disorder as they do not sense properly what is going on in the other person.

This sense can be stimulated through sport and games. By being constantly aware of the other in the child's own space and of the distance between the child and the other, a feeling of delimitation arises which, however, in autistic people does not sufficiently form part of their socioscheme, as we saw in Chapter 5. The space around them is insufficiently explored because of their egocentric perspective. The person himself is central and the other enters the picture only if she has a function in relation to the central person. The same applies to objects in the space around the child. We have seen that a child with a fundamentally egocentric perspective can easily bump into objects due to a lack of awareness of how the world relates to her and how she relates to the world. Within the framework of the socioscheme, there is constant updating of knowledge of surrounding space and of one's location in relation to the things and people within that space.

An autistic person, with his or her impaired socioscheme, is as it were constantly surprised in his or her confrontation with fellow human beings as delimiters of time and space, as delimiters of possibilities and especially as carriers of expectations and wishes.

The firm foothold of proper manners

Children with Asperger's syndrome often absorb information about manners and etiquette with great enthusiasm. It gives them a firm foothold in a strange, incomprehensible world. However, knowledge of the rules of etiquette does not include an insight into when they should and should not be applied. Consequently, these children may come across as excessively polite and even formal in their eagerness to apply the rules.

Rules about proper manners may provide the child with a firm foothold but there is a risk that he is perceived as 'strange' because he does not always apply the rules appropriately.

Martin had learnt that you should kiss people you know well three times, alternating on each cheek. He followed up this advice and carried it out with great care. He gave a well-aimed kiss on the cheek and repeated this twice. But because it felt like a meticulously performed task, it felt unpleasant no matter how well intentioned. Martin did not know that the point was not really to give kisses but to establish contact, to share the emotion that it was pleasant to see each other. No one had ever explained this to him and he was quite surprised that the meaning behind the greeting ritual turned out to be very different from what he had thought. He had taken the non-verbal activity too literally. As it was difficult for Martin to perform the ritual with a light peck on the cheeks, it was more sensible from then on for him to look people in the eye and in this way show that he enjoyed seeing them.

Non-autistic children learn the rules of associating with people initially from their parents and then apply them in practice and check them against their contact with their peers (Bigelow, Tesson and Lewko 1996). Accordingly, the rules change from learnt manners to personally experienced rules of social behaviour and subsequently to a style of contact. In autistic children, these developments do not, or do not sufficiently, take place because they lag behind in their contact with their peers. The rules of social conduct which they apply therefore often remain superficial; they make a distant and cool impression because the rules cannot be fleshed out with feelings that are related to experience in contact with others. The question is whether it is advisable to teach such rules to children in order to prevent them from making the wrong impression in company. This is because an autistic child will not be able to sense properly when and how the rule ought to be applied, let alone when a minor change to the rule is desirable, since the child has no insight into the origin of the rule, the underlying idea. This may be compared with copying a Chinese character. As the language and the script are totally unfamiliar to us, we do not know which stroke is due to the idiosyncrasies of individual handwriting and which stroke is an essential part of the written character. Just to be on the safe side, we copy the entire sign as accurately as possible. The result is that the copied character appears somewhat stiff and stilted.

If the rules of etiquette are devoid of meaning because they are not embedded in social insight, they are not particularly useful in establishing contact. They may at the most serve to keep one's head above water in a social setting. It is important to stimulate children with an autistic disorder to observe other children as this enables them to learn more about how their peers interact with one another. However, in order to be able to use social codes with the proper nuance, friendships are of the utmost importance. In the next chapter, we shall discuss the crucial issue of making friends.

In associating with others during the primary-school period, the child builds up a *social identity*, the image we have of how others think and feel about us. In order to build up a social identity, children have to get sufficient opportunity to practise social interaction. The importance of this is reflected in the growing interest in social skills.

Training programmes for social skills

Children with an autistic disorder have a notable lack of social skills. An obvious remedy appears to be training programmes in social skills. However, this kind of training seems to produce little effect in these children. They are particularly effective for children (mostly girls) who possess a good empathic capacity but not enough assertiveness (Prins 1998). This skill can be learnt by autistic children but tends to be applied wrongly, too rigidly or hardly at all in daily life; think, for instance, of the example earlier in this chapter (pp.200–1) of Steve in the handicrafts group. Training in social skill makes sense only if it refers back to social insight, a developed theory of mind and a developed socioscheme.

A programme such as Steerneman's (1997) seeks to strengthen *social cognition*. It is based on theory of mind (TOM) and does not seek to teach social skills but strives to enhance me–other differentiation and stimulate imagining what goes on in other people's minds. Exercises within this training programme include constant *changes of perspective*. For instance, the children are seated in pairs facing each other. Each pair is given a picture in mosaic which is divided into two halves. One child creates an image and the other must then accurately copy it from the viewpoint of the child facing him. In other words, he has to put himself in the (visual) perspective of the child who produced the image, otherwise the picture would end up upside down.

In another example, two trainers are sitting on the floor and each makes a car from geometric shapes. The two cars are different. The children are asked such questions as: what is different? The analysis is as follows: they are both cars but they look different: everyone has his own image of a car. Next, the children are given the task (from behind a screen) of making a car out of various shapes. The different cars are then compared. This is repeated with other subjects. For every task, there is a discussion stressing the fact that each child apparently has a particular idea, a particular conception, of a particular subject.

Social skills can be developed only on the basis of *social insight*:

Social knowledge→ social insight→ social skills

Where there is no insight, only 'tricks' can be taught that can be used in particular situations and that are often not applied generally to other situations. In providing training in social cognition, it has appeared that as a person's social cognition increases his social skills also increase without the programme being specifically oriented towards this (Steerneman 1995). As an explanation of this effect, Steerneman points out that not only does that child respond more sensitively to the environment but, through interaction, the environment also responds more positively to the child, setting in motion a positive learning process. However, Vermeulen (1999b, 2000a) reports that TOM training in shifts in perspective has little impact on the ability to generalize in real, everyday situations.

The method developed by Dijkshoorn, Pietersen and Dikken (1998) is based on Ringrose and Nijenhuis (1986). They focus on social cognition underlying social skills. One of the principles that play a major role in their therapeutic method is the principle of tit for tat. The children learn to make a move but also to expect a response from the other on a *quid pro quo* basis.

Social skills training programmes have also been devised on the basis of ideas developed by Gordon (1974) and Goldstein (1973). Goldstein's programme was originally designed for people with little education and is frequently used for young people with an intellectual disability.

An essential component of social skills training is associating with peers. This is of fundamental importance for the child's development. Just how important is

Figure 8.2 Stimulating pretend play in a child with PDD-NOS (Steerneman 1997). Reproduced with permission from the author.

clear from research done by Verhulst and others (1990) in which an extensive questionnaire, the Child Behaviour Check List (CBCL), was used to study a wide range of characteristics and behaviours. Having poor relationships with one's peers turned out to be the principal predictor of future problems. Harris (1998) launched a new theory in which she argues that, after predisposition, associating with peers is the main factor in the formation of personality in children. However, Bigelow *et al.* (1996) argue that while peers become increasingly important as the child grows older, the parents continue to play a crucial role in the background.

Within the framework of the socioscheme, social skills ought to be built up on the basis of the degree of me–other differentiation. Autistic children and young people are often still engaged in stages 1 to 4 (me versus not me; not me; object versus human; attachment) listed on p. 120. While most non-autistic children have mastered these developmental tasks by the time they are twelve months old, they take much longer in autistic children. Most training programmes in social skills are therefore too ambitious. It is to be welcomed that efforts are currently being made to devise a specific test for me–other differentiation on the basis of which a programme can be developed (at the University of Nijmegen, Netherlands).

Interacting with others also means forging friendships. In learning how to associate with others, and in particular how to make friends, it is of considerable importance that the child learns to practise the different roles in interaction through play, in particular make-believe. We have already noted that a child with an autistic disorder shows little interest in this.

Focal points

- To children with an autistic disorder, social behaviour is not a matter of course.

- Social skills may become a mere 'trick' due to lack of social insight.

- Children with an autistic disorder have an impaired TOM and accordingly have problems judging what behaviour is appropriate in which situation.

- The child's persistent effort to do his utmost may lead to mental exhaustion.

- Children learn from contacts they observe around them; not only from their own contacts but also from those between others.

- Children with an autistic disorder require more time to follow communication.

- Eye contact requires additional information processing and is consequently often stressful.

- Autistic children are often particularly sensitive to negative signals.

- Looking away may serve to strengthen concentration.

- People with an autistic disorder have less need for other people.

- Children with an autistic disorder seek a hypnotic trance.

- People with autism often have a strong need for privacy.

- Communication with children and in particular with autistic children has its own rules.

- Metacommunication is important, providing an explanation of frameworks of conversation and the intentions of others involved in the conversation.

- Autistic people have problems coping with the multiple meanings of words.

- Children with an autistic disorder often do not understand jokes.

- Children with an autistic disorder run the risk of being teased and bullied at school.

- The autistic child insufficiently 'respects' the other's boundaries because she senses them insufficiently and not because she does not want to do so.

- Rules of etiquette offer a firm foothold for people who have difficulty with social interaction.

- Using rules of etiquette that are not embedded in social insight may come across as formal and stiff, something which often occurs in people with Asperger's syndrome.

- Training in social skills is meaningful only if it is based on social insight.

- Changes in perspective are frequently used in TOM exercises.

Focal points regarding attitude

- Slow down communication to give the child a chance to follow it.

- Protect the child against teasing and bullying.

- Be aware that the child's tone of voice forms part of his disorder.

- Appreciate that the child tries very hard.

- Respect the child's need to look away as an attempt to focus more on contact rather than evade it.

Summary

Children with an autistic disorder have (too) little social insight and, as a result, possess insufficient social skills. If they do possess such skills, they often have difficulty applying them at the right time and in the right manner. Because of defective me–other differentiation, the child has problems imagining what goes on in another person's mind and is unable to acquire sufficient social insight: the socioscheme remains limited. The child senses insufficiently what goes on in another's mind. This leads to impaired communication. The child often takes things too literally and does not understand jokes. He insufficiently respects the other person's boundaries because he does not sense them sufficiently. As rules of etiquette provide a foothold, an autistic child often applies them rather rigidly and comes across as formally polite.

Children with an autistic disorder are less orientated to others because they are often self-sufficient. Their concentration will have to be optimal to understand, follow and take part in social interaction. In order to concentrate better, they regularly look away from their interlocutor for long periods. They are less able to link up with the other person's statements. While they are strongly focused on their parents or carers, they often give the impression that they are not attached to them because they are less able to reciprocate and because they are more self-oriented.

For people with an autistic disorder social intercourse within groups is often even more difficult than individual contact; they therefore often avoid group-oriented activities. Taking turns in conversation causes problems for them because of their lack of empathic capacity and the impaired functioning of their short-term memory, as a result of which they need to stick closely to their own story.

Children with an autistic disorder often encounter problems with the variety of meanings in language; in particular, in understanding and making jokes.

It is important to help these children to develop social skills. However, this is meaningful only if they can refer back to social insight, a developed theory of mind or a developed socioscheme. These tend to be impaired in children with an autistic disorder and this is why training in social insight, in social cognition, will bear more fruit.

9

Forming friendships and relationships

Making friends and forging relationships is one of the principal components of social functioning. For people with an autistic disorder, who already have so much difficulty in superficial social functioning, forming friendships and relationships is much harder. Also, they are somewhat less oriented towards intensive social contact. As a result, few autistic people manage to forge successful, close relationships but people with what is said to be a mild form of autism, Asperger's syndrome, more frequently establish relationships. Above averagely gifted autistic people start a family more often than less gifted ones. In the case of those who have a partner and children, considerable effort is required from both partners to ensure the success and continuation of the relationship.

It is particularly difficult if the condition was not diagnosed in the person's youth, which is still often the case for Asperger's syndrome. It is extremely demanding to provide care to people who have not been diagnosed. Because of years of having had a feeling of failure, they are often embittered and anxious. There is no trust in care and hardly any trust in the parent, who has not managed to raise him or her into a normally functioning human being. The autistic person and those around him become exhausted. This was the case for Irving and his mother, who were mentioned in Chapter 6. To partners of autistic people, the relationship may be particularly burdensome as they wrongly interpret their husband's or wife's behaviour.

Martin's wife was in despair. For years she had tried to change him. Divorce seemed the only solution. She interpreted the fact that he did not change his behaviour as him rejecting her. But gradually she became aware that he was generally not very capable of changing. As long as she saw him as someone who stubbornly wanted to get his own way and was rarely inclined to adjust his pace to that of others, she cherished

> the hope that he would change. But she became exhausted from trying to change him. As soon as she realized that it was Martin's predisposition which caused his behaviour, her hope was rekindled. But her patience ran out once again: the result was social burn-out.

Two elements are of essential importance in forging relationships. First, forming a *secure attachment* in one's youth. As we have seen, in autistic children this is fraught with problems and essentially slower, but it can be achieved. Second, the *formation of friendships* is an important building block for the capacity to develop successful relationships later in life. To translate this into practice, it is necessary to take account of other people which in turn requires having a conception of what goes on in other people's minds (see Table 5.4).

From egocentric behaviour to partnership behaviour

Learning to empathize with others presupposes having solid relationships. The very first one is with the parents, in particular the mother. This is so not only because she is often the main carer and because mother and child are bonded to one another during breastfeeding, but also because in general the mother is more empathic than the father and can give guidance to the child in a world in which he feels structurally a stranger. Through the interaction between mother and child, the child learns to adjust his wishes and desires to those of another person and becomes aware of the extent to which the other is or is not prepared to comply with his wishes.

A child with an autistic disorder has a limited capacity to take account of another person since she cannot sufficiently get into the other's mind and because she has in the meantime probably learnt to get her way through negative behaviour, as we saw in Chapter 7. With this baggage, or rather this lack of baggage, the child is at primary school faced with a new development task: forming friendships. The fact is that children with an autistic disorder are less well equipped to make friends even though they do need friendships in order to make progress towards developing empathy. The relationship with brothers and sisters is also important: it will last throughout life (Boer 1994). What is unique about relationships with siblings is that, on the one hand, it is necessary to get over quarrels because they see each other every day and, on the other hand, it is also possible to carry on together without having settled all arguments (Bigelow *et al.* 1996). For an autistic child, her brothers and sisters are important sources for learning social interaction. For the brothers and sisters, however, it is often a heavy burden to have a brother or sister who is autistic.

The capacity to empathize with other people is stimulated by friendships (Sullivan 1953). Through a friend, we get to know another's world and to penetrate deeper into another's mind. But to be successful in making friends, we have to be able to empathize and take the other's wishes into account. A child has to learn as an individual to meet the other halfway also as an individual with his or her own wishes and feelings. Until the child can do this, the other is largely an 'instrument' in the satisfaction of the child's own needs. Steadily the relationship acquires the character of two individuals who are in contact with one another. Non-autistic children are only capable of genuine *partnership behaviour* from the age of four onwards (Bowlby 1984). This means that the child enters into contact with others as partners and does not see the other as subordinate or exclusively as an instrument serving her own activities. Friendship is reciprocal and based on give and take, taking account of each other and doing things together. The other is no longer viewed as an extension of oneself. On the basis of 'me', the child establishes a relationship with the 'other' who has his or her own thoughts, feelings and wishes. Thus *egocentric thinking* gives way to *empathic thinking*.

As empathic thinking is hampered in autistic children, establishing contacts on the basis of reciprocity, concluding in friendships, will be a cumbersome and often painful task, in the process of which the child constantly has to face 'being different' without really understanding why he is different. From the age of four, when he goes to school, the child is assumed to be forging friendships whereas in this area too the autistic child does not develop on a par with his non-autistic peers. Kees Momma (1996) has given a striking description of how slowly the value of social contact dawns upon the child.

> Yet, I noticed that when I was five I was getting closer to people. I slowly became aware of the nice atmosphere within the family. But I still had problems communicating.

Kanner (1943) gives a similar example of Frederick, for whom it was likewise only by the age of five that he began paying attention to the people around him, to visitors. By the time Kees Momma 'got to know' his family, he should already have been busy making friends. Socially the child is still a toddler, playing without taking account of others, but at primary school he is expected to keep up with others of the same age; even more so in the case of a (highly) gifted child with Asperger's syndrome. The child's high intelligence in one area leads to the expectation that he also comprehends what is happening socially. If it is not the teacher who expects this, then it is the peer group and the other children at school.

Primary school

Primary school is an important period for all children and may for autistic children be a radical and also an anxious period. At primary school, there is little help available with regard to the autistic child's specific sensitive spot: social interaction. Such help is available, for instance, for the child's *learning disorders*, which are not unusual in these children as we saw in Chapter 5. Children with Asperger's syndrome and PDD-NOS usually have a *disharmonic intelligence profile*, meaning that their capacities in various subjects are widely divergent. Usually the difference is between *verbal* and *performal* intelligence. Even more important, however, is the difference between *intellectual* and *social and emotional* development. Because of the growing interest in highly gifted children, there is now increasing attention for children who are emotionally behind but intellectually ahead. They include children with Asperger's syndrome who, although ahead in some intellectual areas, are often structurally underdeveloped in the social and emotional sphere.

> Five-year-old Victor was very withdrawn. He was greatly interested in dinosaurs. It seemed as if he was hardly or not at all aware of the other children in the orphanage where he lived. He took no initiative to play in any way. If invited to join in, he would occasionally stand and watch the others play, without feeling any urge to join them. What he preferred above all was sitting on the sofa with a book.

The learning disorders are in fact not as serious as the contact disorder. Social skills are not taught at school, though they are essential for children in this stage of life and of fundamental importance for children with an autistic disorder.

Children with Asperger's syndrome and PDD-NOS usually go through the ordinary education system for some time without any special help being available at school. Often the child fails at school as he or she begins to display serious behavioural problems and can no longer be kept at school; an alternative form of education will then have to be found. The child's normal and sometimes above average intelligence does not greatly impede learning. Language development is usually normal and arithmetic is no problem either. The learning problems of children with Asperger's syndrome or PDD-NOS are usually not such that they cannot manage in normal education. It is only when the child starts to display serious behavioural problems and the situation at the ordinary school is no longer manageable that recourse must be had to special forms of education. However, even these alternatives are usually not appropriate for the child.

Since the age of five, 14-year-old Robin had had steadily worsening behavioural problems. Time and again he surprised his parents and teachers with his remarkable resistance to particular tasks at school. When his class went swimming, he did not want to join in: 'I'll learn to swim when the water is strong enough to carry me.' Even though he was intelligent, the changeover to secondary school was a complete failure. Within two years, he was downgraded from higher secondary education, for which he had been recommended, via lower secondary education to special secondary education, where his behaviour seriously deteriorated. He should have had no problem learning but because of understimulation combined with a lack of contact with his peer group he ended up in a sharply downward spiral.

Specific education for children who are behind in their development due to predisposition and not to physical or intellectual disability or upbringing is still rare. There are hardly any educational facilities specifically for children with autism, and even less so for those with Asperger's or PDD-NOS. What is of particular importance for them is an assessment of their social and emotional level. *School maturity*, however, is mainly measured by the child's capacity to perform school tasks, evaluating in particular whether the child is able to concentrate sufficiently, can sit still and will not walk about in the classroom. *Social school maturity* has received much less attention. In the meantime, Bar-On (1997) has developed an EQ-I test which measures *emotional intelligence* alongside IQ which measures 'rational' intelligence. This provides a better insight into social and emotional development.

A child who is intellectually ready for education but emotionally not up to the social demands which primary school makes on her easily ends up with problems with the people around her – children and adults – and after some time is at odds with herself.

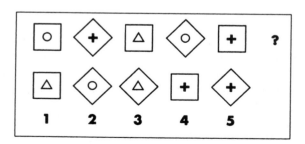

Figure 9.1 Example from an IQ test (Eysenck and Evans 1994). Reproduced with permission from Spectrum. Which of the five figures on the bottom row should go where the question mark is?

Joe, aged five, was eager to play with other children but had little idea how to go about it. He was soon excluded by the others at the kindergarten he was allowed to attend after many failed attempts at various schools. It was virtually impossible to persuade him to engage in constructive play. Instead of choosing activities he enjoyed or in which he could do things together with others, he mainly occupied himself disrupting the others at play. His preferred activity was walking up and down the classroom.

It is important for teachers and classmates to have an insight into what autism is, in particular if an autistic child attends school surrounded by non-autistic children. Vermeulen (2002b) writes of an 'autism-friendly school' with, for instance, clear and specific communication. Knowledge of autism is necessary to understand how upset a child or young person with autism is when the school has been renovated and he or she has to completely re-orient to a new situation. Vermeulen stresses the impact of the interaction: '…just as the whole school affects the pupil, a pupil with autism affects the whole school. The impact of the presence of a pupil with autism reaches beyond the class he or she attends.'

The older the child, the clearer the difference with other children. The child himself continues to grow up, develops further and has a need for contact with others. The quick pace of change in contact or perspective that arises during interaction with others, e.g. in playing together, makes it very hard or indeed impossible for children with an autistic disorder to join in. The terms and conditions of playing together just do not sink in.

Will, aged 14, was delighted that he had a friend who came to his home to play. He really enjoyed it. In his excitement he asked his friend: 'When are you leaving?' His friend felt hurt and replied 'Very soon', and did not stay much longer. Will was disappointed that he left so soon. Will's mother explained that his question had been understood quite differently from how he had intended it. All Will had wanted to know was how much time was left to play with his friend. His mother explained that his question had suggested that Will thought the time had come for his friend to leave. Will was utterly surprised. He had meant his question literally and had no idea that such a different meaning could be attached to it. He thought this was really far-fetched.

Children with an autistic disorder are more self-focused and less contact-oriented but this is not to say that they have no need for contact and do not suffer from their lack of friends. They do have a need for contact with peers, though this is less strong than in other children. Autistic children also have less contact with other children than children without autism (Frith 1989).

A 'buddy' at school who supports the child in her contact with other children can be a great help. Children are often better able than adults to sense that a child with an autistic disorder is 'different' and has a need for more repetition in play as well as clear instructions. While, on the one hand, a brother or sister with an autistic disorder can be a heavy burden on the family, the non-autistic sibling can, on the other hand, help the child to learn how to interact with peers. As time progresses, autistic children perceive with increasing clarity that they deviate from other children. Often, all they want is to be 'ordinary' and they tend to try desperately to behave in such a way that they can join in with their peers. Nevertheless, they do not manage to make friends.

The despair of a child with Asperger's syndrome in its need to make friends was strikingly expressed by nine-year-old George in the film *I am not Stupid* (Fisher 1995). George desperately wanted to have a friend but failed to make friends, and he asked his parents if there was such a thing as 'Friends 'r' us', similar to the toy shop Toys 'r' us.

The constant lack of success in attempts to make friends and the repeated rejections seriously affect the child's self-image. The child perceives that people do not like to play with her, prefer to choose someone else at gymnastics and do not invite her to birthday parties. This also affects the child's intellectual functioning and she usually does not perform optimally, unless she compensates by throwing herself into intellectual work. The consequences of being excluded are equally harmful for the child's emotional development. Gunilla Gerland (2003) blatantly expressed the feeling of being different from others: 'What was wrong with me? Why was I not a real human being?' Her self-image became increasingly damaged as she grew older: 'In the past, when I did not feel like a real human being, I had the feeling I belonged to a different species. Now I still do not feel like a real human being but more like a poor imitation of other people, a kind of faulty copy.'

This need to belong marks a difference with other forms within the autistic spectrum. Children with Kanner's autism have less need for contact with others and therefore suffer less from the lack of it. The 'mild' form of autism which Asperger's syndrome is said to be may well, therefore, be more painful than

Kanner's autism in which children live more by themselves, detached from others. A child with Asperger's syndrome or PDD-NOS is, as it were, caught under a bell jar in the midst of the social process: he sees everything happening around him but does not manage to take part in it. This process, which starts at primary school, continues at secondary school.

Children with an autistic disorder are at a higher risk of being bullied throughout their school years and also later at work.

Bullying

Children of primary-school age form groups of boys and girls. They rarely mix and not for long. This is the period in which the distance between the two sexes seems the widest. The difference between boys and girls, which also becomes accentuated physically, enhances the likelihood of group formation. As a result of the increase in muscular tissue and physical strength, boys feel the need to test their strength against others. There is strong pressure to form a positive *social identity* (Delfos 1999b). At primary school, competitiveness plays an important role and this gives rise to the risk of exclusion.

A child with a disorder is different. This is less noticeable in children with an autistic disorder because there are no visible physical deviations, such as is the case, for instance, in children with Down syndrome. Moreover, children with an autistic disorder function normally in many fields. Others, including their peers, feel that the child is 'different'. Whatever the reason or nature of the child's deviation at primary school, e.g. an unusual external appearance or higher intelligence, the fact of being different is often viewed by peers as unpleasant or even frightening. Peers sometimes find it difficult to cope with this. We even observe this phenomenon when a child goes through the awful experience of losing her father or mother. Alongside all the attention and support, the child will inevitably also be teased about it ('Oh, she's crying again, probably because her mother is dead...'). This is something that adults rarely realize and certainly have difficulty imagining. The basic cause is that it is often shocking to children when one of them loses a parent. It suddenly confronts them with the fact that their own parents can also die. Children who are used to externalizing their problems, and therefore display aggressive, outwardly directed behaviour, may start bullying a child who has lost a parent.

A child who is different from other children is not easily accepted in the group; he is not popular and risks being bullied by children who have a tendency to externalize problems. It should be noted that bullies (using physical force) are more often boys than girls, the ratio being 75 per cent boys to 25 per cent girls. For psychological bullying the ratio is reversed (van der Meer 1993, 1997). Boys, moreover, are on average more attuned to registering negative signals. Usually, therefore, boys receive the negative signals of children with an autistic disorder sooner.

Children with Asperger's syndrome often become withdrawn and anxious in response to their peers. Children with PDD-NOS more often show an aggressive response. In Chapter 12, which deals with aggression, we shall examine why people with an autistic disorder in general respond with little aggression to others.

There is a difference between *teasing*, which is incidental, and *bullying*, which is systematic (van der Meer 1993). Teasing presupposes equal status in the relationship between the teaser and the teased whereas bullying is based on a power difference, making it very difficult for the bullied child to defend himself. In bullying, moreover, there is psychological or physical harm. Being the victim of bullying can lead to major psychological problems and even suicide. Many children who were persistently bullied in their youth try hard throughout their lives to prevent ever being approached negatively again.

Children with an autistic disorder develop a negative self-image as a result of bullying. They measure themselves against others and find themselves wanting, without understanding why. They perceive that they are different, but have no idea why. They notice that they remain on the outside, that they do not do things the way others do, e.g. that their pace in education is often slower. All this harms their self-image, steadily leading to a profound sense of inferiority.

> John continuously evaluated the way his therapy was going, and at one point he said warmly to this therapist: 'A great deal has changed. I still don't manage to do all the things I would like to do, but I no longer feel a loser. Congratulations, that's what you have achieved!'

'Doing your best' often plays a role in children with an autistic disorder. In this respect, there is a difference between children with Asperger's syndrome and those with PDD-NOS. 'Doing one's best' more frequently occurs in children with Asperger's syndrome while children with PDD-NOS more often get bogged down in angry behaviour and resistance. However, it should be borne in mind that there is no sharp line of demarcation and that the PDD-NOS group in fact comprises a number of children whose Asperger's syndrome has not been diagnosed.

It is important to be fully aware that a child with an autistic disorder is susceptible to being bullied. Unfortunately, it is advisable to assume this beforehand and try to protect the child from it as much as possible. The child should first and foremost be helped in finding a proper response to bullying.

Joe, nearly six, had hardly ever been to school. He was very eager, but things always went wrong. Another school was once again tried out but before long he was bullied there. Asked what he did to deal with this, he replied: 'I scream very loudly, and I spit and then they stop.' The therapist responded by saying that this was a very good idea and that it was great that it helped but that it did have a number of disadvantages. For instance, you would not get any friends this way because of course everyone was startled by the screaming and spitting. To Joe this was strange; after all, if they did nothing, he did nothing! The therapist explained that there were other ways of reacting, for example by telling someone who was being unpleasant: 'That's not nice, we can't be friends like that.' At the next session, Joe enthusiastically reported that it worked. The bullying had stopped and it had not been necessary for him to scream and spit.

The child also has to learn to get help so that others can put an end to the bullying. It requires insight and tolerance on the part of the teacher to detect bullying and assess the impotence of the autistic child. Bullying is a response to the way in which the child comes across and her socially awkward behaviour. To someone who cannot sense or comprehend how little a child with an autistic disorder understands of people, it often seems as if the child provokes the behaviour of others. As a result, the child becomes even more isolated as she is not only bullied but also blamed for it. The resulting sense of guilt is something which many people with Asperger's syndrome or PDD-NOS carry with them for the rest of their lives. They constantly have the feeling of doing something wrong unintentionally and being punished for it. Not only because of bullying but also because of rejection in general.

It will probably not be possible to prevent bullying altogether. Bullying is a problem connected with a particular stage of development, especially in boys, which frequently occurs in a particular period, especially in the second half of primary school and the first part of secondary school (Delfos 1999b). Children with deviant behaviour can easily become a target for bullying. Children with Asperger's syndrome and PDD-NOS will not easily get support from other children and also have no idea how to muster such support. Nor will they find it easy to mobilize support from the teacher. As a result, they can easily become isolated, making them even easier targets for bullies.

Notorious bullies appear to have little *empathic capacity*. They are often children with a problematic background who as a child and later as an adult frequently also display criminal behaviour. Their limited empathy is of quite a different type to the impaired empathic capacity of children with an autistic disorder. A child with an autistic disorder will not easily become a bully, although he can be obnoxious towards other children. As we have seen, however, criminal behaviour does not really occur in them. Children with an autistic disorder are *non-empathic* in a naïve, innocent way, without evil or egoistic intentions. Autistic children have little idea of what goes on in others but do not derive any pleasure from hurting or offending someone else, as bullies may. They are in fact very pure children, very sincere. They are not aggressive by nature even though they may on occasion behave quite aggressively. Their lack of empathy covers the entire range of emotions, from pleasant to unpleasant. Children who bully on the basis of a lack of empathic capacity are specifically unaware of the seriousness and intensity of other children's feelings. Children with an autistic disorder are generally unaware of the feelings as such. An autistic child can therefore be very sensitive, very caring, once he knows another's feelings and knows what the other needs. This can be a significant advantage in relationships.

A negative self-image develops as a result of being rejected as a friend and being bullied. The self-image of children with an autistic disorder is strongly underdeveloped, partly because of their problems in recognizing and expressing feelings. At school the child runs the risk of having her self-image shaped by negative experiences. Eventually children with an autistic disorder feel that they are constantly failing and they develop a negative picture of themselves and of the people around them. The film *I'm not Stupid* (Fisher 1995) gives expression to something experienced by so many people with Asperger's syndrome, namely their great need to prove that they are not stupid and that they are worthwhile.

Self-image

The task of the parents in developing the child's self-image is to give the child, in spite of everything, *unconditional* love, support and self-confidence. 'Unconditional' does not mean that everything has to be approved of, quite the contrary; but that the child *as a human being* is not rejected. Unconditional love means making a distinction between the human being and his or her behaviour. There is an enormous difference to a child whether you say to him 'You are really annoying!' or 'What you've done is really annoying!' Giving *I messages* (Gordon 1974) also puts into perspective what is being said, limiting it to the person who says it. 'You're not doing that right' sounds much more general and damning than 'I think that you're not doing that right'. It suggests that other opinions are also possible.

However, it is not easy to give unconditional love. Parents are only human and bringing up a child with an autistic disorder is an extremely heavy burden on them. Bringing up children is a difficult task as it is, even if they have no problem at all and you, as a parent, are in excellent health. The fact is, moreover, that in families with an autistic child there are often additional problems. Not only is it very likely that other children and family members will have autistic features too, conditions such as depressions and rare diseases are also more frequent in these families (Gillberg 1992). Parents have more to cope with than only this child and, as a result, do not always function optimally. In a family with an autistic child, the parents' own dysfunctioning often returns with a vengeance. A tired parent who is in a hurry and in an irritated voice urges the child to get on with it will be faced with a child who goes strongly on the defence and becomes unmanageable. Patience in raising a child with an autistic disorder is absolutely necessary, no matter how difficult this may be.

Seeing the effects of their less than adequate behaviour, parents are at a risk of developing feelings of guilt. This is unfounded, not because they make no mistakes but because it is not possible to live without making mistakes and because the extent to which children with an autistic disorder have problems is not due to the parents' conduct. Of course it is true that the parents' behaviour may help the child and that the child is worse off if the parents do not help it properly. However, parents do not cause an underdeveloped left hemisphere of the brain! The core of the problem lies in the disorder and not in the parents. The other side of the coin is that because of this fact parents have fewer possibilities of influencing the disorder than they would wish.

The relationship the child has with his parents constitutes the link to people in the pre-schooler's environment. In going to primary school, the child switches from an environment with relatively few people with whom he is in contact to a school full of people and a group with which he spends the day in intensive contact. The depth demanded in relationships greatly increases in the primary school period. The child is expected to learn to form friendships.

Developing friendships

Primary schoolchildren are fully occupied forging *friendships*. Friendships evolve around two aspects: the degree of *egocentricity* and that of *continuity*. There are differences between boys and girls with regard to the nature of friendships. According to Rutter and Rutter (1993), the emphasis in girls is usually more on openness and intimacy. Consequently, girls more often have a couple of girlfriends whereas boys more often have a large group of male friends. Girls share more emotional events and more often choose one-to-one relationships; boys compete with one another more physically and they more often associate in groups.

The importance of friendships is beyond dispute. As we have seen, Sullivan (1953) argued that developing a close friendship makes people more receptive to other people's feelings. Selman (1981) designed a classification of friendships according to age.

Table 9.1 Development of friendships (Selman 1981).
Reproduced with permission from Cambridge University Press.

Type of friendship	Period	Nature of friendship
Playmate	Pre-school period	A friend is someone who lives near you and with whom you happen to play
One-way assistance	Early school period	A friend is someone who knows you better than others and who knows what you like and what you don't like; a friend is important because he or she does things you want
Mutual cooperation	Later school period	Greater awareness of reciprocity in relationships; greater willingness to adapt to mutual wishes; no long term – quarrels can easily end a friendship
Intimate mutually sharing relationships	Late childhood years, early adolescence	More closeness, awareness of continuity, the main goal of friendship no longer to prevent getting bored but a possibility for intimacy; conflicts do not necessarily end the relationship

Children with an autistic disorder stay in the first phase for longer, that of *playmates*. In this phase, playing with someone else is more something that arises accidentally. The need to play together is not as strong as in the average child. Because of their limited socioscheme, autistic children have little awareness of others around them. This stands in the way of playing together because in order to let someone in on a game, one has to be aware of the other. In order to really play together, one has to be able to imagine what the other is feeling and thinking, see the other's possibilities to join in and the need for reciprocity in play. The children's book *Vogel* (*Birdie*) (Delfos 1997; see Appendix III for a list of recommended books) explains the egocentric perspective and the need for reciprocity in contact.

Birdie makes long journeys and becomes so preoccupied with himself and his flying skills that he only thinks of himself. On his most distant journey, Birdie discovers that other birds are also important and that the world does not revolve around him.

The nature of the autistic children's play is for a long time more typical of pre-school children than of toddlers, making it difficult for them to adapt to the school environment.

Joe wanted only one thing in the playground: to go around in the cart. Time and again he rushed towards it with determination, pushing children aside if they were in the way. He was not interested in anyone else and thought the others were too childish. But this was in fact what the others thought of him: that his behaviour was childish.

The playing of children with an autistic disorder is often repetitive in character. The repetitions which a baby and a pre-schooler enjoy are in an autistic child often extended into a general way of doing things, from the way he plays to the way he eats. An autistic child often gets stuck for a long time in what Piaget (1972) calls *sensorimotor* play, in which the senses and movement are the most important components. The child repeats successive actions for the pleasure of controlling them. The material with which he plays is of considerable importance. Autistic children are often interested in shiny, rotating objects.

In the period when children go to primary school, the child with an autistic disorder is in specific areas still busy completing her development of the first two years. The playing of non-autistic toddlers is much more varied in nature and the material is of lesser importance. From about the age of two, language begins to play an important part and non-autistic children engage in *make-believe* play in many variations. The materials have become less important than play, but the various roles that are acted out become more important. Vygotsky (1978) gives the example of two sisters who say: 'Let's pretend that we're sisters.' Through this example, he strikingly shows that the fact of having a little sister is not the same as realizing how sisters relate to one another. In their play-acting, the two sisters can explore this.

In this phase, the material is secondary to the activity and is no longer the focus of attention. In play, the child prepares for social interaction. By the time he goes to primary school, these games will become increasingly important. Friends start playing a role in games: cowboy, master, mother, baby. Children act out all roles that are important to them and create a number of roles in which they can work off particular emotions, for instance an aggression game such as 'playing soldiers', or 'playing hospital' after a stay in hospital.

By the time a child with an autistic disorder goes to school, his contact behaviour is determined by the stage he is still in – *accidental contact without personal interest* – and his form of play – *more focused on material and repetition* – does not link up with that of his peers. This forms an impediment to playing together. Because of a number of characteristics, including this playing pattern but often also the child's wooden motor activity or deviant use of language, the child with an autistic disorder is perceived as different by his peers. And 'different' is easily seen as 'wrong', in particular at this young age. The child is rejected and excluded. Initially he is not really aware of this. He is busy reaching a target, perhaps playing in the blocks corner, and registers in particular the moments when this is possible and when he is frustrated in doing so. Playing together is often not appreciated by a child with an autistic disorder because the other has his or her own contribution to make and thereby disrupts the autistic child's playing pattern, or at least this is how the child perceives it. The other child sees the autistic child as dictatorial and uncooperative and is therefore unwilling to play with him.

Selman's (1981) description of phases of friendships in Table 9.1 gives us an indication of how the child ought to be helped. A child with an autistic disorder should be guided to the next stage of development. The first step in this direction is recognizing and acknowledging in which stage the child happens to be. We do not impose things on a baby because we respect that she is not ready for certain things and will develop only with dedication, time and patience. The patience we have for babies is also required for children with an autistic disorder. We often tend to go too fast. We are eager to teach the child to take the feelings and wishes of others into account even though it will be a long time before the child is ready for this, but it is the ultimate goal. Even adults have difficulty taking account of others.

By the time they go to school, autistic children are often still in the first stage of friendships, that of accidental playmates. During the first years at primary school they could move on to the second stage but this is often hampered because they tend to be excluded. They are expected to be in the second stage and to be aware of the qualities of others. This further complicates the transition to subsequent stages.

The second stage, *one-way assistance*, is a stage in which the child registers the fact that other people have qualities that are pleasant and that playing may be more enjoyable if another child joins in. Initially this will be so because the other has toys with which the autistic child wants to play. Accordingly, it is important to teach the child that it is fun to play with other children's toys, that other children have qualities that can make playing more fun and that others can be 'used' in their own play, i.e. may be useful. This takes some effort on our part. We would prefer to skip this stage, refrain from teaching the child to use another child and instead teach him to play together with and take account of the other. However, learning to make friends is something that has to be built up in a number of stages. In the previous chapter it was noted that stimulating me–other differentiation precedes the formation of friendships. It is important, therefore, to first try to make the child develop attachment and experience emotional contact before he can take the next step.

Apart from teaching the child to see the other's qualities and giving him or her a place in his own play, we also have to give attention to the way he plays. A child with an autistic disorder will usually like *repetitive play*. It has to be given ample opportunity for this as it feels happy doing so. If the demands put on the child are too heavy, he will become anxious and angry. Some researchers, e.g. Frith (1989), take the view that repetitive behaviour arises from a lack of activities. They take this view because the behaviour diminishes when the child engages in an activity. In my opinion, however, repetitive behaviour has quite a different function; namely, to reduce anxiety and induce a hypnotic trance. We shall consider this in more detail in Chapter 11 when discussing anxiety.

In order to optimize the child's development, it is important to ensure that the new forms one wishes to stimulate link up with existing forms of play. Here, again, the guiding principle should be that it is better to practise briefly and frequently than to do so a couple of times for longer. It is important to try to develop *make-believe play* with the child. The most basic form of make-believe play may well be 'peekaboo', in which the parent alternately puts a cloth over his or her own face and the baby's. In this game, one pretends very briefly that the baby or oneself is not there. Once the baby is able to pull away the cloth, she will derive great enjoyment from this game. Playing hide and seek is a more refined form of the same game. It is advisable not to look for opportunities to play mummies and daddies too soon but instead to play brief little make-believe games with the child.

Make-believe play can also be used to prepare the child for school, and once the child goes to school it can be used to talk about school through play. Young children prefer to communicate non-verbally and through play rather than a conversation at the table, which is what adults prefer (Delfos 2000).

In Chapter 7 (p.177) I pointed out that in children with autism make-believe play sometimes does not emerge until puberty. Make believe is a very important form of play and it is therefore necessary to pay attention to it when helping children and youngsters with autism. Because of its importance, studies are in progress to investigate whether make-believe play can be developed specifically for autistic children and youngsters.

In the third stage, *mutual cooperation*, friendships involve more collaboration and there is more awareness of reciprocity. In this period, children try to adjust more to their friends' wishes. Continuity in friendship is still limited and friendships can still be easily broken off following a quarrel; however, they are also easily restored.

> Elma, aged nine, had a conflict with an adult. 'It's not easy, quarrelling with grown-ups, it takes them so long and they're angry for a long time. Children just say "shall we be friends again?" and then everything is all right again.'

Children with an autistic disorder face huge obstacles trying to cope with the need for reciprocity. Taking account of the other means being able to imagine what goes on in the other's mind. It means knowing what another person thinks, feels and wants, and what effect your behaviour has on him or her. By the time this demand is made on the child, it is a pre-adolescent in terms of calendar age but, in social and emotional development, he has only just emerged from the toddler stage. Abstract thinking has in the meantime evolved and can be mobilized to exchange explanations about interaction. The child has to learn that he is not (yet) capable in all fields of associating with his peers and that more time and experience is needed to become so. Not every child develops at the same rate in every field. Often, the child herself senses this because children with an autistic disorder prefer to play with younger children. For their development it is better to let them play with younger children rather than expect them to play with their peers. With younger children, they can as it were continue their 'delayed' development. 'Delayed' appears in quotation marks because for the child this is a more optimal rate and as a result the child will develop faster than if she were pushed.

Children with Asperger's syndrome are often particularly interested in trains, town planning or dinosaurs. This can be used to help the child to establish contact with children with the same interest in clubs with a particular focus. The Internet has all kinds of websites where like-minded people can get in touch with each other. There is an increasing number of Internet sites for people with autism that provide opportunities for exchanging contacts (see Appendix II). As she grows older, the autistic child learns more about social relationships and becomes more capable making contacts and friendships.

The fourth stage, *intimate mutually shared relationships*, marks the beginning of emotional relations, of establishing partnerships. The preceding stages prepare for this.

Deepening friendships into relationships

Looking at the description of Selman's (1981) fourth stage (closer, awareness of continuity, the main goal of friendship no longer to prevent getting bored but as a possibility of intimacy, conflicts do not necessarily end the relationship), we immediately understand how essential friendships are for the formation of relationships in (young) adults.

The fourth stage coincides with the onset of the child's biological maturation into a sexually mature individual. Within the framework of this biological maturation, with its hormonal influxes, the problem of calendar age not being synchronous with social and emotional development becomes acute. As a result, the child may get into difficulties. He cannot meet the demand for intimate mutually sharing relationships but he can see around him that he is expected to take part in this. During adolescence, most children with an autistic disorder withdraw within themselves, with the risk of *becoming depressive*. Depression is more likely if the child is of normal or above average intelligence. Adolescents with Asperger's syndrome experience their inability to share fully in social interaction as painful because of their growing insight into social relationships (Happé 1998). Some start smoking hash in an attempt to screen themselves off even more or, on the contrary, to join in with the others and be part of the crowd. Smoking hash and drinking alcohol can be used as a form of *self-medication*. Gunilla Gerland (2003) describes how pleasant it was simply to be part of the crowd by smoking hash with them and getting into the trance so familiar to her, this time not self-induced but generated by the use of cannabis. The other users around her at the most thought that she could get really stoned.

There have been various theories about *addiction*. Nowadays an integrative theory appears the most plausible. Van Dijk (1979) developed a model in which the factors that play a role in addiction are viewed as cogwheels engaging with each other and reinforcing each other's effect.

Van Dijk (1979) posited that the body forms a counter-response to harmful substances by producing counter-agents. To put it more simply, the response to amphetamines, which have an 'accelerating effect', is therefore 'slowing'. The response to smoking cannabis, which has a 'slowing' effect, is therefore 'accelerating'. According to Van Dijk, addiction is a process in which the body craves the drug because it has already produced antidotes to it: the 'anticipatory response'. The elements of the mind/body system reinforce each other. The more is taken of the harmful substance, the more counter-agents are produced and the greater the subsequent craving. But also: the more psychosocial problems there are, the greater the need for the substance of addiction (see Figure 9.2).

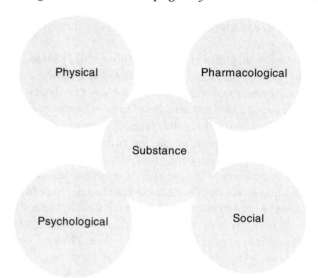

Figure 9.2 Circular model based on Van Dijk (1979). Van Dijk's circles, according to DETOX (Noorlander et al.1993). Reproduced with permission.

Due to smoking hash, the young person becomes increasingly depressive and listless and as a result of the body's counter-response to the substance ends up in an excited or even aggressive state. Noorlander, Rijnders and Wijdeven (1993) have written a clear article about the effects of addictive drugs.

By using drugs, it is easier for children with Asperger's syndrome or PDD-NOS to link up with other youngsters. If a youngster has been unable to make friends during the primary-school period, he or she might well end up joining high-risk groups. The codes of such groups are often quite evident. They have visible rules about hairstyle, use of alcohol and drugs, preferred means of transport, attitudes towards adults and use of language. Conforming to the rules makes joining the group easier. A lonely youngster can try to join the group by following the rules.

Imparting information on the meaning and consequences of drug use is important for all young people. If provided early, it will usually be effective for people with an autistic disorder.

On the threshold of sexuality

Sexuality is an important component in the formation of relationships during adolescence. Also in this respect, young people with an autistic disorder often lag a few years behind their peers. By the time they start thinking about more intimate friendships, their peers are already preoccupied with sexual relationships. For children, sex education is easier to come by than 'friendship education'. In the seemingly straightforward rules of sexuality they seem to find a way of being part of the group. Boys may, for instance, behave towards girls in an inappropriately assertive manner that is seen as sexually 'forward', but they may also find themselves ridiculed by girls because of their awkward behaviour.

> Will, aged 17, had always been excluded by his peers. He saw his friends go around with girls and wanted to have a girlfriend too. He gave a girl a ring as a token of friendship which she accepted but then gave to the boy with whom she was in love. Will felt hurt and did not understand what was wrong with his 'relationship'.

In intimate mutual relationships, there is an expectation, even more so than in other forms of contact, that feelings should be expressed in words. People with an autistic disorder have problems recognizing and verbalizing their own emotions and this applies even more so to emotions they have not experienced themselves.

> Jack, 23, wondered what 'kissing' was all about. 'I know it is lips-lips-push-push, but what are you supposed to feel?'

Isolation and depression

With age, differences among people with an autistic disorder become more pronounced. Some cope extremely well, find a job in which they can apply their particular qualities, and even start a family. For many, adolescence is the most difficult period. There is an acute sense of being isolated while the need to join in social contact has grown stronger. The many attempts made in the past to establish contact have failed and the adolescent with Asperger's syndrome or PDD-NOS is often very depressive.

> After the umpteenth failure to make friends, Alec said bitterly: 'It would be better to look for a friend in a psychiatric institution; I've a better chance to find a soulmate there.'

This is an extremely difficult period for parents. They see their child's sadness and isolation and feel powerless to help. The ability to form relationships partly depends on how the child has learnt to make friends during the school period. In a relationship, everything that has been learnt in earlier stages becomes evident. The scope of the individual's *capacity for attachment* from the baby and pre-school stage, the *capacity to give* from the toddler stage, the *capacity for emotional contact* from the early school period, the *capacity for balanced relationships* from the later school period, the *formation of personal identity* from puberty and the *capacity for sexual contact* is now tested in practice (Delfos 1994, 2001b). At this stage, any disruptions that occurred in earlier stages are therefore clearly visible. In a partner relationship, all these stages become simultaneously evident for the first time.

The combination: Empathic with autistic

Forming relationships is not an easy task for people with an autistic disorder. In order to form relationships, it is necessary to talk about yourself, to engage in *self-disclosure*. Sharing intimate knowledge is quintessential in creating a bond with others. However, self-disclosure is based on awareness of one's own feelings and ways of expressing them. This is a weak spot in people with an autistic disorder. Although they are often verbally gifted and are very skilled in argumentation, and have been referred to as a 'verbal cannon', it is difficult and time-consuming for them to get in touch with their own feelings and align them with behaviour and events. Many people with Asperger's syndrome are good, though slow, at expressing themselves in writing, as witness the autobiographies of Sellin (1995), Grandin (1995b), Gerland (2003) and others, and Segar's survival guide (1997).

It is remarkable that autistic men often choose a partner who is strongly empathic but somewhat emotionally unstable. The naïve down-to-earthness and labile sensitivity compensate each other. In general, people with an autistic disorder are more reliable, purer and more sincere than people on average. They lie less, partly because they cannot sufficiently understand what goes on in other people's minds to manipulate them. An empathic partner helps the autistic person to understand social contact better. However, the empathic partner, because of her strong ability to get into another person's mind, will also have a stronger tendency to manipulate others and will be better at it than people on average. Having a 'pure' partner with whom her own impurity clashes supports her in her struggle not to give in to the temptation to manipulate. Her lability is constrained by her partner's down-to-earth approach. The difference in thinking may come to the fore in various areas. Starting from an attitude of mutual respect, there are surprising possibilities to complement each other.

Alec and Sylvia sometimes threw themselves into an adventure game on the PC. It highlighted their different ways of thinking, with surprising results. Alec even felt that doing computer games together had a therapeutic effect on their relationship. Sylvia systematically explored the virtual environment. When she came up against a wall with drawers, she searched each drawer one by one. Alec had a need for structure but was very chaotic. He frantically looked for structure in that virtual world. While Sylvia was successful when the situation called for a structured approach, Alec found solutions because of his creative way of thinking. It was no problem at all for him to relate seemingly meaningless subjects to each other or to assign a function to subjects that were utterly different from their normal one, e.g. viewing a watch not as a timepiece but as an object with a particular weight and one that could exert force. In this way, he arrived at solutions to situations that Sylvia could never have conceived of.

In Veerle Beel's book about partners of people with an autistic disorder (Beel 2000), she mainly presents women who are divorced from a man assumed to be autistic, without always having been diagnosed. One of these undiagnosed men, moreover, is probably psychopathic rather than autistic. Since these are women who speak up after their divorce, the picture is quite opaque. After a divorce, women will, depending on the stage of the divorce process, rarely speak of their partner with proper nuance, whether he is autistic or not. His negative qualities are accentuated and what emerges as a result is a completely distorted picture of the autistic partner. What is clear in these interviews, however, are the great differences and the extent to which life is governed by guidelines. In conversations with people who are not divorced, there is more evidence of the strength of love and the balance that can be found, no matter how difficult such a relationship may be.

> The apparent peace he radiates, his rational way of dealing with problems, were diametrically opposed to my emotional approach. Of course, this has led to major conflicts between us. But now I see it more as a learning process. Through him I learn to analyse my feelings more objectively.

> There are also aspects to him that are typically autistic and which I love: his structure, his reason. Through him I have become much more independent. Otherwise I would have lost my way in life. Through him I have found myself. And he is so pure. When I see him walking, I recognize his typical posture from a distance. And each time I think: 'Whatever the problem, I would still go for you'. (Beel 2000)

Of her relationship with her autistic husband, the same woman said: 'I see the human being behind the autism.' No matter how well intended, this is in fact speaking about the partner as a case rather than a human being. For a successful relationship, it may well be more accurate to say: 'I see the autism behind the human being.'

A relationship: Learning from life itself

Problems in building up a relationship are often evident from the outset. Starting a relationship requires a subtle approach, which is often too much to ask from people with an autistic disorder. Their lack of experience in contact is quite obvious because they are incapable of small talk. People with Asperger's syndrome tend to get immediately to the point.

> Via a personal ad, Alec had managed to contact a girl by telephone to get acquainted. In their conversation, he asked a number of questions and to his utter surprise the girl said that she did not want meet him because it sounded like going through an interview with a questionnaire, not at all a spontaneous conversation. Alec was surprised. He thought that it was in fact very sensible to ask questions in preparation for a date. Yet, he was not dissatisfied because he had managed to keep her on the phone for a full half hour. He did wonder what 'spontaneous' actually meant. After this had been explained to him, he had a brilliant idea: 'I'm going to do some travelling through the country and start chats with people on the train, then I can practise a bit.' Alec was very creative in arranging a situation in which to practise. This self-developed training programme in social skills proved highly effective.

Asperger (1944) mentions the lack of spontaneity and the strongly intellectual approach as very characteristic for the boys he was working with but also for their parents.

> With the discovery of how relationships work, the need arises to make closer contact. At the course he was attending, John, nearly 30, made contact with women and with one in particular. He began to understand what contact meant. He looked for ways of transposing this insight into

behaviour. This is similar to the behaviour of an adolescent in his first hesitant steps towards contact with girls, but there is an important difference. John's thinking was different and he had become aware of this. He gave the following description of his contact with the young woman he met on the course.

'She is also a kind of example to me. Look, I now have something of a theoretical basis, but because of her I see various theoretical viewpoints in practice. And in this way, I can also examine my own behaviour more closely. In fact, this is sometimes quite frustrating because at times I know better how to approach her (which is nice because then I do not feel so uncertain), I see it clearly and yet I can't do it. For example, when we're having a conversation she talks about all sorts of everyday things such as a film she has seen or something that has happened to her or about someone she knows. But very little happens to me and I also think of quite different things. It would be a bit boring if in an ordinary conversation I tried to explain principles all the time. So I listen to her and search for things in my everyday life that I could tell her. At first I wasn't aware of it, but apparently I have a tendency to place things that are being told to me in a general context, which as it happens is not always a good response to a story told in a nice way.'

Forming a relationship is all the more difficult for an autistic person because the underlying base must remain sincere and balanced. What this means is that building up a relationship not on the basis of genuine feelings but purely for the purpose of not being alone is doomed to fail. In a relationship, it is important to have a balance of give and take. To everyone, forming a relationship is a great, possibly the greatest, challenge in life. To someone with an autistic disorder, it is harder on the one hand because he or she has difficulty getting into the other's mind and, on the other hand, easier because qualities such as loyalty and reliability can be brought into the relationship. It is these qualities in particular that are important in a relationship. An autistic person is often regarded as heartless when he or she fails to sense what is going on in the other person or what something means to another. However, this is quite different from not being prepared to give when the other needs it. We get an idea of this from the way in which Alec approached his partner in their relationship.

When Alec was approaching 30, he managed to start a serious relationship. Either attempts had failed or he had broken them off because they did not seem pure. This time it was right. After some time, Sylvia wanted to meet the therapist he had been seeing regularly. This wish was mutual. The therapist found that Sylvia had not chosen a 'case' but saw the fact that Alec had Asperger's syndrome as one of his peculiarities, such as all people have. She wanted to have a relationship and not be a carer. This was a sound basis and the relationship grew closer and stronger as time went by. After some time, Sylvia wanted to have a meeting with Alec and the therapist together. She wanted to discuss how Alec behaved towards her when she had a problem. When there was something wrong with her and she told Alec, he was always there for her, he would talk to her and support her. However, he never did so on his own initiative. Consequently, she did not know for sure whether Alec really meant it. After all, it was not possible that he was always prepared to do so, or was it? When he heard this, Alec was astounded. After all, if he didn't want to, he wouldn't do it! 'But you never do it on your own initiative', Sylvia replied. 'But I do it when you say so, don't I? If I don't know it, I can't do it', Alec replied. 'But I'd like it very much if you did it off your own bat. I can't always say it', Sylvia said in despair. Alec obviously did not understand this at all. The therapist took a specific example to explain things. 'If Sylvia falls into the water, and you know she can't swim, you go and rescue her, don't you? Then she needn't say while drowning: "I'm drowning because I can't swim, so will you rescue me?" That's what Sylvia is talking about. Sometimes she is in such a state and she feels so awful that she just can't say it and then she wants you to see it and do something about it, without her having to say so.' Alec instantly realized that he would not be capable of this and asked in a worried tone: 'Is this structurally threatening to our relationship?' This intelligent young man had understood perfectly well that this sensing was beyond his reach and wished to know whether it meant that the relationship could not go on.

Life can be very tough for people with Asperger's syndrome. Sometimes they need very long-term help, though not always intensively. Alec, for instance, had no therapeutic help at all for some time, and very little help over a longer period. However, he knew that it was there if he needed it and came to see the therapist at moments in his life when he had problems. The adolescent who spoke in the third person, was very depressive, had no contacts and had an extremely difficult family background had developed into a young man who was capable of feeling happy in a relationship, could use his talents and managed to get a job.

> When Alec had to change jobs because the institute he worked for was being closed down, he was terribly stressed. Sylvia helped him by supporting him through thick and thin, expressing her confidence that he would find another nice job. Alec was enormously grateful to her. It was an incredible experience to him to feel how mutually supportive a relationship could be.

In providing care to adolescents with an autistic disorder, it is important that they receive therapeutic help in which they can talk about contacts and relationships. Having parents in the background who provide support and unconditional love is an important basis on which the adolescent can develop. What is essential is that there remains hope, hope that the situation improves, hope that contacts can eventually develop, and hope that it will prove possible to learn to make friends. The above-mentioned documentary *I'm not Stupid* (Fisher 1995) concludes with the wise words of Mark Fleisher, a young man with Asperger's syndrome:

> I think for anyone with Asperger's Syndrome there is nothing stopping them making progress. Now, it may be a bit slower than some other people, but it doesn't stop them making it. I mean it's like climbing this high mountain and you got really heavy shoes on. Now yes, that is probably gonna mean that you're gonna walk slower, but you still walk on that mountain. You can always set goals and always climb up towards them. And that's really what it is like. No matter how long it takes, there's always hope, that's my belief.

Focal points

- Determine in which stage of making friends the child happens to be.
- Link up with the stage the child is in, in order to stimulate further development.
- Give the child a chance to develop at his own pace, for instance by accepting that he prefers to play with younger children.
- Friendships are necessary if one is to be able to build up relationships later on in life.

- Due to the difference in cognitive and emotional functioning, the child may start to display behavioural problems at school.

- Children with autism are emotionally not mature for school in the ordinary education system.

- Children with an autistic disorder run the risk of being bullied at school.

- The self-image of children with autism is damaged by bullying and by being rejected by their peers.

- In families with autism there are often various disorders, but also particular syndromes.

- Make sure that the child is informed about the meaning and dangers of drugs.

- Make sure the child receives sexual education.

- Autistic people often bond with an empathic partner.

- Working on a relationship demands considerable effort from autistic people and the non-autistic partner makes many painful wrong interpretations.

- Autistic people have a naïve purity; strongly empathic people, however, can be very manipulative.

Focal points regarding attitude

- Patience.

- Development always remains possible.

- Respect the purity of autistic people.

Summary

Forming a secure attachment and forming friendships are two important building blocks in forging relationships as life unfolds. Making friends is a developmental task with which children are faced at primary school. A child with an autistic disorder does not develop socially in line with her calendar age. Her intelligence profile is not evenly balanced. It may be that the child goes to primary school while socially she still functions at the level of a baby or a pre-schooler. At primary school, this problem is often not recognized and as a result the child may start to display serious behavioural problems. A child with Asperger's syndrome or PDD-NOS often does have a need for friendships but is unable to make and keep friends. When the child enters primary school, she should be able to change over from egocentric functioning to partnership behaviour. A child with an autistic disorder is not sufficiently capable of this.

Children at primary school sense that a child with an autistic disorder is 'different' and children who are 'different' run a great risk of being bullied at school. Bullying has a negative effect on the child's self-image. During adolescence in particular, youngsters with an autistic disorder, for instance Asperger's syndrome, are at risk of becoming depressive.

Children with an autistic disorder stay for much longer in the first phases of friendship formation that typically belong to the pre-school years. Depending on the stage in which the child happens to be, proper help should be provided. In adolescents with an autistic disorder the ability to start relationships is severely impaired. There is a danger that they will link up with high-risk groups because these have clear rules of conduct that make becoming part of the group easier.

Relationships of people with an autistic disorder are often mutually complementary, meaning that the autistic man or woman often enters into a relationship with a highly empathic partner. They complement one another and keep each other in balance.

10

Resistance to change

People with an autistic disorder are not very flexible. Often, they stick rigidly to a particular pattern. They have a *one-track mind*. Autistic children have great difficulty with change; an object that has been moved from its usual place is enough to cause considerable anxiety and provoke resistance combined with aggressive behaviour and screaming. Because of this resistance, it is often very hard to deal with the child or adult in everyday life. Parents become exhausted because of the constant fighting about ordinary everyday things: a new pair of pyjamas, going to the hairdressers or buying shoes.

Change and unpredictability

As we saw in Chapter 2, *resistance to change* does not mean that nothing new is undertaken but that there is resistance to interruptions of one's own activity or programme. The underlying cause is that a change requires adjustment, processing new stimuli, which poses a problem to people with an autistic disorder. Consequently, unexpected, unannounced changes in particular meet with resistance.

Resistance to change occurs in many areas. In many children, for instance, there is resistance when they are offered a new type of food. This gives rise to the one-sided and limited eating pattern to which we referred in Chapter 3. The problem with resistance is not that the subject that changes is so important, or that the new subject is not wanted. Often it is not specific resistance to what is going to happen but an inner need to keep things as they are. Every change – even for the better – is unpleasant to an autistic person.

Jack was aware that new things evoked strong resistance in him. He was surprised that this was also the case if the new thing was something nice. He could never really be happy about something new. Music was the only exception. He could go into raptures about a new combination of sounds. In fact, all new things were like a heavy suitcase to him and he was tired of having to carry so many suitcases.

A change breaks off the present on the way to the future. In its deepest sense, a change eventually leads to the end, to death. Birger Sellin (1995) ceased speaking from the age of two. When he was 18, he expressed this anxiety when he wrote the following lines:

I don't want to be inside me anymore

I have eyes to see, and that's why I've been terribly scared

That's why I didn't want to speak anymore

I was scared of the end of the way and my existence as a human being.

Resistance to change is fed by two aspects. First, the brain structure, which is such that new stimuli are not easily processed, as we saw in Chapter 2.

Mary, aged 20, was completely disoriented when she had to swap her bed and room with her brother for one night. She woke up in the middle of the night and roamed around the room in total panic, screaming for her parents because she had no idea where she was.

The second aspect is the unpredictability of what is going to happen due to poor orientation towards people and a concomitant impaired orientation to time and space, as we saw in Chapter 5. This induces a basic fear triggered by the new event that is about to happen. The child's solution is to put up resistance to the change and endlessly ask questions about what is going to happen.

Eight-year-old Maureen wanted to know every morning what was going to happen that day. In great detail, she asked about every action that would be taking place. Her parents did their best to answer her questions, perfectly aware that they were caused by anxiety. That year they wanted to spend their holiday in a different location than usual.

Until then, they had always gone to the same place. Now they wanted to move from place to place. They did not know whether this would be possible with Maureen. Their first concern was that they did not know what answers they would have to give during the holiday to Maureen's questions about what was going to happen that day, as this would not be known beforehand. The advice given was to explain to her what the holiday entailed and to answer her questions in the morning as follows: 'This is a holiday in which we don't know in the morning what we're going to do, but we do know we're going to have fun.' No matter how uncertain this approach, it does provide a structure, i.e. the fact that it is not known what is going to happen. It proved effective. Children with an autistic disorder are bad at coping with change, but a holiday often does not produce the disquiet which other situations and even ordinary everyday situations bring about. It is possible to build up in their thinking the idea that 'This is a period in which it is not clear how things will develop. It's no use asking about it because they don't have an answer to it.'

The endless asking of questions is not so much intended to obtain an answer but to contain anxiety. Parents notice this because the child hardly waits for an answer before repeating the question. It should be borne in mind that this may also be connected with a language problem in that the child may not (yet) be able to formulate the question he or she wants to ask. Adults often make the mistake of assuming that when a child is capable of pronouncing the words of a language he is also able to express his personal concerns. This is certainly not the case up to the age of about ten, and this is true of children with and without an autistic disorder. For instance, because of their inability to put into words what they actually want to ask, children may ask *repetitive questions*, repeating the same question after they have already received an answer. It is not unusual for parents to interpret such behaviour as a lack of attention and they often respond by saying that they have already given an answer and that the child should listen. A child that always poses the same question may be one that does not listen properly but will more often be a child who tries to get a particular answer without being able to formulate the right question. Even though the child is given an extensive answer, she repeats the question hoping to get the desired answer. Repetitive questions are frequent in children without an autistic disorder up to the age of about eight. It continues for much longer in autistic children and with much greater intensity. As a child with an autistic disorder often has a general problem with putting his feelings into words, he will more frequently have recourse to repetitive questions. It is advisable to help the child to formulate the right question by trying to guess what it is the child wishes to know. The example of Peter in Chapter 7, with his series of questions about the strength and speed of animals, illustrates this. He was not able to formulate the underlying question about fighting and instead posed a series of very similar questions.

Similarly, another's 'no' may be misunderstood by children with an autistic disorder. The 'no' is construed as a definite reply and the nuance that 'no' now may become 'yes' later sometimes eludes them (Peeters 1996). Because it is misunderstood, the 'no' may provoke disproportionate resistance.

Resistance to change is often at its most intense when something is not going ahead. When an autistic child hears or notices that an intended plan is not going ahead, he or she may be extremely upset, become anxious and put up resistance. One of the reasons is that when something is not going ahead, the question is what is going to happen instead, and this triggers anxiety. The poor capacity to imagine what goes on in other people's minds also means that it is difficult for children with an autistic disorder to predict what is going to happen. If something is not going ahead, the autistic person faces a black hole because he or she cannot imagine what is going to happen. This anxiety may be attenuated by not first telling him or her what is not going ahead but by starting with an explanation of what *is* going to happen: first create security before evoking insecurity.

Sam was always terribly upset when something that had been planned was not going ahead. At such moments, he could even become very aggressive and scare those around him. He was normally a mild-mannered boy. Due to his expressive language disorder, he had problems communicating what was bothering him. Any change provoked great anxiety. Accordingly, his parents were advised first to tell him what was going to happen and why this was good, and only then explain that the other thing was not going ahead and why. Announcing and explaining what is going to happen creates security. Of course, this does not solve everything. Sometimes Sam wanted something to go ahead not because he was resistant to the change, but simply because he wanted it so much. In this case, he – as others called it – stubbornly persisted. This, in fact, is not stubbornness. A child who is capable of expressing himself starts arguing and in this way may get his way and what he wanted *does* go ahead; an autistic youngster with an expressive language disorder such as Sam's does not have this possibility and remains bogged down in 'stubborn' resistance.

We often see the same – imperturbable, aggressive – behaviour in young children before they are able to use language to express themselves. From the moment they can speak, their aggressive behaviour often diminishes. Aggression is in principle related to anxiety, as we shall see in the next chapter. It is therefore advisable to deal with the anxiety instead of merely trying to counter the aggression. *Aggression management* is of course important but it is not the solution to the fundamental problem of anxiety. At the same time as and after practising aggression management, it is necessary to investigate the anxiety. We shall come back to this in the next chapter.

Force of habit

Resistance to change is in fact a deep-seated need to hold on to the familiar, the habitual. The fact is that human beings are quintessentially conservative. Change usually provokes resistance. In its profoundest form, we see this in our attitude to suicide. While no one has consciously chosen to live, there must be something very seriously wrong for a human being to choose death. People tenaciously hold on to life even under the most atrocious circumstances. In less extreme forms, we see this in the resistance which a merger may provoke in workers. In general, people wish to maintain the situation as they know it. This is particularly true for autistic people who also anxiously want to keep their own activities unchanged. They show resistance not only when someone else demands or causes a change; their resistance to change is very strong in general.

The underlying cause of resistance to change in autistic people is that the unpredictability of what is going to happen arouses anxiety. Disrupting a fixed pattern of events immediately evokes anxiety. An exception to the rule means that the situation becomes unpredictable and incomprehensible. One of the possible responses to this is resistance, whether the change is pleasant or unpleasant. If the exception is not applied the next time, this raises all kinds of questions. Every child wants to understand how his or her world is structured. It is often very exhausting for the parents to cope with this flood of questions, and they may therefore decide to make no more exceptions. In this way they further reinforce the pattern and they themselves also become less flexible as a result. The child's rigidity will only increase in his or her interaction with the parents. The development of patterns is characteristic of autistic children, with one pattern replacing another. Rather than attempting to get rid of all patterns, it is preferable to *turn change into a pattern* (Wing 2001).

Resistance to change diminishes as the person grows older, partly because of increasing knowledge about all the things that may happen. Nevertheless, force of habit remains an important factor. Holding on to habits is a major strategy in controlling the anxiety that is never far away. Embarking upon something new arouses anxiety because it entails unpredictability and unfamiliarity. In trying to fight anxiety, holding on to *habits* and to what is familiar seems to offer more security than new things, even if the new thing would be better and more secure. One characteristic of habits is that they are known and familiar and therefore give a sense of security. This applies to people in general and not specifically to autistic people.

Once the author was mugged. The mugger tried to grab her notebook. The attack was repeated within a couple of minutes. To reduce the risk of being mugged again, it made more sense to avoid a particular bus stop. It would have been safer to use an earlier bus stop, at the same walking distance from the destination. Nevertheless, an effort had to be made to break with the habit of using the familiar stop. The security lay not in the place as such, which was actually less safe, but in the familiarity of the habit.

If a habit proves to be unsafe, it nevertheless takes considerable effort to give it up. This is because the habit feels secure due to its familiarity, while the new behaviour might be more secure but is not sensed as such because it is unfamiliar. In autistic people this is often a very strong phenomenon. Only when the new behaviour has become familiar can it offer the sense of security that would persuade the child to change over to it completely. A sudden changeover arouses too much anxiety.

There are two ways of dealing with this resistance to change. The first is through gradual transition: allowing someone to slowly grow familiar with the new situation or the new behaviour.

Sam's parents needed a year to get him used to the transition from a cot to a bed. They let him lie in the bed for a bit every evening until he had got used to it and dared to sleep in the big bed.

The other way to teach new behaviour is to implement the change in one go. This may evoke enormous anxiety and therefore resistance. Apart from the fact that such an attempt is usually fiercely resisted by the child, it is not advisable to apply this in many different situations because of the very strong anxiety it arouses. There are particular situations in which it is desirable and possible to implement such a change in one go. The first condition to doing so is to be sure that the child will (eventually) find the new situation more pleasant than the old one. It is recommended as much as possible to apply the method of gradual familiarization in cases where the new situation is necessary but will not be pleasant. Before using the method of 'throwing the child in the deep end', one will have to be absolutely certain that the child will find the new situation pleasant. In *behavioural therapy*, this method is called *flooding*: a sudden intense exposure to the anxiety-evoking situation, i.e. the new behaviour or the new situation. Applying this behavioural therapy technique appears to be particularly appropriate for some anxieties, but quite the opposite for others. The second condition for implementing new behaviour instantly is that it should be possible to explain to the child what is going to happen and why it is a change for the better. The third condition is that the change can be carried out swiftly and the child can experience the result swiftly without having to be anxious and tense for a long time about what is going to happen. The fourth – equally necessary – condition is metacommunicative in nature: explaining to the child that one would prefer not to expose him to change, that it is not the intention to inflict pain or punishment, but that the change is necessary, because the child cannot grasp the new situation and rejects it from the outset. It is important to explain the reason for the change and to show understanding for the child's anxiety. It is also important to invite the child initially and after all explanations to carry out the change himself or to let it happen voluntarily. In this way the child may be able to try out the new behaviour or situation by himself so that he can experience some control of the situation and his reserves can be mobilized. This sense of being able to exercise control is the exact 'antidote' to the strong sense of powerlessness that the child feels when overwhelmed by anxiety.

Resistance to different foods

Resistance to change is a basic problem which arises in a wide range of fields, including eating. This resistance may be caused by two factors. The first is resistance to what is new and the anxiety of having to let go of what is familiar. What is new in food is its taste and texture, the structure of the food in the mouth. The second factor may well be that the new food cannot yet be properly digested. For example, children in general do not like Brussels sprouts, but adults do. It appears that when this vegetable is cooked gases are released that cannot yet be properly processed in the child's body. Children's dislike of sprouts may well be determined by the wisdom of the body. This does not mean that one should do everything children say but that some modesty on the part of adults is called for in respect of the child's opinion.

It may be that the 'wisdom of the body', to which we referred in Chapter 3, is one reason why autistic children have such difficulty getting used to new food. They probably have an immature immune system and therefore need more time to digest a particular type of food. In deeply autistic children, there are initially almost always serious eating problems, ranging from difficulty swallowing to problems of metabolism. Kanner (1943) repeatedly refers to such problems in the young autistic children with whom he worked.

Ronald's mother was in despair. She was convinced that there was something wrong with her three-week-old son. 'There is something wrong with his throat', she kept on saying in desperation. The doctor could not find anything wrong but Ronald's problems swallowing shortly after birth were in fact the first sign that the child had serious developmental problems. He lagged behind considerably and eventually turned out to be severely autistic.

In spite of their eating problems and resistance to new food, autistic children with a one-sided and limited eating pattern appear to be healthier, fitter and more energetic than one would expect (Wing 2001).

It is also possible that the process of getting used to new foods, for which all children need time, requires more time in autistic children because the body is not geared to rapid changes. Presenting food which the body cannot yet digest properly at a too-early stage, for instance offering the first sandwich too early, might well cause a dislike of that food, as a result of which resistance to it may persist even when the food can be digested. Thus a *negative association* will have developed which will unnecessarily affect behaviour. We shall see how important associations are for autistic people and how prevalent they can be in their lives.

In order to take both aspects into account – resistance to and familiarization with new things – it is advisable not to force eating. It is in any case not possible, because the child frenetically and wilfully continues to resist. It is more sensible to present new food gradually and explain to the child what it is for. No matter how young the child, the explanation will find its way to the child's brain. One way of teaching the child to eat new food is by combining it with the taste of familiar food; for example, some apple sauce. This applies only if there is more resistance to the new taste than to the nature of the food. The advantage of this form of teaching, *conditioning*, is that the new food will be more easily accepted. A disadvantage is that through such conditioning the new food becomes linked with the old, i.e. a strong association develops between the two. As a result, it becomes almost impossible for the child to consume them separately. When there is a great deal that is unfamiliar and the world looks threatening, associations are sometimes the only way to create security.

In order to prevent excessively strong associations, the *shaping process* is useful. This involves changing over from old to new behaviour in small steps, from the unwanted to the wanted. For instance, one could offer the new food each time with a little bit less apple sauce. This approach forms part of behavioural therapy and is the basis of *Discrete Trial Training* (DTT) and *Applied Behaviour Analysis* (ABA) based on the ideas of Lovaas (1987).

Resistance resulting from hypersensitivity

Resistance to change may also be connected with hypersensitivity to particular stimuli. Getting dressed is often a problem for autistic children. They may put up resistance to particular clothes and refuse to give up specific clothing even if completely threadbare. Often this is a question of tactile sense. An autistic child may be hypersensitive to how particular fabrics feel and because of this some clothes may feel very unpleasant to the skin. This is one of the reasons why some autistic children resist putting on clean clothes. The clean clothes feel stiffer and rougher to the skin and worn clothes feel much softer. Sensitivity to such irritation can sometimes be dealt with through massage. If a child is hypersensitive, it is useful to examine together with her which fabrics she likes and which ones she does not, and adapt the child's set of clothes to this as much as possible. It is important to point out to the child that the irritability may eventually disappear and that all kinds of fabrics will then become acceptable. This prevents negative associations leading to resistance to particular clothes or materials. Once the sensitivity has diminished, the negative association can be overcome through behavioural therapy (see Chapter 13). If this is done at an earlier stage, the child's predisposition would not be being respected and her resistance would intensify.

In autistic people, various senses may be hypersensitive. For instance, many autistic children resist having their hair cut, which may be due to a hypersensitivity of the scalp. Anyone who has ever worn their hair in a ponytail knows very well how in the evening one feels every single hair when the ponytail is loosened. This may be similar to what autistic children experience. Many cannot bear having their hair cut. The surroundings have to be familiar and the hair must be cut with care in order to be tolerated.

Two-year-old Ronald always screamed at the top of his voice when his hair had to be cut. One day he became so upset that his eyes started rolling. His mother rushed him to the doctor who diagnosed psychosis and prescribed medication. Ronald's mother gave up taking him to the hairdresser and his older sister began cutting her little brother's hair. The advice was to cut a little bit each time so that Ronald did not have to go through the unpleasant sensation of his hair being cut for very long. This he tolerated much better.

Cutting of the hair has a deeper meaning. At the beginning of a psychosis, for instance, people often cut off their hair. The Bible tells the story of Samson and Delilah. Samson's hair is said to be the source of his strength and Delilah wanted to cut it when he was asleep so that he would not notice.

It is advisable regularly to cut off small bits of hair rather than a lot in one go. In general, massage may be helpful to speed up the development of coping with the irritation to the skin. Presumably, maturation also plays a role here and it appears that the sensitivity diminishes as the child grows older (Momma 1996; Wing 2001).

Bob loved climbing into bed with his parents in the morning but he did not want to lie against his mother if she wore short pyjamas because then he felt the hairs on her legs pricking his skin. His mother could not even imagine that one could feel something like that.

Terrorizing or panicking

The behaviour of autistic people may come across as terrorizing. The intransigent self-oriented behaviour with no account taken of others is the most problematic to cope with in everyday life. The autistic child takes no account of the time by which the people around him or her are governed. This may give rise to major problems in the morning, for instance, when there is a tight daily schedule at home.

This problem is fed from four sources:

1. The need to complete one's own programme in order to prevent anxiety.

2. High distractibility.

3. Limited sense of time.

4. Impaired capacity to imagine what goes on in other people's minds and taking less notice of other people.

The first source is the strong need of the autistic child to carry out the programme he has in mind; the child cannot escape this because to do so produces anxiety. The second reason is the fact that the child is very easily distracted, for instance when getting dressed and consequently digressing towards other activities. The third and most important source is the child's limited awareness of time. Autistic children in general do not have a sharp sense of time because, as we have seen, this sense is related to the people around us. A fourth source of this behaviour lies in the fact that autistic children attach less importance to what goes on in another's mind because they are less able to imagine other people's thoughts and feelings and therefore care less about what the other person wants.

The anxiety becomes apparent very soon to people who live or deal with an autistic person every day. To those who are not used to autistic people, the behaviour very quickly comes across as demanding, spoilt, authoritarian and terrorizing.

The behaviour which an autistic person displays when faced with change is often perceived as consciously chosen behaviour rather than as an expression of impotence. Other people may feel terrorized as a result. The reasons for this are the apparent unreasonableness of the behaviour, the fact that the other cannot empathize with such behaviour and the intransigence of the child's behaviour. It seems as though the autistic person wants nothing else but to be a dictator imposing his will on those around him, as though he wants to control everything out of sheer egoism. However, the opposite is true; autistic people have the feeling that they cannot control anything, that everything is beyond their control. The child feels powerless, not powerful. These children have the feeling that everything happens to them without them having much influence over events, even though they try. Their *locus of control* is strongly external. This concept, developed by Rotter (1966), indicates a person's ideas with regard to the connection between his or her behaviour and its consequences. One's locus of control shows where one places the control of events and situations. For the child's development, it is important to observe where the child places the locus of control. If it is internal, inside the child herself, the child has the feeling that she can exercise control over circumstances herself. If the locus of control is external, outside the child, she will feel at the mercy of accident and circumstance. While in the first case – internal – the child has a feeling of power, in the second – external – she will experience powerlessness. If a child always situates the locus of control externally, this may lead to *learnt helplessness* (Seligman 1975): the child has the idea that she cannot help herself and that she is structurally dependant on others.

An autistic person has very restricted ideas about how he or she relates to the other, and makes serious mistakes in this respect. Within the confines of his defective theory of mind (TOM), he nevertheless tries to keep the situation under control. Since the child cannot properly imagine another person's thoughts and feelings, this also means that he cannot imagine that another person may have solutions which he does not know himself. Accordingly, an autistic child will not find it easy to appeal to others for help, other than asking or demanding that something be done the way he has it in mind.

Considering the way power is experienced, we can say that autistic people experience a great deal of powerlessness and little power. They have an externally situated locus of control. The people around them feel so strongly governed by their behaviour that they have the impression that the autistic person is very powerful.

The locus of control can be influenced by the environment. In fact, it is quite sensitive to influence from the environment, including culture. The TOM should store information on the effect of one's behaviour on others, and the locus of control can be located internally on the basis of such experience. This is limited in autistic people, giving rise to a sense of powerlessness and helplessness. Recalling the three types mentioned by Wing (Chapter 4), we note, on the basis of intelligence and other factors, a decreasing helplessness with increasing intelligence, from *aloof* via *passive* to *active but odd*. One reason for this is that with increasing intelligence, insight into one's own functioning and that of others increases, and the TOM expands accordingly.

An autistic person's behaviour is not based on an – egoistic – evaluation of the effect his behaviour will have on others but on *social egocentricity*, an inherent incapacity to take account of others. In other words, the child does not display the behaviour on purpose to annoy someone else. His behaviour springs from powerlessness. The autistic person wants to contain the anxiety constantly evoked in him by carrying out a 'programme' which he has thought up. As this programme has the function of attenuating anxiety, it can easily degenerate into a *ritual* of sequential actions. Rituals have a calming, anxiety-reducing effect.

Ritualized programmes

Rituals are actions that are constantly carried out in a fixed sequence, e.g. first put on pyjamas, then brush teeth, then put chair next to bed, then get into bed and get tucked in.

A ritual is not a need to do things inherently in a particular manner but a way of keeping the anxiety that is never far away under control through predictability of events. The repetition inherent in the ritual has a 'hypnotizing' effect and therefore feels pleasant and calming. The chain of actions is connected with a sequence of feelings.

Even as a child, Linda loved endlessly brushing her hair. By the time she reached puberty, tension at home increased and her brushing increased proportionately. She could spend hours brushing her hair. The same applied to having a shower. At a time when young people in their puberty are preoccupied by their appearance, Linda's interest in all aspects of her appearance increased enormously. She spent hours brushing her hair, having a shower, choosing her clothes and ironing. By focusing so much attention on her appearance, Linda tried to cope with the anxiety of associating with her peers.

Putting a stop to the ritual not only interrupts the action but also the feeling. One of the principal emotional aspects of a ritual is *relaxation*. Interrupting it therefore produces tension. We can see this in the autistic child in the form of anxiety, sometimes panic, anger and resistance.

The concatenation of actions originally arose from a desired result combined with a pleasant feeling. Research by theoreticians such as Thorndike, Watson and Skinner in the last century has clearly shown how a sequence of sometimes meaningless acts can develop. Skinner (1974) speaks of strengthening behaviour through the 'law of effect'. A striking example is the pigeon which he tried to teach to get food by pressing a lever. Before the pigeon discovered the lever, it had done all kinds of things, stepping up and down, making a pirouette, hopping and similar movements. The fact that after this range of behaviour food was provided as a reward ensured that the pigeon executed this series of successive factually meaningless actions whenever it wanted to have food. It was not clear to the pigeon that all it had to do was press the lever. The pigeon had formed a ritual on the basis of associations developed over time to which it attributed a causal link.

The autistic child is actively engaged in *fighting anxiety*, involving all kinds of subjects evoking anxiety (see Chapter 11 where the workings of anxiety are explained in detail), while those around the child have no idea about this. Consequently, they are virtually unable to help the child fight anxiety in any other way than through the ritual. Parents understand ordinary anxieties about eating, sleeping, etc. better because the reasons are often more evident. They can help the child overcome her anxiety because they can follow her reasoning and see that she lacks knowledge and is therefore not sufficiently able to deal with the anxiety on her own. The parents can help the child to cope with her anxiety by providing knowledge and protection. The rituals of autistic people are based on *associations* that have arisen through simultaneity or succession of events. These associations are completely unclear to others who were not present at the time or who failed to see what was happening to the child. Consequently, parents and others can easily become annoyed by the seemingly senseless acts the child wishes to perform, indeed feels she *must* perform. Kees Momma (1996) gives an excellent description in his book about how these associations determine his life. Drawing is one of his main hobbies, and he has a great talent for it.

> But when I had experienced something awful, I would tear up the drawing I had made the day the incident had occurred. I did this because I would otherwise have been reminded of the awful experience. Moreover, because of the event the drawing had lost its value and I could no longer look at it with any sense of enjoyment. (Momma 1996)

Figure 10.1 Drawing of the inside of a cathedral (Momma 1996, p.157). Reproduced with permission.

Associative thinking can give rise to a great deal of anxiety. Normally this form of thinking diminishes in young children as they become capable of putting their feelings into words and ask questions so that adults can reassure them with their knowledge. Since the autistic child has difficulty putting her feelings and thoughts into words, she is often left all alone with her anxieties and feelings.

Associative and magical thinking

Because of their deficient knowledge and especially their inability to put thoughts and feelings into words, autistic people maintain early forms of thought for longer. One of the principal forms is associative thinking, as I mentioned above. This occurs in everyone and is an essential mode of thought. For autistic people, many things continue to exist through association because they have too little knowledge and insight to test occurrences against reality and break away from a formed association through new knowledge. I shall outline certain modes of thought in early childhood that help us to gain a better understanding of autistic thinking.

Laying causal links on the basis of a succession of events is one of the first forms of *causal thinking*. A causal link between events is established because the events occur quickly one after another. If a cat screeches the moment a child puts on a sweater, the child thinks the cat screeches *because* he puts on a sweater. This is called *parasyntactic thinking*. The cause is attributed to the first event because it occurred a fraction of a second earlier. As the child grows older and acquires more knowledge, parasyntactic thinking moves into the background and makes place for realistic, causal thinking with regard to events that do actually cause each other in chronological succession. Adults, however, do not entirely abandon parasyntactic thinking. It re-emerges at times when we feel insecure or anxious and do not properly understand a situation. One example is thunderstorms. If a door falls shut during a clap of thunder, we may conclude that the thunder caused the door to shut. Autistic people are often in such a startled state, causing insecurity and lack of understanding. Parasyntactic thinking (two events immediately following each other) and associative thinking (events occurring simultaneously are therefore frequently encountered in autistic people well beyond the age at which children normally use this mode of thought. A similar development can be observed in egocentric thinking, in which the child perceives himself as the central figure in events. In general, this mode of thinking greatly diminishes as the child grows older, in particular from the age of about four. Egocentric thinking may take the form of *magical thinking* in which the child perceives events occurring because he wishes them or provokes them in a negative sense. During the primary-school period, this mode of thinking is important as a way of warding off undesirable events.

Magical thinking can be observed when a child walking on a pavement has to skip a slab with each step to prevent something awful from happening or, on the contrary, to bring about something pleasant. It can provide a sense of security. Grandma's necklace 'helps' to keep away nasty dreams; the lucky stone 'protects' against bad luck. When adults admit that they have such feelings (and many adults still do), we call it superstition. Adults are certainly not free of magical thinking, because otherwise there would be no such things as lotteries and gambling.

For much longer than their non-autistic peers, autistic children take things literally and engage in magical, parasyntactic and associative thinking. The problem is not so much that they think in this way, but that on the basis of 'inner statistics' regarding their age we do not expect it. We know that this is what young children do and we take it into account. We can easily get the wrong expectation, in particular from intelligent and highly intelligent people with autism, such as those with Asperger's syndrome. Their great intelligence, greater than ours in particular areas, causes us to expect that their thinking is evenly developed in all fields, although this is not the case. When communication fails or the child displays unexpected behaviour, it is useful to realize that the child may well be following a different thinking strategy to yours. It is advisable to try and find out what this strategy is, e.g. by asking about the reason for the behaviour. When doing so, we should bear in mind that an autistic child cannot always quickly put this into words but needs time to find the right words to explain things. Think of Martin from Chapter 8, who indicated that it was not so much a question of inability but of pace. It is the pace problem that leads to difficulties in everyday social interaction in which demands are made on autistic people.

Allergic to 'must'

Resistance to change also arises in a very problematic area; namely, when the child is told she *must* do something. In particular at school and in the community this causes considerable problems. When still a child, someone with an autistic disorder will already stand out because of her strong resistance to carrying out tasks she is given. They seem *allergic to imposed obligations* and are often wrongly considered to be lazy. This applies especially when something has to be done under pressure of time (Wing 1998). This causes major problems, in particular at school. Sometimes heavy pressure such as at an examination does produce the necessary concentration (Asperger 1944) but in most cases exercising pressure has an adverse effect.

'Must do' entails two aspects that are of a particular importance in connection with an autistic disorder: it involves a *change* and a *limit in activity and in time*.

When there is resistance to an imposed obligation it is not so much the authoritarian aspect that is significant. Children with an autistic disorder do not really have an authority complex in the sense of resisting the fact that somebody else is their superior. In general, they do not 'measure' personal and social properties and therefore do not perceive others as authoritative. Quite the contrary, in their behaviour they often make too little distinction in regard to age. Even if well brought up, they tend to treat adults and children on a par.

While six-year-old Joe was a likeable and intelligent little boy, the adults at his new school soon became annoyed about his attitude towards them. Several teachers thought he was rude because of the way he refused to listen to anything teachers other than his own said. Joe did not think there was anything wrong with this: 'You are not my teacher so you have nothing to say about me.' It was beyond his grasp that among the teachers there is joint responsibility for the children. Something that does not need to be explained to children without an autistic disorder because they sense it themselves was unknown territory to Joe.

Someone who asks an autistic person to do something usually meets with an abrupt 'no'. This reply helps the autistic person to gain time to think about what is expected of him or her. The pace of other people's lives is too quick, which becomes apparent when someone else suddenly invades the autistic person's activity and life with his or her question. The autistic person tries to slow this down by saying 'no'. The result is that both sides are left with a statement that is difficult to reverse. Often another attempt is made to persuade the autistic person to answer the question or carry out the task. This does not stimulate thinking but switches the thinking process 'off'. Almost as a reflex action, he or she will stick to this 'no'. The autistic person needs time to switch the thinking process to 'on' instead of 'off'. Autistic people need time to evaluate the situation and this is possible only if they get a chance to think things over. The thinking process stagnates if the other continues to try to persuade or convince the autistic person.

Resistance to imposed obligations is one of the hardest aspects of dealing with autistic people. It is an enormous burden for parents to get their child to do the things that need to be done. Siblings often feel that they are treated very unfairly because their autistic brother or sister always manages to evade doing particular tasks which they then have to do. Teachers are often close to despair when, exercising self-control, patience and perseverance, they try to get the child to do something. For partners it is often stressful to have to go through the long process of carrying on intense discussions before decisions are taken and tasks carried out. The children concerned do have insight into their own condition and often suffer from the fact that they cannot get themselves to carry out tasks. Some become physically ill from the tension of being unable to bring themselves to take the action necessary.

Although he was only six years old, Joe was prepared to take a critical look at himself. He did not want to do things someone else asked him to do. At school this proved to be an insurmountable problem. Sometimes he was forced to do something and later realized that he had nevertheless learnt from it. 'You have to force me, otherwise I won't do it and then I don't learn anything.'

Some autistic children end up in an untenable position. They like going to school and love all the things they can play with there. They also want to have friends to play with. But their resistance to obligations is so strong that going to school becomes extremely problematic.

Six-year-old Joe has little school experience apart from a number of failed attempts. He has also been unlucky as not every school has been suitable and not every teacher has understood him. For him the circumstances have to be just right. If he is not understood and the circumstances are not particularly favourable, things soon go seriously wrong. Nevertheless, it is important to make it possible for him to go to school. He is highly gifted and could certainly learn a few more things by himself, but he is lagging behind emotionally and this is also becoming apparent in the cognitive field. In a conversation with Joe, he succinctly pointed out what was expected of him: 'At school they try to force me to do things and I don't want that.' The answer was equally brief: 'There's no other way Joe, it's either school and being forced or no school at all.' Joe burst into tears and said that he did want to go and therefore opted for being forced to do things. The question is to what extent he will manage to do this and also whether it is good for him to have to function under coercion. Sometimes the combination of highly gifted and Asperger is more problematic than Kanner's autism, in which everything is much clearer and there is hardly any discussion about the child's possibilities and impossibilities.

An obligation implies a relationship to the other. This means that people who tend to ask a great deal from others will soon meet with resistance from autistic people. Sometimes the resistance to disrupting their own programme is so strong that it gives rise to major problems in relationships. Living together with a partner entails a structural infringement of one's own programme. To many autistic people, this is a major problem. Some impose strict rules on the partner, limiting the partner's freedom of movement. Others cannot bring themselves to live together with someone else and feel particularly threatened when their partner wants to have children. Having children means a constant violation of one's own programme and causes constant obligations.

Autistic people, and in particular young autistic children, are not really aware of what goes on in other people. Obligations imposed on them disrupt their own activities and their own plans, completely putting them out. The boundaries are drawn by someone else. Because of their lack of orientation towards other people, this overwhelms them. It means that they have to embark on something else and interrupt or break off their own activity, and to this they put up natural resistance. As they have problems understanding how other people think and feel, another's interests will not motivate them in any way to interrupt their own activity. Their own state of mind is the principal motive for their actions. Consequently, their behaviour is strongly self-orientated and even seems egoistic. It is difficult to interrupt or break off an activity, especially if it is a pleasant one. Accordingly, it is of the utmost importance to explain to children with an autistic disorder that they do not live in a vacuum but in relation to others just like everyone else, and that this always makes a certain demand on people. It should be explained that this restricts one's freedom and limits one's own activities. It should further be pointed out that tasks which have to be carried out at school lead to more possibilities later in life.

What 'later' means exactly is difficult to fathom for autistic people because, as we saw in Chapter 5, there is little conception of time in their socioscheme. This lack of awareness of time is often remedied by putting up a clock near the child so that he can look at it to follow time passing (as recommended in the TEACCH programme). If, for example by using pictograms indicating the next activity, the clock shows when the time for a particular activity has passed, this may help to make the unpredictable world predictable. In actual fact, this is what clocks, diaries and calendars are generally used for.

Children with an autistic disorder have an impaired internal sense of time. This is why indicating time externally may be helpful. However, this does not solve the internal problems. Explaining to the child that it is not the teacher's intention to annoy her but to teach the group particular skills and provide the children with knowledge within a particular period of time helps to motivate the child to look at the clock. The result will be that the clock is no longer viewed as an isolated phenomenon. Slowly the child will become aware of the connection between time and the people around her. This process will be slow and it will take time, patience and regular explanations in order to embed this connection into the child's *socioscheme*.

In this way, an external clock can be used to gradually develop an inner awareness of the passage of time. In Chapter 5 we saw that the limited awareness of time in autistic children is a consequence of their impaired me–other differentiation. Explaining to the child about how he relates to other people and the consequences of this for the passage of time stimulates his me–other differentiation, helping him to develop a sense of time.

Joe had considerable problems with the passage of time. As a result, the end of the play hour surprised him and evoked strong resistance. There was a clock on the wall of the therapist's room, not particularly high or low, a clock that was easy to read. The therapist used it to indicate to Joe that time was passing, for instance to point out that there were still ten minutes left and that he had another ten minutes if he had anything in mind he still wanted to do. Joe slowly developed a sense of time and one day he even started sobbing while looking at the clock saying: 'Now I only have a quarter of an hour left to play and then it's over.'

Planning activities and keeping appointments

Because of their poor orientation in time and space, people with Asperger's syndrome are often bad at planning their activities and have problems keeping appointments.

> In the first years of therapy, Alec was never on time. Regularly he would turn up a day late or an hour late or a day early and was completely surprised that he had no appointment at that time. He also frequently forgot his appointments. If the therapist had not been aware of Alec's difficulty in orienting in time, she might have thought that he lacked sufficient motivation, which was certainly not the case. Eventually, the therapist's patience was rewarded by continuity of the therapy. Alec's awareness of time became progressively stronger and his mistakes about the time of his appointment became less and less frequent.

One theory of autism assumes that difficulty in planning and organizing things is the core of the problem (the planning and executive function, or EF). According to this view, this lack of organization means, for instance, that autistic people get bogged down in detail and put up resistance to change. This theory has lost ground, partly because it is not so much planning that is a problem but social cognition. As social insight increases, planning and organization improve. In this respect, the TOM has proved to be a better explanatory model. The difficulty with planning and organization seems to be more an effect than a cause.

As a result of poor orientation to the surrounding world, specifically to the people around, people with Asperger's syndrome and also those with autistic features have little experience in planning day-to-day activities.

> In spite of his intelligence and strong motivation, John was not used to planning tasks. Structuring the morning ritual into strict time slots to teach him to estimate how long each component lasted helped him to avoid getting constantly stuck in the morning through frustrating loss of time. The knowledge one would normally have expected him to have was lacking, and imparting that knowledge at a time when he was ready for it – in fact much later than usual – had a positive effect.

Arranging things is also a task which plays a special role in people with Asperger's syndrome. On the one hand, they can be overly neat and tidy: everything always has to be in the same place and everything must always be cleared up. Others are sometimes so disturbed by their perfectionism that the task of clearing up becomes too much of a burden. It hampers them in their other activities. For instance, it is not possible to study before the room has been cleared up but at the same time they cannot bring themselves to clear up the room.

> Charles's main activity was going through the newspapers and cutting out the bits that interested him. At times when things went less well with him, he got behind with the papers. Sometimes they piled up for months. At such times, Charles lacked the courage to tackle the pile but at the same time found it impossible to throw any away or start any new activities. Eventually, when things got better, he would deal with the pile of papers and steadily work his way through them. Consequently, Charles's state of mind could be measured by the height of the pile.

The many obligations combined with the inability to set about these tasks means that even doing nice things does not produce any pleasure because it is overshadowed by feelings of guilt about matters left undone.

In autistic people we encounter tendencies to arrange and collect things, such as Charles's archive of newspaper cuttings. This helps them to cope with the chaos surrounding them. The perfectionism of many people with Asperger's syndrome is connected with this. A small scratch on a musical instrument, the long search for the best bargain, doubts about the right purchase, all these reflect an attempt to get a grip on the situation.

The perfectionism of people with an autistic disorder can be a real burden to them. They choose quality rather than quantity, which in a work situation may be an advantage or a drawback. It is important that they get a job in which their talent can be properly used, where it can be an asset rather than a liability. Perfectionism is a characteristic which many people appreciate and even envy, but they usually do not show this and criticize perfectionist tendencies. People with Asperger's syndrome or Asperger features may come to see their talent as a weakness because their perfectionism regularly gets in the way. In Sweden, a manager took up this idea and constructed a company with a team of people with Asperger's syndrome because they are more precise in their work and more reliable.

> Jerome had always thought of himself as a perfectionist and viewed this as a negative quality. He resisted his own perfectionism, causing himself a great deal of stress. Because of his resistance, he did not manage to use his perfectionism as a talent and only fight the excesses. In other words, he failed to come to terms with his own predisposition.

Arranging things is an activity which generally causes contentment. We see this tendency emerging from about the age of two (Montessori 1973) when children start deriving pleasure from sorting and arranging beads and similar objects. The world of advertising makes enthusiastic use of this urge, with stickers and pictures for children to collect. At the end of the primary-school period, this urge to arrange things reaches a climax in collecting. We observe this more frequently in boys than in girls. In light of this tendency, it is less surprising to see that many autistic people are collectors. They collect meaningful and meaningless things. Many of the collections are connected with technical subjects. Trains, for instance, are very popular as objects to be 'collected' and studied.

Vermeulen (1999b) notes that collecting follows a particular course of development: first collecting objects, then collecting for the sake of collecting, next focused attention on a theme with collecting serving to gather information, and finally composing mental collections of information such as facts and data.

In social interaction in the Western world, where people have to be punctual for appointments, unlike in many non-Western cultures where punctuality is less important, people with Asperger's syndrome often get into difficulty in contacts with the people around them. Either they are completely unreliable in keeping appointments or they are excessively punctual and sharply criticize those around them when they are only slightly late. An additional problem is that making appointments is tantamount to making a commitment at some point in the future, which to people with Asperger's syndrome is less certain.

> Jack had enormous difficulty with appointments. Making an appointment meant committing yourself and he did not know in advance whether he would be able to keep the appointment. Joanna, on the other hand, had a very great need to know what she was letting herself in for and could hardly bear it that Jack never wanted to commit himself to a date with her. It gave her the feeling that their relationship was non-committal. This in turn surprised Jack who only meant that he could not look into the future and was worried that he would be unable to stick to the date.

Learning to make realistic plans is therefore of considerable importance to people with Asperger's syndrome. It helps them to make life more manageable and predictable. It also means that they will achieve more and fail less. In learning to make plans, it is important to ensure that it is not someone else who makes the plan but that the individual concerned learns to estimate how much time a particular activity will require. In the transitional period, it is necessary that others do the planning but the aim, particularly for persons with normal or above average intelligence, is to be able eventually do so themselves.

Punishment and reward

Because of the behavioural problems with which an autistic child confronts her environment, the people around her feel a strong need to influence the child's behaviour. As a result of the huge resistance to change, resulting in tasks remaining undone; the lack of an overall vision, leading to jobs piling up; or the need to carry out tasks in a specific fixed order, people with Asperger's syndrome may come into conflict with those around them. As such behaviour can often not be admitted, it has to be stopped in order to protect the person concerned and to keep the situation for the people around them tolerable.

The fact is that such behaviour cannot always be kept within acceptable bounds. This is not to say that the behaviour should be accepted but that the underlying anxiety should be uncovered so that something can be done about it. Here, again, it is clear that providing an explanation about what is going on is of primary importance. Clarity ensures that the anxiety diminishes.

Educators often try to modify behaviour though *punishment*. However, punishment does not appear to have a positive effect on children's development; quite the contrary. New behaviour cannot be taught through punishment; at best, the undesirable behaviour is halted temporarily. This may be a desirable and necessary result. Children need boundaries and clarity, and punishment can fulfil that role. However, there are various different forms of punishment one of which is damaging and another is not; one harms the child and another offers him security. Punishment involving a disruption of love, a rejection of the child himself and not just his behaviour, is in principle negative. Punishment which provides clarity about the boundaries of acceptable behaviour without rejecting the child himself may offer the child security.

Putting an end to a particular behaviour, however, is different from curing the child of the undesirable behaviour, which is in fact the ultimate aim. Punishment certainly does not lead to learning desired new behaviour. Strict disciplinary measures by parents may stimulate aggressive conduct in children, more so in boys than in girls (Deater-Deckard and Dodge 1997). It appears, however, that in a culture where hitting children is common practice and is not accompanied by lovelessness, it does not necessarily encourage aggression and need not harm children's self-image.

New behaviour is taught by *reinforcing* desired behaviour, e.g. through rewards. In order to teach new behaviour, it is necessary to constantly reward the desired behaviour. This can then be reinforced by applying an unpredictable pattern of rewards. A *variable reinforcement scheme* — sometimes with and sometimes without reward — is highly conducive to reinforcing behaviour. A variable reinforcement scheme involves, for instance, sometimes paying attention to the behaviour and sometimes not, sometimes rewarding it and at other times not. The parents' cry of despair 'We have tried everything but nothing helps!' is indicative of reinforcement of behaviour on the basis of a variable scheme, with one method at one time and another method at other times. If this is applied to undesired behaviour, it often unintentionally reinforces such behaviours. No child asks for negative attention, he or she only wants positive attention, but if he or she cannot gain that, then even negative attention is more rewarding than none. This is why *negative attention* or punishment also reinforces behaviour, and there is a risk that while punishment stops the behaviour for the moment, it also reinforces it for the future.

Behaviour is to an important extent shaped through a process of conditioning in which a habit develops between human being, stimulus from the environment, reinforcement and behaviour. This is how habits arise. If one wishes to change a habit, something will have to be changed in the stimulus–behaviour–reinforcement chain. If a child learns that he gets his way by incessant nagging, parents reinforce this behaviour and teach the child to pursue his wishes through nagging.

Behaviour can be altered through *extinction*, i.e. extinguishing behaviour by *ignoring* it. Not only rewarding but also disapproving of behaviour acts as a reinforcer. If one wishes to bring about a change in behaviour, desired behaviour should therefore be reinforced and undesirable behaviour ignored rather than punished.

Why is it that punishment is such a widespread strategy in bringing up children? One reason is probably that punishment can put an immediate end to undesirable behaviour and thus satisfy the wish of the person who is confronted with it. Another reason is that undesired behaviour often evokes helpless anger in carers and punishment may serve as an outlet for that anger.

If we wish to bring about a change in behaviour, it is important to bear in mind that this can be achieved only by applying three rules. A permanent change in behaviour can *always* and *only* be brought about by these three rules. The three rules should be implemented in chronological order: first stop behaviour, then look for alternative desired behaviour and reinforce it, and finally ignore the undesirable behaviour.

1.   *Behaviour can be stopped* through punishment or corrective measures, and the likelihood of the behaviour decreases as the chance of being caught increases.

2.   *New behaviour* can only be taught by reinforcing it. Reinforcement can take the form of a reward, both material and immaterial. In order to ensure that the new behaviour is learnt, it should initially be reinforced each time. Once it has been learnt it can be further strengthened through variable reinforcement, sometimes being rewarded and sometimes not.

3.   Ensuring that the child *unlearns behaviour* can be achieved only by ignoring and thereby extinguishing it.

Undesirable behaviour is sometimes so serious that it cannot be ignored and it will therefore be necessary first to stop it through punishment. No matter how unpleasant the punishment, it does not teach new behaviour nor alter undesirable behaviour. On the contrary, punishment is in principle a reinforcer even though it is not rewarding. The chance that the behaviour recurs is greater rather than smaller. We often see this happening in the form of escalation of behaviour. Undesirable behaviour can sometimes not be ignored, but applying the first rule is not enough. Desired behaviour can be taught only by reinforcing it. This means that it cannot be learnt simply by someone demanding it or through instruction or example. It is learnt through reinforcement, in particular through reward. Locke (1632–1704; see Gay 1964) noted in the seventeenth century that flattery and praise are the strongest reinforcers; what nowadays we call 'reinforcing someone's self-image'. In fact, the behaviour should be reinforced each time it is displayed. If we want to ensure that the behaviour becomes firmly embedded in the behavioural repertoire, we must subsequently sometimes reinforce it and sometimes not. We can observe this effect arising, for instance, in gambling or highly addictive computer games. If we reinforce the new desired behaviour, the undesired behaviour diminishes in quantity and quality. We can then start to apply the third rule, i.e. ignoring the undesired behaviour. Application of the three rules together can bring about genuine modification of behaviour but only if the three steps are applied in the right order: first *stopping* behaviour, then *reinforcing* alternative behaviour and finally *ignoring* undesired behaviour.

It is clear from the nature of the rules that the desired behaviour should be displayed if a child is to learn it. It should therefore already be present and potentially feasible.

Thirteen-year-old Tim had some features of autism. His father was desperate and told the therapist that Tim was not susceptible to any learning, quite contrary to prevailing views of autism. On the computer they had activated a screensaver in which a sentence scrolled across the screen whenever the PC was in standby. Tim typed in the most disgusting words to scroll across the screen. This was considered inappropriate in Tim's family and his father wanted it to stop. After many remarks and comments, Tim's father typed in a sentence himself: 'Why is that necessary?' The response was a flood of swearwords scrolling in the screensaver. 'You see', he told the therapist, 'he just can't be taught anything'. The therapist inquired what had happened since. 'Well, what a coincidence, he hasn't done it since.' 'How long has it been?' the therapist asked. 'About two or three weeks.' In other words, Tim had certainly responded positively and displayed the desired behaviour. Adults often do not notice this and do not reward the positive behaviour. It is only when the child does something wrong again that the parent reacts. 'Sometime soon your son will do something that is not right and you will comment on it and then he will come up with a sentence you have heard before but you may this time understand its significance: "You only say something when I do something wrong; you never say anything when I do things right"' the therapist told Tim's father.

Many parents have heard the sentence quoted in the example. It indicates how easily parents pass over a change in behaviour and fail to reinforce it, fail to apply rule 2, so that behaviour cannot change. The reason why parents fail to notice the improved behaviour is that the child's response to being told off is often very intense and negative. After this, the parents fail to notice that the message has certainly come across and that the child has adapted her behaviour. This is why after applying rule 1 (stopping/punishing) it is important to pay attention to whether the desired behaviour is displayed so that it can be reinforced.

In children with autism, punishment usually has a negative effect. Often they are not susceptible to flattery or disapproval because they have little understanding of the impact of their behaviour. Since these children have difficulty understanding what goes on in other people's minds, they do not really pay much attention to others. Moreover, their lack of orientation towards others is low. In their socioscheme there is little information about the other and the effect of their own behaviour on the other. They feel that punishment is an enormous injustice and they can become extremely angry as a result. We shall discuss this in some detail in Chapter 12 on aggression. At the same time, these children run the risk of developing feelings of inferiority when they learn about their behaviour and that of others. In the next chapter, we shall consider the consequences of these feelings for the self-image and behaviour of people with autism.

Special attention should be given to the fact that children with an autistic disorder are easy prey for their peers and can be incited into undesirable behaviour by them. For teachers, for instance, it is therefore advisable first to find out whether that has been the case before considering punishment.

> Will was very eager to make friends. This made him easy prey for a group of young delinquents who used him as a drugs courier.

People live by their *preferred behaviour* (Delfos 2004b). In children with autism their preferential behaviour is often associated with anxiety reduction; it is behaviour that serves as a *strategy in anxiety reduction*. So, in order to change the undesirable behaviour into new behaviour, this new behaviour should work as a strategy in anxiety reduction, otherwise it will never be automated. Under stress the preferential behaviour will emerge.

The burnt-out family

An autistic child is a heavy burden on the family and the risk of *burn-out* is always present because of the constant demands made by the child. The child needs a great deal of attention and care, often right from birth. We have already mentioned eating and crying problems. Yet these problems do not apply to all children with a contact disorder. Children with an autistic disorder and below average intelligence often sleep a lot and cry very little. Children with an autistic disorder and normal or above average intelligence often cry frequently during the first year. These babies have particular difficulty falling and remaining asleep, which are two of the sleep phases which babies have to learn. It puts enormous strain on the parent's perseverance to guide the child through this stage, and support and understanding from the family are of essential importance.

Bob's parents suffered from nervous exhaustion a year and a half after his birth. Bob's severe sleeping problems kept them busy day and night. His father even went cycling with Bob sitting in a little chair on his handlebars supported by a cushion on the handlebars in order to get him to sleep. Their social life had become greatly restricted and their friends were beginning to protest that they had the feeling that they were no longer around.

Parents are often advised by people around them to just let the baby cry. In practice, however, this is not feasible. From the way the child cries, the parents hear how badly he needs them. Autistic children often have all kinds of 'tricks' to fall asleep. For instance, they may rhythmically bang their head before falling asleep or rock their head from left to right. When parents try to stop these 'tricks', it becomes more difficult for the child to fall asleep. As these babies often find mild vibrations pleasant, they like being picked up and rocked. Parents often spend whole nights walking up and down with the baby in their arms to calm him down, but in the end this is impossible to keep up. As the baby may like mild vibrations, it may help to put a music box against his cheek and let it play. However, this is possible only if the child is not hypersensitive to sound. Helping and teaching the child to fall asleep is an important educational task for these babies because sleep is conducive to the maturational process of the baby's brain (see also Chapter 2).

A child with an autistic disorder has a decisive influence on the family. The fact that the family is actually 'governed' by the child's anxieties is not always immediately clear. Often, the child does not look anxious but angry, spoilt or self-willed. This is why members of the family feel personally responsible for his or her behaviour. The same thing happens at school. There is a strong risk of burn-out when people take the child's behaviour personally. They think the behaviour is aimed at them personally and feel hurt, have the feeling that they are failing, and attempt to guide the child's behaviour in a different direction and then adapt their own behaviour. As the child's behaviour is not personal but impersonal and not controlled by the environment but by an inner anxiety, this intervention cannot be successful. This further reinforces the personal hurt and the feeling of failure, with the risk of leading the child and those around her down a negative spiral. Anger in the environment also enhances the child's anxiety and consequently her undesired behaviour.

> One of the main pitfalls in interaction between autistic and non-autistic people is not only that the autistic person wrongly evaluates the other's behaviour but also that the non-autistic person does the same and feels personally affected by something that is not meant personally.

Burn-out also arises because, as a result of the incessant appeal which the child makes for their attention, the carers never get any breathing space, never have a chance to withdraw and just empty their minds completely. In Chapter 8 we explained how self-reflection on one's own thoughts and feelings contributes to burn-out.

A burnt-out family has no energy left to cope adequately with the situation. The most difficult thing when dealing with an autistic child is for the other people around the child to remain patient and not take the behaviour personally. These qualities are of fundamental importance to enable the child to grow up under optimum conditions and to keep the support which the family and the people around can provide as strong as possible. However, this requires understanding, trust and some stability. Accordingly, it is necessary for the family to get outside help. This can be obtained by exchanging experiences with other parents. There are associations (see Appendix II) whose activities include organizing such contacts among parents. But what is needed above all is practical help. There are homes for the temporary accommodation of autistic children, enabling the family to recover and giving the child an opportunity to be with other children under expert supervision and guidance.

Suggestions for upbringing may focus, for instance, on preventing rituals by not getting the child used to only one pair of shoes or one way of going to bed. Providing guidance through this type of advice can prevent problems. Most people with Kanner's autism cannot live on their own and are dependent on institutional care. Children with Asperger's syndrome can function independently but run the risk of becoming completely isolated from the onset of adolescence. The parents remain their most important operating base. The responsibility of parents of an autistic child reaches much further than adulthood.

Dealing with resistance to change

There are two important causes that play a part in autistic people's resistance to change. The first is when someone says that something is not going ahead. This in fact is a change imposed from outside. It may trigger a great deal of resistance and aggression. This is because hearing that something is not going ahead can cause the autistic person to fall into a black hole because he or she cannot foresee what is going to happen instead. Even if, after saying that something is *not* going ahead, something is announced that is *nice and pleasant*, this is not registered as the first shock has already been inflicted. Consequently, one should first explain what is going to happen and only then that the other thing is not going ahead, and why not.

The second possible source of resistance is the personal need to prevent an unpleasant feeling. People with autism, in particular children, can often feel extremely unhappy. In order not to have that feeling, they are sometimes very active in producing a pleasant state, e.g. a *trance*. An intrusion into an activity that produces this state evokes resistance to change because the pleasant feeling has been interrupted. In order to ensure that this resistance does not escalate and the pleasant feeling is not disrupted, it is advisable to link up with it and once the link has been established slowly announce the new activity. An added advantage is that the pace is thereby slowed down, something that is of great importance to autistic people.

When someone puts up resistance, we tend to exert more pressure or provide justifications. The fact is that both are counterproductive. Behaviour arising out of resistance to change is not fighting what the other does but an inner, almost reflexive response. If the person concerned is given some time to recover from the initial reaction, things become much easier. See also the example of Tim given on page 293.

Table 10.1 Coping with resistance to change	
Reasons for resistance	*Coping strategies*
Unpredictability of what is going to happen	Announce what is going to happen and only then what is not going to happen
Preventing an unpleasant feeling	Try to link up with an ongoing activity and fade the new activity into the old
To sum up: no justification and no insistence; both are counterproductive	

In the next two chapters, we shall examine the meaning of anxiety and aggression and ways of dealing with them.

Focal points

- Resistance to change is in fact a deep-seated need to hold on to what is familiar, to a habit.

- Parents of autistic children become exhausted from the fights for ordinary everyday things, a new pair of pyjamas, going to the hairdresser's or buying shoes.

- Resistance to change occurs in all fields, e.g. in eating new food.

- The newness of new food may be its taste but also its texture; changing over to food with a coarser texture is often problematic.

- Changes make the world more unpredictable.

- As they cannot properly formulate their questions, autistic children continue asking repetitive questions for longer than other children; they keep asking the same question even when the answer has already been given.

- Children with an autistic disorder often have difficulty putting their thoughts and feelings into words.

- Behaviour can be modified through 'shaping', which involves redirecting behaviour towards desired behaviour in small steps.

- A great deal of learning is acquired through association of one thing with another.

- Many autistic children resist having their hair cut.

- If the child resists having his hair cut, try to cut his hair for a short space of time and at regular intervals in a secure environment, preferably at home, rather than waiting till the hair has grown long and has to be cut in one go.

- Autistic people may be hypersensitive in several of their senses.

- Together with the child, find out which fabrics feel pleasant to the skin and which ones do not.

- Once the child is no longer hypersensitive, try through behavioural therapy to break through any negative associations the child has built up.

- Sensory hypersensitivity decreases as the child gets older.

- For autistic children, exceptions to a rule are often a reason for asking endless questions about justification.

- If parents start to give in to their child's resistance, they are reinforcing the child's pattern of behaviour.

- Anxiety can be expressed in several ways. The most usual reactions to anxiety are hyperactivity, aggression, withdrawal and shyness.

- Holding on to what is familiar and to habits seems to offer more security than a new situation.

- Something new can be introduced at a stroke only if one is certain that the child will like it and will not be anxious for long, and that the change can be carried through swiftly and the reason why the change takes place can be explained to the child.

- The behaviour of autistic people may come across as terrorizing but in fact arises out of a sense of powerlessness.

- Children with autism have a limited sense of time.

- Autistic children attach less importance to what goes on in other people as they are insufficiently able to imagine what goes on in others' minds and therefore pay less attention to what others want.

- A ritual is not an inherent need to do things in a particular manner but a way of keeping the anxiety that lurks around the corner at bay by controlling the predictability of events. The repetition incorporated in the ritual has at it were a 'hypnotizing' effect.

- Breaking through the ritual not only disrupts the action but also the sense of security.

- The rituals of autistic people are based on associations. Associative thinking is an important form of thinking for people with an autistic disorder.

- Obligation means change and marks a boundary in activity and time. Every change is in fact a step closer to death.

- A request addressed to an autistic person usually meets with 'no'. This 'no' helps him or her to gain time to think about what to do. The thinking process requires time to switch to 'on' instead of 'off'.

- By hanging a clock on the wall, the child can follow the passage of time.

- Poor orientation in time and space means that people with Asperger's syndrome are often bad at planning their activities and frequently have trouble keeping appointments.

- Perfectionism is a virtue that can degenerate into a vice.

- Learning to make realistic plans is of considerable importance for people with Asperger's syndrome, making their lives manageable and more predictable.

- Carers often try to modify behaviour through punishment. Punishment merely ensures that the behaviour stops and that the chance of it recurring decreases as the risk of being caught increases. New behaviour is learnt through reinforcement. Behaviour can be unlearnt only by extinguishing and ignoring it.

- It is not that children ask for negative attention, they just do not know how to elicit positive attention.

- A family with an autistic child is at risk of burn-out.

- Babies have to learn to fall asleep and remain asleep. Autistic children often have difficulty mastering these skills. Mild vibrations are often pleasant to them. One way may be to put a music box against their cheek.

- Parents and carers can easily take an autistic child's behaviour personally and thus feel hurt by it.

Focal points regarding attitude

- Be aware that people with an autistic disorder have great difficulty with 'obligations', and do not label them as lazy.

- Autistic children are actively engaged in fighting anxiety.

- There is a difference between not wanting to keep appointments and lacking a sense of time causing one not to keep appointments.

- Avoid taking something personally when it is not meant as such.

- Be aware of the risk of burn-out to the family.

Summary

People with an autistic disorder resist changes imposed by others. Their brain has difficulty processing the pace of change, and changes render their world unpredictable. A habit, often ensuing from particular associations, gives a stronger sense of security than something new if imposed from outside. Their resistance to change leads to resistance to tasks imposed from the outside. Their automatic 'no' is intended to try and gain time to grasp the situation. Resistance emerges in all fields, also for instance to new food. Techniques of behavioural therapy can bring about a change in behaviour. No such change can be brought about through punishment but only by reinforcing the desired and ignoring the undesired behaviour.

Sensorial hypersensitivity may cause difficulty with subjects such as clothes, sound or haircuts.

Autistic people's lack of a sense of time means that they are poor at planning and are often bad at keeping appointments or tend to keep to them too stringently.

Taking things personally is one of the major pitfalls in interaction among people, and in particular between autistic and non-autistic people.

11

Coping with anxiety and obsession

A prominent feature of people with an autistic disorder, in particular children, is their anxiety. Among the many researchers who have emphasized this aspect, Niko and Elisabeth Tinbergen (1985) even pointed to anxiety as the principal cause of the lack of speech. Waterhouse (2000) emphasized the importance of anxiety in autistic disorders. Possibly there is a basic hormonal structure causing continuous underlying anxiety. In people with autism, this problem is presumably connected with immaturity of the hormone system. Moreover, as the child grows up there are all kinds of factors that may enhance anxiety. In this chapter, I shall explain how hormones play a role in anxiety. I shall present a model in which the relation between anxiety, aggression and depression is clarified. I have developed this model and presented it in an earlier publication (Delfos 2004a). It is based on the findings of research which have been combined in a comprehensive explanatory framework. Once again, an appeal is made to the reader's patience: I shall first present the state of knowledge about anxiety before we can go on to examine how it operates in autistic people and what can be done about it.

Anxiety as a basic motive

In Chapter 5 we explained that an impaired *sociocheme* causes a lack of inner structure. As a result, the child does not have appropriate inner resources to understand the behaviour of people around her and the changes that take place continuously. Without this inner structure, the child is at the mercy of her anxiety. As soon as her balance is disturbed, e.g. when the programme which the child has in mind is disrupted, anxiety may be triggered. Because of the unpredictability of events, anxiety about the unknown always lies around the corner. Situations that do not entail any surprises for the average child may be completely unpredictable to an autistic child. In babies, we see this anxiety emerge as soon as they do not understand what is happening and are afraid that their carer will leave them. Often, it is this anxiety that causes babies to cry during the first three months. The child is anxious, experiences a need that is not satisfied and still possesses insufficient means of communicating his wishes to those looking after him. Even Watson (1924), who was convinced that all behaviour was learnt behaviour, even love, considered anxiety as an innately present basic emotion.

In autistic people, especially children, anxiety is quicker to emerge; but the older the child, the more she understands how things work. Also, those around her understand the child and her anxiety better and are better able to respond. Anxiety diminishes with the increase in possibilities of communication, at least if the carers intuitively respond to the child's needs.

When a child, young person or adult with an autistic disorder becomes anxious, his or her response will primarily depend on individual temperament. The response to anxiety may be aggression or withdrawn, anxious behaviour.

Anxiety is indelibly linked with aggression and depression. To clarify this connection, I outline below the anxiety scheme presented in detail in Delfos (2004a), where the consequences for psychosomatic diseases are presented in a psychosomatics model. Appendix V (in electronic form; for access information see p. 13) gives a more extensive explanation of the scheme, with references to research which are not included in this chapter.

If we wish to understand the behaviour of children with an autistic disorder, it is necessary to take a closer look at anxiety. This will help us to understand better the flapping hands, obsessions and outbursts of anger. Armed with this knowledge, we can help these children to display behaviour that solves their problems, rather than fruitlessly try to teach them to adapt.

Anxiety and stress

Anxiety and stress are interrelated. Stress is in fact a form of 'danger', by which we mean both a physical and a psychological threat. Table 11.1 outlines the various forms of danger, with examples.

In reaction to danger, the brain gives a signal to produce hormones, triggering a chain reaction in the body. *Anxiety, aggression* (here we mean specifically physical aggression) and *depression* can be brought together in a single hormonal model, at the same time illustrating the differences between men and women with regard to anxiety, aggression and depression. The model is reproduced in Figure 11.1.

The point of departure of the model is the fact that humans respond to danger. *Detection* of danger is not a conscious process but *perceiving* is: it means that the information has been transmitted to consciousness. Danger may entail a physical threat but also a negative thought. Danger activates the stress system (HPA: hypothalamic-pituitary-adrenocortical system) and makes the body produce stress hormones, including adrenalin. A number of physical processes are set in motion, enabling the person concerned to take action. The heartbeat accelerates, causing

Table 11.1 Forms of danger

Form	Example
External direct physical danger	Someone who is about to hit me
External indirect physical danger	A fire breaking out
Internal direct physical danger	A sudden pain in my body
Internal indirect physical danger	A symptom such as fever
External direct psychological danger	Someone who threatens me verbally or pressure exerted by another person (stress)
External indirect psychological danger	Arachnophobia
Internal direct psychological danger	A negative thought emerging
Internal indirect psychological danger	Pressure I experience myself (stress)

the blood to be pumped faster through the body and oxygen to be carried faster to the muscles to fight or take flight, and to the head to stimulate thinking. Respiration intensifies to get more oxygen into the lungs. The pupils dilate to be able to take in more visual information. The body is brought into a general state of *arousal*, enabling it to face the danger through the *fight or flight* response (Selye 1976).

Danger → production of stress hormones

Humans react to these hormones with emotional alertness, *anxiety* (Damasio 1994). The intensity of the emotion depends on the quantity of hormones produced, not on the danger. Some produce many hormones in the face of a relatively minor danger and will therefore experience strong anxiety. Others produce fewer hormones in the face of a relatively major danger and will consequently feel less anxiety. The quantity of hormones produced depends on a number of factors; including the *unconscious* evaluation of the danger by the amygdala, *conscious* evaluation of danger, predispositional factors determining the extent to which stress hormones are produced, and the individual's past experience. Years of exposure to stress may lead to habituation, causing the body to maintain stress hormone production at a constantly higher level than normal (Kendall-Tackett 2000). In case of danger, production will therefore be extremely high. Unconscious and conscious evaluation of danger determine the need to produce hormones while predisposition and habituation largely determine the quantity of hormones produced.

Danger → stress hormones → anxiety

After the danger–(stress) hormones–anxiety sequence, there are two possible paths. The individual may become *active* (taking action) or have a *passive* reaction (inaction). Taking action always *reduces anxiety*, inaction *increases anxiety*. Action may take the form of a physical activity, fight or flight; but any activity in fact reduces anxiety, even pacing up and down, singing or vacuuming or, for instance, squeezing stress balls. Stress balls have been developed as a simple way of calming down. By squeezing these stress balls, action is taken; no matter how mild, it is a physical activity 'using up' hormones and diminishing anxiety.

The most effective action is that which fights the danger or removes it. Action can be a physical activity such as running away but it can also be a constructive thought. Inaction is nearly impossible in humans: they do not support an emptiness and fill the emptiness with their own monsters. Thus, inaction leads to an increase in anxiety and the risk of 'brooding', i.e. forming negative thoughts which again constitute a danger and again trigger the production of stress hormones, ending up in a vicious circle.

Action → anxiety decrease

Inaction → anxiety increase

This often happens when we go to sleep. In bed, in the dark, there is a lack of stimuli (light off, lying still, silence) as a result of which the hormones cannot be converted into activity and are instead converted into brooding. This explains why children become more difficult to handle when they have to go to bed. They sense that lying in the dark makes them afraid and makes them have unpleasant thoughts. This is in particular the case if the body is in an aroused state before going to sleep. After a busy day, working late or an exciting situation, it is difficult to go to sleep right away. In fact, the substances first have to be 'used up'.

Action is a form of behaviour with two components. First, it has to be possible to carry it out, for which one needs adrenergic hormones, *adrenalin* in particular. Second, it has to be effectively carried out, for which one needs androgenes, *testosterone* in particular. There should be a balance between testosterone and adrenalin. If there is too much adrenalin in the body in relation to testosterone, one cannot perform a particular behaviour. One may want to but remains as it were stuck to one's chair. This causes an enormous increase in anxiety. If there is too much testosterone in relation to adrenalin one could move into action but one is unable to carry it out, leading to the feeling of as it were 'exploding' without being able to do anything. This feeling in itself leads to the sensation of 'danger' and, in turn, can trigger the production of adrenalin. The result is that an 'explosion' can also occur in behaviour.

If there is sufficient testosterone and adrenalin, it is possible to take action. If both are at a high level, *aggression* may occur. Aggression can be viewed as an extreme form of action. The hormone testosterone is linked with aggression. Roughly speaking, the more testosterone, the more aggression, and the less testosterone, the more anxiety.

If we have too much adrenalin (and other stress hormones) in our body in relation to testosterone, this is harmful to the body. The body initially tries to get rid of the adrenalin by moving into action, as action restores the hormone balance. This could even be the natural reaction of trembling after a stressful event. If we have too little testosterone, we cannot move into action. If adrenalin is not translated into action, it may become harmful to the body. *Psychosomatic symptoms* may be the result of this process. For the psychosomatic component of anxiety-aggression-depression, see the psychosomatic model (Delfos 2004a; 2004b). However, a more detailed discussion of this subject is beyond the scope of this book.

If, due to excitement, the body has produced too much adrenalin, it tries to get rid of the excess hormones, for instance through perspiration; hence *breaking out in a cold sweat*. If there is still too much, it is converted into other substances and these can shut down the body. Then the anxiety changes into *depression*. The extreme form of inaction is, therefore, depression.

Action → extreme form – aggression

Inaction → extreme form – depression

The process makes it clear why jogging may be an effective form of therapy for depression. In the depressive state, the substances are not 'used up'. Production continues in the body, leading to a negative spiral. If the substances are 'used up', e.g. through running, the negative spiral is broken and the depression can diminish. The effect of taking action is always evident when, in the face of anxiety or stress, we begin to do something; even if it is just pacing up and down or clearing up a few things, it immediately makes us feel a bit better.

Obviously, the action we take does not always solve everything. The most effective approach is of course any action that actually reduces the danger. Nevertheless, bringing about some reduction of anxiety through physical activity is positive in itself, even if only to boost our flow of thoughts.

Testosterone is a hormone that is not easily produced, although it is to some extent also produced under stress. We are therefore dependent on the quantity of testosterone present in the body. If one has too little testosterone in relation to adrenalin, one will not be able to move into action. The standard level of testosterone in men is nine to twenty times higher than in women. As a result, men have a tendency to move into action in the face of danger whereas women tend towards inaction (see Figure 11.1).

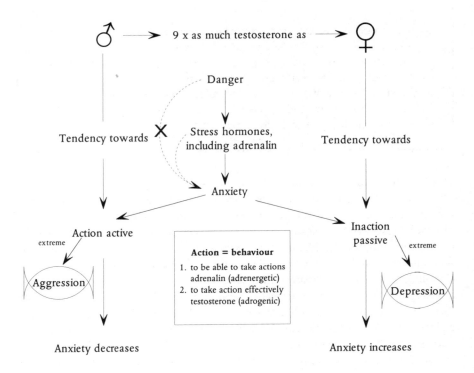

Figure 11.1 Anxiety scheme 1 (Delfos 2004a).

Since aggression, which is linked to testosterone, can be viewed as the most extreme form of action in the face of danger, it is not surprising that problems of aggression occur significantly more often in men. Men are not less fearful as such but are often more effective in dissolving their fear because they tend to move into action. On average, men are much more solution-oriented than women. Because men act, they experience less anxiety and for shorter periods. In fact, they have an effective method of getting rid of feelings of anxiety. Women are less inclined to act and as a result feel more anxiety and for longer. The most extreme form of inaction is depression. Someone with a depression is listless and can hardly be persuaded to move. Women therefore have depressive problems much more frequently than men.

A typical, simple example of the way adrenalin and depression work is lying in. Sleeping late is wonderful, in particular when one is physically very tired. If we then get up, we feel fit and the day normally starts in a pleasant mood. However, if instead of getting up we stay in bed for a bit longer, the situation shortly afterwards is not quite as pleasant. Later

> again, one begins to unpleasant, one starts to brood and the mood may become sombre. This is in fact a miniature version of depression. The probable cause is that the body produces adrenergic hormones when we have slept enough, enabling us to move into action. If we fail to do so, the situation is slowly reversed, the adrenergic substances are not converted into activity and, as a result, a noxious quantity of adrenalin develops in the body in relation to the other hormones.

One way in which an excess of stress hormones, excitatory substances, can be converted is through movement. *Hyperactivity* is a possible form of this, but *obsessive behaviour* may also be of this type. This we can observe in children with an autistic disorder. Obsessive behaviour increases as stress or anxiety increase (Frith 1989), as we have indicated in Chapter 5. Children with an autistic disorder may start flapping their hands, quick rotary movements of the hands. These movements, like clapping their hands, increase with excitement. The excitement occurs both in anxiety and in positive excitement because adrenalin plays a part in both (Schachter and Singer 1962). The research by Gillberg and Ehlers (1998) provides a clear indication of the disrupted balance of the hormonal system in connection with anxiety. They note that people with an autistic disorder have a lot of degrading substances in their body, produced from the excitatory substances. Given a structural feeling of anxiety that can be so easily evoked by all kinds of occurrences in the lives of autistic children, it is to be expected that they convert a considerable quantity of these degrading substances in their body.

If autistic people cannot use language to express themselves and cannot communicate through language what motivates them and what they want, the urge to move increases. Just as people who can speak normally may start pacing the room up and down or fidgeting with their foot, autistic people often need even more activity to control their anxiety and excitement. Birger Sellin (1995) had, according to his father, become completely beside himself after a journey. Sellin, who cannot speak but can write, makes it clear, however, that the trip offered him so much beauty that he was filled with excitement. This is how he expresses it:

> How else should I cope with such an experience? It is simply the excitement of not being able to answer those who can talk.

In terms of action, there is a difference between men and women. Men have a stronger tendency towards action to deal with the danger and initiate physical activity sooner. Women, on the other hand, have a greater tendency to act by seeking security and help when faced with danger. Under the influence of the oxytocin hormone, women will be more inclined to look after the nest, the children or the housework and talk to their female friends (Taylor *et al.* 2000). If we take the consequence of this difference in action between man and women seriously, we can better understand a number of problems between men and women. We often see this pattern (working versus talking) arising when men and women are in stressful situations. The most painful among these is possibly the loss of a child, probably the strongest grief known to humans. The risk of divorce is particularly serious in this situation (75%). The cause of the divorce is the different way in which the man and the woman respond to the pain of the loss of their child. Women blame men for 'escaping' into their work and not talking with them about their child. Women do not sufficiently realize that working is a strategy for the man to alleviate his pain about the loss, just as talking fulfils the same function for women. These are two solutions to the problem, rather than one, and the two pieces together can solve the puzzle. The same pattern can be observed when a partner dies, for instance. Men who are widowed tend to concentrate on their work and neglect their family; women tend to focus on their family and neglect their work (Worden 1996).

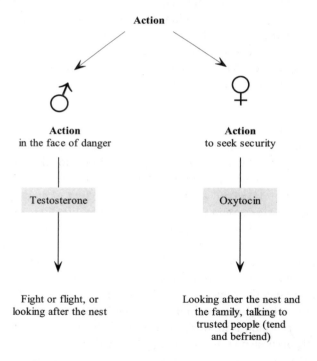

Figure 11.2 Anxiety scheme 2 (Delfos 2004a).

We probably find the same pattern of gender differences in autistic children. Significantly more boys than girls have the autistic disorders with which we are concerned here, Asperger's syndrome and PDD-NOS. Given this fact, it is no surprise that there is a strong focus on aggression and physical activity. In the example of Linda (Chapter 10) we saw that she started combing her hair and ironing her clothes, which can be viewed as 'nest activities'. Maureen (Chapter 10) also spent hours combing her hair and playing with her dolls. Both displayed the more 'female' solution in response to danger. However, I am not aware of any research in which this phenomenon has been investigated more closely.

Fight or flight can be seen as two basic responses to stress, two coping mechanisms mainly found in men. Because of their physical predominance and orientation, they have a stronger tendency towards a physical response to stress. Women tend to respond less physically and their reactions to stress are therefore more social and psychological in nature. This response has been mentioned above, *tend and befriend*. The two basic responses of women are being nice and being a victim. Both are strategies protecting against attack. One does not attack victims or people who are nice. In the animal kingdom, we observe this for instance in the case of a puppy which, when taken for a walk, may meet a larger dog. The puppy presses itself against the ground to indicate that it is the smaller, inferior one and the larger dog need not attack it. Women's most common coping mechanisms are therefore 'nice' or 'victim' (Delfos 2004b).

Signs of anxiety

The cause of anxiety is certainly not always easy to recognize and discover. There are various sources for the feeling of anxiety. A predispositionally excessive *hormone production* causing a state of arousal without a clearly discernible cause in the current situation brings about a pervasive, vague feeling of anxiety. In this case, there is no discernible cause in the events in the child's life. A second source is the *associations* which can link one subject to another and may adhere to a particular emotion, in this case anxiety. These associations are not always discernible as a source of anxiety either. Finally, there is the autistic person's *course of life*, which may be such that conflict, confrontation and contact with people in the immediate surroundings frequently trigger anxiety. These are often easier to discover because the people around the autistic child have experienced a conflict with it. Social anxiety and fear of failure are forms of anxiety derived from these situations that also frequently occur in non-autistic people. We shall discuss these forms of anxiety in Chapter 13 when considering non-autistic contact problems.

In the chapters of this book, we have encountered various forms of behaviour connected with anxiety in a child with an autistic disorder. They are in fact various forms of activity, of action, to prevent and reduce anxiety. Some forms of behaviour serve both functions; it is indicated that it is very strongly the case with *self-hypnotic behaviour*. Both forms are summarized in Table 11.2.

We shall discuss both forms and the way they are expressed. It is important to bear in mind that a great deal of the behaviour of autistic people is a form of *stress management* and that it is therefore not easy to control if the source, i.e. anxiety, is not treated or removed.

Preventing anxiety

Anxiety is an important issue in people with autism. This is particularly true for people with Asperger's syndrome and PDD-NOS. However, anxiety is less clear if it takes the form of aggression rather than visible anxiety. People with an autistic disorder are very actively engaged in trying to prevent anxiety. There are several ways in which they do so:

- resistance, opposition to change
- extreme focus on the mother
- defence against strangers
- extreme shyness with strangers
- stiffening oneself on being touched
- closeness to ensure availability when in distress; demanding behaviour
- avoidance of social situations
- withdrawal from social situations
- self-isolation
- doing one's best
- adaptation
- self-hypnotic behaviour.

A number of these are discussed below.

Resistance to change

Their resistance to change, which can take the form of very strong opposition, is one of the ways in which autistic children try to avert new stimuli and keep their world predictable. This is because every change carries the risk that the new situation is going to be unpleasant or induce anxiety. The resistance put up by people with an autistic disorder is one way of keeping their situation as free of stress as possible. As the person grows older, his or her knowledge increases and with it insight into the nature of new situations. Consequently, the resistance may diminish though in some situations it will actually increase if knowledge has provided the insight that the new situation may be stressful.

Extreme attachment to the mother

A second way in which an autistic child may try to prevent anxiety is to make sure he stays close to – usually – the mother. In general, an autistic child is very detached from his surroundings but at the same time it is extremely focused on the mother. The child badly needs the mother in order to cope with the utterly incomprehensible world.

Anxiety is an emotion triggered by danger. We have already noted that autistic children have a keener perception of danger than an average child. Accordingly, there are many stimuli, many situations that may evoke a feeling of anxiety in autistic children. Sullivan (1953) speaks of an almost telepathic bond between mother and baby. In autistic babies, this bond may mean that they perceive the mother's negative moods and stress more keenly than the average baby.

> At the age of two, Ronald was still extremely focused on his mother. When she went to the toilet, he had to go with her for otherwise he would get into a panic. If he woke up at night, he calmed down only when his mother came. Only when he was three did this behaviour diminish and it seemed that Ronald had become aware that his mother was available to help him without always being around him. What an average baby learns in less than one year took him three years.

Resistance to strangers

On the basis of their anxiety, autistic children also put up resistance to strangers, keeping them at arm's length and not easily letting them into their world. When they are older, they may still be extremely shy of strangers. In babies this is even evident physically, when they stiffen on being touched. Because of a heightened sense of touch, being touched may feel like pain. Stiffening stimulates the other person into letting go, keeping their distance, and in this way the child protects herself against the danger of touch.

It is to be expected that children with an autistic disorder become extra-sensitive to signals emitted by the mother. In reaction to the parent's stress, the general response of children is not keeping their distance but, on the contrary, clinging to them. The child wishes to keep the parent nearby just in case he gets into distress. His behaviour is very demanding. For the parent, in particular the mother, this means that at the very moment she needs extra peace and quiet because she is tense, the child appeals to her more than at other times. The effect may be that the mother is at a greater risk of burn-out. Consequently, extra care should be given to a mother of an autistic child when she experiences stress due to circumstances.

This extreme orientation towards the mother is due in particular to a lack of knowledge of and insight into social relations. Just as we explain to a baby that her mother will be coming back and that there is no need to be afraid, we will have to explain this to an autistic child over and over again and for a longer period to ensure that she builds up trust in social situations and processes. This is necessary not only when leaving the room but also when coming back. When the mother returns and the child's anxiety proves unfounded, it is important to make the child aware of this. In this way, the new awareness is checked against reality and can be embedded in the child's mind. Anxiety is kept alive by avoidance and can be extinguished by checking against reality. This requires repetition as the working memory of autistic children is weak and things are less easily retained.

> One way of teaching a child that he is not being left behind, helpless, when the carer leaves the room is by playing 'coming and going' games. One of the most usual games parents play to teach this to their children is by briefly putting a cloth over the child's head and removing it again (playing peekaboo).

Just as peekaboo teaches children about the permanence of people, playing hide and seek teaches them that people continue to be present or findable even if they are out of sight.

> Herbert ended up in a children's home at the age of six. He reverted to baby-like behaviour and whined while the child minders just could not discover what was wrong. In play therapy two years later his favourite game was playing hide and seek. He kept on playing that he had to be found. This game took up a large part of his time and was repeated during many sessions. Part of the game was that the therapist expressed her (acted) despair about not being able to find Herbert. He visibly and audibly enjoyed hearing her say this in his hiding place. Herbert suffered from autistiform behaviour which was all the more serious as his life had been such that he had early on lost what little security he had.

Playing hide and seek can evoke a great deal of anxiety in autistic children, and this is why they tend to avoid the game. Although her calendar age might suggest that the child is ready for it, this is in fact not the case because of her mental age. Because of her extremely delayed development in the social sphere, it may be helpful to insert intermediate stages between putting a cloth on the child's head and playing hide and seek, in order to prepare her for playing hide and seek. The aim should be to make the child aware of the availability of help without the helper always being near at hand and visible.

An example of such a game is putting the child in one room and the mother in another room and then to see how quickly she can be with the child when he calls for help. This can be repeated at various locations indoors and outdoors. If the child knows how to use a telephone, this can also be used to practise the game. The situation should also be reversed, with the mother calling the child. Next, the child can be taught that this should only be performed if the child genuinely needs it. This can be clarified by the mother calling the child while the child is busy doing something else and the mother does not really need the child. In this situation, the child is needlessly disrupted in his activity. It is important to repeat this performance several times with the child in the role of the caller and the called in order to make him aware of the way in which calling can be used in practice.

In this way, the child learns that he does not need the helper to be very near him in order to face possible danger but also that he can mobilize help and that the helper is prepared to provide help even if he or she is not present at the time the situation arises. As the person providing help is often the mother, these exercises may serve to prevent burn-out in the child's mother.

Attachment plays an important role in anxious children. They want to stay near their parents, often the mother. In children with an autistic disorder it is more difficult to bring about mutual attachment because they are slow in developing a socioscheme. They need to know that help will be at hand when they are in distress and they are not (yet) sufficiently focused on the inherent proximity of their carers. It is more a question of availability than of a need for contact.

The difference between need for contact and need for availability can be observed when a pre-schooler is happily playing on his own in the room where the mother is sitting nearby. There is no problem as long as the mother sits on the couch and quietly watches the child play. However, as soon as she starts reading a book or making a telephone call, the child draws the mother's attention. This is not out of a need for getting her attention or playing with her. Quite the contrary, the child would rather continue his own play. The reason why he tries to mobilize the mother is because he feels perfectly well that her availability diminishes as soon as she starts reading or phoning.

The need to keep carers available in order to be able to cope with possible distress may bring the child into conflict with her various needs. On the one hand, the child wants to distance herself from the parent and continue her own activity; on the other hand she craves the parent's proximity to feel more secure.

Anxious children have difficulty going to their peers' birthday parties. The mother offers to take the child there but once they have arrived at the friend's front door the child loses all courage. On the one hand, he wants to go to the party but on the other hand he wants to keep the mother near in case of need. The cause is often that the child is parting with his mother in an unknown situation. Often things work out better if the child is collected from home and leaves his mother behind at a familiar place.

Avoiding social situations

Social situations elicit a great deal of anxiety, especially in autistic children. Going to stay with other people, for instance, may be a major problem. Homesickness is not so much a longing for the people you have left behind as the anxiety that they will not be at hand when something goes wrong. Hans Asperger (1944) expressed surprise at the overwhelming feelings of homesickness in autistic children staying at his institute. At the time, Bowlby's (1984) attachment theory had not yet been published, but it is this theory that makes it easier to understand homesickness in the light of the need of children to have their attachment figure available in case they get into distress. The children at Asperger's institute had been cut off from their parents, their attachment figures, and their anxiety was therefore very strong, particularly in the alien surroundings of the institute. Asperger at first found this hard to understand because these children did not seem to be very attached to their parents. Consequently, Asperger wondered whether this was perhaps connected to an attachment to objects at home rather than the people.

In the above example of the birthday party, the availability of a mother you leave behind on the doorstep is less evident than of a mother you leave behind at home. In the latter case, you know exactly where she is and how to reach her. The same applies to working mothers. Once the child has seen where the parent works, knows where the telephone is and can conjure up an image of where her mother is at a given moment, her anxiety about her mother's departure for work will diminish. Once the child has successfully tried to reach her, this has a favourable effect on her anxiety. The arrival of the mobile telephone is a welcome development for anxious children because now they can mobilize their parents whenever they want. It is not that they have a need to speak to their parents all the time, but it is important to have this possibility. What counts is the parent's availability when the child feels in distress. The need to mobilize the parent diminishes once it knows the parent can be reached.

As children with an autistic disorder are often anxious, they can make heavy demands on those looking after them.

Maureen was usually ready for school on time. Although she was fifteen years old, she was still very restless when waiting for the school bus. She would sit on the stairs near her mother and continuously talk to her. Through this contact, Maureen tried to keep her insecurity under control. She remained in contact with her mother who was her main attachment figure and whom she wanted to keep close. Her mother, however, felt imprisoned in her daughter's constant presence and the demand she made on her.

What such demanding children in fact seek is availability, not proximity. It is important to teach the child to make this distinction. Through play the child can be taught that mother remains available even if she is out of sight. We have already mentioned the example of calling each other from adjacent rooms.

While children with an autistic disorder desire proximity and may be very demanding, they do not easily ask for help, as we saw in the previous chapter. The autistic child is more likely to give someone else an order and want it to be carried out in the way he has in mind. It is more a question of 'demanding' than 'asking for help'. In the following chapter, we shall examine this lack of asking for help in autistic children.

It is social situations in particular that evoke a great deal of anxiety. As social situations are difficult to understand, a child with an autistic disorder will often avoid such situations and withdraw from social settings. Her growing intelligence will ensure that through thought she gains a steadily better understanding of social interaction, and this will lead to more social contact. We also observe this in the three types of children mentioned by Lorna Wing (2001), the *aloof* autistic child, the *passive* child and the *active but odd* child. These three types of children represent an increase in intelligence and thereby in the possibilities of understanding social interaction, which effectively leads to an increase in social participation. A withdrawn child with an autistic disorder usually has low intelligence. If the child has average or above average intelligence, it means that a lack of sensing and empathy with people and concomitantly evaluating social situations can be compensated for by intellectually understanding social interaction.

No matter how capable the child becomes in evaluating social interaction, it remains problematic. This applies particularly to functioning in groups because there the social situation is extremely complex. Alec expressed this through his strong dislike of groups (Chapter 8). The difficulties involved in social situations are one reason why a child with an autistic disorder often tends to withdraw from social contact. Avoidance can thus take the form of isolating oneself and withdrawing from the social world, even through self-hypnotic behaviour. Consciousness is, as it were, 'toned down' to a lower level, diminishing the perception of stimuli. Gunilla Gerland (2003) illustrates this with a clear example.

> With a hissing sound, the teacher's pointer came down heavily on the open page of my book but I hardly batted an eyelid. I sat there withdrawn within myself, and my nervous system was not working sufficiently to react.

Self-hypnotic behaviour

Since anxiety plays such an important part in an autistic person's life, averting feelings of anxiety is an important activity. People with an autistic disorder therefore try to distract themselves from anxiety. Self-hypnotic behaviour is a prominent example of this but so also is the tendency to focus on pleasant things. Carrying out tasks, having obligations and any duties in general are therefore activities they want to avoid. They concentrate completely on a pleasant subject, thereby excluding unpleasant ones. In connection with autism, Wing (2001) therefore speaks of a *problem of motivation* rather than one of concentration.

Children have enormous *resilience* based on the hope that their situation will improve and on excellent stress management. Children seem to be better able to get through serious situations than adults.

> Five-year-old Joe was playing with an adult. The latter wished to discuss a painful subject. 'No, I don't want to talk about that now', Joe said. However, the adult persisted, saying to Joe: 'When I play with you, I can't help thinking about it all the time.' But Joe replied: 'So you should think "table, table, table", that's what I always do and then it just goes away.' At this early age of five, Joe had already thought up an Indian mantra.

One day when we have a better understanding of how consciousness works and can measure this in the brain, we will probably find that autistic people are very strongly focused on one single subject. This may take the form of a *trance*. Disrupting that activity causes problems and may lead to aggression, as we shall see in the following chapter.

Adaptation

Because of their experience of always being off the mark in contacts, while at the same time perceiving that the difference seems so small, children with Asperger's syndrome and PDD-NOS tend to try to adapt themselves and do their very best. For them, adaptation is a problem because of their resistance to change and their difficulty sensing what the other person would find agreeable. Consequently, 'adaptation' takes the form of 'doing your best'. Constantly doing his or her best without this resulting in being part of the group profoundly harms the child's self-image. As a result, people with an autistic disorder often have difficulty coping with criticism. They have carefully 'thought out' much social interaction and cannot easily imagine that they are making a 'mistake', but above all it affects their self-image. Criticism by others is often completely in line with their own feeling of always doing things wrong, always being off the mark in social interaction, thereby causing a great deal of pain.

Their attempts to reduce anxiety about social situations by adapting themselves and trying to behave in the way they think the others would wish result in behaviour that comes across as artificial, leading more often to rejection than acceptance. Accepting oneself, improving one's social insight and learning to cope with the disorder and the way in which others react to it is more fruitful than forever doing one's best. Trying to do one's best also leads to high levels of stress, triggering the danger-hormones–anxiety sequence, with all that this entails.

Forms of behaviour to reduce anxiety

If anxiety nevertheless arises, the autistic person will try to attenuate it. We have already mentioned various ways of coping with anxiety, including 'flapping hands' and having obsessions. The forms of behaviour to reduce anxiety are:

- hyperactivity

- flapping hands

- rocking or fidgeting

- obsessions and compulsions

- rituals

- stereotyped behaviour

- rational reaction

- understanding intellectually

- asking questions repeatedly

- argumentation

- arranging things

- self-hypnotic behaviour.

These are the non-aggressive forms. Aggression as an outlet for anxiety will be discussed in the next chapter. We shall now briefly consider the various forms. Self-hypnotic behaviour has already been discussed above under the heading 'Preventing anxiety'.

Hyperactivity

One of the most common ways of reducing anxiety is hyperactivity. If we can interpret an autistic child's behaviour as signs of anxiety, we will be less inclined to restrict his or her behaviour but, in particular, more inclined to trace the source of the behaviour and try to remove the anxiety. This does not mean that the behaviour may not or cannot be channelled. It is necessary to teach children to contain their behaviour. It gives them peace of mind but it does not solve the problem and can at the most have a short-lasting effect. Attention should also be given to the child's distress.

Patrick always returned home from school in a state of excitement. As soon as he was home, he would start to tell his story. At such times he was always full of movement, never sitting still for a moment. What he liked best was, while telling his story, to lean on the dining room table with his hands spread out, alternately jumping from his left to his right foot. For his parents it was sometimes quite tiring to listen to him and at the same time have this restless image in front of them. His mother would say: 'Patrick, I'd love to listen to you but I'm getting a bit dizzy from the way you jump around, could you just stop for a moment while you're telling your story?' At first, Patrick just continued as though he had not heard anything. Later on he would stop telling his story when his mother said something like that; he would get angry and go away to do something else. His mother kept on emphasizing that she would very much like to hear what he had to say and after some time Patrick stopped jumping up and down during his story if asked to stop. After a while, he no longer jumped up and down when he returned home from school and started telling his story.

Training a child to keep her hyperactivity in check does not mean that the activity will diminish in all situations but only in situations when attention is drawn to it. The activity is a healthy outlet for the child's anxiety and excitement and should not be completely controlled. If one wishes to do something about the hyperactivity, one should go about it selectively. Rather than trying to influence all behaviour, it is better to try and modify only the behaviour that is important to the child or those around her. The hyperactivity may in fact mask other problems, such as a psychotic condition.

Maureen's hyperactivity increased with the onset of physical puberty. She could be extremely active and very restless. However, this activity was not the same as it had been in the past. Her sleep at night was seriously affected. She regularly seemed to lose touch with reality. Her hyperactivity was now accompanied by a psychotic reaction. At this point, it was important not only to get the hyperactivity under control but also, and in particular, its psychotic nature. She was given medication in order to deal with the rush she ended up in as a result of the hormonal changes typical of puberty.

Imagine a psychotic person on a train: as long as the train is standing in the station, he is talking and chatting but as soon as it starts moving he falls silent. It is the waiting that makes him restless, and the movement, in particular the rhythm, of the train has a calming effect.

The 'flapping' and hand clapping which we often observe in autistic children is a specific form of hyperactivity. The reason why it is the hands that are subject to this activity is probably connected with the fact that they can be moved with the greatest ease. Rocking in a chair and fidgeting with the feet fulfil a comparable function but 'flapping' the feet is much more difficult to perform. When autistic children have to sit still, they often tend to fidget or rock to and fro. If they are stopped, their movements increase. This does not mean that they cannot sit still by themselves but only that this is more difficult for them if they are anxious or excited.

Obsession and compulsion

Obsessions and compulsions are compulsive phenomena. Obsessions include compulsive thoughts and compulsive brooding. Compulsions are compulsive actions often resulting from compulsive thoughts. Well-known examples are checking whether the gas has been turned off or the door has been closed.

Compulsive actions arising out of obsessive and especially compulsive behaviour are intended to ward off anxiety and have a calming effect. Consequently, it is in fact not possible for children and adults with a tendency towards obsessive behaviour to function completely without these obsessions, in particular at times of great stress. Medication may sometimes help (Grandin 1992; Ditmars 1995).

As we have mentioned before, these are *compulsive actions* rather than *obsessions* (Gillberg 1992). The aspect of action being taken to diminish anxiety, which we referred to above, is particularly evident.

Obsessions may focus on harmless subjects but also subjects that are important to the person concerned or his or her surroundings. Rather than trying to stop the obsession, it is better to try and redirect it towards a more innocent subject.

Jack had always been obsessive, especially in taking decisions. Should he buy this synthesizer or that one? Often he became quite literally ill from the decision-making process, involving everyone around him, including shop assistants, in his panic. When he started having girlfriends, the obsession focused on aspects of the girlfriend. A physical characteristic could bring him to despair and convince him that he felt no love for the girl as he would otherwise probably not be so upset by that particular physical feature. As he became better at having relationships, the nature of his obsession deepened. While he had initially focused on external physical characteristics, in Joanna's case he concentrated on collecting data indicating whether or not he was in love with her, whether the relationship would or would not last, whether she was or was not a true partner for life.

Frith indicates that at the time she was writing (1989) little was known about the compulsive acts of autistic people and that no attention was being given to this because it was not quite clear what role this aspect played in the context of autism. She doubted that the problems of obsessions were a secondary symptom, serving as a strategy to be able to cope in a world that did not make sense. If this were the case, these symptoms would have to disappear once it started to make more sense. These views suggest that Frith thought that the content of compulsive acts was what mattered whereas I take the view that it is the action as such that matters and not the content, and that the contents do not serve as a symbol for something else. My interpretation is that compulsive acts are forms of behaviour serving as a lightning conductor for the autistic person's anxiety. Frith (1989) indicated that there could be a connection with anxiety when she pointed out that the obsessions increase under stress or under circumstances in which the child can do little and anxiety becomes apparent in the form of restlessness.

Bert developed an obsession with lamp-posts. It began as an innocent pastime while sitting in the car. He controlled his anxiety and restlessness during car trips by counting lamp-posts, In this way, his interest in lamp-posts became associated with calming down and this enhanced his interest in lamp-posts. Soon it was impossible for him not to pay attention to lamp-posts and eventually it developed into an obsession.

Rituals

As we have seen, rituals are patterns of acts around a particular subject. In principle, they are necessary and agreeable patterns. One of the best-known rituals in children in general is the *bed ritual*. Before the child can go to sleep, a series of actions needs to be performed, including telling a story. Rituals are a way of being active to diminish tension. If one wishes to do something about this behaviour, one should be aware that the tension would have to be removed or an alternative form of behaviour thought up. It is not possible to always prevent tension as it is simply a fact of life.

> Linda had always gone through an elaborate ritual before going to sleep, including combing her hair. When as an adolescent she got a boyfriend, her attention to her appearance increased enormously. She was extremely concerned about the way she looked and would get up during the night and spend hours ironing the clothes she intended to wear the next day. Her mother wanted her to go back to bed but this was quite impossible for her because she was still so tense about the relationship with her boyfriend.
>
> If staying awake was the main reason for difficulty with this behaviour, Linda's mother could have been advised simply to accept that Linda coped with her stress in this way even though it cost her some sleep. At the same time, Linda should have been given an insight into her own behaviour so that she would have other means of controlling it.

Linda is an adolescent, and the view that the *Socratic method of question and answer instead of just telling things* is the best approach also applies to her. If someone is questioned, he or she is obliged to think: thinking is 'switched on'. If you tell a person something, he or she will mainly be listening rather than thinking: thinking is 'switched off'. Adolescents in particular have a strong need to form an opinion rather than have one imposed on them. This is also an important form of communication for autistic people, even though we have a tendency to tell them everything and assume they know nothing. By asking questions, one's intellectual powers are activated. If Linda were given the time to verbalize her feelings, she could possibly discover by herself what function her rituals serve. Through such self-acquired insight, she would, now that she has become an adolescent with a reasonable level of intelligence, be better able to control her behaviour than through any knowledge derived from what her mother tells her. Moreover, this process is slower, includes more repeated thoughts and links up more closely with knowledge already present, increasing the chance that it will be retained.

Rituals may serve to ward off anxiety but they may also start to lead a life of their own. They may lead to habits which, if they cannot be performed, evoke anxiety *because* they are not performed. The source of anxiety which the ritual was originally meant to control is often no longer relevant and the ritual is used partly as a habit and partly as a way of diminishing anxiety, as a kind of 'tranquillizer'. The difference between habit and warding off anxiety becomes apparent when there is stress. At times of stress, the frequency, duration and intensity of the ritual increases. The apparently meaningless acts thus serve a function, not because of their content but as a way of warding off anxiety, a 'tranquillizer'. Disrupting a ritual evokes anxiety, further enhancing the intensity of the ritual at that particular moment.

Life without any ritual is not possible. If one wishes to put an end to a ritual, the situation should be fairly stable, there should be no stress factors and the environment should not exert excessive pressure to halt it. It should therefore be done preferably in a situation in which the need of the environment to put an end to the ritual is not overly strong. As in the case of obsessions, the focus ought to be on adapting the ritual rather than making it disappear.

Stereotyped behaviour is probably a special form of ritual, a combination of ritual and movement; for instance, rhythmically shifting from one foot to the other or moving an object to and fro always in the same way. According to some, stereotyped movements result from boredom, as they tend to stop when the person concerned starts to engage in an activity (Frith 1989). If we look upon them as a part of the *anxiety scheme*, however, we believe that such behaviour is intended to reduce the feeling of anxiety by doing something. It is evident that this anxiety also diminishes when there is 'genuine' activity as this likewise reduces anxiety, as we saw with the example of psychotic talking while the train is standing still. The view that stereotyped behaviour is connected with anxiety rather than boredom is borne out by the fact that suppressing such behaviour increases stress (Wing 2001). An additional element is the pleasant hypnotic effect produced by stereotyped behaviour.

Peeters (1996) mentions a number of steps to examine whether repetitive and stereotyped behaviour can or should be treated.

1. Objective description of the behaviour.

2. How did it develop?

3. Is it necessary and urgent to alter the behaviour?

4. Where, when and with whom does it occur?

5. What are the consequences of the behaviour for the child?

6. How serious is the child's autism and is the child's developmental level high enough to be able to cope with the situation in which the behavioural problems occur?

7. Now that we have sufficient data to understand the behaviour, what can we do about it?

There is a similarity between stereotyped behaviour and *Tourette's syndrome*, the multiple tic syndrome. Tics resemble stereotyped behaviour. However, tics are less controllable. They are involuntary behaviours controlled by the brain. However, tics may (like obsession, rituals and stereotyped behaviour) increase under fatigue and stress. In Chapter 4 we found another indication that these forms of behaviour belong to the same 'family', when we noted that autistic disorders and Tourette's syndrome often occur together.

Rational response, intellectual comprehension and argumentation

A world in which social interaction is difficult to understand is a frightening world. Associating with people is one of the main tasks in life, right from babyhood. If one does not sense what someone else's behaviour means and how one should behave, one feels the need to collect knowledge about this and intellectually try to understand the situation. We have already mentioned the function of looking away in order to enhance concentration during conversation. Repeating questions can be a way of compensating for a lack of sensing what is happening by expanding one's knowledge. The need to comprehend *intellectually* what is happening may counterbalance the lack of sensing what is going on. People with Asperger's syndrome, in particular, can endlessly reason and argue (Wing 2001); they respond rationally instead of emotionally.

People who expend their energy in this way are often reproached that they are 'not emotional', 'hide behind reason', 'have little feeling'. This is evidence that there is no respect for the way in which people with an autistic disorder or with autistic characteristics attempt to cope with the incomprehensible world. *Arranging things* also meets this need of getting a grip on the situation. For people living with autistic persons it can be quite exhausting to put up with this incessant reasoning and argumentation.

Six-year-old Eric really wanted to have a particular toy from the playroom. He asked if he could have it. He did not take 'no' for an answer: 'But I want it!' The answer that the toys were meant for all children who came to play there did not satisfy him. 'Here, the rule is that all the toys stay in the playroom and can't be lent out, and in this way everything stays in the playroom for everyone to play with. So you can't take any toys with you.'

'But I'm sure they wouldn't notice anything if it wasn't there', Eric replied, surprised.

'But you noticed that it was there', the therapist replied.

'Yes, but if it hadn't been there, I wouldn't have noticed it', said Eric, who was not easily put off.

'You like it, and if it hadn't been here you wouldn't have had the nice feeling you now have because you can play with it'.

'Yes, but I have a little car just like this at home and you can have that one', said Eric.

'If this car wasn't more fun you wouldn't want to swap it: you keep your car, this car stays in the playroom'.

Stopping such argumentation is not particularly helpful as a solution to the problem. Thinking is a solution to making the incomprehensible world comprehensible. It is advisable to go along with this rational approach, respond to the need to understand, and insert information about feelings-related matters in one's replies.

In Chapters 5 and 10 we described arranging things as an activity that helps one to cope with chaos and as an activity that fits in with children's need to collect things. Arranging things has a calming effect. A well-known phenomenon is, for instance, that by arranging things one creates order in a physical chaos, and one's mind is 'cleared' at the same time. Arranging things is therefore conducive to reducing restlessness, it may diminish anxiety and at the same time help one to think more clearly.

Feelings of inferiority, jealousy and depression

Children with an autistic disorder perceive that they are different. Possibly this is, as with 'the boy with the salt' from Chapter 3, knowledge that is present from the outset and does not arise only from the response of the child's environment. The child perceives this difference without understanding exactly why and how. It may fill the child with a profound feeling of *inferiority* and may lead to *jealousy*. It may be fed by behaviour which he or she observes being appreciated in other children, or by his or her own behaviour that is not appreciated by others. If autistic children are intelligent, the problem is even more acute because they have insight in many fields, but this is too limited to be able to understand what happens in contact with people. As a result of associating with others, strong feelings of inferiority may develop, seriously affecting their self-image. This is often the case in children with Asperger's syndrome. Since the child can be very dominant in his or her behaviour, which is something we associate more with such terms as 'assertive' and 'self-assured' than with 'anxious', people around the child are hardly aware that over time the child's self-image is seriously damaged. By the time the child enters adolescence, these feelings of inferiority may lead to a severely depressive mood.

In the above-mentioned documentary *I'm not Stupid* (Fisher 1995), Marc Fleisher makes it clear that all his life he has been busy proving that he is not stupid. He was bullied as a child because he was so often off the mark in social contact. He dreams of going to university to study mathematics. Realizing his dream is therefore hugely important for his self-image.

Observing that others make and retain contact so easily can evoke strong jealousy in children with Asperger's syndrome. Their feeling of being different and not being part of a certain social context can become channelled in specific ways. They may focus their attention negatively on someone else's particular quality, characteristic or possession. Their jealousy thus becomes channelled and can even become an obsession as in the example below.

Kees Momma (1996), an autistic Dutchman, made it clear in his autobiography that the fact that others could speak English triggered strong feelings of jealousy in him. He refused to have anything to do with people who spoke English and avoided the school when he found out that there were children of English parents at the school. 'I wanted every English-speaking person to just disappear from my environment. The fact that they could speak the language and I could not was very frustrating for me.'

The never-ending assault on their self-image by others and themselves can make autistic children increasingly anxious. If we place this in the framework of the anxiety scheme, it becomes clear why I posited in Chapter 9 that adolescents with Asperger's syndrome often struggle with *depression*. Given that people with autism have less testosterone available than average, aggression will be a less obvious outlet than depression. Awareness of problems in contact with people increases. Their anxiety and grief increases. If they do not get help, they run the risk of ending up in a downward spiral in which activity steadily diminishes and depression sets in.

Children and adults with an autistic disorder often suffer from *social anxiety* and *fear of failure*. These anxieties do not ensue from the autistic disorder itself but are the consequence of a breakdown of social interaction and failure in skills at school. These anxieties will be considered in more detail in Chapter 13 when we shall discuss anxiety arising out of environmental factors and examine the behavioural therapy that is among the most effective methods in treating anxiety.

Table 11.2 summarizes the various methods of preventing and reducing anxiety.

Table 11.2 Ways in which autistic people cope with anxiety	
Preventing anxiety	*Reducing anxiety*
Resistance, opposition to change	Hyperactivity
Extreme focus on the mother	Hand flapping
Defence against strangers	Rocking or fidgeting
Extreme shyness	Obsessions and compulsions
Stiffening when touched	Rituals
Proximity to ensure availability when in distress, demanding behaviour	Stereotyped behaviour
Avoidance of social situations	Rational response
Withdrawal from social situations	Intellectual understanding
Isolation	Argumentation
Doing one's best	Asking repeated questions about what is going to happen
Adaptation	Arranging things
Self-hypnotic behaviour	Self-hypnotic behaviour

Appendix V (in electronic form; for access information see p.13) the anxiety model explains in more detail and a scientific basis is established to underpin it.

A more harmful response to experiencing anxiety is taking action in a more extreme form, in aggression. In this case, the environment suffers. We shall discuss aggression in the following chapter.

Focal points

- Anxiety is characteristic of autistic people.

- In autistic children there may be basic immaturity of hormonal structure, entailing constantly present underlying anxiety.

- An impaired socioscheme leads to a lack of inner structure, leaving the child with few certainties.

- Communication is necessary to cope with the child's anxiety.

- A baby still has inadequate capacities to communicate his wishes to those looking after him and may therefore cry frequently, in particular during the first months of life.

- Anxiety diminishes as communicative possibilities increase.

- The response to anxiety primarily depends on temperament.

- The response to anxiety may be aggression or withdrawn, anxious behaviour.

- Anxiety is indelibly linked with aggression and depression.

- In response to danger, stress hormones are produced that translate into anxiety.

- Anxiety may trigger action or inaction.

- Action reduces anxiety; inaction enhances anxiety.

- Aggression is an extreme form of action; depression is an extreme form of inaction.

- Men more often have aggression problems; women, depression problems.

- Men have a greater tendency to take action in the face of danger and more quickly engage in physical activity. Women, on the other hand, have a stronger tendency to seek security and help in the face of danger.

- Anxiety is connected with the production of hormones, associations with anxious situations and life experience.

- The following are forms of behaviour to prevent anxiety: resistance to change, extreme focus on the mother, defence against strangers, extreme shyness, proximity to ensure availability in distress, avoidance of social situations, withdrawal from social situations, doing one's best, adaptation, isolation, self-hypnotic behaviour and stiffening when touched.

- The following are forms of behaviour to reduce anxiety: hyperactivity, flapping the hands, rocking or fidgeting, obsessions and compulsions, rituals, stereotyped behaviour, responding rationally, understanding intellectually, arguing, repeatedly asking the same question and arranging things.

- People looking after autistic children run the risk of burn-out by constantly having to be physically and mentally available to the child.

- Playing hide and seek is one way of training children in the idea of being available without being visible.

- The demanding behaviour of autistic children is connected with availability, not proximity.

- Children with an autistic disorder will find it less easy to ask for help because asking for help implies that you are aware that the other person has solutions which you do not know yourself.

- Children have enormous resilience, based on hope.

- Children have excellent stress management.

- Children with an autistic disorder can easily get into a trance.

- Children with an autistic disorder will 'adapt' eventually.

- Children with an autistic disorder often try their very best.

- The self-image of autistic children becomes damaged over time.

- Rituals are, in principle, necessary and pleasant patterns. One of the best-known rituals in children is the bed ritual.

- Children with an autistic disorder perceive that they are different.

- Children and adults with an autistic disorder often suffer from social anxiety and fear of failure.

- People with an autistic disorder may develop jealousy with regard to subjects they find important but in which they fail.

- Autistic adolescents have a high risk of depression.

Focal points regarding attitude

- One should not want to influence all behaviour but try to modify the behaviour that is meaningful to the child and the environment.

- Problematic behaviour increases under stress.

- People with an autistic disorder use thinking to compensate for their lack of sensing. Reproaching them for being rational or having little feeling is a sign of a lack of respect.

- Start from the assumption that the autistic person does his or her best.

- Action reduces anxiety; therefore, do not just take the autistic child's activity away from him or her.

Summary

Anxiety is an important source of problematic behaviour in autistic people. Obsessions, rituals and aggressive behaviour are to a large extent fed by anxiety. The anxiety model describes the chain of biological and mental reactions connected with anxiety. Unconscious evaluation of danger, in the form of a physical or psychological threat which may also include a thought, triggers the production of hormones in the body which give rise to the emotion of anxiety. This leads to 'action' or 'inaction' which, respectively, lead to a reduction or an increase of anxiety. Children with an autistic disorder suffer a great deal of anxiety, partly due to their problem in understanding social situations. The autistic child displays many forms of action to prevent or reduce anxiety. To prevent anxiety and anxious situations, the child shows resistance to change, an extreme focus on the mother, withdrawal from social situations, adaptation, and extreme shyness, is defensive with strangers, stiffens on being touched and does his or her best. To reduce anxiety, a child with an autistic disorder may become hyperactive, flap his or her hands, rock or fidget on a chair, develop obsessive behaviour or rituals, display stereotyped behaviour, try to understand things intellectually, ask repeated questions about what is going to happen, respond rationally, argue or start to arrange things. The autistic child's constant perception of being different can strongly affect his or her self-image and lead to feelings of inferiority. Poor functioning in social situations and at school may result in fear of failure and social anxiety. Feelings of inferiority and jealousy may emerge. As a result of this, autistic people risk developing depression.

12

Coping with aggression

In the previous chapter we saw that aggression is one of the forms in which anxiety may be expressed. To the people around the child, it is often less evident that the aggression conceals underlying anxiety. Anxiety that is visible in the child's eyes and translates into panic, crying or withdrawal is a signal to the environment that help should be offered. Aggression suggests power rather than powerlessness. Just as anxiety seems to indicate weakness, aggression is equated with strength. When we see someone cry, our first reaction is to get closer, to offer comfort and help. The first reaction to aggression is to avoid the aggressive person or stop this behaviour. The aggressive person is viewed as an opponent and almost never as someone who does not want to have the negative behaviour either. An aggressive child is easily regarded as badly brought up.

> Joe's mother was seriously ill in hospital. He was almost unmanageable in the restaurant, screaming and pushing chairs around. The disapproving glances from the people in the restaurant left no doubt about their conclusion that Joe was a badly brought-up little boy, instead of an anxious boy screaming to express his fear of losing his mother.

Aggression appears as consciously chosen behaviour, especially in the eyes of those against whom it is directed. People want to stop the aggressive behaviour on the assumption that the person displaying it does not want to stop. Often people have no idea that the aggressive person and others have the same opinion about the behaviour, namely that it is not good; nor is this in any way evident when one observes aggressive conduct. In particular for children with an autistic disorder, an aggressive outburst is often a way of expressing panic. For instance, Gunilla

Gerland (2003) indicates that she could get into a panic by a sudden 'insight' that the present and the past are linked. Her normal feeling was different: every situation was new and unique and had nothing to do with the past. She gave vent to this panic in an intense outburst of anger while to those around her there appeared to be no reason at all for her aggressive behaviour.

> Sam could be overcome by sudden fits of aggression against the driver of the coach taking him to the day care centre. People just could not get him to say what was the matter.

Aggression and sexuality

In general, autistic people are not particularly aggressive by nature, although they can have sudden, fierce aggressive outbursts.

In Chapter 3, I mentioned the *Geschwind hypothesis,* which posits that testosterone has a major impact on the development of the foetus in the womb. According to this hypothesis, the influence of testosterone occurs in three areas. A high testosterone level while the foetus is developing in the womb causes:

1. inhibition of the left hemisphere of the brain to the benefit of the right

2. diminished functioning of the immune system and

3. a higher testosterone level after birth.

Various combinations of these three factors are possible, and the three do not necessarily play an equally significant role. In particular, the two factors prior to birth (1 and 2) and the one after birth (3) can probably function in relative independence from one another. Of these three factors, one could say that the first two play an important role in autism while the third does not.

The testosterone level after birth underpins aggression, as we saw in the previous chapter, but also sexuality. Although I have come across little research on sexuality in autistic people, it is my view, in line with Asperger (1944), that sexuality does not play a predominant role in autistic people. In his work, Asperger came across many autistic children who were an only child. He suggested that these children had inherited their autism or autistic features from their parents. He reported reduced intimacy in these parents and wondered whether this could be the cause of having few children. If one reads between the lines, Asperger here seems to suggest a weaker sex drive. Further research has not confirmed the view that autistic children are usually their parents' only child (Wing 1997). On the other hand, it has been reported that autism involves lower fertility (Gent *et al.* 1997). In this regard, it would be interesting to investigate whether in families with autistic children there is more often a smaller number of children and a wider spread in birth years. It is my contention that both the aggressive urge and the sexual urge are weaker than average. Here I do not mean a reduced need for intimacy but rather a relatively weak sex drive underpinned by a lower than average testosterone level. As far as I am aware, however, this has never been investigated.

What emerges from the author's own experience with autistic people is that there is a weaker sexual urge and more slowly developing sexuality. Little or no mention is made of this in publications about autism. The fact is, of course, that sexuality is a sensitive subject, highly susceptible to value judgements. If I state that I assume that autistic people have a lower than average sexual urge, I run the risk that this is easily considered to be a 'bad' quality, not very masculine, for autistic men. Nevertheless, I would advocate that this subject be researched without making any value judgements. On the contrary, in a heterosexual relationship a lower sex drive may well be an advantage rather than a disadvantage.

I raise this subject because aggression and sexuality *are* interconnected, no matter how difficult people often find it to accept this. In our opinion, autistic people are below average in both aggression and sexuality. If, in the field of aggression, it can be argued that among autistic people there is in principle no criminal behaviour (Attwood 1998), we can also state with regard to sexuality that it is less likely that there are paedophiles or sexual abusers among autistic people.

My basic contention is that in disorders within the autistic spectrum aggression plays a less important role and in the disorder related to it, PDD-NOS, where there are autistic features without the complete syndrome, aggression plays a more important part. In theory, it could be that the third factor (testosterone level after birth) does play a role in people with PDD-NOS.

In autistic people, aggression is not directed against another person; it is not aggression for the sake of aggression. One reason why in the literature autistic people are often called a *vulnerable group* is the fact that they are rarely aggressive or assertive: they defend themselves only when threatened in their territory. Rather, they tend to be friendly, sincere and anxious.

Their aggression mainly springs from anxiety and increases at times of stress. Gunilla Gerland (2003) clearly puts it as follows: 'I could not recognize those feelings, that kind of aggressiveness, within myself. What others regarded as anger in me was usually sheer anxiety.'

Aggression is often connected with an insufficient ability to express oneself. For aggressive children who do not speak, aggression is often the only way in which they can make something clear. Temple Grandin has described this with remarkable clarity (Grandin 1995b, Chapter 5). In normally developing young children, we find that their angry outbursts and hitting of others also diminishes once they can use language to express themselves, from about the age of three.

Autistic sources of aggression

There are two sources of aggression specifically connected with the autistic disorder: aggression arising from *resistance to change* and that arising from *misunderstanding in communication*. Apart from these, there are forms of behaviour that are disagreeable rather than aggressive. Because of anxiety about social contacts, a child with an autistic disorder may display ill-mannered and unfriendly behaviour *vis-à-vis* strangers. The opposite, extreme friendliness, also occurs, sometimes even in the same child. In Chapter 10 we saw that this is comparable with shyness in pre-schoolers. Lack of knowledge about how things work in the real world can also lead regularly to autistic children feeling irritated.

In the following example of Joe's behaviour, we can see the process of restlessness due to stress (successfully performing a difficult task at school), leading to naughtiness (folding a paper plane and throwing it) and then to aggressive behaviour that is fed by a misunderstanding in communication.

> Joe had been at a new school for a couple of weeks. He had just carried out a task and had finished it. It took him a great deal of effort to complete it properly. He folded the paper on which he had been working into a plane and threw it into the classroom. It landed near another child's table. Joe walked towards it. In the meantime, the child picked up the plane in order to give it to Joe whereupon Joe screamed at the child: 'Take your bloody hands off my plane!'

Joe was completely absorbed by his plane. The other child, who had nothing but good intentions, disrupted his preoccupation with the plane. Joe had little experience in interacting with children and much of it had been rather negative. He was startled by having his 'programme' disrupted, which triggered aggressively coloured behaviour. This unexpected behaviour in children with an autistic disorder can be quite frightening to other children.

Resistance to change

We have seen that children with an autistic disorder can put up strong resistance to change. Outlining a programme of events can be a way of helping them to overcome their anxiety about the unpredictability of the world around them.

Moreover, they are strongly pleasure-driven and are eager to do pleasurable things and without interruption. Disrupting their programme, their activity, can therefore provoke aggression. Children who have a tendency to take action in the face of danger will tend towards active resistance to a change whereas in others it translates into passive resistance. Active resistance may turn into aggression if the inner 'programme' is not restored or if the anxiety is not brought under control in some other way. In Chapter 10, I mentioned a number of ways of dealing with resistance to change. The aggression resulting from this resistance is difficult to contain. The child shows obnoxious, aggressive behaviour and the parent often does not know how to turn the tide by removing the anxiety as it is not clear what the source is of the child's behaviour. However, the parent will try to stop the aggressive behaviour and consequently it often escalates, with the child becoming angry and hysterical, making the parent feel powerless. The result is that a pattern may develop in which the parents, at the end of their tether, give in to the child, thereby reinforcing his undesirable behaviour instead of containing it (see also Chapter 10). The behaviour then becomes rampant like a tumour. After a year has passed, the child's behaviour will be virtually unmanageable. Parents and child become entangled in a pattern in which both are enormously restricted in their freedom of action.

Breaking through this aggression takes a great deal of care and patience. Under normal circumstances, it is often impossible in a family or at school to muster this patience. Some activities cannot be deferred, e.g. when the child has to be collected to be taken to school. Another problem is that the behaviour itself, the time pressure on the carers and the lack of understanding from the people around the family can provoke additional tension in the carer. Because of this, the carer is eager for the behaviour to stop and his sympathy for the child's behaviour diminishes. This quickening pace clashes with what is happening in the child. She senses the tension in the carer. As we noted above, children with an autistic disorder can be particularly sensitive to signs of stress in those looking after them. It makes the child (even) more anxious, further reinforcing her behaviour. The behaviour undesired by parents and child intensifies. The contact between them maintains the tension, and breaking off this contact may diminish the tension. One therefore often sees children walking away angrily in an attempt to break through the situation. The parent often runs after the child. However, it is wiser to leave the child alone for a while and keep one's distance so that the child can recover somewhat. If there is sufficient patience and sympathy left, which is desirable but not always humanly feasible, *metacommunication* is a good way of breaking through the situation. The main thing is to establish an alliance with the child towards the undesirable behaviour: 'You're very angry now and I do know what you want, but it can't be done now because you have to go to school. I know that you don't want to be angry but I can't solve the problem for you now.'

One should then wait a bit, maintain a silence and give the child time for the angry mood to pass. Adults usually want to stop the behaviour immediately, but this often works like a red rag to a bull. What an autistic person needs above all is to *unhurry*, to slow down the pace.

Putting his own feelings into words helps a child to understand the relation between his behaviour and another's behaviour. This applies even more so to children with an autistic disorder. When people have become adult, we tend to think that there is complete insight and we are angry, disappointed or saddened if this proves not to be the case. For autistic adults, even more so than for people in general, the fact is that there is no such thing as complete insight.

It is important not to burden children with the feelings of adults. On the other hand, it is also important that children realize what their behaviour provokes in adults. It is important for children, and therefore also for children with an autistic disorder, to see that their parents do not remain unaffected by their behaviour. Children with an autistic disorder often do not understand the feelings they provoke, but the display of them can bring them into contact with reality. The fact that they fail to understand the feelings and behaviour of their parents has two main causes.

The first is that the child will not understand the parents' feelings if she cannot experience these feelings herself. Awareness of the existence of emotions they do not have themselves only dawns upon autistic children many years later. As the child has no cognition (recognition) of the emotion, she soon feels that she is being treated unfairly. The way the child sees it, the adult assumes a negative or corrective attitude completely out of the blue.

A second important reason why such children do not understand their parents' behaviour is that they take it too personally. It again requires explanations to ensure that the child comprehends the feelings and impotence of the parent, carer or teacher.

An aggressive child is in fact a child who is upset. He needs a limit to be set to his grief or despair. At such moments, the child needs structure with warmth. If this cannot be provided via the above-mentioned methods (blowing off steam, leaving the child alone, slowing the pace, establishing an alliance, providing an explanation, touching), sometimes the only thing that will help is to hold the child tightly. It may be necessary to protect the child from himself or from the environment, to ensure that the behaviour stops and that the child does not get any more upset than he is.

This tight clasping should not be done in an aggressive manner or with aggressive intent. The child should at the same time be told that the adult could not think of anything else to do to halt the child's aggression. It should be clear to the child that the adult does this out of a sense of powerlessness and not out of a need for power. This remedy should be used only as a last resort because this physical difference in power leaves the child feeling impotent and helpless.

In the treatment of autism, holding the person tightly has led to application of *holding therapy*: holding the child tightly until it calms down. It was originally developed by psychiatrist Martha Welch and is applied to teach autistic children to tolerate being touched. In a plea against this therapy, Claire Sainsbury (2000) argues that from a scientific viewpoint this theory is no longer of any relevance because it is rarely applied any more and every autistic person who has to undergo holding therapy is one too many. She describes the distressing fear of autistic children undergoing the treatment. It frightens them, harms their trust in people and breaks their will, and this is not what we want to achieve. While the treatment has been compared with the 'squeeze machine' developed by Temple Grandin, an autistic woman, there is a fundamental difference. Grandin developed her machine to simulate hugging but the quantity of pressure exerted is completely under the control of the person undergoing the therapy. She also indicates that holding therapy may be stressful and harmful (Grandin 1995b). She points out that holding works because it brings about neurological desensitization to touch, but this can be achieved through far less stressful methods. In her article, Grandin mentions studies showing that exerting deep touch pressure has a calming effect (Grandin 2000).

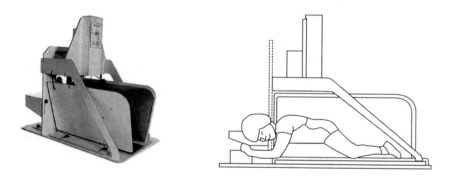

Figure 12.1 Temple Grandin's squeeze machine (www.therafin.com/squeezemachine.htm). Reproduced with permission from the Therafin Corporation.

In my opinion, the difference in response to superficial pressure and deep pressure applied to the skin is indicative of the need to register signals. In Chapter 5, I explained that sensory sensitivity may compensate for the lack of inner schemes. An optimum amount of information has to be gleaned from the environment. In this way we can also explain the different response to superficial and deep pressure. The outside, the surface, is particularly sensitive to registering signals.

Time and again, new therapies emerge claiming miraculous cures for autism, even though this is not possible. The Son-Rise programme is one such therapy, completely focusing on making contact with the child and understanding his or her world. However, the method is very intensive and, even though it offers a great deal to the individual child, requires considerable effort from those around him or her. Attention for other children in the family suffers as a result. The progress that can be achieved is greater than would be the case without this specific attention but seems disproportionate to the efforts which all members of the family, volunteers and professionals are asked to make.

Where there has been a conflict, it is advisable afterwards to come back to what actually happened. At such moments, the child's intention and knowledge can be called upon to find alternative solutions to the aggression should it recur. It is sensible to prepare the child for a recurrence of aggression. No matter how good the parents' and child's intentions are, there is a risk that the behaviour will re-emerge. It may seem discouraging to be prepared for future aggression, but it is realistic. In this way, the child's powers can in the future be mobilized and the child will not have the same sense of failure when aggression does recur. Aggression is fed by the body, as we saw in the previous chapter, and this means that it is also possible to teach the child to feel aggression setting in and keep it under control.

Children love playing computer games. Particular games are very suitable to be used to teach the child to feel aggression welling up inside. These include platform games (if you manage to get through one level you can go on to the next), games of skill and shooting games. These happen to be the type of games boys aged between 6 and 14 like to play (Delfos 2003b). While playing such games, the child's mood changes from cheerful, excited, happy and proud when he is successful to angry, moody and frustrated when things do not go the way he wants. These emotions occur in interaction with the computer and are independent of inter-human contact. The advantage is that the emotions can be discussed and treated without being encumbered by the interpersonal tension inherent in human conflict. Through the child's physical and emotional response to the computer, he can learn how body and mind work together and learn through his body to recognize the emotion before it reaches an irreversible stage.

> Example: 'Isn't that strange, a moment ago you were so happy that you were doing well and now you're beginning to get fed up just because one thing doesn't work out the way you want.'
>
> As time passes, the child will gradually become familiar with his own reactions and can apply himself to preventing an outburst. Total prevention is not possible, and the question is whether that is in fact necessary. Aggression is also a – sometimes necessary or unavoidable – way of expressing the underlying anxiety.

Misunderstanding social interaction

A second major source of aggression is failure to understand and, accordingly, misunderstanding social interaction in general and communication in particular. In previous chapters, I have tried to make it clear that verbal and non-verbal communication can provide major obstacles for people with an autistic disorder as regards social interaction and other people's feelings (see the list on p.148). In the present chapter, I consider specific situations that may elicit aggression in autistic children. They invariably concern communication problems at metacommunicative level, as a result of which the autistic child fails properly to evaluate the other person's intention. These communication problems are:

- Inability to evaluate other people's intentions properly
- Projecting one's own thoughts and feelings onto another
- Taking literally what another says
- Feeling treated unfairly.

In Chapter 8 we indicated the conditions for communication in children and their importance for autistic children. Children with an autistic disorder often prefer, and are better at, interacting with adults than with their peers because adults possess more knowledge, have more extensive statistics on human behaviour, are less egocentric and are consequently more likely to sympathize with the fact that the child is different.

When children go to school, problems with communicating with their peers become apparent and conflicts with the environment increase.

Major problems may arise because a child with an autistic disorder is unaware that another child does not know what is going on in her mind. Accordingly, a failure to fulfil her wish can be interpreted by an autistic child as a deliberate decision made by the other child. The other's good intention is not sensed and is wrongly interpreted. The autistic child assumes that the other knows perfectly well what she has in mind. As soon as the other child fails to fulfil her wishes, the autistic child feels unfairly treated and can become angry. The fact is that from the autistic child's point of view this anger is perfectly justified. From the other's position, the anger is totally uncalled for, completely out of the blue.

A psychologist temporarily replaced the teacher in a class with autistic children. No matter how hard she tried and how well intentioned she was, one conflict after another arose. In a class of non-autistic children there is considerable unrest and conflict among the children when a teacher is replaced. In this case, the children constantly became angry with the psychologist. For instance, a child was waiting near the psychologist/teacher's table. She had no idea what the boy wanted. When she asked him, the boy became irritable: he wanted 'frog paper'. She had no idea what it was and this made the boy terribly angry. The problem was that he just could not imagine that the psychologist did not know this and he therefore assumed she was doing this deliberately. He assumed that the psychologist refused to give him frog paper on purpose. He saw no reason at all why he could not get the paper and therefore, quite rightly from his perspective, he felt treated unfairly.

Through the projection of the child's own thoughts to the other, many conflicts can arise in this way which, from the autistic child's point of view, are completely justified, as we saw in the colour-blindness test in Chapter 8. For the others, the anger comes completely out of the blue.

Joe was sitting in a restaurant completely absorbed in his favourite comic strip. When someone dropped a cup, it disrupted his concentration. Furious, he got up and went from table to table to find out who had dropped the cup which had interrupted his reading.

When people are aware how an autistic child experiences fairness and how this affects the emergence of aggression, they remain motivated to get the child out of her constrained thinking. Through metacommunication, the right intention can be conveyed and the misunderstanding clarified.

Normal aggression

For children, aggression is a normal form of expression. It is not always necessary to control or counter it. However, this is often necessary for aggression ensuing from autistic problems because it brings the child into constant conflict with his environment. Sometimes the child has to be protected against his own aggression or others need to be protected against it. Moreover, after the bout of aggression the child has no automatic awareness that the situation could also be perceived differently. For non-autistic children, an aggressive outburst may serve as a release, after which they can again think clearly and begin to see things in perspective. The awareness enabling children to view their own anger in perspective after such a release is often lacking in autistic children. Consequently, an autistic child, more than non-autistic children, needs an explanation and help from others in order to learn to assess the situation more accurately.

Children with an autistic disorder generally make little distinction between situations. They adapt their behaviour very little, or not at all, to the different social situation that may arise, as Joe, for example, could get equally angry with his peers, the teacher or complete strangers in a restaurant. The environment is rarely prepared for this form of aggression. Though a non-autistic child might slap her mother at home, she is most unlikely to do the same at school in the teacher's presence. To children with an autistic disorder, this makes little difference. This applies in particular if the aggression arises from an autistic source such as resistance to change.

While growing up, children learn how the world functions and become aware that things do not always work out the way they want. As the child's insight into social interaction increases, excessive aggression diminishes, while aggression in the more usual form of normal frustration or anger increases. The latter form of aggression is much easier to control both for the child and for the adult. It is important, therefore, to continue to appeal to the *controllability* of behaviour because it increases with age. There is a risk that the parents and the environment get stuck in a pattern of action and thought, whereas new forms of behaviour have become possible. Not all aggression is autistically controlled. Indeed, the aggression will be less and less autistically determined as insight into social situations grows.

Controllability of behaviour is not always easy to discern. However, close observation will make it clear which forms of aggression are controllable. One sign of the controllability of behaviour is when, during an outburst of aggression, children keep on furtively checking how the other person reacts. Such glances signify knowledge about the effect of their own behaviour on others. Another sign is when the child looks as if he is more angry than in despair.

Autistically determined aggression often comes unexpectedly as a complete surprise to another person. Often, the other has no idea what is the matter. If these feelings are elicited, the autistic child's behaviour is probably less easy to control. By controllability we mean not only controllable by the other person but also, and especially, controllable by the child himself. Such aggression can be stopped, for instance, by telling the child off. The aggression can also be worked off if channelled in a different way, perhaps by hitting a cushion or jogging. In the more controllable form of aggression, the source of aggression can be traced so that it can be dealt with at a deeper level.

It is important to remain alert to the potential of the behaviour of children with an autistic disorder to grow. We have already noted that aggression can end up in patterns that can be broken through. However, patterns evolve in social interaction that elicit habitual behaviour, which often persists for longer than necessary.

> In her book, Lorna Wing (2001) gives the example of a boy who refused to have a bath. He fiercely resisted this and his parents had long since given up trying to put him in the bath. As a result, the washing ritual had become very complicated, but the parents had resigned themselves to this. The pattern was no longer a subject for discussion. It was therefore with utter surprise that one day they found their child playing happily in the bath with the *au pair* standing next to it. She did not know that the child could not be put in the bath. It was not clear what had triggered this revolution. Possibly the problem had solved itself in the meantime, or possibly the anxiety ritual had been broken through because a completely new link had entered the chain: the *au pair*.

Parents and carers should realize that patterns can develop between child and adults that are more reversible than they sometimes appear. It is therefore important to keep on trying to change things.

All alone in the world

Children with an autistic disorder who use aggression as a way of expressing themselves often behave as though aggression is the only means by which things can be stopped. The root of the problem is the characteristic feature of these disorders: the lack of me–other differentiation and the incapacity to imagine what goes on in other people's minds. Children with an autistic disorder control their environment. They give verbal or non-verbal orders to the people around them. They make demands on their environment, and the people around them may seem to be instruments in their lives. Sometimes it appears as if the children do not realize that they are people, with whom you live together, from whom you learn, with whom you play or whom you meet.

In the following example, seven-year-old Joe behaves more like someone in a position of authority wishing to teach another child a lesson than like a child that is angry with another. He gets really angry only when the teacher stops him.

> Joe came running out of the school bus. There was a conflict going on between him and another boy. Joe ran after the boy. The teacher stopped him with her arm. Beside himself, Joe screamed: 'He called me a shithead!' The teacher replied: 'He mustn't do that, he will be punished for it, but you mustn't hurt him either', whereupon Joe spontaneously kissed the teacher on her arm.

Joe's kiss shows that this basically very friendly boy is sincerely grateful for the unexpected help the teacher offers him. His feeling of having been treated unfairly is acknowledged and the teacher furthermore offers a solution. He gives her a kiss on the arm that stops him out of gratitude for the limit she sets and the solution she provides. If she had not responded to his hurt feelings with this simple but highly respectful intervention and had merely wanted to stop his aggressive behaviour, he would probably have bitten her on the arm.

Asking for help

A child with an autistic disorder finds it less easy to seek help. As he cannot properly imagine something he does not know himself, he will have problems imagining someone else might have a solution; he only knows his own solutions. This inability is one of the three components of the triad, namely the lack of imagination. The child cannot easily surrender to someone else's control as he has problems getting into the other person's mind and therefore has no clear picture about how another person could be helpful in solving his problems. In other words, he can involve the other person only as an instrument towards a solution which he himself can think up and comprehend and in a way he can foresee. That someone else may have other possibilities for a solution which the autistic child does not know himself is outside the autistic person's grasp, even if he is sufficiently intelligent. With advancing age, knowledge increases and with it the range of knowledge about other people's possibilities and also the fact that they may be capable of coming up with unexpected solutions that may prove helpful. At the same time, the chance that another's help will be solicited increases. Here I do not mean seeking help with a specific task but generally asking for help because he does not know how something should be done and assumes that the other person might have an idea.

Another, deeper cause of these problems of autistic people who do not seek other people's help – in addition to their incapacity to imagine what goes on in another person's mind – is that they are not, or hardly, aware of the other person. In a situation of distress, an autistic child will sooner adopt aggressive behaviour if she has no other answer; not only because the child does not have an inclination to seek someone else's help but also because she cannot even conceive of this idea. From her restricted socioscheme, her limited awareness of the people around her, the child insufficiently perceives these people as potential helpers: indeed, she is not really aware of their existence. Children with an autistic disorder have a tendency to solve their own problems.

> Bob, nearly five, was sitting in the sand pit on the camping site. He was waving his spade dangerously at the other children playing in the sand. Bob was building a sandcastle and the other children were joining in and making constant changes. This drove him to despair. He wanted to be alone in the sand pit and wanted everyone else to disappear, because he did not tolerate others interfering with what he was doing. He started screaming as though aggression was the only way to solve the situation. His mother rushed up and immediately tried to get the children away from him. She stood between Bob and the other children because she knew from experience that he would not stop. It had not occurred to him that he could seek help.

Because of their incapacity to get into other people's minds, children with autism do not fundamentally view an adult as an adult but more as an equal or even someone subordinate in their own world. This is why a child with an autistic disorder may seem rude towards adults. Within his socioscheme, he has little awareness of status. When closely observed, their 'rudeness' is not challenging but rather calm and self-assured. It gives a somewhat arrogant rather than aggressive impression. Many people with Asperger's syndrome are therefore seen as haughty and arrogant. This may, moreover, also be connected with their affected language which may seem somewhat pedantic.

Combination of autistic characteristics and ADHD

Within the anxiety model (Chapter 11) we saw that activity and aggressiveness may be attempts to cope with feelings of anxiety and danger. Children with an autistic disorder display a great deal of such behaviour because the world around them can seem strange and frightening. Since *hyperactivity* and *aggressive behaviour* (*externalizing behaviour*) are normal expressions of problematic behaviour, we encounter it in many children. Comorbidity (concurrence of disorders) of autism and ADHD (attention deficit hyperactivity disorder) may occur. About 15 per cent of children with Asperger's syndrome also have ADHD (Eisenmajer *et al.* 1996).

Children with autistic characteristics, with PDD-NOS, may be wrongly diagnosed with ADHD and *vice versa*. Children who display agitated and uncontrolled behaviour due to environmental factors are often diagnosed with ADHD whereas in actual fact they are more likely to have a hyperactive reaction to living conditions and life events (Delfos 2004a). Consequently, it is useful to highlight a number of differences in the nature and extent of externalizing behaviour.

Although the diagnosis of ADHD is often used to label lively, hyperactive children, it is advisable to limit this diagnosis to children who have a disorder in the rate of maturation of the central nervous system (Delfos 2004a). If we had to specify the difference, to the extent possible, between ADHD and autistic disorder, we could say that in the case of ADHD there is delayed maturation which may eventually be remedied and may cover a wide range of aspects, from language disorders to hyperactivity. This maturation may encompass the entire central nervous system, without specifically leading to an imbalance between the right and left hemispheres. Autism, on the other hand, involves profoundly limited maturation which in some areas within this limitation is also very slow. As both disorders relate to maturation of the nervous system, there may be overlapping characteristics. This certainly applies to hyperactivity.

In children with ADHD, however, there is structural hyperactivity which occurs in many situations, frequently and protractedly. In contrast, children with an autistic disorder have short spurts of hyperactivity which are specifically focused on reducing anxiety. In ADHD, there appears to be more a structural immaturity of the hormone system as a result of which the child is structurally stimulated into action, into activity. In the light of the anxiety model in Chapter 11, we could say that anxiety must underlie the structurally hyperactive behaviour of children with ADHD (incessant action). If the action, the fact of being active, diminishes during puberty and adulthood, people who still have ADHD but no longer display hyperactive behaviour therefore often appear to suffer from *generalized anxiety disorder* (GAD) or *depression*. Restraining the action without solving the underlying problems or with the hormonal immaturity still present will expose the anxiety. Generalized anxiety is also characterized by indeterminate diffuse anxiety, which is without a clear focus on a particular subject. If anxiety is intense or protracted without the danger being averted or without the action 'using up' the hormones, it eventually leads to depression, as we saw in the anxiety model in the previous chapter.

In the following chapter, which concludes the second part of this book, *What can we do about it?*, we shall discuss forms of anxiety that do not ensue directly from the autistic disorder but may arise from the vicissitudes of life; in particular, confrontation with other aspects of society.

Focal points

- Aggression in autistic people is not consciously chosen. One should therefore not make the mistake of thinking that they themselves agree with it.

- Parents of children with an autistic disorder often meet with disapproving looks from other people. They are considered responsible for their children's behaviour.

- Aggression in autistic people is mostly controlled by anxiety.

- Two important sources of aggression in people with an autistic disorder are 'resistance to change' and 'misunderstanding communication'.

- Attempts to stop aggressive resistance often cause the situation to escalate.

- The child often attempts to prevent the situation from escalating by walking away.

- Without putting too much pressure on them, children should be confronted with the reality of the effect which their behaviour has on their parents and carers.

- Children with an autistic disorder in general prefer to associate with younger children or with adults rather than their peers.

- Children with an autistic disorder easily feel unfairly treated.

- Children with an autistic disorder often take the behaviour of the people around them too personally.

- In general, a child with an autistic disorder makes little distinction between situations and between people.

- 'Normal' aggression is more controllable than 'autistic' aggression.

- A behavioural pattern between parents and children may stabilize when the need for the pattern no longer exists.

- It is important to continue to have recourse to the controllability of behaviour as it increases as the person grows older.

- Children with an autistic disorder control their environment.

- Children with an autistic disorder do not easily ask for help but involve others to be instrumental in a solution which they can think up and comprehend themselves in a way they can foresee.

- Children with an autistic disorder do not easily conceive of the idea that someone else might be able to help.

- It is necessary to give an explanation about the possibility of someone else providing help.

- Hyperactivity and aggressive behaviour are normal expressions of problematic behaviour and occur in many children with various disorders and problems.

Focal points regarding attitude

- Make sure to be an ally rather than an opponent.

- Slow down the pace: autistic people need you to 'unhurry'.

- Create a structure founded in warmth.

- Have patience.

- Have the courage to verbalize one's own impotence.

Summary

People witnessing an outburst of aggression often fail to see that it masks anxiety. Aggression is construed as involving power rather than impotence. In general, autistic children are not particularly aggressive although they can display fierce and sudden fits of aggression. Aggression in autistic people is mostly caused by anxiety and arises as a result of resistance to change or of misunderstood communication.

Aggression resulting from resistance to change is hard to restrain. A pattern may develop between parents and child in which the former give in to the child's behaviour which after some time becomes virtually unmanageable. Breaking through this pattern requires major efforts.

In the event of an outburst of anger, slowing the pace, waiting a while, being calm, giving the outburst a chance to pass and creating distance often work better than attempting to stop the behaviour immediately. Metacommunication and explaining the parent's powerlessness to the child may also help to break through the situation. A second important source of aggression is failure to understand social interaction. Problems such as projection of one's own thoughts and feelings onto the other person, taking literally what the other says, feeling unfairly treated and being unable to evaluate the intention of others can trigger an aggressive reaction in autistic children. Children with an autistic disorder are hardly, or not at all, aware of other people and of the help they might be able to offer in particular situations. Consequently, they appeal to others only for solutions they have thought out themselves. Becaue of their limited socioscheme, autistic children insufficiently perceive the people around them as helpers. They tend to solve their own problems.

Apart from autistically controlled aggression, there is also 'normal' aggression. It is more controllable than the former. As the child grows up, he gains more insight and his autistically controlled aggression diminishes. However, the child and the people looking after him may have become entangled in a pattern, as a result of which aggression persists. The people around the child should remain alert to this possibility so that full use is made of the potential for growth and control. Hyperactivity and aggression are expressions of problematic behaviour in general. They occur in many disorders and many problems.

13

Acquired social anxiety

In addition to their anxieties that ensue from the autistic disorder itself, children with an autistic disorder have anxieties which result from confrontations with society, *acquired anxieties*, in particular in contact with people. This chapter examines such acquired anxieties. These anxieties extend to increasing numbers of people and situations and are fed by thoughts, *cognition*, connected with social situations.

It is often difficult for other people to persuade children with an autistic disorder to do something. They are strongly maladjusted in the sense that they are often unable to meet the social demands imposed upon them. As a result of their difficulty with social interaction, they regularly get into conflict with the people around them. Their efforts to make contact are often shipwrecked by a lack of understanding in their environment. This inflicts wounds which slowly wear them out, as water steadily hollows out a rock. Their knowledge and skill in social situations grow far too little and too slowly in relation to the demands which the environments makes on them, first, due to their autistic disorder and second, because they avoid social situations. In this respect groups, as Alec has noted (Chapter 8), are the most threatening element but at the same time that which is most desired, as Martin has expressed it.

The avoidance of social situations makes contact with peers even more difficult than it already is because of the autistic disorder. Accordingly, anxiety increases. The child needs a great deal of support to enter into social situations. Training programmes in social skills seem to be useful in helping the child in this regard, although I have already pointed out that they will bear little fruit if they are not based on developing, stimulating and reinforcing social insight (Chapter 8).

Labelling anxiety through cognition
It is characteristic of children with an autistic disorder that they struggle with anxiety with which they try to cope by keeping their environment under control,

displaying externalizing behaviour or by reducing their anxiety through obsessions and rituals. The anxiety is, to a large extent, controlled autistically. Part of the anxiety, however, is not an anxiety controlled by predisposition but an acquired anxiety. These children, for instance, run the risk of developing a *social phobia*. They are anxious about social situations and increasingly avoid them. This risk will increase with age if the help offered is inappropriate or insufficient. A child with an autistic disorder who, because of a lack of knowledge, shows inhibited or even rude behaviour in his contact with people, will increasingly be excluded and feel that he does not belong. Eventually he is increasingly reluctant to take part in social situations, he becomes anxious and tries to avoid them.

Such anxiety should first of all be treated by reducing the source through the stimulation of social insight, which is the core of the autistic condition. At the same time, the consequences of the acquired anxiety – development of social phobic behaviour – can be treated. For the latter, *(cognitive) behaviour therapy* is particularly suited.

People often find it difficult to place an anxiety that is physically triggered. Schachter (1968) discovered that people cannot bear having states of mind they do not understand. They look for explanations for a state of excitement, of arousal. Schachter's *labelling theory* provides an explanation of how this works in people. People have a need to examine their state of mind in order to find an explanation for their physical sensations. This was ingeniously demonstrated by Schachter and Singer's experiments (1962). In the experiments, they gave their subjects correct or incorrect information about the physical sensations they would undergo as a result of an injection. Those who had been correctly informed about the physical sensations were hardly affected, or not at all, by events in their surroundings. Those who had received incorrect information attributed their physical processes to their surroundings. In this way, they had a satisfactory explanation for the state of arousal in which they found themselves as a result of the injection. Awareness of what was happening in their body made them less dependent on their surroundings.

The aim of Schachter and Singer's research (1962) was to investigate the cognitions – thoughts – connected with arousal. They injected their subjects with epinephrine (adrenalin). This substance puts the body in a state of arousal and excitement: increased heartbeat, dilated pupils, sweating, etc. These general physiological changes occur in both negative and positive emotions. Next, some of the subjects were given correct information about the physical reactions that were to be expected. Other subjects were given inaccurate information. They were told that they would be injected with a substance which would enable them to perceive black–white contrasts more sharply. They were told nothing about heartbeat or other physical reactions. The subjects were then, individually, taken to a waiting room with only one person present there. That person was, unbeknown to the subject, a member of the research team who displayed cheerful or playful behaviour or exactly the opposite: angry, irritated behaviour. The results indicated that those who had been directly informed about their physical state were hardly affected, or not at all, by the behaviour of the person present in the waiting room. Those who had been incorrectly informed were influenced. They were cheerful or irritated depending on the other's behaviour. Lack of clarity about the physical state makes a person dependent on stimuli from the environment and leads to the physical sensations being attributed to the environment, as these experiments showed.

In order to find an explanation for a state of excitement which he is in, a child will link particular subjects with the anxiety. The anxiety 'attaches' to the subjects that are connected with the situation in which the excitement arose. Imparting information about the physiological condition and the feeling of anxiety that subsequently attaches to subjects may help the child to reduce the anxiety to realistic proportions. Using the anxiety model discussed in Chapter 11, we may posit that activity reduces anxiety, even if it does not immediately solve the problem. It means that the anxiety is cut down to size, the panic diminishes and the child, and people in general, are able to reflect on the situation better.

Just how this can be explained to the child depends, of course, on her age (Delfos 2000). It is important to use an experience the child has gone through herself in explaining things to her. The child has been afraid in the past but she did not know what was the matter. This fear, this anxiety, focused on subjects of the occurrence, and this is how the anxiety has spread.

Eric, do you still remember that you used to refuse to wear those blue trousers? At first you really liked them. Then you fell off the swing and you didn't dare to go on the swing any more. Your heart was pounding every time you saw a swing. Also, you didn't want to put on the trousers which you had worn at the time, as if it were the trousers' fault that you had fallen off. Now you know that you stepped off the swing too quickly and this is why you fell down. Whenever you saw those trousers, you got scared again and your heart started beating very fast. Actually, there was no need for this, but at the time you didn't know it. You liked those trousers and you were happy that you could wear them again once you knew that the trousers had nothing to do with it. Well this is the same as...

The adrenergic substances are converted by an activity. As we noted above, men have a greater tendency to take action and therefore suffer less from anxiety, and for shorter periods. Women are less inclined to act and therefore feel more anxiety, but for longer periods. When they do act they are, moreover, more inclined to seek security and help rather than pursuing an activity to deal with the danger.

Relaxation is important to cope with anxiety and return to clear thinking. A child with a strong social anxiety is hardly able to relax. His tension diminishes somewhat when he is alone but even at such moments his incessant self-reflection causes him to have unpleasant feelings.

A girl in her puberty with generalized – ever-present – anxiety did not know what relaxation was. She had never experienced it. Therefore, the instruction to relax in no way linked up with her own personal world. What she did know was that she experienced less tension when she was alone in her room. She became even less tense if she had an animal on her lap, her guinea pig or her cat. She was stimulated to do this more frequently and feel what the difference was compared with other situations. This served as a way of teaching her to relax.

Children with an autistic disorder frequently struggle with feelings of anxiety. However, they are often also quite experienced in seeking relaxation. They develop behaviour that may put them in a state of trance. People around them are not always aware of the fact that this is in fact stress management and often they see the child as egocentric, even egoistic, in search of her own pleasure.

When Joe's mother died, Joe was full of grief. During the first seven years of his life, his mother had given him everything she could. He had been showered with love and attention. He felt the enormity of his grief well up and asked if he could go to his favourite theme park. To superficial outsiders, it might have seemed as if Joe had already forgotten his grief or that it hardly affected him and that he was abusing the attention being focused on him by asking to go on an excursion. Nothing could be further from the truth. His uncle suggested they could look at pictures of the theme park, but Joe said that this didn't help, that he could not enter it in this way; that he did not want to think of his mother's death and was looking for distraction. Joe was aware that the huge grief should be counterbalanced by something equally enormous in order to distract him and therefore asked to go to this theme park, which had in fact also been his last major excursion with his mother.

Anxiety has two components. The first is the body's metabolism. The other relates to cognition – thoughts – that are generated in order to place the anxiety. These thoughts are in line with the anxiety or are aligned to the anxiety and consequently are negative in character. The thoughts become linked with the anxiety through a *conditioning process* and can subsequently evoke the anxiety again independently. We have already mentioned that Kees Momma (1996) has described how, for example, by tearing up drawings he tried to prevent feelings of anxiety and negative memories from emerging (Chapter 10).

These are thoughts that remain largely internal and are not expressed, causing the child to be inhibited in his or her functioning. One of the most usual responses to anxiety is avoiding the subject of the anxiety. However, the anxiety can be maintained as a result of the avoidance and the subject associated with the anxiety spreads unchecked. If the thoughts are not externalized and situations are avoided, there is no testing against reality, and the anxiety persists as a result. It seems as though the anxiety is well founded. By testing it against reality, one can discover that the anxiety is ill-founded or that it arises only in some situations. One reason why anxiety is maintained is that there is not enough testing against reality. It is important to offer the child possibilities to do such testing without thereby enhancing the anxiety. The testing should result in an experience showing the child that the anxiety is not applicable. It is important for the child to think this over afterwards so that the new thought can take hold: 'I was scared but afterwards this turned out to be unfounded' or 'I was scared but because I took these measures the situation proved manageable'. In this way, thoughts can help to test more realistically what one's own role in an occurrence is. Gradually the child will develop more confidence in her ability to cope with anxious situations and this will restore the child's self-image. The child's view of the world will then become more realistic and less frightening.

Anxious thoughts often concern the child's self-image and usually take the form of a rejection.

'I am not going to school any more', Peter said when he had the feeling that he had been bullied by all his peers at the new school (described in Chapter 8). His understanding was that the children at this school did not like him and wanted to bully him. Because of this, his anxiety about school increased and eventually led to a school phobia, a fear of going to school. Thoughts that label anxiety often hamper social functioning. Peter's cognition was wrong. A better construction would have been: the children at this school do not understand my jokes and this is why they do not laugh at them. On the basis of this cognition, Peter would have been more likely to modify his joke-telling behaviour and not reject the school as a whole.

Self-appreciation and self-confidence are often deeply affected by anxiety cognitions. The aim of *cognitive behaviour therapy* is to modify these cognitions which makes it highly suitable for these problems.

Medication or therapy

Hormones and neuro-transmitters (the body's and brain's 'messengers') play a major role in anxiety problems and medication can influence them. Various psychopharmaceuticals are available for the treatment of anxiety. However, it is not directly appropriate to apply them systematically to children and young people who are still developing because of the side effects and disruptions to normal development, as we mentioned in Chapter 11 (Ditmars 1995). Moreover, psychopharmaceuticals taken for anxiety often have an addictive effect. The disorder is not cured by medication and tends to recur after medication is discontinued. However, the advantage of medication is that anxiety is reduced and a situation created in which the child can learn to cope with anxious situations. It may have a positive impact in the case of social anxiety and panic attacks. The fact is, however, that medication is not as likely to be prescribed for anxiety as, for instance, for ADHD. This may be connected with the fact that hyperactive behaviour is more troublesome to other people than anxious behaviour. Anxiety is principally troublesome to the person concerned. Moreover, anxiety appears to be something one can overcome more easily than hyperactivity, and a child with anxiety is more often expected to get the anxiety under control. The question is also to what extent gender plays a part in this connection and whether help will be provided sooner for boys displaying more externalized behaviour, annoying to the people around them, than for girls who display more internalized behaviour.

The most successful form of treatment for anxiety appears to be behaviour therapy, and in particular cognitive behaviour therapy (Emmelkamp 1995). Behaviour therapy offers not only short-term help but also a strategy to cope with future problems oneself. Medication, it has been argued (Rotter 1966), does not really affect the *locus of control* whereas behaviour therapy does. Learning a strategy to cope with anxiety ensures that the child is more capable of dealing with anxious situations in the future, and the locus of control in this case shifts so that it is more internally located. When taking medication, the child attributes the change in behaviour to the medication and therefore is less inclined to think that he can influence his behaviour. The locus of control will become more external.

Despite the fact that they are always trying to control their environment for their own purpose, children with an autistic disorder feel powerless in bringing about what they really want. They have an extreme need to exercise control over themselves and those around them. If they acquire more anxiety than they are already experiencing because of their autistic predisposition (which seeks to make life predictable), their need to gain control over the situation intensifies. This need is already present because of its autistic source and is further aggravated by anxiety sustained in everyday life.

In the course of behaviour therapy, the child will learn to put her own influence, her own role in events more in perspective and the locus of control will accordingly shift in the direction of a more realistic, internal position. It appears, furthermore, that behaviour therapy does effectively modify the functioning of the brain just as medication does (Baxter, cited in Staff 1996). It has a favourable impact on metabolism in the brain.

Behaviour therapy

Behaviour therapies have proved their worth in particular in the field of anxiety. This form of therapy goes back to research by Watson (1928) who investigated how anxiety develops. His famous experiment was with an eleven-month-old boy, 'Little Albert'. Albert was conditioned to fear a white rabbit. While he was sitting in his bed, a white rabbit was placed near him. Next, a loud noise was suddenly produced, which greatly startled him. In this way, the presence, movement and touch of the white rabbit was linked to an unpleasant, loud, sudden noise. Albert developed an anxiety, namely fear of the white rabbit. Watson discovered that the anxiety spread from the white rabbit to everything white, furry or moving on the bed. Jones (1924) carried out research that is considered the basis of behaviour therapy. Through a little boy, Peter, who was afraid of rabbits, Jones investigated how this fear could be overcome. Peter was given a positive reinforcer (an element reinforcing behaviour: in Peter's case it was sweets) when seeing a rabbit. The rabbit was brought ever closer until Peter was no longer afraid and caressed the rabbit without any anxiety. On the basis of this research, a new method was developed to overcome anxiety through a behaviour modification method, known as *systematic desensitization*. In this method, the person concerned slowly learns to associate a feeling of relaxation with the object of anxiety. In this way, the anxiety gradually disappears. This method laid the basis for the development of behaviour-therapeutic techniques to counter anxiety.

These techniques are useful to treat excesses of anxiety problems such as *phobias* in general and *agoraphobia* (fear of open spaces) in particular. In his overview of forms of treatment under behaviour therapy, Emmelkamp (1995; Arntz and Bögels 1995) indicates that his research has shown that behaviour therapy is highly effective for anxiety problems. Current behaviour therapy has developed in the direction of cognitive therapies.

The focus of cognitive therapy is the cognition (thinking) of the person concerned. People's behaviour is viewed as being controlled by their cognition. These cognitive behaviour therapies are particularly useful for children with anxieties. If the anxiety is controlled by predisposition, however, they are only ways of learning to cope with the anxiety without removing it. The hormone balance is not structurally influenced by behaviour therapy, although in the long term adaptation may occur with a lower level of response. Conversely, the body may also adapt when someone suffers from a great deal of stress for a protracted period. When undergoing prolonged stress, the body will adapt and generate a higher level of response (Prins, Kaloupek and Keane 1995). As a result, the body produces a high level of stress hormones in response to minor danger, with a concomitantly disproportionate increase in anxiety.

Through cognitive behaviour therapy, a child can learn to cope with the thoughts constantly evoked by her anxiety. It can help the child to control her anxiety.

The cognitive tendency within behaviour therapy, founded by Ellis (1973) and Beck (1985), starts from the assumption that humans are hampered in their behaviour by wrong cognitions, thinking errors. Within this tendency, Beck (1989) has listed the thinking errors that may affect self-image, distort reality and provoke or maintain anxiety. These thinking errors occur frequently in the cognition of children with anxiety.

1. *All-or-nothing thinking*: you look at things in absolute, black-and-white categories: 'I never do anything right.'

2. *Labelling*: you identify with your mistakes or properties: 'I am just an awful person doing a thing like that.'

3. *Exaggeration:* viewing one negative event as a repeating pattern of failures: 'I always do that!'

4. *Mental filtering:* a tendency to transform neutral or positive experiences into negative ones, and to do so constantly: 'She seemed nice but of course she only feels sorry for me.'

5. *Mind reading:* assuming that others have negative thoughts about you: 'Of course he thinks that I am being childish.'

6. *Fortune telling:* like a fortune teller, predicting that things will turn out badly: 'I am bound to start stuttering when it's my turn in school.'

7. *Emotional reasoning:* you reason from how you feel: 'I feel inferior, so I really must be': 'I feel ridiculous, so I really must be.'

8. *'Ought to' thinking:* criticizing yourself or others with principles, obligations, threats, or other strict demands. This form of thinking is underpinned by words such as 'must' or 'ought to': 'I should really be a bit nicer.'

9. *Self-reproach:* blaming yourself for something for which you are not, or not solely, responsible: 'If only I hadn't quarrelled, that accident would not have happened.'

For children with an autistic disorder who possess language ability and have normal or above average intelligence, cognitive behaviour therapy is eminently suited to deal with *acquired anxiety*. However, one should not expect that this treatment completely keeps the anxiety under control or can reduce the autistic disorder: it can deal with the acquired *social anxiety* but not with the anxiety that is autistically controlled. A necessary condition for this is that cognitions can be fitted in with the existing *socioscheme*. As in social skills training, it can be argued that behaviour therapy can be successful only to the extent that it can be underpinned by social insight. One of the things which is emphasized in cognitive therapies is the internal logic of cognitions and the lack of testing against reality ('It's not logical that you are worried about getting a bad mark at school. You have prepared your lessons and when you do so you always get high marks'). In analyses, use is often made of statistical principles ('What's the chance of that bridge collapsing when you drive across it?'). To treat children with Asperger's syndrome, the therapist needs above average intelligence, and a great deal of patience and perseverance to teach them to cope with the anxiety in this way. Their inventiveness in argumentation with regard to anxiety is quite considerable, and they always find counter arguments. However, they have a great need to cope rationally with their anxiety because it is the only way in which they can. It means that once the therapist has successfully gone through some of the objects of anxiety, the autistic person will have acquired a thinking strategy which he or she can use to cope with anxieties in the future without outside help. The nature of the therapy, the use made of thinking, fits in with the asset people with Asperger's syndrome possess: their ability to think logically.

When a child learns to view cognitions not as established truths but ideas that can be called into question, she will suffer less from the burden of these cognitions. It is even more important that the child learns to accept that her predisposition gives rise to the formation of substances in the body which feed cognitions. Consequently, the child will sooner recognize cognitions generated by anxiety for what they are and be able to suppress them. It is easier to deal with the realistic cognition 'I am of a nervous disposition' than with the socially inhibiting cognition 'Nobody likes me'.

It is necessary, finally, for the child to learn to act when he feels anxious so that his anxiety can diminish. This refers to acting both in the physical sense of moving into action and in terms of thinking and language by becoming more assertive. If the child is not sufficiently assertive, he may benefit from assertiveness training or a training programme in social skills. In the case of children with an autistic disorder, such training should take the form of stimulating social insight and enhancing knowledge of social situations, as otherwise the programme of training in social skills can have no or little effect, as we saw in Chapter 8.

Depression

Children with anxiety problems are at a risk of developing depression as they grow up. During puberty, children with an autistic disorder, in particular those with Asperger's syndrome and PDD-NOS, run the risk of developing depressive feelings. Depressive feelings during the childhood years and youth are different from those in adults (Delfos 2004a). In children, the picture is not so much one of slow, listless behaviour than of busy, hyperactive and irritable behaviour. Within the anxiety scheme, they still are very much on the acting side. The transition to depressive feelings as observed in adults usually arises during adolescence. It is necessary to detect depressive feelings promptly, with a change in appetite and sleep pattern being important markers. In such cases, special attention should be given to two areas: undertaking activities, remaining in motion (as discussed in the anxiety model in Chapter 11) and converting self-destructive thoughts to self- supporting thoughts.

When symptoms of depression become apparent, it is important to break through the situation as soon as possible because, as the body adapts to the negative situation, an increasing number of negative ideas are formed which in turn produce more stress hormones and evoke anxiety, while the body becomes steadily less able to transform these substances into activity.

The strength of the parent

When bringing up an anxious child, parents soon find out that it is little use in trying to force the child to get over his or her anxiety. There is strong resistance and the anxiety calls for protection. Parents try to find out why their child is so afraid, and this is something that can rarely be successful in the case of autistically controlled anxiety but will produce fair results in socially acquired anxiety.

If the children have sufficient verbal skills to verbalize what moves them, the parents can, by reasoning with the child, help him or her to cope with the anxiety. However, the problem is often that a child with an autistic disorder does not conceive of the idea of sharing her emotions with others and seeking the help of others in dealing with the problem.

Since cognition is often far removed from reality and produces a greatly exaggerated picture, parents can through their own powers of reasoning manage to reassure the child. Parents can apply their life experience and knowledge to help their child to develop better thoughts with regard to subjects of anxiety. This is possible only if they do so respectfully, linking up with the child, and refrain from trivializing the anxiety. Parents with good verbal and logical skills have more chance of helping their child. They are bound to fail if they do not possess such skills or if they fail to take their child's anxiety seriously enough.

With this focus on socially acquired and ordinary everyday anxiety which everyone has to deal with in life, we conclude this chapter. It is followed by an epilogue in which we place autism in a social context.

Focal points

- Children with an autistic disorder have, in addition to anxieties arising out of the autistic disorder – those resulting from their confrontation with society – acquired anxieties, in particular in contact with people.

- Anxiety is evoked by a physical response and people want to understand this response. They want to 'label' their anxiety.

- In seeking an explanation of a physical response, the child will connect 'subjects' with the anxiety.

- One of the most usual reactions to anxiety is avoidance of the subject to which anxiety has become linked.

- In order to reduce the anxiety, it is important literally and figuratively to move into action.

- Children with an autistic disorder are often good at relaxation, even getting into a trance.

- If anxiety cognitions are not expressed and if situations are avoided, there is no testing against reality and anxieties may persist and aggravate.

- After an anxious situation has been successfully dealt with, it is important to have feedback about the truth content of the cognitions.

- Cognitive behaviour therapy is one of the most effective ways to treat acquired anxiety.

- Cognitive behaviour therapy is highly suited for children with an autistic disorder and normal or above average intelligence.

- In the formation of anxiety cognitions, thinking errors may occur.

- If a child learns that the cognitions that have been formed are not established truths but can be questioned as ideas, he or she will be able to change these cognitions.

- Medication for anxiety is less suited to young children.

- Children with autism, in particular Asperger's syndrome and PDD-NOS, are at risk of developing depressive feelings.

- Parents can apply their life experience and knowledge in order to help the child to form better thoughts with regard to subjects of anxiety.

Focal points regarding attitude

- Do not trivialize the child's anxieties but take them seriously.

- Together with the child, search for the source of the anxiety.

- Try to test the anxiety against reality.

- Make sure the child moves into action so as to diminish the anxiety.

Summary

Alongside anxieties that directly result from the autistic disorder, anxieties may arise which develop in the course of life, and in particular in confrontation with people in social situations. In children with an autistic disorder, knowledge and skill in social situations increase far too little in relation to what is demanded of them. This is caused first by their autism and second by their avoidance of social situations as a result of their autism.

Cognitive behaviour therapy may be an effective means of treating such anxieties. Through cognitive behaviour therapy, the child builds up a more realistic conception of his or her own influence and role in events. Anxiety arises due to a physical response. In order to be able to explain this response and the anxiety, the anxiety will attach to a subject associated with the situation in which the response emerged. These may be subjects which originally had nothing to do with the source of anxiety. Providing information about the physical and cognitive response may help the child to reduce the anxiety to realistic proportions.

Children with anxiety problems are at a risk of developing depression when older. In children, this manifests itself not so much in slow, listless behaviour but rather in excited, hyperactive and irritable behaviour. The transition to depressive feelings evident in adults in most cases arises only in adolescence. It is important to detect depressive feelings in time.

A child with an autistic disorder will not easily conceive the idea that others could be applied to for help when they feel anxious. Consequently, parents should be alert to this and should try to find out why the child is so anxious. This will be easier to trace in the case of socially acquired anxiety than in autistically controlled anxiety. Parents can apply their life experience to knowledge to help the child gain a more realistic perception of situations and thus get their anxiety under control.

14

Epilogue

Having come to the end of this book on autistic disorders, we turn our attention to the significance of disorders for our society. After the attention of researchers had been focused for a long time on the impact of the environment on children's development, there is now renewed attention for predisposition and the maturation of the central nervous system. Interest in autism is growing. Diagnosis is more common and sometimes appears to assume epidemic proportions. Presumably there are many erroneous diagnoses. Given the characteristics of our modern society, this need not cause surprise. Society is strongly oriented towards communication and through the Internet contact can be established with anywhere in the world in a fraction of a second. It is therefore not surprising that people who deviate somewhat in social and communicative respects immediately stand out and are approached with less tolerance. It may well be that they are labelled sooner than would be the case in a less communication-oriented world.

In this century, when genetic material is progressively being mapped, the focus will increasingly be on the genetic background of behaviour. Knowledge about this aspect is growing exponentially: whereas it used to be thought that humans had 100,000 genes, it now appears that they only have 30,000. The mapping of the human *genome* will never be able to record the incredible variety in human potential, no matter how much progress is made in our knowledge. Just look, for instance, at the number of languages and words that can be produced from the 26 letters of the Roman alphabet. In autistic disorders, there will certainly not be one sole gene which offers an explanation for the disorder. Asperger (1944) spoke of a *polygenetic origin* and recent research has shown that various genes spread over multiple chromosomes (Consortium 1998). There are bound to be genes and groups of genes that are dominant, with the presence of one gene among these being sufficient in itself to give rise to a particular feature. However, it will be more often a question of recessive genes and mixed forms that are responsible for the pattern of behaviour. Since maturation plays such an important part in the development of autism, however, many aspects will be formed in direct interaction with the environment. The 'interactive' genes will probably play a major role.

This brings us to the importance of the environment for the development of autistic children. If the 'wild boy of Aveyron', the badly neglected feral who hardly functioned as a human being, had been discovered in the woods earlier or if he had not been abandoned by his parents, how much more could he have developed? If Kees Momma had benefited from the unremitting devotion of his parents, what would his development have been like? Upbringing is and remains important.

The fact that autism is connected with a genetic structure, does not mean that we can put autistic people in a cage to be gawped at as a curiosity or treat them like the village idiot, as was the case in the Middle Ages. We hope that this book has at least made two things clear: problematic autistic features can be discerned in all human beings and autism also has a different, valuable side: that of purity and honesty, of a naïve, non-manipulative, social life. Characteristics that are less generously distributed among other human beings!

We tend to have a negative judgement of anything that deviates. Something we don't know often frightens us. This is where *xenophobia*, fear of foreigners comes from, leading to discrimination. Autistic people are strangers in a non-autistic world. For a very long time, we tried to keep people who deviated from the norm at a distance. We put them in homes, in the woods, far away from us. Next, we tried to integrate them in ordinary society. How civilized a society is can be judged by the way it deals with people who deviate from the average. In the meantime, we have learnt from autistic people that they form *part* of the *range* of human variety, not a *deviation*. To give an example I often use to put human diversity into perspective: from a lion's viewpoint, all humans are the spitting image of each other.

It is salutary to realize that people with an autistic disorder probably try much harder to understand the non-autistic world than the other way round.

I hope that I have managed to give a respectful and probing description and insight of how strange the world looks through the eyes of autistic people and have at the same time shown something of the beauty of that world, the strength that goes with the weakness, 'les qualités de ses défauts' (Igor van Krogten). If the book is meant to serve as an aid towards understanding autistic disorder, I hope that it also offers a possibility for non-autistic people to learn from those with autism in order to attain a better quality of life and more sincere contact with other people.

Diagnoses

AI.A. Autism and related disorders

AI. A.1 Autism, PDD (Pervasive Developmental Disorder)

According to the diagnostic criteria of DSM-IV (APA 1994), there is a total of 12 items, six of which should be present in order to be able to diagnose a disorder as autism, with at least two from A, *social interaction*, one from B, *impairment in verbal and non-verbal communication*, and one from C, *restricted repetitive and stereotyped patterns of behaviour, activities and interests* (Box AI.1).

Box AI.1 Criteria for autism according to DSM-IV (APA 1994).
Reproduced with permission.

A. Social interaction

1. Marked impairment in the use of multiple non-verbal behaviours such as eye-to-eye gaze, facial expression and gestures to regulate social interaction.

2. Failure to develop peer relationships appropriate to developmental level.

3. A lack of spontaneous seeking to share enjoyment, experience or achievements.

4. Lack of social or emotional reciprocity. Autistic people seem unaware of the existence or feelings of others. They deal with other people as though they were objects.

B. Impairment in verbal and non-verbal communication

1. Delay in the development of verbal communication, not accompanied by an attempt to compensate through alternative modes of communication such as gestures. Sometimes a total lack of verbal communication.

2. In individuals with adequate speech, a marked impairment in the ability to initiate or sustain a conversation with others.

3. Strange use of form or content in language, for instance echolalia, stereotyped speech, repetitions, mixing up of personal pronouns and idiosyncratic language.

Box AI.1 continued

4. Lack of make-believe play and varied forms of play.

C. Restricted repetitive and stereotyped patterns of behaviour, activities and interests

1. Preoccupation with one or more stereotyped patterns of behaviour.

2. Inflexible adherence to specific, non-functional rituals or routines.

3. Stereotyped, repetitive body movements.

4. Persistent preoccupation with parts of objects.

ICD-10 (WHO 1992) mentions three areas of psychopathology:

- qualitative disorders of social interaction

- patterns of communication

- restricted, stereotyped and repetitive behaviour.

ICD-10 indicates that this may be combined with a range of non-specific problems such as phobias, sleeping and eating disturbances, temper tantrums and (self-directed) aggression.

The Dutch Autism Association (NVA) uses the following working definition:

Persons with an 'autistic disorder' means persons whose development is disturbed or has been disturbed due to:

A DISTURBANCE IN SOCIAL CONTACT, IN PARTICULAR IN SOCIAL RECIPROCITY
This contact disturbance can take very different forms in practice. Some people are very passive and hardly involved in the world around them while others cannot keep their distance and make demands on others in an often bizarre manner. There is also severe limitation of the insight into what others feel and think and of understanding social situations.

A DISTURBANCE IN VERBAL AND NON-VERBAL COMMUNICATION
Some people do not speak at all; others are deceptively eloquent; in between these extremes are all possible intermediate forms. However, communication is mostly one-way. People find it difficult to understand facial expressions and gestures, which may be a source of confusion.

A DISTURBANCE IN POWER OF IMAGINATION
This disturbance of the powers of imagination (impaired capacity to imagine something and assign meaning to it) may take the form, for

instance, of a total lack of imagination or of empathy but also of excessive imagination overwhelming the individual.

A MARKEDLY LIMITED REPERTOIRE OF INTERESTS AND ACTIVITIES

The individual focuses exclusively on particular objects, subjects or activities (e.g. rotating wheels, trains or opening and closing doors). He or she may be so totally preoccupied or obsessed by this that any interest in other matters is totally inadequate, severely hampering development and intensifying isolation.

AI. A.2: PDD-NOS (pervasive developmental disorder not otherwise specified) or atypical autism

According to DSM-IV, this category should be used if there is a serious and pervasive deficiency in the development of reciprocal social interaction or verbal and non-verbal communicative skills, or if there is stereotyped behaviour, interests and activities while the criteria are not met for a specific pervasive developmental disturbance, schizophrenia, schizotypical personality disorder or deviant personality disorder. This category includes 'atypical autism patterns' that do not meet the criteria of autistic disorder because of later onset, atypical symptoms, too few symptoms, or all of these.

DSM-IV also indicates that a total of three (or more) items should be present from the DSM-IV list under autism (see Box AI.1), from A, B and C, with at least one from A. However, the problems must be such that they otherwise do not meet the criteria for other pervasive disorders.

ICD-10 uses the subcategory of *atypical autism* if abnormal behaviour and impaired development are manifest only after the age of three years and if there are characteristics of abnormal functioning in one or two areas of reciprocal social interaction, communication or restricted, stereotyped and repetitive behaviour. According to the criteria of ICD-10, atypical autism occurs in particular in severely intellectually disabled persons and persons with a serious developmental disorder in *receptive language*.

AI. A.3: Asperger's syndrome

Various diagnostic criteria have been developed and described for Asperger's syndrome, including those according to DSM-IV and ICD-10; characteristics according to Wing (2001) and Gillberg and Gillberg (1989); and an overview by Delfos.

The characteristics of Asperger's syndrome, according to DSM-IV, correspond to those of autism described under headings A, social interaction and C, restricted repetitive and stereotyped behaviour, activities and interests.

According to DSM-IV, there is no delay in language development as described under the heading B for autism. According to DSM-IV, there is no delay in cognitive development either. The disorder causes significant problems in social and professional areas and other important areas of functioning.

ICD-10 indicates that it is not clear whether this disorder is distinct from autism. The three areas mentioned under autism apply here as well. In Asperger's syndrome, there is no general delay or lag in language or cognitive development. Asperger's syndrome often includes awkward motor activity. The boy/girl ratio is 8:1. The deviant pattern of behaviour persists up to and including adolescence and adulthood. Another characteristic is that at the beginning of adulthood there may be occasional psychotic episodes.

Wing (2001; Burgoine and Wing 1983) mentions six characteristics of Asperger's syndrome (Box AI.2). The most significant divergence from DSM-IV is movements and postures, which Wing considers core problems of Asperger's syndrome, whereas DSM-IV does not mention these.

Box AI.2 Characteristics of Asperger's syndrome (Burgoine and Wing 1983, Wing 2001).

- Lack of empathy
- Naïve, inappropriate, one-sided interaction
- Little or no ability to make friends
- Pedantic, repetitive speech
- Poor non-verbal communication
- Intense absorption in certain subjects
- Clumsy and ill-coordinated movements and odd postures

Gillberg and Gillberg (1989) mention six different criteria, indicating patterns of behaviour that may occur in each case (Box AI.3). Consequently, their outline is more complete than the features mentioned by Wing. They also mention motor problems as core problems in Asperger's syndrome.

In an overview of the characteristics, the author presents not only necessary characteristics but also common and possible characteristics that may occur in Asperger's syndrome (Box AI.4). This distinction makes it possible to identify between primary and secondary characteristics.

Box AI.3 Characteristics of Asperger's syndrome (Gillberg and Gillberg 1989). Reproduced with permission from Blackwell Publishing.

1. Social impairment (extreme egocentricity)

(at least two of the following)

a.   Inability to interact with peers

b.   Lack of desire to interact with peers

c.   Lack of appreciation of social clues

d.   Socially and emotionally inappropriate behaviour

2. Narrow interest

(at least one of the following)

a.   Exclusion of other activities

b.   Repetitive adherence

c.   More rote than meaning

3. Repetitive routines

(at least one of the following)

a.   Concerning themselves

b.   Concerning others

4. Speech and language peculiarities

(at least three of the following)

a.   Delayed language development

b.   Superficially perfect expressive language

c.   Formal pedantic language

d.   Odd prosody, peculiar voice characteristics

e.   Impairment of comprehension, including misinterpretations of literal/implied meanings

5. Non-verbal communication problems

(at least one of the following)

a.   Limited use of gestures

b.   Clumsy/gauche body language

c.   Limited facial expression

d.   Inappropriate expression

e.   Peculiar stiff gaze

6. Motor clumsiness

Poor performance on neural-developmental examination

Box AI.4 Characteristics of Asperger's syndrome.

Necessary characteristics
- Difficulty comprehending and appreciating social interaction
- Difficulty imagining what goes on in other people's minds
- Egocentric thinking
- Difficulty making and keeping friends
- An eye for detail
- Difficulty expressing feelings and thoughts in words

Common characteristics
- Reasoning instead of feeling
- Non-smooth motor activity
- Difficulty with left–right coordination
- Intense anxiety
- Obsessions and compulsions
- Stereotyped behaviour
- Sudden tantrums
- Better in abstract than language thinking or *vice versa*
- Unstoppable flood of words
- Careful formulation
- Walking on tiptoe during first years
- Food allergy, eczema or airway problems during first year
- Phobic behaviour
- Often failing to understand jokes

Possible additional characteristics
- Special interests
- Dyslexia, language problems
- Writing problems (motor function)
- Writing problems (formulation problem)
- Creative skills (music, drawing)
- Highly intelligent on the abstract side
- Repetitive behaviour
- Coercive behaviour
- Left-handed

AI. A.4: high functioning autism (HFA)

People with HFA have the pattern of autism but their intelligence level is normal, i.e. >85. From a scientific viewpoint, there are doubts whether HFA and Asperger's syndrome are in fact separate conditions.

AI. A.5: Rett's syndrome (Box AI.5)

In Rett's syndrome, motor and social problems in the autistic person are preceded by normal development during the first 5 to 48 months. In this syndrome there is a loss of proper motor and social functioning. It is found almost exclusively in girls. If the onset was preceded by a fairly long period of normal functioning, the term *disintegrative developmental disorder* is used. The one condition is not subsequent on the other because Rett's syndrome has so far been encountered almost exclusively in women, while the disintegrative disorder occurs in men and women, with the former in the majority as in almost all forms, except Rett's syndrome.

ICD-10 describes Rett's syndrome as follows:

> Rett's syndrome is a condition, so far found only in girls, in which apparently normal early development is followed by partial or complete loss of

---

Box AI.5 Criteria for Rett's syndrome according to DSM-IV (APA 1994). Reproduced with permission.

A. All of the following:

1. Apparently normal prenatal and perinatal development

2. Apparently normal psychomotor development through the first 5 months after birth

3. Normal head circumference at birth

B. Onset of all of the following after the period of normal development:

1. Deceleration of head growth between ages 5 and 48 months

2. Loss of previously acquired purposeful hand skills between ages 5 and 30 months with the subsequent development of stereotyped hand movements (e.g. hand wringing or hand washing)

3. Loss of social engagement early in the course (although often social interaction develops later)

4. Appearance of poorly coordinated gait or trunk movements

5. Severely impaired expressive and receptive language development with severe psychomotor retardation

---

speech and of skills in locomotion and use of hands, together with deceleration in head growth, usually with an onset between 7 and 24 months. Loss of purposive hand movements, hand-wringing and hyperventilation are characteristic. Social and play development are arrested, but social interest tends to be maintained. From the age of four, development of the trunk becomes deviant. Mental retardation results almost invariably.

Box AI.6 Criteria for disintegrative disorder according to DSM-IV (APA 1994). Reproduced with permission.

A. **Apparently normal development for at least the first 2 years after birth as manifested by the presence of age-appropriate verbal and nonverbal communication, social relationships, play, and adaptive behavior.**

B. **Significant loss of previously acquired skills (before age 10 years) in at least two of the following areas:**

1. Expressive or receptive language

2. Social skills or adaptive behavior

3. Bowel or bladder control

4. Play

5. Motor skills

C. **Abnormalities of functioning in at least two of the following areas:**

1. Qualitative impairment in social interaction (e.g., impairment in nonverbal behaviors, failure to develop peer relationships, lack of social or emotional reciprocity)

2. Qualitative impairments in communication (e.g., delay or lack of spoken language, inability to initiate or sustain a conversation, stereotyped and repetitive use of language, lack of varied make believe play)

3. Restricted, repetitive, and stereotyped patterns of behavior, interests, and activities, including motor stereotypies and mannerisms

D. **The disturbance is not better accounted for by another specific pervasive developmental disorder**

AI. A.6: Disintegrative developmental disorder (Box AI.6)

Initial normal development is followed by acute *psychosis*, becoming chronic, between the ages of three and ten. In general, disintegrative developmental disorder has the same characteristics as autism but it also involves a loss of skills which were already present, as in Rett's syndrome. In most cases, cortical degeneration is diagnosed after a couple of years. Accordingly, it is regarded as one of the organic psychoses.

ICD-10 also mentions the loss of skills previously acquired, following initially normal development. According to ICD-10 it includes loss of interest in the environment, which is not the case in Rett's syndrome. Moreover, there are stereotyped, repetitive movements and abnormal behaviour, similar to autism, in social interaction and communication.

AI.B. Related disorders

AI.B.1 Alexithymia

Alexithymia comprises a range of cognitive and affective impairments, characterized by:

1. Difficulty recognizing, identifying and describing feelings

2. Difficulty distinguishing between feelings and physical sensations associated with emotional arousal

3. Limited emotional imaginative processes (few dreams and fantasies)

4. Concrete and reality-based thought processes (Taylor *et al.* 1990; Hendryx, Haviland and Shaw 1991).

AI.B. 2: McDD (multiple complex developmental disorder)

McDD has been described by Cohen, Paul and Volkmar (Cohen, Paul and Volkmar 1987; Cohen *et al.* 1994). It is a condition comprising both autistic and schizophrenic characteristics, with the schizophrenic, affective features prevailing. Children with McDD may become autistic or schizophrenic or outgrow the condition. Intense emotions such as anxiety and aggression may play an important part and at the same time there is detachment from the environment.

McDD involves a more psychotic way of being (interpretation based on Buitelaar and van der Gaag 1998). A total of five (or more) characteristics from headings 1, 2 and 3, with at least one item from 1, one from 2 and one from 3, is required for a diagnosis (Box AI.7). In the meantime, ideas about McDD develop,

---

Box AI.7 Criteria for McDD (Buitelaar and van der Gaag 1998).
Reproduced with permission from the author.

1. Impaired regulation of states of mind and anxieties

A. Unusual or odd anxieties and phobias or frequent idiosyncratic or bizarre anxiety reactions

B. Recurrent panic episodes or being flooded by anxiety

C. Episodes of behavioural disorganization punctuated by markedly immature, primitive or violent behaviour

2. Impaired social behaviour

A. Social disinterest, avoidance or withdrawal

B. Markedly disturbed and/or ambivalent attachments

3. The presence of thought disorder

A. Irrationality, magical thinking, sudden intrusion on normal thought processes, bizarre ideas, neologisms or repetitions of nonsense words

B. Perplexity and being easily confused

C. Overvalued ideas including fantasies of omnipotence, paranoid preoccupations, overengagement with fantasy figures, referential ideation

---

and Van der Gaag (in press) points out that thinking disorders become the more prominent concept with McDD as regulation of affect. The social impairment seems to be a more general feature of anxiety rather than a specific feature of McDD.

AI.B.3: NLD (non-verbal learning disability)

The diagnosis of non-verbal learning disability (NLD) has been developed from neuropsychology. Diagnosis covers children who have more difficulty processing what they see than what they hear. In intelligence tests, these children score highly in the verbal area (language development) but lower in the performal area (spatial comprehension). NLD involves functional disturbances of the right hemisphere of the brain. Children affected have good language performance but weak spatial thinking and calculating. There are also problems in motor function and writing and there is resistance to new situations. Development is by leaps and bounds. It is said to be a disturbance of 'wiring' caused by a deficiency of white matter, the protective layer surrounding nerve fibres. If the protective layer is missing or insufficient or degraded, stimuli are inadequately transmitted.

Volkmar and Klin (1998) list the characteristics of the NLD intelligence profile (Box AI.8).

Box AI.8 Assets and deficits in the NLD profile (Volkmar and Klin 1998). Reproduced with permission from Springer.

Deficits	*Assets*
Tactile and visual spatial perception	Auditive perception
Visual-motor integration	Verbal skill
Visual memory	Verbal memory
Novel learning	Rote learning
Prosody	Articulation
Verbal content	Vocabulary
Pragmatics	Verbal output

Smeets and van de Wiel (1996) described the following characteristics of children with NLD:

- little urge to explore things at young age
- following initial arrest, swift language/speech development in the pre-school stage
- slow motor and manual skill development
- little play, in particular with sensopathic and construction material
- abundant talking, but language/thought development is slow in the toddler stage
- limited capacity of social evaluation (constantly rushing into everything and then coming unstuck)
- great difficulty with new situations.

AI.B.4: Hyperlexia

Another related diagnosis is hyperlexia, which involves a strong development in word recognition but impaired development in comprehension of meaning. This diagnosis is rare.

AI.B.5: Visual thinking

Visual thinking is a diagnosis which is closely connected with autistic diagnoses but with a different point of departure. The scientific status of this diagnosis is debatable. The list of characteristics/symptoms is so elaborate and diffuse that it covers many problems but also ordinary behaviour. Briefly, visual thinkers understand a text by conjuring up a picture of it, a visual image. Archiving data in the brain also passes through visual images rather than words. Children with visual thinking display the following characteristics (visual thinking criteria at primary-school level):

SPEECH

- poor articulation
- garbled speech (mumbling)
- stumbling over words
- mangling words
- intense gesticulation when relating something.

LISTENING

- attentive listening lags behind exploratory vision
- decelerated or accelerated response to instructions and tasks
- tendency to only half listen
- difficulty processing oral information (remembering instructions but losing the thread in long instructions)
- many misunderstandings (understanding things said too literally; taking personally reprimands meant for others).

LANGUAGE DEVELOPMENT

- difficulty linking words to images
- word-finding problems ('the thingy which…')
- odd use of words
- little logical thread in the stories they tell (jumping from one thought to another, starting at the end or somewhere in the middle, incoherent stories)
- rather limited though original vocabulary.

MOTOR DEVELOPMENT

- poor fine motor activity
- accident prone
- clumsy
- difficulty learning to ride a bicycle, swim, write, etc.
- no sense of rhythm.

ORIENTATION IN TIME AND SPACE

- poor sense of time
- difficulty with spatial orientation
- mixing up left with right
- difficulty keeping things in order or sequence.

OTHER CHARACTERISTICS

- delayed development (cognitive/affective/physical)
- too infantile
- exhausted, in particular when a holiday approaches
- low stress tolerance
- fluctuating pattern of performance
- changeable, easily distracted
- difficulty finishing things
- dependent on circumstances (system/structure from the environment)
- impulsive/associative
- strong perseverance (for survival)
- flights of fancy, including lying
- difficulty expressing feelings/emotions in words
- wild imagination, inventive, original
- dreamy/withdrawn (living in a world of their own)
- (hyper)sensitive/emotionally vulnerable

- exaggerated sense of fairness
- empathic/strong sense of social justice
- often a loner among siblings
- low frustration tolerance
- stubborn/obstinate
- messy/chaotic
- difficulty keeping appointments and sticking to rules
- undisciplined
- forgetful.

Internet addresses

An overview of several Internet addresses is included in this appendix. When drawing up the appendix, what was apparent was the enormous amount of information on the Internet about autism and Asperger's syndrome. The selection made here gives access to this enormous pool of information from various points of view.

The Internet is a medium that is very susceptible to change. It is possible that the websites mentioned here are not accessible all the time, have in the meantime disappeared or the addresses have changed. It is hoped that the websites selected are stable.

AII.1 Associations

Autism Society of America (ASA)

http://www.autism-society.org

The National Autistic Society (NAS)

http://www.nas.org.uk

This is a large English site for people with Asperger's syndrome. It contains much information and includes full text articles, including Sainsbury's article on the detrimental effects of holding therapy for autistic children.

Autism Europe

http://www.autismeurope.arc.be

This is the website of the European umbrella organization of 71 parents' associations in Europe. There are also links to websites of parents' associations in Belgium, Finland, France, Great Britain, the Netherlands, Northern Ireland, Spain, Sweden and Switzerland.

Autism France, Pro Aid Autisme

http://www.surzone.com/proaidautisme/

French website about autism.

Autism Germany, Autismus

http://www.autismus.de/

German website about autism.

Autism, The Netherlands, Nederlandse Vereniging voor Autisme

http://www.autisme-nva.nl

Dutch website about autism.

AII.2 Information about autism

O.A.S.I.S. (Online Asperger Syndrome Information and Support)

http://www.udel.edu/bkirby/asperger

This website has a lot of information and links relating to Asperger and HFA. The site has been compiled by parents in cooperation with the University of Delaware. Many of the sites are aimed at carers, parents and teachers.

Questionnaire about Asperger syndrome, Tony Attwood

http://www.udel.edu/bkirby/asperger/aspergerscaleAttwood.html

The Australian test for Asperger's syndrome can be found on this site (by Tony Attwood). It is a questionnaire where characteristics of the child can be scored.

The Center for the Study of Autism

http://www.autism.org

This American research centre provides information about autism to parents and professionals and carries out research into the effect of various therapies. A lot of this research is done together with the Autism Research Institute in San Diego, California. The site gives information about autism sub-groups and related syndromes, important subjects, treatment, some articles, a summary of the books by Temple Grandin, information for siblings, interviews and links to other sites.

Homepage of the Asperger Syndrome Coalition of the United States, Inc.

http://www.asperger.org

This site is especially interesting because it refers to books and sometimes entire articles. There are a number of articles by Gillberg and Attwood posted on this site. The site is more suited to professionals and parents who have gone into the problem in more detail.

Homepage of the Asperger Support Network

http://home.vicnet.net.au/~asperger/

An Australian site with information and meeting points for parents with children with Asperger's syndrome.

Autism Resources

http://autism-resources.com

A site with many links, generally regarded as the most complete site about autism. Includes many links to online papers.

Tony Attwood's homepage

http://tonyattwood.com.au

Tony Attwood is the author of the book *Asperger's Syndrome, A Guide for Parents and Professionals*. Information about the book is given on this homepage, an overview of conferences and lectures, Internet links and a number of summaries of articles.

Independent Living on the Autistic Spectrum

http://www.inlv.demon.nl

This site was set up by Martijn Dekker, who himself has an HFA autistic disorder. It is also a platform where people with HFA and Asperger's syndrome can meet.

Guidelines for Education, Karen Williams

http://www.udel.edu/bkirby/asperger/karen_williams_guidelines.html

This site contains an article by Karen Williams about guidelines for teachers on how to deal with children with Asperger's syndrome in the classroom. A brief summary is included in Appendix IIA.

Holding therapy: An autistic perspective

http://www.nas.org.uk/nas/jsp/polopoly.jsp?d=364&a=2179

Article by C. Sainsbury (2000) about the danger of holding therapy.

Social Cognitive Processing in Individuals with Autism Spectrum Disorders: A Hot Theory of Mind Deficit

http://trainland.tripod.com/verity.htm

An article by V. Bottroff (1999) about the 'hot' and 'cold' theory of mind. Other papers from the 99th autism conference can be found on: http://trainland.tripod.com/autism99.htm.

Coping: A Survival Guide for People with Asperger Syndrome

http://www.asperger-marriage.info/survguide/chapter0.html

A survival guide written by Marc Segar (1997).

Summary of Karen Williams' article

This is a brief summary of the article by Karen Williams (1995) on guidelines for teachers on how to deal with children with Asperger's syndrome in the classroom. The complete article is posted on the Internet at the following address: www.udel.edu/bkirby/asperger/karen_williams_guidelines.html.

Karen Williams mentions a number of focal points for teachers who have pupils with Asperger's syndrome:

1. *Resistance to change* (enhance the predictability of the situation; limit changes; offer clear routines; avoid surprises, prepare thoroughly to changes; practise new situations beforehand).

2. *Impairment in social interaction* (protect against bullying and teasing; involve classmates for help and support; bring out the child's qualities; practise associating with peers; teach social skills; set up a buddy system; foster involvement with others).

3. *Restricted range of interests* (limit and mark off the time spent on a particular area of interest; reinforce desired behaviour through compliments; use areas of interest in class work; try to broaden the child's repertoire of interests).

4. *Poor concentration* (provide a large amount of external structure; set time limits; lessen homework; provide assistance to supplement class work; seat the child at the front of the class and direct frequent questions to the child to maintain his or her attention; work out a non-verbal signal with the child to retain his or her attention; seat the child's buddy next to him or her; actively encourage the child to focus on the real world).

5. *Poor motor skills* (provide additional physical education; help with writing; avoid competitive sports; take account of slower writing rhythm).

6. *Learning difficulties* (create an individualized programme; do not assume that the child understands something just because he or she parrots back what he or she has heard; capitalize on these children's exceptional memory; take account of their difficulty understanding meaning, emotional nuances and relationship issues when reading books; take account of their problems with

written assignments, such as repetition or misunderstood meanings of words; take account of the fact that despite excellent reading skills understanding of texts may be slow; ask them to carry out their work carefully even if it is outside their area of interest).

7. *Emotional vulnerability* (prevent outbursts by ensuring predictability of the situation; help the child to prevent being overwhelmed by agreeing rules on what to do if he or she feels stressed; keep one's voice calm and even; pay attention to changes in behaviour which may announce shifts in mood; collaborate with other carers; bear in mind that adolescents with Asperger's syndrome are highly susceptible to depression; make sure that the child has a supporting staff member with whom he or she can talk every day; prevent the child from being overwhelmed by school tasks by offering help: because of their emotional vulnerability, these children need a school environment which enables them to do well).

Books

An overview of books on autism is given in this appendix. Specialized literature on the subject has not been included except for classic books and articles. An attempt has been made to draw up a list of books which can be used immediately. They have been set out alphabetically per subject. A brief description is provided for each book.

AIII.1 Autism and related disorders, general

Asperger, H. (1944) 'Autistic psychopathy in childhood.' Translated and annotated by Uta Frith. In U. Frith (ed.) (1997) *Autism and Asperger Syndrome.* **Cambridge: Cambridge University Press.**

The problems of autism are set out in this article in an intelligent and respectful manner. It is one of the two pioneer articles. The problems encountered in Asperger's syndrome are also described, which is one of the reasons why the syndrome was given the name of this pioneer.

Attwood, T. (1998) *Asperger's Syndrome: A Guide for Parents and Professionals.* **London: Jessica Kingsley Publishers.**

This very readable and respectful book about Asperger's syndrome gives a description and analysis of its characteristics. Many practical strategies are described to limit the effects of the disorder. Includes a lot of information for parents and carers.

Frith, U. (1989, second edition 2003) *Autism: Explaining the Enigma.* **Oxford, Blackwell Publishers.**

This book presents the psychological background to autism. The theory of mind and central coherence theories are explained here. This very readable book is regarded as a classic in the field of autism. In 2003, the revised second edition appeared in which a chapter was added about the importance of self-awareness.

Frith, U. (ed.) (1997) *Autism and Asperger Syndrome.* **Cambridge: Cambridge University Press.**

A collection of chapters by scientists about Asperger's syndrome. It provides a summary of the background and history. The original article by Hans Asperger of 1944, translated into English by Uta Frith, is included.

Happé, F.G.E. (1998) *Autism: An Introduction to Psychological Theory.* **Cambridge, MA: Harvard University Press.**

Introduction to the theory of autism. Excellent overview and critical description of the various theories with regard to autism. Used as a textbook.

Kanner, L. (1943) 'Autistic disturbances of affective contact.' *Nervous Child 2,* **217–50.**

This is the first article written about autism. Kanner describes eleven children (eight boys and three girls) who appear to have the same 'fascinating peculiarities'. Apart from strange 'features' in the family that have an influence on development, Kanner concludes that these children were born with an innate incapacity for ordinary, biologically controlled affective contact with people, just as other children are born with physical or intellectual disabilities.

Vermeulen, P. (1999) *Autistic Thinking – This is the Title.* **London: Jessica Kingsley Publishers.**

This is about how autistic people think. Vermeulen postulates that people with autism have a different type of intelligence. He describes the way that autistic people think in details and explains that, in his view, this is why autistic people consequently cannot meet the demands of society. The book is based on the central coherence theory.

Wing, L. (2001) *The Autistic Spectrum. A Parents' Guide to Understanding and Helping your Child.* **Berkeley, CA: Ulysses Press.**

An excellent overview of the whole autistic spectrum. Practical and useful for parents and carers. The book consists of two parts: 1. What is the autistic spectrum? 2. Upbringing, guidance and treatment.

AIII.2 Autism and related disorders, personal accounts

Claiborne Park, C. (1967) *The Siege. The First Eight Years of an Autistic Child.* **Boston/New York: Little, Brown and Co.**

A classic work in trying to understand autism. The impressive fight of a mother for her autistic daughter Jessy.

Claiborne Park, C. (2001) *Exiting Nirvana.* Boston/New York: Little, Brown and Co. Sequel to *The Siege* about Jessy, an autistic girl, growing up and becoming an adult.

Gerland, G. (2003) *A Real Person. Life on the Outside.* London: Souvenir Press Ltd.
Autobiography of an autistic woman. A moving story in which the isolation and difference felt by autistic people is clearly described. Written like a good novel without being romanticized.

Grandin, T. (1995) *Thinking in Pictures and Other Reports from My Life with Autism.* New York: Doubleday.
Both autobiographical and scientific, Temple Grandin's book deals with the problems that autistic people encounter.

Segar, M. (1997) *Coping: A Survival Guide for People with Asperger Syndrome.* www.asperger-marriage.info/survguide/chapter0.html
Based on his own experience, Marc Segar has written a 'survival guide' for young people with Asperger's syndrome. He did not benefit from it as he committed suicide.

Sellin, B. (1995) *I Don't Want to be Inside Me Anymore: Messages from an Autistic Mind.* New York: Basic Books.
Selection of texts by Birger Sellin, an autistic young man who has not spoken since the age of two and communicated by computer only from the age of 17. Before that time, it was not known that he could read and write. The texts are prefaced by an introduction to autism and a brief biography of Birger Sellin by Michael Klonovsky. The pain and emotion of an autistic individual imprisoned in his inability to communicate through language is movingly portrayed.

Stehli, A. (1995) *Dancing in the Rain. Stories of Exceptional Progress by Parents of a Child with Special Needs.* Westport, CT: Georgiana Organization Inc.
Annabel Stehli describes her struggle to understand her child and find the right therapy for her. She had to come to terms with Bettelheim's view that prevailed at the time which blamed the mother as the cause of the child's autism.

AIII.3 Books for children

Delfos, M.F. (1997) *Vogel. Over Omgaan met Leeftijdgenoten.* [Birdie. Interacting with Children Your Own Age] Bussum: Pereboom.
Birdie goes on long journeys and becomes so full of himself and his flying prowess that he no longer cares for the birds around him. On his longest journey, Birdie discovers that other birds are also important and need space. *Vogel* is a therapeutic book to be read aloud to children from 4 to 12. The idea is to show children that all human beings are equally important and have their own individual world. Only available in Dutch.

Delfos, M.F. (2003) *De Wereld van Luuk. Over Autisme.* **[Luke's World. About Autism] Bussum: Pereboom.**

This book clearly explains to children what autism is all about. The trouble that Luke has making friends, his need to walk around in old clothing, his collection and his fear are described. Apart from the story to be read aloud, text boxes are inserted with explanations for parents and carers. Only available in Dutch.

Delfos, M.F. (2003) *Merel is Bang. Over Angst.* **[Merle is Frightened. About Fear] Bussum: Pereboom.**

Merel is frightened without exactly knowing why. She has to go and stay with someone and finds it very scary. Apart from the story to be read aloud, there are text boxes with explanations for parents and carers. Only available in Dutch.

Vermeulen, P. (2000) *I am Special.* **London: Jessica Kingsley Publishers.**

Exercise book for autistic young people (aged 10–12) of average intelligence. The book is read and the exercises completed together with a parent or carer. The idea is to explain to autistic people themselves what autism is.

References

Aarons, M. and Gittens, T. (2000) *Autisme. Werkboek Sociale Vaardigheden.* Adapted by H. Roeyers. Leuven/Leusden: Acco.

Achterberg, G. (1984) 'Glas.' In *Verzamelde Gedichten.* Amsterdam: Querido.

Aguiar, A. and Bailargeon, R. (1999) 'Perseveration and problem solving in infancy.' *Advances in Child Development and Behavior 27,* 135–138.

Ainsworth, M.D.S., Blehar, M.C., Waters, E. and Wall, S. (1978) *Patterns of Attachment, A Psychological Study of the Strange Situation.* Hillsdale, NJ: Erlbaum.

Albert, D.J., Walsh, M.L. and Jonik, R.H. (1993) 'Aggression in humans: What is its biological foundation?' *Neuroscience and Biobehavioral Reviews 17,* 4, 405–25.

Angold, A., Costello, E.J., Erkanli, A. and Worthman, C.M. (1999) 'Pubertal changes in hormone levels and depression in girls.' *Psychological Medicine 29,* 5, 1043–53.

APA (American Psychiatric Association) (1994) *Diagnostic and Statistical Manual of Mental Disorders Fourth Edition.* Washington DC: American Psychiatric Association.

Archer, J. (1991) 'The influence of testosterone on human aggression.' *British Journal of Psychology 82,* 1, 1–28.

Archer, J. (1994) 'Testosterone and aggression.' *Journal of Offender Rehabilitation 21,* 3–4, 3–39.

Arntz, A. and Bögels, S. (1995) 'Cognitieve therapie bij angststoornissen: Een overzicht.' In J.A. den Boer and H.G.M. Westenberg (eds) *Leerboek Angststoornissen. Een Neurobiologische Benadering.* Utrecht: De Tijdstroom.

Aronson, M., Hagberg, B. and Gillberg, C. (1997) 'Attention deficits and autistic spectrum problems in children exposed to alcohol during gestation: A follow-up study.' *Developmental Medicine and Child Neurology 39,* 9, 583–7.

Asperger, H. (1944) 'Autistic psychopathy in childhood.' Translated and annotated by Uta Frith. In U. Frith (ed.) (1997) *Autism and Asperger Syndrome.* Cambridge: Cambridge University Press.

Attwood, T. (1998) *Aspergers's Syndrome: A Guide for Parents and Professionals.* London: Jessica Kingsley Publishers.

Autisme Team Gelderland (2000) *Vragenlijst ten Behoeve van Diagnostisch Onderzoek naar Pervasieve Ontwikkelingsstoornissen.* Autisme Team Gelderland: Arnhem.

Bailey, A., Phillips, W. and Rutter. M. (1996) 'Autism: Towards an integration of clinical, genetic, neuropsychological, and neurobiological perspectives.' *Journal of Child Psychology and Psychiatry 37,* 1, 89–126.

Baird, G., Charman, T., Baron-Cohen, S., Cox, A., Swettenham, J., Wheelwright, S. and Drew, A. (2000) 'A screening instrument for autism at 18 months of age: A 6 year follow-up study.' *Child Adolescent Psychiatry 39*, 694–702.

Banks, T. and Dabbs Jr., J.M. (1996) 'Salivary testosterone and cortisol in a delinquent and violent urban subculture.' *Journal of Social Psychology 136*, 1, 49–56.

Bar-On, R. (1997) *Bar-On Emotional Quotient Inventory. Technical Manual.* Toronto: Multi-Health Systems.

Baron-Cohen, S. (1989) 'The autistic child's theory of mind: A case of specifc developmental delay.' *Journal of Child Psychology and Psychiatry 30*, 285–97.

Baron-Cohen, S. (1990) 'Autism: A specific disorder of "mind-blindness".' *International Review of Psychiatry 2*, 79–88.

Baron-Cohen, S. (2000) 'Is Asperger syndrome/high-functioning autism necessarily a disability?' *Development and Psychopathology 12*, 489–500.

Baron-Cohen, S. (2003) *The Essential Difference. Men, Women and the Extreme Male Brain.* London: Allen Lane, Penguin Books.

Baron-Cohen, S. and Hammer, J. (1997) 'Parents of children with Asperger syndrome: What is the cognitive phenotype?' *Journal of Cognitive Neuroscience 9*, 4, 548–54.

Baron-Cohen, S., Wheelwright, S. and Jolliffe, T. (1997) 'Is there a "language of the eyes"? Evidence from normal adults, and adults with autism or Asperger syndrome.' *Visual Cognition 4*, 3, 311–31.

Baron-Cohen, S., Jolliffe, T., Mortimore, C. and Robertson, M. (1997) 'Another advanced test of theory of mind: evidence from very high functioning adults with autism or Asperger syndrome.' *Journal of Child Psychology and Psychiatry 38*, 7, 813–22.

Baron-Cohen, S., Campbell, R., Karmiloff-Smith, A., Grant, J. and Walker, J. (1995) 'Are children with autism blind to the mentalistic significance of the eyes?' *British Journal of Developmental Psychology 13*, 379–98.

Baron-Cohen, S., Ring, H.A., Wheelwright, S., Bullmore, E.T., Brammer, M.J., Simmons, A. and Williams, S.C. (1999) 'Social intelligence in the normal and autistic brain: An fMRI study.' *European Journal of Neuroscience 11*, 6, 1891–8.

Baron-Cohen, S., Cox, A., Baird, G., Swettenham, J., Nightingale, N., Morgan, K., Auriol, D. and Charman, T. (1996) 'Psychological markers in the detection of autism in infancy in a large population.' *British Journal of Psychiatry 161*, 839–43.

Barrett, S., Beck, J.C., Bernier, R., Bisson, E., Braun, T.A. Casavant, T.L. *et al.* (1999) 'An autosomal genomic screen for autism. Collaborative linkage study of autism.' *American Journal of Medical Genetics 15*, 88, 6, 609–15.

Bauman, M.L. (1996) 'Brief report: Neuroanatomic observations of the brain in pervasive developmental disorders.' *Journal of Autism and Developmental Disorders 26*, 2, 199–203.

Bauman, M.L. and Kemper, T.L. (1994) 'The neuroanatomy of the brain in autism.' In M.L. Bauman and T.L. Kemper (eds) *The Neurobiology of Autism.* Baltimore: The Johns Hopkins University Press.

Beatty, W.W. (1984) 'Hormonal organization of sex differences in play fighting and spatial behavior.' In G.J. De Vries, J.P. De Bruin, H.B.M. Uylings and M.A. Corners (eds) *Progress in Brain Research 61*, 315–30.

Beck, A.T. (1985) *Anxiety Disorders and Phobias.* New York: Basic Books.

Beck, A.T. (1989) *Love is Never Enough.* New York: HarperPerennial.

Beel, V. (2000) *Dag, Vreemde Man. Over Partners met Autisme.* Gent: Vlaamse Dienst Autisme, EPO.

Bender, L. (1947) 'Childhood schizophrenia. Clinical study of one hundred schizophrenic childen.' *Journal of Orthopsychiatry 17,* 1, 40–56.

Berckelaer-Onnes, I. van (1992) *Leven naar de letter. Inaugurele rede.* Groningen: Wolters-Noordhoff.

Berckelaer-Onnes, I. van (1999) 'De details van Ina Berckelaer-Onnes.' *Psychologie 18,* 34–7.

Berckelaer-Onnes, I. van and Hoekman, J. (1991) *Auti-R-schaal. Handleiding en Verantwoording.* Lisse: Swets and Zeitlinger.

Berenbaum, S.A. and Hines, M. (1992) 'Early androgens are related to childhood sex-typed toy preferences.' *Psychological Science 3,* 3, 203–6.

Bergman, B. and Brismar, B. (1994) 'Hormone levels and personality traits in abusive and suicidal male alcoholics.' *Alcoholism: Clinical and Experimental Research 18,* 311–16.

Bernards, J.A. and Bouman, L.N. (1993) *Fysiologie van de Mens.* Utrecht/Antwerpen: Bohn, Scheltema and Holkema.

Bernhardt, P.C., Dabbs Jr., J.M., Fielden, J.A. and Lutter, C.D. (1998) 'Testosterone changes during vicarious experiences of winning and losing among fans at sporting events.' *Physiology and Behavior 65,* 1, 59–62.

Berversdorf, D. and Hughes, J. (2000) 'A neural network model of decreased context utilization in Autism Spectrum Disorder.' Sixth Congress of Autism Europe, Glasgow.

Bettelheim, B. (1956) 'Childhood schizophrenia as a reaction to extreme situations.' *Journal of Orthopsychiatry 26,* 507–18.

Bettelheim, B. (1967) *The Empty Fortress: Infantile Autism and the Birth of the Self.* New York: The Free Press.

Bettelheim, B. (1977) *Die Geburt des Selbst.* [The Empty Fortress] Erfolgreiche Therapie autistischer Kinder. München: Kindler Verlag GmbH.

Bettison, S. (1997) 'The long-term effects of auditory training on children with autism.' Comment in *Journal of Autism and Developmental Disorders 27,* 3, 347–8.

Biddulph, S. (2003) *Raising boys. Why boys are different – and how to help them become happy and well-balanced men.* London: Thorsons.

Bigelow, B.J., Tesson, G. and Lewko, J.H. (1996) *Learning the Rules. The Anatomy of Children's Relationships.* New York/London: Guilford Press.

Björkqvist, K. and Niemelä, P. (1992) 'New trends in the study of female aggression.' In K. Björkqvist and P.K. Niemelä (eds) *Of Mice and Women: Aspects of Female Aggression.* San Diego, CA: Academic Press.

Blakemore-Brown, L. (2002) *Reweaving the Autistic Tapestry. Autism, Asperger syndrome and ADHD.* London: Jessica Kingsley Publishers.

Bleuler, E. (1908) 'The prognosis of dementia praecox. The group of schizophrenias.' English translation in J. Cutting and M. Sheperd (eds) (1987) *The Clinical Roots of the Schizophrenia Concept.* Cambridge: Cambridge University Press.

Boer, F. (1994) *Een Gegeven Relatie. Over Broers en Zussen.* Amsterdam: Prometheus.

Bottroff, V. (1999) *Social Cognitive Processing in Individuals with Autism Spectrum Disorders: A Hot Theory of Mind Deficit.* http://trainland.tripod.com/verity.htm

Boucher, J. (1981) 'Memory for recent events in autistic children.' *Journal of Autism and Developmental Disorders 11*, 3, 293–301.

Bower, G.H. (1981) 'Mood and memory.' *American Psychologist 36*, 129–48.

Bowlby, J. (1984) *Attachment and Loss Volume I, Revised Edition.* London: Penguin Books.

Bowler, D.M., Matthews, N.J. and Gardiner, J.M. (1997) 'Asperger's syndrome and memory: Similarity to autism but not amnesia.' *Neuropsychologia 35*, 1, 65–70.

Buck, R. and Ginsburg, B. (1997) 'Communicative genes and the evolution of empathy.' In W. Ickes (ed.) *Empathic Accuracy.* New York/London: Guilford Press.

Buitelaar, J.K. and Gaag, R.J. van der (1998) 'Diagnostic rules for children with PDD-NOS and Multiple Complex Developmental Disorder.' *Journal of Child Psychology and Psychiatry 39*, 6, 911–19.

Burger, R.A. (2003) *Autism and the Immune System.* www.genevacentre.org/html/ burger.html

Burgoine, E. and Wing, L. (1983) 'Identical triplets with Asperger's syndrome.' *British Journal of Psychiatry 143*, 261–5.

Burke, H.L. and Yeo, R.A. (1994) 'Systematic variations in callosal morphology: The effects of age, gender, hand preference, and anatomic asymmetry.' *Neuropsychology 8*, 4, 563–71.

Cahill, L., Haier, R.J., White, N.S., Fallon, J., Kilpatrick, L.C., Potkin, S.G. and Alkire, M.T. (2001) 'Sex-related difference in amygdala activity during emotionally infuenced memory storage.' *Neurobiology of Learning and Memory, 75*, 1, 1–9.

Cannon, W.B. (1932) *The Wisdom of the Body.* New York: Norton.

Castle, J., Groothues, C., Bredenkamp, D., Beckett, C., O'Connor, T., Rutter, M. and the ERA Study Team (1999) 'Effects of qualities of early institutional care on cognitive attainment.' *American Journal of Orthopsychiatry 69*, 4, 424–37.

Chakrabarti, S. and Fombonne, E. (2001) 'Pervasive developmental disorders in preschool children.' *Jama 27*, 285, 24, 3093–9.

Coe, C.L., Hayashi, K.T. and Levine, S. (1988) 'Hormones and behavior at puberty: Activation or concatenation? Development during the transition to adolescence.' In M.R. Gunnar and W.A. Collins (eds) *Minnesota Symposia on Child Psychology 21*, 17–41. Hillsdale: Lawrence Erlbaum Associates.

Cohen, D.J., Paul, R. and Volkmar, F.R. (1987) 'Issues in the classifcation of pervasive developmental disorders and associated conditions.' In D.J. Cohen and A.M. Donnellan (eds) *Handbook of Autism and Pervasive Developmental Disorders.* New York: Wiley and Sons.

Cohen, D.J., Towbin, K.E., Mayes, L. and Volkmar, F.R. (1994) 'Developmental psychopathology of Multiple Developmental Disorder.' In S.L. Friedman and H.C. Haywood (eds) *Developmental Followup: Concepts, Genres, Domains and Methods.* New York: Academic Press.

Cohn, L.D. (1991) 'Sex differences in the course of personality development: A meta-analysis.' *Psychological Bulletin 109*, 252–66.

Collaer, M.L. and Hines, M. (1995) 'Human behavioral sex differences: A role for gonadal hormones during early development?' *Psychological Bulletin 118*, 55–107.

Connellan, J., Baron-Cohen, S., Wheelwright, S., Ba'tki, A. and Ahluwalia, J. (2001) 'Sex differences in human neonatal social perception.' *Infant Behavior and Development 23*, 113–18.

Consortium (International Molecular Genetic Study of Autist Consortium) (1998) 'A full genome screen for autism with evidence for linkage to a region on chromosome 7q.' *Human Molecular Genetics 7*, 3, 571–8.

Constantino, J.N., Grosz, D., Saenger, P., Chandler, D.W., Nandi, R. and Earls, F.J. (1993) 'Testosterone and aggression in children.' *Journal of the American Academy of Child and Adolescent Psychiatry 32*, 6, 1217–22.

Cumming, D.C., Brunsting, L.A., Strich, G., Ries, A.L. and Rebar, R.W. (1986) 'Reproductive hormone increases in response to acute exercise in men.' *Medical Science in Sports and Exercise 18*, 369–73.

Dabbs, J.M. (1990) 'Age and seasonal variation in serum testosterone concentration among men.' *Chronobiology International 7*, 3, 245–9.

Dabbs, J.M. (1992) 'Testosterone and occupational achievement.' *Social Forces 70*, 3, 813–24.

Dabbs, J.M. (1993) 'Salivary testosterone measurements in behavioral studies. Saliva as a diagnostic fluid.' In D. Malamud and L.A. Tabak (eds) *Annals of the New York Academy of Sciences 694*, 177–83.

Dabbs, J.M. (1997) 'Testosterone, smiling, and facial appearance.' *Journal of Nonverbal Behavior 21*, 1.

Dabbs, J.M. and Hargrove, M.F. (1997) 'Age, testosterone, and behavior among female prison inmates.' *Psychosomatic Medicine 59*, 5, 477–80.

Dabbs, J.M. and Hopper, C.H. (1990) 'Cortisol, arousal, and personality in two groups of normal men.' *Personality and Individual Differences 11*, 931–5.

Dabbs, J.M., Hopper, C.H. and Jurkovic, G.J. (1990) 'Testosterone and personality among college students and military veterans.' *Personality and Individual Differences 11*, 12, 1263–69.

Dabbs, J.M., Jurkovic, G.J. and Frady, R.L. (1991) 'Salivary testosterone and cortisol among late adolescent male offenders.' *Journal of Abnormal Child Psychology 19*, 4, 469–78.

Dabbs, J.M., La Rue, D. and Williams, P.M. (1990) 'Testosterone and occupational choice: Actors, ministers, and other men.' *Journal of Personality and Social Psychology 59*, 6, 1261–5.

Damasio, A.R. (1994) *Descartes' Error: Emotion, Reason and the Human Brain.* New York: Putnam.

Damasio, A.R. (1999) *The Feeling of what Happens. Body and Emotion in the Making of Consciousness.* San Diego/New York/London: Harcourt.

Damasio, A.R. and Maurer, R.G. (1978) 'A neurological model for childhood autism.' *Archives of Neurology 35*, 777–86.

Damon, W. (1988) *The Moral Child. Nurturing Children's Natural Moral Growth.* New York/London: The Free Press.

Dawson, G. and Lewey, A. (1989) 'Arousal, attention and socioemotional impairments of individuals with autism.' In G. Dawson (ed.) *Autism, Nature, Diagnosis and Treatment.* New York: Guilford Press.

Deater-Deckard, K. and Dodge, K.A. (1997) 'Externalizing behavior problems and discipline revisited: Nonlinear effects and variation by culture, context, and gender.' *Psychological Inquiry 8*, 3, 161–75.

Dekker, M. (2001) 'On our own terms: Emerging autistic culture.' *Independent Living,* www.inlv.demon.nl.

Delfos, M.F. (1993) 'Postpartum mood disturbances. The menstrual and emotional cycle.' Conference paper presented at International Marcé Conference, November.

Delfos, M.F. (1994) 'De ontwikkeling van intimiteit. [The development of intimacy] Een ontwikkelingspsychologisch model gekoppeld aan een model van de gevolgen van seksueel misbruik.' *Tijdschrift voor Seksuologie*, December, 18, 282–92.

Delfos, M.F. (1996) 'Jongens, de zorgenkindjes van de toekomst.' [Boys, the care problem of the future] *Psychologie 15*, June, 16–17.

Delfos, M.F. (1997) *Vogel. Over Omgaan met Leeftijdgenoten.* [Birdie. Interacting with Children Your Own Age] Bussum: Pereboom.

Delfos, M.F. (1999a) *Le parent insaisissable et l'urgence d'écrire.* Amsterdam: Rodopi.

Delfos, M.F. (1999b) *Ontwikkeling in Vogelvlucht. Ontwikkeling van Kinderen en Adolescenten.* Lisse: Swets and Zeitlinger.

Delfos, M.F. (2000) *Are You Listening to Me? Communicating with Children between Four and Twelve Years Old.* Amsterdam: SWP.

Delfos, M.F. (2001a) 'Borderline, a changing pattern.' In M.F. Delfos and N. Visscher (eds) *(Foster)Children and Odd Behaviour?! On 13 Themes.* Amsterdam: SWP.

Delfos, M.F. (2001b) 'The developmental damage to children as a result of the violation of their rights.' In J.C.M. Willems (ed.) *Developmental and Autonomy Rights of Children: Empowering Caregivers and Communities.* Antwerpen/Groningen/Oxford: Intersentia.

Delfos, M.F. (2002a) 'Afscheid van het normale kind.' [Goodbye to the normal child] *Pedagogiek in Praktijk Magazine 5*, 28–31.

Delfos, M.F. (2002b) 'Autisme in het voortgezet onderwijs.' [Autism in Secondary School] In H. Schoots (ed.) *Handboek Leerlingbegeleiding.* Alphen a/d Rijn: Kluwer, 2195, 1–14.

Delfos, M.F. (2002c) 'Autisme: Het socioschema als verklaringsmodel.' [Autism: The socioscheme as explanatory model] *Wetenschappelijk Tijdschrift Autisme (WTA) 2*, 20–34.

Delfos, M.F. (2003a, fourth revised edition, original edition 1996) *Kinderen in Ontwikkeling. Stoornissen en Belemmeringen.* [Developing children. Disorders and Impediments] Lisse: Swets and Zeitlinger.

Delfos, M.F. (2003b) 'The conquered giant. The use of computers in play therapy.' In F.J. Maarsse, A.E. Akkerman, A.N. Brand and L.J.M. Mulder (eds) *Computers in Psychology 7.* Lisse: Swets and Zeitlinger.

Delfos, M.F. (2003c) *De Wereld van Luuk. Over Autisme.* [Luke's World. About Autism] Bussum: Pereboom.

Delfos, M.F. (2003d) *Merel is Bang. Over Angst.* [Merle is Frightened. About Fear] Bussum: Pereboom.

Delfos, M.F. (2004a, first published in Dutch in 1997) *Children and Behavioural Problems. Anxiety, Aggression, Depression and AD/HD. A Biopsychological Model with Guidelines for Diagnostics and Treatment.* London: Jessica Kingsley Publishers.

Delfos, M.F. (2004b) *De Schoonheid van het Verschil. Waarom Mannen en Vrouwen Verschillend én Hetzelfde zijn.* [The Beauty Difference. Why Men and Women are Different and the Same] Lisse: Harcourt Book Publishers.

Delfos, M.F. (in preparation) *Writing disorders device.*

Dennen, J.M.G. van der (1992) 'The sociobiology of behavioural sex differences. II: Sex differences in sexual and aggressive behavioural systems.' In J.M.G. van der Dennen (ed.) *The Nature of the Sexes. The Sociobiology of Sex Differences and the Battle of the Sexes.* Groningen: Origin Press.

Derks, J. (2002) Personal communication.

Didden, R., Palmen, A.M.J.W. and Arts, M.C.M. (2002) 'Communicatieve vaardigheden bij kinderen en jongeren met autisme.' In B.E.B.M. Huskens and R. Didden (eds) *Behandelingsstrategieën bij Kinderen en Jongeren met Autisme.* Houten/Diegem: Bohn Stafeu Van Loghum.

Dijk, W.K. van (1979) 'De miskende alcoholist.' *Nederlands Tijdschrift voor Geneeskunde 123,* 2, 1228–36.

Dijkshoorn, P., Pietersen, W. and Dikken, G. (1998) *Kinderen met een Contactstoornis. Een Groepsbehandeling voor PDD-NOS-Kinderen en hun Ouders.* Lisse: Swets and Zeitlinger.

Ditmars, N. van (1995) *Autisme en geneesmiddelen.* Utrecht: Publicaties Wetenschapswinkel Geneesmiddelen.

Donnellan, A.M. (ed.) (1985) *Classic Readings in Autism.* New York: Teachers College, Columbia University.

Donovan, B.T. (1985) *Hormones and Human Behaviour: The Scientifc Basis of Psychiatry.* Cambridge: Cambridge University Press.

Doornen, L. van (2000) 'Stress: Mind the body.' *De Psycholoog 35,* 3, 114–18.

Duyndam, J. (2001) 'De stuipen op het lijf. Over goede en slechte empathie.' *Tijdschrift voor Humanistiek 2,* 5, 16–23.

Eagly, A.H. and Steffen, V.J. (1986) 'Gender and aggressive behavior: A meta-analytic review of the social psychological literature.' *Psychological Bulletin 100,* 309–30.

Edelman, G.M. (1991) *Bright Air, Brilliant Fire. On the Matter of the Mind.* New York: Basic Books.

Egaas, B., Courchesne, E. and Saitoh, O. (1995) 'Reduced size of corpus callosum in autism.' *Archives of Neurology 52,* 794–801.

Eisenberg, N. and Fabes, R.A. (1991) 'Prosocial behavior and empathy: A multimethod developmental perspective.' In M.S. Clark (ed.) *Prosocial Behavior. Review of personality and social psychology 12,* 34–61.

Eisenberg, N., Murphy, B.C. and Shepard, S. (1997) 'The development of empathic accuracy.' In W. Ickes (ed.) *Empathic Accuracy.* New York/London: Guilford Press.

Eisenmajer, R., Prior, M., Leekman, S., Wing, L., Gould, J., Welham, M. and Ong, B. (1996) 'Comparison of clinical symptoms in autism and Asperger's Syndrome.' *Journal of the American Academy of Child and Adolescent Psychiatry 35,* 1523–31.

Elbers, E. (1991) 'Context en suggestie bij het ondervragen van jonge kinderen.' *Gezin 3*, 4, 234–243.

Eliot, L. (1999) *Early Intelligence. How the Brain and Mind Develop in the First Five Years of Life.* Middlesex: Penguin Books.

Ellis, A. (1973) *Humanistic Psychotherapy.* New York: McGraw-Hill.

Emmelkamp, P.M.G. (1995) 'Gedragstherapeutische behandeling van angststoornissen.' In J.A. den Boer and H.G.M. Westenberg (eds) *Leerboek Angststoornissen. Een Neurobiologische Benadering.* Utrecht: De Tijdstroom.

Eysenck, H.J. and Evans, D. (1994) *Test Your IQ.* London: Thorsons/Harper Collins. Translated by Jan van Rooij.

Farrant A., Blades, M. and Boucher, J. (1999) 'Recall readiness in children with autism.' *Journal of Autism and Developmental Disorders 29*, 5, 359–66.

Federici, F. (1998) *Help for the Hopeless Child: A Guide for Families.* Alexandria: Federici and Associates.

Fenenga, M. (1993) *Autistische Kinderen op School. Handreikingen voor de Aanpak van Autistische Leerlingen.* Amsterdam/Duivendrecht: Paedologisch Instituut De Pionier.

Field, T. (1981) 'Early development of the preterm offspring of teenage mothers.' In K. Scott, T. Field and E. Robertson (eds) *Teenage Parents and their Offspring.* New York: Grune and Stratton.

Field, T.M. (1995) 'Massage therapy for infants and children.' *Journal of Developmental and Behavioral Pediatrics 16*, 105–11.

Field, T.M. (1996) 'Touch therapies for pain management and stress reduction.' In R.J. Resnick and H.R. Ronald (eds) *Health Psychology through the Life Span: Practice and Research Opportunities.* Washington DC: American Psychological Association.

Fisher, J.H. (1995) *I'm not Stupid.* BBC documentary.

Flavell, J.H. (1985) *Cognitive Development* (second edition). Englewood Cliffs, NJ: Prentice Hall.

Fraiberg, S.H. (1959) *The Magic Years: Understanding and Handling the Problems of Early Childhood.* New York: Scribner.

Freud, S. (1947) *Abriss der Psychoanalyse. Gesammelte Werke, Band XVII.* London: Imago.

Friedman, M.J., Charney, D.S. and Deutsch, A.Y. (eds) (1995) *Neurobiological and Clinical Consequences of Stress. From Normal Adaptation to Post-Traumatic Stress Disorder.* Philadelphia/ New York: Lippincott-Raven.

Frith, C.D. (1992) *The Cognitive Neuropsychology of Schizophrenia.* New Jersey: Lawrence Erlbaum.

Frith, U. (1989) *Autism. Explaining the Enigma.* Oxford: Blackwell Publishers.

Frith, U. (ed.) (1997a) *Autism and Asperger Syndrome.* Cambridge: Cambridge University Press.

Frith, U. (1997b) 'Asperger and his syndrome.' In U. Frith (ed.) *Autism and Asperger Syndrome.* Cambridge: Cambridge University Press.

Frith, U. (2003) *Autism. Explaining the Enigma. Second Edition.* Oxford: Blackwell Publishers.

Frith, U. and Happé, F. (1994) 'Autism: Beyond Theory of Mind.' *Cognition 50*, 115–32.

Frye, I.B.M. (1968) *Fremde unter uns. Autisten, ihre Erziehung, ihr Lebenslauf.* Meppel: Boom en Zoon.

Furby, L. and Wilke, M. (1982) 'Some characteristics of infants' preferred toys.' *Journal of Genetic Psychology 141*, 207–210.

Gaag, R.J. van der (in press) 'Multiple complex Developmental Disorders. een verkenning aan de grenzen van het Autistische Spectrum.' In M.F. Delfos (ed.) *Asperger in meervoud.* Amsterdam: SWP.

Galjaard, H. (1994) *Alle Mensen zijn Ongelijk. De Verschillen en Overeenkomsten Tussen Mensen: Hun Erfelijke Aanleg, Gezondheid, Gedrag en Prestaties.* Amsterdam: Muntinga.

Gallagher, L., Becker, K., Kearney, G., Dunlop, A., Stallings, R., Green, A., Fitzgerald, M. and Gill, M. (2003) Brief Report: A Case of Autism Associated with del(2)(q32.1q32.2) or (q32.2q32.3). *Journal of Autism and Developmental Disorders 33*, 1, 105–8.

Gay, P. (ed.) (1964) *John Locke on Education.* New York: Bureau of Publications, Teacher's College, Columbia University.

Geest, J. van der (2001) *Looking into autism. Eye movements and gaze behavior of autistic children.* Rotterdam: Proefschrift Erasmus Universiteit.

Geest, J. van der, Kemner, C., Camfferman, G., Verbaten, M.N. and Van Engeland, H. (2002) 'Looking at images with human figures: Comparison between autistic and normal children.' *Journal of Autism and Developmental Disorders 32*, 2, 69–75.

Gent, T. van, Heijnen, C.J. and Treffers, P.D.A. (1997) 'Autism and the immune system.' *Journal of Child Psychology and Psychiatry and Allied Disciplines 38*, 3, 337–49.

Gerland, G. (2000) 'Personal accounts for people with autism.' Sixth Congress of Autism Europe, Glasgow.

Gerland, G. (2003) *A Real Person. Life on the Outside.* London: Souvenir Press Ltd.

Geschwind, N. and Behan, P. (1982) 'Left-handedness: Association with immune disease, migraine, and developmental learning disorder.' In *Proceedings of the National Academy of Sciences.* Washington: The National Academy of Sciences.

Geschwind, N. and Behan, P.O. (1984) 'Laterality, hormones and immunity.' In N. Geschwind and A.M. Galaburda (eds) *Cerebral Dominance. The Biological Foundations.* Cambridge, MA and London, England: Harvard University Press.

Gesell, A. (1965) *Developmental Diagnosis: Normal and Abnormal Child Development: Clinical Methods and Pediatrics.* New York: Amatruda, Catherine Strunk.

Gesell, A. and Ilg, F. (1949) *Child Development.* New York: Harper and Row.

Ghaziuddin, M. and Butler, E. (1998) 'Clumsiness in autism and Asperger's syndrome: A further report.' *Journal of Intellectual Disability Research 42*, 43–8.

Ghaziuddin, M. and Gerstein, L. (1996) 'Pedantic speaking style differentiates Asperger's syndrome from high-functioning autism.' *Journal of Autism and Developmental Disorders 26*, 6, 585–95.

Ghaziuddin, M., Tsai, L. and Ghaziuddin, N. (1991) 'Brief report: Violence in Asperger syndrome – A critique.' *Journal of Autism and Developmental Disorders 21*, 349–354.

Gillberg, C. (1989) 'Asperger's syndrome in 23 Swedish children.' *Developmental Medicine and Child Neurology 31*, 520–31.

Gillberg, C.L. (1992) 'The Emanuel Miller Memorial Lecture 1991. Autism and autistic-like conditions: Subclasses among disorders of empathy.' *The Journal of Child Psychology and Psychiatry and Allied Disciplines 33*, 5, 813–42.

Gillberg, C. (1997) 'Clinical and neurobiological aspects of Asperger syndrome in six family studies.' In U. Frith (ed.) *Autism and Asperger Syndrome*. Cambridge: Cambridge University Press.

Gillberg, C.L. (2000) 'An overview of the biology of autism.' Sixth Congress of Autism Europe, Glasgow.

Gillberg, C. and Ehlers, S. (1998) 'Five high functioning people with autism and Asperger syndrome: A literature review.' In E. Schopler, G.B. Mesibov and L.J. Kunce (eds) *Asperger syndrome or High Functioning Autism?* New York/London: Plenum Press.

Gillberg, C. and Gillberg, C. (1989) 'Asperger's syndrome. Some epidemological considerations: A research note.' *Journal of Child Psychology and Psychiatry 30*, 631–8.

Gillberg, C., Nordin, V. and Ehlers, S. (1996) 'Early detection of autism. Diagnostic instruments for clinicians.' *European Journal of Child and Adolescent Psychiatry 5*, 2, 67–74.

Gillberg, C., Terenius, L. and Lönnerholm, G. (1985) 'Endorphin activity in childhood psychosis. Spinal fluid levels in 24 cases.' *Archives of General Psychiatry 42*, 78–783.

Goldberg, J., Szatmari, P. and Nahmias, C. (1999) 'Imaging of autism: Lessons from the past to guide studies in the future.' *Canadian Journal of Psychiatry 44*, 8, 793–801.

Goldstein, A.P. (1973) *Structured Learning Therapy. Towards a Psychotherapy for the Poor*. New York: Academic Press.

Gomez, J. (1991) *Psychological and Psychiatric Problems in Men*. London/New York: Routledge.

Gordon, T. (1974) *P.E.T Parent Effectiveness Training: The Tested New Way to Raise Responsible Children*. New York: Wyden.

Grandin, T. (1992) 'An inside view of autism.' In E. Schopler and G.V. Mesibov (eds) *High Functioning Individuals with Autism*. New York: Plenum Press. www.autism.org/temple/inside.html.

Grandin, T. (1995a) 'The learning style of people with autism: An autobiography.' In K.A. Quill (ed.) *Teaching Children with Autism. Strategies to Enhance Communication and Socialization*. New York/London: Delmar Publishers.

Grandin, T. (1995b) *Thinking in Pictures and Other Reports from My Life with Autism*. New York: Doubleday.

Granger, D.A., Weisz, J.R., McCracken, J.T., Kauneckis, D. and Ikeda, S.C. (1994) 'Testosterone and conduct problems.' *Journal of the American Academy of Child and Adolescent Psychiatry 33*, 6, 908.

Gray, A., Jackson, D.N. and McKinlay, J.B. (1991) 'The relation between dominance, anger, and hormones in normally aging men: Results from the Massachusetts Male Aging Study.' *Psychosomatic Medicine 53*, 4, 375–85.

Gray, P. (1999) *Psychology*. New York: Worth.

Hadders-Algra, M. and Groothuis, A.M. (1999) 'Quality of general movements in infancy is related to neurological dysfunction, ADHD, and aggressive behaviour.' *Developmental Medicine and Child Neurology 41*, 6, 381–91.

Hadders-Algra, M., Klip-Van den Nieuwendijk, M.A.A. and van Eykern, L.A. (1997) 'Assessment of general movements: Towards a better understanding of a sensitive method to evaluate brain function in young infants.' *Developmental Medicine and Child Neurology 39*, 2, 88–98.

Halpern, C.T., Udry, J.R., Campbell, B. and Suchindran, C. (1993a) 'Relationships between aggression and pubertal increases in testosterone: A panel analysis of adolescent males.' *Social Biology 40*, 1–2, 8–24.

Halpern, C.T., Udry, J.R., Campbell, B. and Suchindran, C. (1993b) 'Testosterone and pubertal development as predictors of sexual activity: A panel analysis of adolescent males.' *Psychosomatic Medicine 55*, 5, 436–47.

Hamilton, L.W. and Timmons, R. (1990) *Principles of Behavioral Pharmacology.* Englewood Cliffs, NJ: Prentice Hall.

Hamstra-Bletz, E. and Bie, J. de (1985) 'Diagnostiek van het dysgrafsch handschrift bij leerlingen uit het gewoon lager onderwijs.' In A.J.W.M. Thomassen, G.P. Van Galen and L.F.W. De Klerk (eds) *Studies over de Schrijfmotoriek.* Lisse: Swets and Zeitlinger.

Happé, F.G.E. (1997) 'The autobiographical writings of three Aspergers syndrome adults: Problems of interpretation and implications for theory.' In U. Frith (ed.) *Autism and Asperger Syndrome.* Cambridge: Cambridge University Press.

Happé, F.G.E. (1998) *Autism. An Introduction to Psychological Theory.* Cambridge, MA: Harvard University Press.

Harris, J.R. (1998) *The Nurture Assumption – Why Children Turn Out the Way They Do.* New York: John Wiley and Sons.

Haveman, M. and Reijnders, R. (2002) 'Meer autisme of betere detectie?' *Wetenschappelijk Tijdschrift Autisme 1*, 4–12.

Hellige, J.B. (1993) *Hemispheric Asymmetry. What's Right and What's Left.* Cambridge/London: Harvard University Press.

Hendryx, M.S., Haviland, M.G. and Shaw, D.G. (1991) 'Dimension of alexithymia and their relationships to anxiety and depression.' *Journal of Personality Assessment 56*, 227–37.

Henry, J.P. and Stephens, P.M. (1977) *Stress, Health, and the Social Environment.* New York: Springer.

Herlitz, A., Nilsson, L.G. and Bäckman, L. (1997) 'Gender differences in episodic memory.' *Memory and Cognition 25*, 801–11.

Hill, E. and Frith, U. (2003) 'Understanding Autism: Insights from Mind and Brain.' *Philosophical Transactions of the Royal Society 358*, 275–427.

Hobson, P. (1993) 'Understanding persons: The role of affect.' In S. Baron-Cohen, H. Tager-Flusberg and D.J. Cohen (eds) *Understanding Other Minds. Perspectives from Autism.* Oxford/New York: Oxford University Press.

Hoffman, M.L. (1984) 'Empathy, its limitations, and its role in a comprehensive moral theory.' In W.M. Kurtines and J.L. Gewirtz (eds) *Morality, Moral Behavior and Moral Development.* New York: Wiley and Sons.

Hoksbergen, R., Van Dijkum, C., Ter Laak, J., Rijk, K. and Stoutjesdijk, F. (2002) 'Institutional Autistic Syndrome bij Roemeense adoptiekinderen.' *Tijdschrift voor Orthopedagogiek 41*, 143–55.

Holmstrom, R. (1992) 'Female aggression among the great apes: A psychoanalytic perspective.' In K. Björkqvist and P. Niemelä (eds) *Of Mice and Women: Aspects of Female Aggression.* San Diego, CA: Academic Press.

Hornsveld, H. (1996) *Farewell to the Hyperventilation Syndrome.* Amsterdam: Proefschrift.

Hovers, M. (1996) 'Gestresst meisje groeit minder hard.' *Eindhovens Dagblad,* 4 September, 21.

Howard, M.A., Cowell, P.E., Boucher, J., Broks, P., Mayes, A., Farrant, A. and Roberts, N. (2000) 'Convergent neuroanatomical and behavioral evidence of an amygdala hypothesis of autism.' *Neuroreport 11,* 13, 2931–5.

Hrdy, S.B. (2000) *Moederschap. Een Natuurlijke Geschiedenis.* Utrecht: Het Spectrum.

Hynd, G.W., Semrud-Clikeman, M., Lorys, A.R., Novey, E.S., Eliopulos, D. Lyntinen, H. (1991) 'Corpus callosum morphology in attention deficit-hyperactivity disorder: Morphometric analysis of MRI.' Special Series: Attention deficit disorder.' *Journal of Learning Disabilities 24,* 3, 141–6.

Ishihara, S. (1954) *Tests for colour-blindness.* Tokyo: Kaneharah Suppan Co., Ltd.

James, A.L. and Barry, R.J. (1980) 'A review of psychophysiology in early onset psychosis.' *Schizophrenia Bulletin 6,* 506–25.

Jiang, H.K., Wang, J.Y. and Lin, J.C. (2000) 'The central mechanism of hypothalamic-pituitary-adrenocortical system hyperfunction in depressed patients.' *European Archives of Psychiatry and Clinical Neuroscience 54,* 2, 227–34.

Jones, M.C. (1924) 'The elimination of children's fears.' *Journal of Experimental Psychology 7,* 383–90.

Jung, C.G. (1975) *The Archetypes and the Unconscious.* London: Routledge.

Kalat, J.W. (1998) *Biological Psychology.* Pacific Grove, CA: Brooks/Cole Publishing Company.

Kanner, L. (1943) 'Autistic disturbances of affective contact.' *Nervous Child 2,* 217–50.

Kanner, L. (1958) *In Defense of Mothers: How to Bring up Children in Spite of the More Zealous Psychologists.* Springfeld, IL: Thomas.

Kanner, L. (1969) Speech for the American Psychiatric Association. In R.C. Sullivan (ed.) (1994) Advocate, 26, 4.

Kaplan, L. (1990) *Das Mona-Lisa-Syndrom: Männer die wie Frauen Fühlen.* Düsseldorf: Econ.

Kaplan, H.I. and Sadock, B.J. (eds) (1995) *Comprehensive Textbook of Psychiatry/VI. Volume 1.* Baltimore, MD: Williams and Williams.

Kars, L. (1996) 'Neurologisch onderzoek.' In M.A.H. Mulders., M.A.T. Hansen and C.J.A. Roosen (eds) *Autisme: Aanpassen en Veranderen. Handboek voor de Ambulante Praktijk.* Assen: Van Gorcum.

Kendall-Tackett, K.A. (2000) 'Physiological correlates of childhood abuse: Chronic hyperarousal in PTSD, depression, and irritable bowel syndrome.' *Child Abuse and Neglect 24,* 6, 799–810.

Korvatska, E., Van de Water, J., Anders, T.F. and Gershwin, M.E. (2002) 'Genetic and immunologic considerations in autism.' *Neurobiology of Disease 9,* 2, 107–25.

Krech, D., Crutchfeld, R.S. and Ballachey, E.L. (1962) *Individual in Society.* New York: McGraw-Hill.

Krevans, J. and Gibbs, J.C. (1996) 'Parents' use of inductive discipline: Relations to children's empathy and prosocial behavior.' *Child Development 67*, 3263–77.

Kubey, R.L. and Larson, R. (1990) 'The use and experience of the new video media among children and young adolescents.' *Communication Research 17*, 107–30.

Kunce, L. and Mesibov, G.B. (1998) 'Educational approaches to high-funcioning autism and asperger syndrome.' In E. Schopler, G.B. Mesibov and L.J. Kunce (eds) *Asperger Syndrome or High Functioning Autism?* New York/London: Plenum Press.

Lafeber, C. (1984) *Psychotische Kinderen. Opvoedings- en Behandelingsmogelijkheden van Autistische en Symbiotische Kinderen.* Rotterdam: Lemniscaat.

Lam, C-M. (1997) 'A cultural perspective on the study of Chinese adolescent development.' *Child and Adolescent Social Work Journal 14*, 2, 95–113.

Langeveld, M.J. (1969) *The Columbus Picture Analysis of Growth Towards Maturity. A Series of 24 Pictures and a Manual.* Basel/New York: S. Karger.

Leslie, A. (1987) 'Pretense and representation: Origin of "theory" of mind.' *Psychological Review 94*, 4, 412–26.

Lincoln, A., Courchesne, E., Allen, M., Hanson, E. and Ene, M. (1998) 'Neurobiology of Asperger syndrome, seven case studies and quantitative magnetic resonance imaging findings.' In E. Schopler, G.B. Mesibov and L.J. Kunce (eds) *Asperger Syndrome or High Functioning Autism?* New York/London: Plenum Press.

Loevinger, J. (1990) 'Ego development in adolescence.' In R.E. Muuss (ed.) *Adolescent Behavior and Society.* New York: McGraw-Hill.

Lovaas, O.I. (1974) *Perspectives in Behavior Modifcation with Deviant Children.* Englewood Cliffs, NJ: Prentice Hall.

Lovaas, O.I. (1987) 'Behavioral treatment and normal educational and intellectual functioning in young autistic children.' *Journal of Consulting and Clinical Psychology 55*, 3–9.

Lovaas, O.I. (1996) 'The UCLA Young Autism Model of Service Delivery.' In C. Maurice (ed.) *Behavioral Intervention for Young Children with Autism.* Austin: Pro-Ed.

Mahler, M. (1968) *On Human Symbiosis and the Viscissitudes of Individuation.* New York: International Universities Press.

Manning, J.T. and Taylor, R.P. (2001) 'Second to fourth digit ratio and male ability in sport: Implications for sexual selection in humans.' *Evolution and Human Behavior 22*, 1, 61–9.

Manning, J.T., Baron-Cohen, S., Wheelright, S. and Sanders, G. (2001) 'The 2nd to 4th digit ratio and autism.' *Developmental Medicine and Child Neurology 43*, 3, 160–4.

Manning, J.T., Scutt, D., Wilson, J. and Lewis-Jones, D.I. (1998) 'The ratio of 2nd to 4th digit length: A predictor of sperm numbers and concentrations of testosterone, luteinizing hormone and oestrogen.' *Human Reproduction 13*, 11, 3000–4.

Manning, J.T., Barley, L., Walton, J., Lewis-Jones, D.I., Trivers, R.L., Singh, D. *et al.* (2000) 'The 2nd:4th digit ratio, sexual dimorphism, population differences, and reproductive success, evidence for sexually antagonistic genes?' *Evolution and Human Behavior 21*, 3, 163–83.

McBurnett, K., Lahey, B.B., Rathouz, P.J. and Loeber, R. (2000) 'Low salivary cortisol and persistent agression in boys referred for disruptive behavior.' *Archives of General Psychiatry 57*, 38–41.

McDougle, C.J. (1998) '13 repetitive thoughts and behaviors in pervasive developmental disorders.' In E. Schopler, G.B. Mesibov and L.J. Kunce (eds) *Asperger Syndrome or High Functioning Autism?* New York/London: Plenum Press.

Medscape (2000) 'Update on the neurobiology of depression.' *Psychiatry and Mental Health Treatment Updates.* http://medscape.com/viewprogram/142

Meer, B. van der (1993) 'Een vijfsporenaanpak van het pestprobleem op school.' *Bulletin Nederlandse Vereniging voor Adolescentenzorg 11*, 3, 20–9.

Meer, B. van der (1997) *Pesten op School. Lessuggesties voor Leerkrachten.* Assen: Van Gorcum.

Meltzoff, A.N. (1985) 'Immediate and deferred imitation in fourteen- and twenty-four-month-old infants.' *Child Development 56*, 62–72.

Meltzoff, A.N. (1988a) 'Infant imitation and memory: Nine-month-olds in immediate and deferred tests.' *Child Development 59*, 217, 225.

Meltzoff, A.N. (1988b) 'Infant imitation after a 1-week delay: Long term memory for novel acts and multiple stimuli.' *Developmental Psychology 24*, 4, 470–6.

Merimee, T.J., Russell, B., Quinn, S. and Riley, W. (1991) 'Hormone and receptor studies: Relationship to linear growth in childhood and puberty.' *Journal of Clinical Endocrinology and Metabolism 73*, 5, 1031–7.

Mesibov, G.B., Schopler, E., Schaffer, B. and Landrus, R. (1988) 'Individualized assessment and treatment for autistic and developmental disabled children.' *Adolescent and Adult Psychoeducational Profile 4.*

Mesman, J. (2000) *Preadolescent Internalizing and Externalizing Psychopathy.* Rotterdam: Erasmus Universiteit.

Meyer-Bahlburg, H.F.L., Feldman, J.F., Cohen, P. and Ehrhardt, A.A. (1988) 'Perinatal factors in the development of gender-related play behavior: Sex hormones versus pregnancy complications.' *Psychiatry 51*, 260–71.

Millward, C., Powell, S., Messer, D. and Jordan, R. (2000) 'Recall for self and other in autism: Children's memory for events experienced by themselves and their peers.' *Journal of Autism and Developmental Disorders 30*, 1, 15–28.

Moffaert, M. van and Finoulst, M. (2001) *Vrouwen, humeuren en hormonen.* Antwerpen/Baarn: Houtekiet.

Moffit, T.E. (1990) 'The neuropsychology of juvenile delinquency: A critical review.' In M. Tonry and N. Morris (eds) *Crime and Justice: A Review of the Literature.* Chicago, IL: University of Chicago Press.

Moffit, T.E. (1993) 'Adolescent-limited and life-course persistent antisocial behavior: A developmental taxonomy.' *Psychological Review 100*, 674–701.

Momma, K. (1996) *En toen Verscheen een Regenboog. Hoe ik mijn Autistische Leven Ervaar.* [And then there was a rainbow. The way I experience my autistic life] Amsterdam: Ooievaar.

Montessori, M. (1973) *From Childhood to Adolescence.* New York: Schocken Books.

Morgan, C.T. (1965) *Physiological Psychology.* New York: McGraw-Hill.

Moss, J.I. (2001) 'Many Gulf War illnesses may be autoimmune disorders caused by the chemical and biological stressors pyridostigmine bromide, and adrenaline.' *Medical Hypotheses 56*, 2, 155–7.

Mostert, M.P. (2001) 'Facilitated communication since 1955, a review of published studies.' *Journal of Autism and Developmental Disorders 31*, 287–313.

Newman, D.L., Tellegen, A. and Bouchard Jr., T.J. (1998) 'Individual differences in adult ego development. Sources of infuence in twins reared apart.' *Journal of Personality Psychology 74*, 985–95.

Noorlander, E., Rijnders, W. and Wijdeven, R. (1993) *De Cirkels van Van Dijk (Volgens Detox Utrecht)* [Van Dijk's circles]. Utrecht: Detoxication Institute.

Nordin, V. and Gillberg, C. (1998) 'The long-term course of autistic disorders: Update on follow-up studies.' *Acta Psychiatrica Scandinavica 97*, 2, 99–108.

Olweus, D., Mattson, A., Schaling, D. and Low, H. (1980) 'Testosterone, aggression, physical, and personality dimensions in normal adolescent males.' *Psychosomatic Medicine 42*, 352–269.

Oord, E.J.C.G. van den (1993) *A Genetic Study of Problem Behaviour in Children.* Rotterdam: Proefschrift.

Ozonoff, S., Pennington, B.F. and Rogers, S.J. (1991) 'Executive function deficits in high-functioning autistic individuals: Relationship to theory of mind.' *Journal of Child Psychology and Psychiatry 32*, 7, 1081–105.

Parham, P. (2000) *The Immune System.* New York/London: Garland Publishing.

Passmore, R. and Robson, J.S. (1973) *A companion to medical studies. Vol.1. Anatomy, biochemistry, physiology and related subjects.* Oxford: Blackwell Scientific Publications.

Peeters, T. (1996) *Autisme. Van Begrijpen tot Begeleiden.* Antwerpen/Baarn: Hadewijch.

Pennington, B.F. and Ozonoff, S. (1996) 'Executive functions and developmental psychopathology.' *Journal of Child Psychology and Psychiatry 37*, 1, 51–87.

Peters, T.J. and Guitar, B. (1991) *Stuttering: An Integrated Approach to its Nature and Treatment.* Baltimore, MD: Williams and Wilkins.

Piaget, J. (1972) *The Child's Conception of the World.* Totowa, NJ: Littlefeld Adams.

Pine, D.S., Cohen, P., Gurley, D., Brook, J. and Ma, Y. (1998) 'The risk for early-adulthood anxiety and depressive disorders in adolescents with anxiety and depressive disorders.' *Archives of General Psychiatry 55*, 56–64.

Piven, J., Bailey, J., Ranson, B.J. and Arndt, S. (1997) 'An MRI study of the corpus callosum in autism.' *American Journal of Psychiatry 154*, 1041–56.

Piven, M.F., Vranic, D., Nanclares, V., Plebst, C. and Strakstein, S.E. (1999) 'An MRI study of the corpus callosum and cerebellum in mentally retarded autistic individuals.' *Journal of Neuropsychiatry and Clinical Neuroscience 11*, 4, 470–4.

Premack, D. and Woodruff, G. (1978) 'Does the chimpanzee have a theory of mind?' *The Behavioral and Brain Sciences 4*, 515–26.

Prins, P. (1998) 'Sociale vaardigheidstraining bij kinderen in de basisschoolleeftijd: Programma's, effectiviteit en indicatiestelling.' In A. Collot d'Escury-Koenings, T. Snaterse and E. Mackaay-Cramer (eds) *Sociale Vaardigheidstrainingen voor Kinderen. Indicaties, Effecten and Knelpunten.* Lisse: Swets and Zeitlinger.

Prins, A., Kaloupek, D.G. and Keane, T.M. (1995) 'Psychophysiological evidence for autonomic arousal and startle in traumatized adult populations.' In M.J. Friedman, D.S.

Charney and A.Y. Deutsch (eds) *Neurobiological and Clinical Consequences of Stress. From Normal Adaptation to Post-Traumatic Stress Disorder.* Philadelphia/New York: Lippincott-Raven.

Putz, R. and Pabst, R. (eds) (1993) *Sobotta Atlas of Human Anatomy, Twentieth Edition.* Munich: Urban und Schwarzenberg.

Rahe, R.H., Karson, S., Howard, N.S., Rubin, R.T. and Poland, R.E. (1990) 'Psychological and physiological assessments on American hostages freed from captivity in Iran.' *Psychosomatic Medicine 52*, 1, 1–16.

Raine, A. (1993) *The Psychopathology of Crime: Criminal Behavior as a Clinical Disorder.* San Diego, CA: Academic Press.

Raine, A., Lencz, T., Birhrle, S., LaCasse, L. and Coletti, P. (2000) 'Reduced prefrontal gray matter volume and reduced autonomic activity in antisocial personality disorder.' *Archives of General Psychiatry 57*, 2, 119–27.

Ramaekers, G. and Njiokiktjien, C. (1991) *Pediatric Behavioral Neurology. Vol. 3: The Child's Corpus Callosum.* Amsterdam: Suyi Publications.

Renner, P., Klinger, L.G. and Klinger, M.R. (2000) 'Implicit and explicit memory in autism: Is autism an amnesic disorder?' *Journal of Autism and Developmental Disorders 30*, 1, 3–14.

Ricks, D.M. and Wing, L. (1975) 'Language, communication and the use of symbols in normal and autistic children.' *Journal of Autism and Childhood Schizophrenia 5*, 191–221.

Rieffe, C., Meerum Terwogt, M. and Stockman, L. (2000) 'Understanding atypical emotions among children with autism.' *Journal of Autism and Developmental Disorders 30*, 3, 195–203.

Riksen-Walraven, J.M.A. (1994) 'De sensitieve opvoeder: Dimensies en determinanten van opvoedingsgedrag.' In C.J.M. Lindner-Middendorp, D.A. Ramakers, D.A. Flikweert, R.F.B. Geus and M. Bleeksma (eds) *Gehecht aan Goede Relaties: de Betekenis van Gehechtheid en Goede Relaties voor Verstandelijk Gehandicapte Mensen.* Assen: Van Gorcum, Dekker and van de Vegt.

Rimland, B. (1990) 'Sound sensitivity in autism.' *Autism Research Review International 4*, 1–6.

Ringrose, H.J. and Nijenhuis, E.H. (1986) *Bang zijn voor andere kinderen. Omgaña en therapie met socigl onhandige kinderen: een werkboek.* Groningen: Wolters-Noordhoff.

Robinson, S.J. and Manning, J.T. (2000) 'The ratio of 2nd to 4th digit length and male homosexuality.' *Evolution and Human Behavior 21*, 5, 333–45.

Rotter, J.B. (1966) 'Generalized expectancies for internal versus external control of reinforcement.' *Psychological Monographs 80*, 1, 609.

Rovee-Collier, C. and Fagan, J. (1981) 'The retrieval of memory in early infancy.' In L.P. Lipsitt (ed.) *Advances in Infancy Research 1.* Norwood, NJ: Ablex.

Rovee-Collier, C. and Gerhardstein, P. (1997) 'The development of infant memory.' In N. Cowan and C. Hulme (eds) *The Development of Memory in Childhood.* Brighton: Psychology Press Publishers.

Rutter, M. (1985) 'The treatment of autistic children.' *Journal of Child Psychology and Psychiatry 2*, 193–214.

Rutter, M. and Rutter, M. (1993) *Developing Minds. Challenge and Continuity across the Life Span.* London: Penguin Books.

Rutter, M. and Schopler, E. (1988) 'Autism and pervasive developmental disorders.' In M. Rutter, A.H. Hussain Tuma and I.S. Lann (eds) *Assessment and Diagnosis in Child Psychopathology.* London: David Fulton Publishers.

Rutter, M., Hussain Tuma, A.H. and Lann, I.S. (1988) *Assessment and Diagnosis in Child Psychopathology.* London: David Fulton Publishers.

Rutter, M., Andersen-Wood, L., Beckett, C., Bredenkamp, D., Castle, J., Groothues, C., Kreppner, J., Keaveney, L., Lord, C., O'Connor, T.G. and The English and Romanian Adoptees (ERA) Study Team (1999) 'Quasi-autistic patterns following severe early global privation.' *Journal of Child Psychology and Psychiatry 40,* 4, 537–49.

Ruwaard, D., Gijsen, R. and Verkleij, H. (1993) 'Chronische aspecifeke respiratoire aandoeningen.' In *Volksgezondheid Toekomst Verkenning. De Gezondheidstoestand van de Nederelandse Bevolking in de Periode 1950–2010.* [Public health. Future Exploration. The Health of the Dutch people in the period 1950–2010. Report of the Dutch Ministry of Public Health. 395–401.

Sacks, O. (1984) *A Leg to Stand On.* London: Duckworth.

Sainsbury, C. (2000) *Holding Therapy: An Autistic Perspective.* www.nas.org.uk/jsp/polopoly. jsp?d=364&a=2179

Sartre, J-P. (1943/1971) *L'être et le néant.* Paris: Gallimard.

Scerbo, A.S. and Kolko, D.J. (1994) 'Salivary testosterone and cortisol in disruptive children: Relationship to aggressive, hyperactive, and internalizing behaviors.' *Journal of the American Academy of Child and Adolescent Psychiatry 33,* 8, 1174–84.

Scerbo, A.S. and Kolko, D.J. (1995) '"Testosterone and aggression": Reply.' *Journal of the American Academy of Child and Adolescent Psychiatry 34,* 5, 535–6.

Schachtel, E. (1973) *Metamorphosis.* New York: Basic Books.

Schachter, S. (1968) *The Psychology of Affiliation: Experimental Studies of the Sources of Gregariousness.* Stanford, CA: Stanford University Press.

Schachter, S. and Singer, J.E. (1962) 'Cognitive, social and physiological determinants of emotional states.' *Psychological Review 69,* 379–99.

Schopler, E. and Mesibov, G.B. (1988) *Diagnosis and Assessment in Autism.* New York/London: Plenum Press.

Schopler, E. and Reichler, R. (1979) 'Individualized assessment and treatment for autistic and developmentally disabled children.' Psychoeducational Profile, Vol. 1. Baltimore: University Park Press.

Schopler, E., Mesibov, G.B. and Kunce, L.J. (eds) (1998) *Asperger Syndrome or High Functioning Autism?* New York/London: Plenum Press.

Schreck, K.A. and Mulick, J.A. (2000) 'Parental report of sleep problems in children with autism.' *Journal of Autism and Developmental Disorders 30,* 2, 127–35.

Segar, M. (1997) *Coping: A Survival Guide for People with Asperger Syndrome.* www.asperger-marriage.info/survguide/chapter0.html

Seligman, M.E.P. (1975) *Helplessness: On Depression, Development, and Death.* San Francisco, CA: Freeman.

Sellin, B. (1995) *I don't Want to be Inside Me Anymore: Messages from an Autistic Mind.* New York: Basic Books.

Selman, R. (1981) 'The child as friendship philosopher.' In S.A. Asher and M. Gottman (eds) *The Development of Children's Friendships.* Cambridge: Cambridge University Press.

Selye, H. (1976) *The Stress of Life.* New York: McGraw-Hill.

Semrud-Clikeman, M., Filipek, P.A., Biederman, J., Steingard, R., Kennedy, D., Renshaw, P. and Bekken, K. (1994) 'Attention-deficit hyperactivity disorder: Magnetic resonance imaging morphometric analysis of the corpus callosum.' *Journal of the American Academy of Child and Adolescent Psychiatry 33*, 6, 875–81.

Sigman, M. and Ungerer, J.A. (1984) 'Attachment behaviors in autistic children.' *Journal of Autism and Developmental Disorders 14*, 231–44.

Sigman, M., Mundy, P., Sherman, T. and Ungerer, J. (1986) 'Social interactions of autistic, mentally retarded and normal children and their caregivers.' *Journal of Child Psychology and Psychiatry 27*, 647–56.

Silberg, J., Pickles, A., Rutter, M., Hewitt, J., Simonoff, E., Maes, H., Carbonneau, R., Murelle, L., Foley, D. and Eaves, L. (1999) 'The infuence of genetic factors and life stress on depression among adolescent girls.' *Archives of General Psychiatry 56*, 3, 225–32.

Skinner, B.F. (1974) *About Behaviorism.* Chicago, IL: Rand.

Skuse, D.H., James, R.S., Bishop, D.V.M., Coppin, B., Dalton, P., Asmodt-Leeper, G. *et al.* (1997) 'Evidence from Turner's syndrome of an imprinted x-linked locus affecting cognitive function.' *Nature 387*, 705–8.

Slap, G.B., Khalid, N., Paikoff, R.L., Brooks-Gunn, J. and Warren, M.P. (1994) 'Evolving self-image, pubertal manifestations, and pubertal hormones: Preliminary findings in young adolescent girls.' *Journal of Adolescent Health 15*, 4, 327–35.

Smeets, C.J. and van de Wiel, M.C.W.M. (1996) 'Non-verbal learning disabilities. Implicaties voor behandeling bij het neuropsychologisch syndroom NLD.' *Tijdschrift voor Remedial Teaching 3*, 23–6.

Smith, B.D., Meyers, M.B. and Kline, R. (1989) 'For better or for worse: Left-handedness, pathology, and talent.' *Journal of Clinical and Experimental Neuropsychology 11*, 6, 944–58.

Sparrow, S.S., Balla, D.A. and Cicchetti, D.V. (1984) *Vineland Social Maturity Scale.* Circle Pines, MI: American Guidance Service.

Staff, P.T. (1996) 'Neuroscience 1, philosophy 0.' *Psychology Today,* July/August, 18.

Steerneman, P. (1995) 'Een sociale cognitietraining voor kinderen met problemen in sociale situaties.' In A. Collot d'Escury-Koenings, T. Snaterse and E. Mackaay-Cramer (eds) *Sociale Vaardigheidstrainingen voor kinderen. Indicaties, Effecten and Knelpunten.* Lisse: Swets and Zeitlinger.

Steerneman, P. (1997) *Leren denken en leren begrijpen van emoties. Groepsbehandeling van kinderen.* Leuven, Apeldoorn: Garant.

Steerneman, P. (2001) 'Lacking social skills: Hereditary or (not) learned?' In M.F. Delfos and N. Visscher (eds) *(Foster) Children and Odd Behaviour?! On 13 Themes.* Amsterdam: SWP.

Steerneman, P., Meesters, C. and Muris, P. (2000) *Tom Test.* Garant: Leuven/Apeldoorn.

Stehli, A. (1995) *Dancing in the Rain. Stories of Exceptional Progress by Parents of a Child with Special Needs.* Westport, CT: Georgiana Organization Inc.

Steiger, A., Bardeleben, U. Von, Wiedemann, K., Holsboer, F. (1991) 'Sleep EEG and nocturnal secretion of testosterone and cortisol in patients with major endogenous depression during acute phase and after remission.' *Journal of Psychiatric Research 25*, 4, 169–77.

Storey, A.E., Walsh, C.J., Quinten, R.L. and Wynne-Edwards, K.E. (2000) 'Hormonal correlates of paternal responsiveness in new and expectant fathers.' *Evolution and Human Behavior 21*, 79–96.

Sullivan, H.S. (1953) *The Interpersonal Theory of Psychiatry.* New York: W.W. Norton and Co.

Sullivan, M.W. (1982) 'Reactivation: Priming forgotten memories in infants.' *Child Development 53*, 516.

Tannen, D. (1990) *You Just Don't Understand.* New York: William Morrow.

Tanner, J. (1978) *Fetus into Man: Physical Growth from Conception to Maturity.* Cambridge, MA: Harvard University Press.

Tantam, D. (1997) 'Asperger's syndrome in adulthood.' In U. Frith (ed.) *Autism and Asperger's Syndrome.* Cambridge: Cambridge University Press.

Taylor, G.J., Bagby, R.M., Ryan, D.P. and Parker, J.D. (1990) 'Validation of the alexithymia construct: A measurement-based approach.' *Canadian Journal of Psychiatry 35*, 290–7.

Taylor, S.E., Klein, L.C., Lewis, B.P., Gruenewald, T.L., Gurung, R.A. and Updegraff, J.A. (2000) 'Biobehavioral responses to stress in females: Tend-and-befriend, not fight-or-flight.' *Psychological Review 107*, 3, 411–29.

Thomas, A. and Chess, C. (1977) *Temperament and Development.* New York: Brunner and Mazel.

Tinbergen, N. and Tinbergen, E. (1985) *Autistic Children. New Hope for a Cure.* London: Allen and Unwin.

Treffers, P. and Westenberg, P.M. (1997) CZAL, Curium Zinaanvullijst. Kinderpsychiatrisch Instituut Curium. Lisse: Swets and Zeitlinger.

Tremblay, R.E. (1998) 'De ontwikkeling en preventie van fysieke agressie.' In W. Koops and W. Slot (eds) *Van Lastig tot Misdadig.* Houten/Diegem: Bohn Stafeu Van Loghum.

Varendi, H., Porter, R.H. and Winberg, J. (1997) 'Natural odour preferences of newborn infants change over time.' *Acta Paediatrica 86*, 9, 985–90.

Varendi, H., Christensson, K., Porter, R.H. and Winberg, J. (1998) 'Soothing effect of amniotic fluid smell in newborn infants.' *Early Human Development 51*, 47–55.

Verhulst, F.C. and Akkerhuis, G.W. (1986) 'Mental health in Dutch children. (III): Behavioral-emotional problems reported by teachers of children aged 4–12.' *Acta Psychiatrica Scandinavia 73*, 330.

Verhulst, F.C., Versluis-den Bieman, H.J.M., Ende, J. van der, Berden, G.F.M.G. and Sanders-Woudstra, J.A.R. (1990) 'Problem behavior in international adoptees: Diagnosis of child psychiatric disorders.' *Journal of the American Academy of Child and Adolescent Psychiatry 29*, 420–8.

Vermeulen, P. (1999a) *Brein Bedriegt. Als Autisme niet op Autisme Lijkt.* Gent/Berchem: Vlaamse Dienst Autisme/EPO.

Vermeulen, P. (1999b) *Autistic Thinking – This is the Title.* London: Jessica Kingsley Publishers.

Vermeulen, P. (2000a) *Een Gesloten Boek. Autisme en Emoties.* Leuven/Leusden: Acco.

Vermeulen, P. (2000b) *I am Special.* London: Jessica Kingsley Publishers.

Vermeulen, P. (2001) *Beter Vroeg dan Laat en Beter Laat dan Nooit. De Onderkenning van Autisme bij Normaal tot Hoogbegaafde Personen.* Berchem: EPO.

Vermeulen, P. (2002a) 'Lecture at the conference: A strange world.' Logacom: Amsterdam, 5 March.

Vermeulen, P. (2002b) *Voor alle Duidelijkheid. Leerlingen met Autisme in het Gewoon Onderwijs.* Berchem: EPO.

Verpoorten, R.A.W., Noens, I.L.J. and Berckelaer-Onnes, I.A. van (1999/2001) *De ComVoor – Voorlopers in Communicatie. Experimentele Versie.* Leiden: Universiteit Leiden.

Virgilio, G. (1986) *Maturation of the CNS and Evoked Potentials.* Amsterdam: Excerpta Medica.

Volkmar, F.R. and Klin, A. (1998) 'Six Asperger syndrome and Nonverbal Learning disabilities.' In E. Schopler, G.B. Mesibov and L.J. Kunce (eds) *Asperger Syndrome or High Functioning Autism?* New York/London: Plenum Press.

Volkmar, F. and Nelson, I. (1990) 'Seizure disorder in autism.' In C. Gillberg (ed.) *Diagnosis and Treatment of Autism.* New York: Plenum Press.

Vrij, A. (1998) *De Psychologie van de Leugenaar.* Lisse: Swets and Zeitlinger.

Vygotsky, L.S. (1962) [1934] *Thought and Language.* Cambridge, MA: MIT Press. (Original work published 1934.)

Vygotsky, L.S. (1978) *Mind in Society. The Development of Higher Psychological Processes.* Cambridge: Harvard University Press.

Waterhouse, S. (2000) *A Positive Approach to Autism.* London: Jessica Kingsley Publishers.

Watson, J.B. (1924) *Behaviorism.* New York: Norton.

Watson, J.B. (1928) *The Psychological Care of the Infant and Child.* New York: Norton.

Westenberg, P.M., Cohn, L.D. and Blasi, A. (eds) (1998) *Personality Development: Theoretical, Empirical, and Clinical Analyses of Loevinger's Conception of Ego Development.* Mahwah, NJ: Erlbaum.

Westenberg, P.M., Drewes, M.J., Siebelink, R.M., Treffers, Ph.D.A., Jonckheer, J. and Goedhart, A.W. (2001) *Zinnenaanvultest Curium, ZALC. Handleiding.* Lisse: Swets and Zeitlinger.

Wheeler, G., Cumming, D., Burnham, R., Maclean, I., Sloley, B.D., Bhambhani, Y. and Steadward, R.D. (1994) 'Testosterone, cortisol and catecholamine responses to exercise and autonomic dysrefexia in elite quadiplegic athletes.' *Paraplegia 32,* 292–9.

WHO (World Health Organization) (1992) *International Statistical Classification of Diseases and Related Health Problems, Tenth Edition.* Geneva: World Health Organization.

Wilkins, L., Fleischmann, W. and Howard, J.E. (1940) 'Macrogenitosomia precox associated with hyperplasia of the androgenic tissue of the adrenal and death from corticoadrenal insuffiency.' *Endocrinology 26,* 3, 387.

Williams, K. (1995) 'Understanding the Student with Asperger's Syndrome: Guidelines for Teachers.' *Focus on Autistic Behavior 10*, 2. www.udel.edu/bkirby/asperger/ karen_williams_guidelines.html.

Windle, M. (1994) 'Temperamental inhibition and activation: Hormonal and psychosocial correlates and associated psychiatric disorders.' *Personality and Individual Differences 17*, 1, 61–70.

Wing, L. (1981a) 'Asperger's syndrome: A clinical account.' *Psychological Medicine 11*, 115–30.

Wing, L. (1981b) 'Language, social and cognitive impairments in autism and severe mental retardation.' *Journal of Autism and Developmental Disorders 11*, 1, 31–45.

Wing, L. (1988) 'The continuum of autistic characteristics.' In E. Schopler and G.B. Mesibov (eds) *Diagnoses and Assessment in Autism*. New York: Plenum Press.

Wing, L. (1992) 'Manifestations of social problems in high functioning autistic people.' In E. Schopler and G.B. Mesibov (eds) *High Functioning Individuals with Autism*. New York: Plenum Press.

Wing, L. (1996) *The Autistic Spectrum: A Guide for Parents and Professionals*. London: Constable and Company Limited.

Wing, L. (1997) 'The relation between Asperger's syndrome and Kanner's autism.' In U. Frith (ed.) *Autism and Asperger Syndrome*. Cambridge: Cambridge University Press.

Wing, L. (1998) 'The history of Asperger's syndrome.' In E. Schopler, G.B. Mesibov and L.J. Kunce (eds) *Asperger Syndrome or High Functioning Autism?* New York/London: Plenum Press.

Wing, L. (2001) *The Autistic Spectrum. A Parents' Guide to Understanding and Helping your Child*. Berkeley, CA: Ulysses Press.

Wing, L. and Gould, J. (1979) 'Severe impairments of social interaction and associated abnormalities in children: Epidemiology and classification.' *Journal of Autism and Developmental Disorders 9*, 11–29.

Worden, J.W. (1996) *Children and Grief. When a Parent Dies*. New York/London: Guilford Press.

Yirmiya, N., Kasari. C., Sigman, M. and Mundy, P. (1989) 'Facial expressions of affect in autistic, mentally retarded and normal children.' *Journal of Child Psychology and Psychiatry 5*, 725–35.

Yirmiya, N., Sigman, M., Kasari, C. and Mundy, P. (1992) 'Empathy and cognition in high functioning children with autism.' *Child Development 63*, 150–60.

Zeiger, R.S. and Heller, S. (1995) 'The development and prediction of atopy in high-risk children: Follow-up at age seven years in a prospective randomized study of combined maternal and infant food allergen avoidance.' *Journal of Allergy and Clinical Immunology 95*, (6), 1179–91.

Subject index

Author index

Aarons, M. 101, 168
Achterberg, G. 28
Aguiar, A. 196
Ainsworth, M.D.S. 188, 189
American Psychiatric
  Association (APA) 45, 59,
  69, 86, 87, 88, 365,
  371, 372
Arntz, A. 357
Aronson, M. 84
Asperger, H. 17, 18, 19, 23,
  24, 25, 48, 49, 60, 61,
  64, 68, 71, 81, 85, 86,
  98, 100, 108, 112, 115,
  134, 137, 146, 154,
  166, 178, 181, 205,
  208, 216, 262, 283,
  315, 316, 333, 385, 386
Attwood, T. 73, 98, 122,
  125, 145, 208, 334,
  380, 381, 385
Autisme Team Gelderland
  101

Bailey, A. 107, 108, 114,
  115
Baird, G. 97
Bar-On, R. 244
Baron-Cohen, S. 25, 49, 73,
  86, 89, 100, 107, 108,
  109, 110, 111, 112,
  115, 118, 128, 131,
  168, 176, 205, 207
Barrett, S. 23
Bauman, 41, 42
Baxter, L. 356
Beck, A.T. 357
Beel, V. 100, 261

Bender, L. 127
Berckelaer-Onnes, I. 100,
  101, 107, 133, 144
Bernards, J.A. 78
Berversdorf, D. 126
Bettelheim, B. 23, 129, 165
Bettison, S. 142
Bigelow, B.J. 234, 237, 241
Bleuler, E. 17, 18
Boer, F. 241
Bottroff, V. 128, 381
Boucher, J. 125
Bower, G.H. 127
Bowlby, J. 50, 169, 187,
  188, 242, 317
Bowler, D.M. 126
Broca, P. 69
Buck, R. 129
Buitelaar, J.K. 90, 373, 374
Burgione, E. 368
Burke, H.L. 74

Cahill, L. 72
Chakrabarti, S. 97
Clairborne Park, C. 386,
  387
Cohen, D.J. 373
Cohn, L.D. 74
Connellan, J. 136
Consortium (International
  Molecular Genetic Study
  of Autist Consortium) 23,
  363
Constantino, J.N. 78

Dabbs, J.M. 78
Damasio, A.R. 56, 62, 86,
  116, 128, 304
Damon, W. 73, 74
Dawson, G. 191
Deater-Deckard, K. 290
Dekker, M. 76, 209, 381

Delfos, M.F. 21, 26, 27, 43,
  45, 47, 55, 58, 59, 60,
  76, 77, 78, 79, 90, 110,
  133, 138, 140, 153,
  155, 169, 170, 180,
  188, 189, 195, 196,
  207, 220, 221, 230,
  247, 249, 252, 255,
  260, 302, 303, 306,
  307, 309, 310, 339,
  346, 352, 359, 367,
  370, 387, 388
Dennen, J.M.G. 75, 78
Derks, J. 139
Didden, R. 113
Dijk, van, W.K. 257, 258
Dijkshoorn, P. 236
Ditmars, N. 321, 355
Duyndam, J. 65, 66

Edelman, G.M. 62
Eisenberg, N. 65, 66, 72,
  79, 128, 216
Eisenmajer, R. 346
Elbers, E. 149, 219
Eliot, L. 41
Ellis, A. 357
Emmelkamp, P.M.G. 356,
  357
Evans, D. 244
Eysenck, H.J. 244

Farrant, A. 125
Fenenga, M. 227
Field, T. 190, 194, 205
Fisher, J.H. 68, 132, 167,
  246, 250, 265, 327
Flavell, J.H. 64, 65, 126,
  186
Fleisher, M. 68, 265, 327
Fombonne, E. 97
Fraiberg, S.H. 228
Freud, S. 63